P9-ECJ-894

DISCIPLINED MINDS

A CRITICAL LOOK AT SALARIED PROFESSIONALS AND THE SOUL-BATTERING SYSTEM THAT SHAPES THEIR LIVES

JEFF SCHMIDT

ROWMAN & LITTLEFIELD PUBLISHERS, INC.

Lanham • Boulder • New York • Oxford

ROWMAN & LITTLEFIELD PUBLISHERS, INC.

Published in the United States of America
by Rowman & Littlefield Publishers, Inc.
A wholly owned subsidary of The Rowman & Littlefield Publishing Group, Inc.
4501 Forbes Boulevard, Suite 200, Lanham, Maryland 20706
www.rowmanlittlefield.com

PO Box 317
Oxford
OX2 9RU, UK

Copyright © 2000 by Jeff Schmidt
First paperback printing 2001.

All rights reserved. No part of this publication may be reproduced,
stored in a retrieval system, or transmitted in any form or by any
means, electrical, mechanical, photocopying, recording, or otherwise,
without the prior permission of the publisher.

British Library Cataloguing in Publication Information Available

The hardback edition of this book was catalogued by the Library of Congress as follows:

Schmidt, Jeff, 1946–
   Disciplined minds : a critical look at salaried professionals and the soul-battering
system that shapes their lives / Jeff Schmidt.
      p.   cm.
   Includes bibliographical references and index.
   1. Professions—Social aspects—United States. 2. Professional education—United States.
   3. Quality of work life—United States. I. Title.

HT687.S35 2000
305.5'53'0973—dc21   99-053464

ISBN 13: 978-0-7425-1685-4

Printed in the United States of America

For my daughter,
Joshua Rose

CONTENTS

ACKNOWLEDGMENTS

Many people helped to create this book.

The always-inspiring Stanley Aronowitz, an extraordinarily insightful social critic whom I've had the pleasure of knowing for many years, did a great deal to make the book a reality. His comments on the manuscript helped to improve the book's content, and his generosity and principled solidarity played a crucial role in getting it published.

My parents, Esther and Jerry Schmidt, gave me more than moral support. My mother has been a lifelong role model for treating people decently, and the values inherent in her example helped shape this book. My father's long-standing activism taught me that action is the bottom line. His spirited suggestions on all facets of the book project always reminded me to keep the big picture in mind.

Jean Kumagai made important contributions to the book on all levels, from the basic ideas to the subtle details of how they are expressed. Her insight into today's society and culture was invaluable. Matt Siegel also made invaluable contributions to all aspects of the project. His independent thinking often led me to rethink ideas or to present them more clearly. Chris Mohr gave me scores of good editing suggestions and shared his knowledge of the publishing industry. Bill Sweet read the manuscript with a sharp eye and offered many thoughtful suggestions, both broad and detailed. I first met my friends Jean, Matt, Chris and Bill when they were hired at *Physics Today* magazine and thus became my coworkers. Our many fruitful discussions about topics in the book, and about their own projects, made our workdays more interesting and more satisfying.

Others who contributed generously of their time and who offered support and valuable suggestions include Charlotte Miller, Daniel Gladstone (another friend from the *Physics Today* workplace), William DiFazio, Michael Bérubé, Noam Chomsky, Liane Scott, Michael Balter, Eric Chase, Maude Covalt, Sam Ma, Cecily Stewart, Margaret Boeringer, Frank Potter, Pat Kerig, Ted Werntz, Robin Hanson, Robert N. Proctor, Fred Dolan, Alak Ray, Keith Skotnes, Marlowe Hood (another friend from the magazine), Shawna Vogel, Michael Neuschatz and Barbara Dixon.

The Education and Employment Statistics division of the American Institute of Physics, just down the hall from the *Physics Today* offices, provided lots of useful data.

Phil Mattera of the National Writers Union set an example for all unionists, and indeed for all workers, by looking critically not only at the terms of production, but also at what was being produced: He helped me get a great book contract and gave me excellent suggestions for improving the manuscript.

Dean Birkenkamp, my editor at Rowman & Littlefield, is everything a writer could want. He has maintained his own social vision and high standards of personal conduct within an increasingly corporate publishing industry that sees such priorities as inefficient at best. Dean was enthusiastic about the book and signed it up promptly. He offered wise global and detailed suggestions and worked closely with me at each step in the publishing process.

It was not easy. . . . It needed . . . a sort of athleticism of mind, an ability at one moment to make the most delicate use of logic and at the next to be unconscious of the crudest logical errors. Stupidity was as necessary as intelligence, and as difficult to attain.

George Orwell, *1984*

INTRODUCTION

This book is stolen. Written in part on stolen time, that is. I felt I had no choice but to do it that way. Like millions of others who work for a living, I was giving most of my prime time to my employer. My job simply didn't leave me enough energy for a major project of my own, and no one was about to hire me to pursue my own vision, especially given my irreverent attitude toward employers. I was working in New York City as an editor at a glossy science magazine, but my job, like most professional jobs, was not intellectually challenging and allowed only the most constrained creativity. I knew that if I were not contending with real intellectual challenges and exercising real creativity—and if I were not doing anything to shape the world according to my own ideals—life would be unsatisfying, not to mention stressful and unexciting. The thought of just accepting my situation seemed insane. So I began spending some office time on my own work, dumped my TV to reappropriate some of my time at home, and wrote this book. Not coincidentally, it is about professionals, their role in society, and the hidden battle over personal identity that rages in professional education and employment.

The predicament I was in will sound painfully familiar to many professionals. Indeed, generally speaking, professionals today are not happy campers. After years of worshiping work, many seemingly successful professionals are disheartened and burned out, not because of their 70-hour workweeks, but because their salaries are all they have to show for their life-consuming efforts. They long for psychic rewards, but their employers' emphasis on control and the bottom line is giving them only increased workloads, closer scrutiny by management and unprecedented anxiety about job security. In this way the cold reality of employer priorities has led to personal crises for many of this country's 21 million professionals.

Burned-out professionals may not be immediately obvious to the casual observer, because typically they stay on the job and maintain their usual high level of output. But they feel like they are just going through the motions. They have less genuine curiosity about their work, feel less motivated to do it and get less pleasure from it. The emotional numbness inevitably spreads from their work lives into their personal lives. According to Herbert J. Freudenberger, the New York psychologist who coined the term burnout in the mid-1970s, the personal consequences are wide-ranging and profound: cynicism, disconnection, loss of vitality and authenticity, decreased enjoyment of family life, anger, strained relationship with spouse or partner, divorce, obsessive behavior such as "workaholism," chronic fatigue, poor eating habits, neglect of friends, social isolation, loneliness—and the list of symptoms goes on. Freudenberger tells me he has seen a big increase in career burnout among professionals in the past twenty years. Ironically, such depression is most likely to hit the most devoted professionals—those who have been the most deeply involved in their work. You can't burn out if you've never been on fire.

The problem shows no sign of easing. In fact, the ranks of troubled professionals are swelling as members of Generation X finish school and rack up a few years in the workforce. Many Xers, having observed the unfulfilling work ethic of their baby boom predecessors, want their own working lives to be fun and meaningful from the get-go. Starting out with priorities that took boomers a decade to figure out, but in no better position to act on those priorities, Xers are simply having career crises at an earlier age. Clearly, there is an urgent need to understand why career work so often fails to fulfill its promise.

I argue that the hidden root of much career dissatisfaction is the professional's lack of control over the "political" component of his or her creative work. Explaining this component is a major focus of this book. Today's disillusioned professionals entered their fields expecting to do work that would "make a difference" in the world and add meaning to their lives. In this book I show that, in fact, professional education and employment push people to accept a role in which they do *not* make a significant difference, a politically subordinate role. I describe how the intellectual boot camp known as graduate or professional school, with its cold-blooded expulsions and creeping indoctrination, systematically grinds down the student's spirit and ultimately produces obedient thinkers—highly educated employees who do their assigned work without questioning its goals. I call upon students and professionals to engage in just such questioning, not only for their own happiness, but for society's sake as well.

This book shows that professional education is a battle for the very identity of the individual, as is professional employment. It shows how students and working professionals face intense pressure to compromise their ideals and sideline their commitment to work for a better world. And it explores what individuals can do to resist this pressure, hold on to their values and pursue their social visions. People usually don't think of school and work in terms of such a high-stakes struggle. But if they did, they would be able to explain why so many professional training programs seem more abusive than enlightening, and why so many jobs seem more frustrating than fulfilling.

I decided to write this book when I was in graduate school myself, getting a PhD in physics, and was upset to see many of the best people dropping out or

Non Sequitur by Wiley

© 1995 The Washington Post Writers Group. Reprinted with permission.

being kicked out. Simply put, those students most concerned about others were the most likely to disappear, whereas their self-centered, narrowly focused peers were set for success. The most friendly, sympathetic and loyal individuals, those who stubbornly continued to value human contact, were handicapped in the competition. They were at a disadvantage not only because their attention was divided, but also because their beliefs about big-picture issues such as justice and social impact caused them to stop, think and question. Their hesitation and contemplation slowed them down, tempered their enthusiasm and drew attention to their deviant priorities, putting them at a disadvantage relative to their unquestioning, gung-ho classmates. Employers, too, I realized, favored people who kept their concerns about the big picture nicely under control, always in a position of secondary importance relative to the assigned work at hand. Thus I saw education and employment as a self-consistent, but deeply flawed, system. I wrote this book in the hope of exposing the problem more completely and thereby forcing change.

A system that turns potentially independent thinkers into politically subordinate clones is as bad for society as it is for the stunted individuals. It bolsters the power of the corporations and other hierarchical organizations, undermining democracy. As I will explain in detail, it does this by producing people who are useful to hierarchies, and only to hierarchies: uncritical employees ready and able to extend the reach of their employers' will. At the same time, a system in which individuals do not make a significant difference at their point of deepest involvement in society—that is, at work—undermines efforts to build a culture of real democracy. And in a subordinating system, organizations are more likely to shortchange or even abuse clients, because employees who know their place are not effective at challenging their employers' policies, even when those policies adversely affect the quality of their own work on behalf of clients.

This book is intended for a broad range of professionals, nonprofessionals and students, and for anyone interested in how today's society works. It is for students who wonder why graduate or professional school is so abusive. It is for nonprofessionals who wonder why the professionals at work are so often insufferable, and who want to be treated with greater respect. It is for socially concerned professionals who wonder why their liberal colleagues behave so damn conservatively in the workplace. (Chapter 1 explains how professionals are fundamentally conservative even though liberalism is the dominant ideology in the professions.) It is for individuals who are frustrated by the restrictions on their work and troubled by the resulting role they play—or don't play—in the world. It is also for those who simply find their careers much less fulfilling than they had expected and aren't exactly sure why.

Disillusioned lawyers, doctors, financial analysts, journalists, teachers, social workers, scientists, engineers and other highly educated employees are looking for a deeper understanding of why their lives are stressful and feel incomplete. My hope is that readers will find such an understanding in these pages, along with effective strategies for corrective action. If you are a professional, coming to understand the political nature of what you do, as part of an honest re-assessment of what it really means to be a professional, can be liberating. It can help you recover your long-forgotten social goals and begin to pursue them immediately, giving your life greater meaning and eliminating a major source of stress. It can help you become a savvy player in the workplace and reclaim some lost autonomy. And, ironically, it can help you command greater respect from management and receive greater recognition and reward, without necessarily working harder.

If you are a student, understanding the political nature of professional work can help you hold on to your values and moral integrity as you navigate the minefields of professional training and, later, employment. For students trying to get through professional training intact, this book can serve as something of a survival guide, explaining the frightening experiences and warning of what lies in store.

If you are a nonprofessional, you experience even more lack of control, un-fulfilling work, insecurity and other sources of stress than do professionals. As a consequence, the toll on your physical and psychological well-being is even greater than that suffered by professionals. If you want to act individually or collectively to improve your situation, then it pays to know what makes your professional coworkers tick. Such awareness can help you figure out which people you can trust and how far you can trust them. When professional and non-professional employees maintain solidarity in the workplace, they can cover for each other and get more concessions from their employer. But any alliance between unequal partners is doubly risky for the less powerful party—in this case the nonprofessionals, who are at the bottom of the workplace hierarchy. By understanding professionals, you reduce the chances of being double-crossed by them. You'll be treated with more respect, too.

Whatever your occupation, you have to deal with a variety of professionals when you are off the job. Most of these professionals work for others, not directly for you. Whether you visit an HMO, send kids to school, request a government service, see a counselor, get assistance from a social worker, deal with a lawyer, file a consumer complaint or contact a local TV station or newspaper, understanding the political nature of professional work will help you get better service. If you are involved in an independent organization working for social change, you have to contend not only with professionals in the corporations or agencies that your group confronts, but also with professionals advising your own organization. Groups that simply trust professionals without truly understanding them are very likely to be misdirected or sold out by those professionals.

And, of course, everyone deals with professionals indirectly, too. For instance, newspapers, magazines, radio and television are filled with supposedly objective news reports, analyses and studies prepared by professionals. What should you believe? To truly understand the output of these or other professionals, you first need to understand the political nature of the professional's role at work.

The political nature of professional work is this book's unifying theme. To make the case that the professional's work is inherently political, I examine not only professionals and what they do (part one: chapters 1 to 6), but also the system that prepares them to do it (part two: chapters 7 to 13) and the battle that one must fight to be politically independent (part three: chapters 14 to 16).

My hope is that whether you are a professional, a nonprofessional or a student, you will find here an unsettling but empowering new way of looking at yourself, your colleagues, the institution that employs or trains you, and society as a whole. This book strives to arm you with a very practical analytical tool that you can use to your advantage in whatever individual and collective struggles you find yourself in as an employee, student, organization member, consumer or citizen.

A note on pronouns. To make less frequent use of phrases such as "he or she," in part one I will sometimes use female pronouns instead, and in part two I will sometimes use male pronouns instead. Today most professionals are women, and the female majority, which stood at 53% in 1997, is growing. Women have long made up large majorities in professions with relatively low social status and salary; thus teachers, social workers, registered nurses and librarians have been said to labor in the subprofessions. But today the proportion of women is increasing throughout the professions. Nearly half the students now in medical school and law school, for example, are women, up from about 9% in 1970.

A note on references. Many of the references listed at the end of each chapter make for fascinating reading. I encourage you to look further into topics in this book that interest you, and so I have given lots of references and have spelled things out to make them as easy as possible to look up. Time spent with these materials will surely be thought provoking, informative and entertaining.

PART ONE

PROFESSIONALS

❶

TIMID PROFESSIONALS

"No two people are allowed to read the same thing," I said above the noise, gesturing toward the other passengers on the crowded subway car. My out-of-town visitor glanced around the clattering train. Indeed, the commuters hurtling toward their jobs in Manhattan's office buildings, restaurants, shops and other workplaces were reading such a wide variety of material that my joke almost held up. That typical weekday morning found riders engrossed in all kinds of magazines, paperback books, the *Daily News*, the *Post*, the *Times*, office documents, a software instruction book and, yes, the Bible. Those who weren't reading were listening to headphones, talking to others or, apparently, just thinking.

Seeing this every day on the subway set me up for a surprise one morning when I went to catch a suburban commuter train to Manhattan. I had stayed overnight in Westchester County, an upscale New York City suburb where many executives and professionals live. I would be riding into the city with lawyers headed for big corporate law firms, financial analysts going to investment banks, editors bound for publishing conglomerates, as well as accountants, journalists, doctors, architects, engineers, public relations specialists and a host of other professionals. Boarding the train felt something like entering a library. There were no conversations even though nearly all the seats were occupied. Almost everyone was reading. But the dozens of passengers were reading only two things: the *New York Times* and the *Wall Street Journal*. I could have formulated another joke about allowed reading matter, but the scene was too spooky, like the aftermath of an invasion of the body snatchers: everyone dressed the same, in suits, sitting silently in neat rows and columns, each holding up a large newspaper, absorbing the same information.

A herd of independent minds?[1] Something seemed very wrong with this picture. It was obvious that when the subway riders and the suburban train riders converged at the workplace, the people who showed the greatest diversity in their dress, behavior and thought—the nonprofessionals—would be asked to do the least creative work, while the most regimented people would be assigned the creative tasks. This seemed just the opposite of what one might expect. And even more disturbingly, it indicated that people who do creative work are not necessarily independent thinkers.

Evidence that professionals are not independent thinkers has been around for a long time but has generally been ignored, in part because people don't know how to make sense of it. The Vietnam War produced some revealing examples, which are worth looking back at.

On 12 January 1971, the federal government indicted Philip Berrigan and other East Coast antiwar activists on felony charges of plotting to impede the Vietnam War through violent action. The activists' agenda supposedly included blowing up underground heating pipes in Washington to shut down government buildings, kidnapping presidential adviser Henry Kissinger to ransom him for concessions on the war and raiding draft boards to destroy records and slow down the draft.

The Justice Department prosecutors chose to hold the conspiracy trial in Harrisburg, Pennsylvania, a conservative area where a randomly chosen jury would be heavily against the defendants. However, before the jury was selected at what came to be known as the Harrisburg-7 trial, a group of left-leaning social scientists supporting the defendants interviewed a large number of registered voters in the area to try to figure out how to get a sympathetic jury there. They discovered, among other things, that college-educated people were more likely than others to be conservative and to trust the government. Thus, in court, during the three weeks that it took to examine 465 potential jurors and pick a panel of 12, lawyers for the defense quietly favored skilled blue-collar workers and white-collar workers without a lot of formal education—nonprofessionals, although the sociologists and lawyers apparently never used that term.

The lawyers were uneasy doing this, however, because it went against their intuition. The notion of closed-minded hard hats and open-minded intellectuals is widespread and is reinforced by mass-media characters like loading-dock worker Archie Bunker and his college-student son-in-law, "pinko" Mike. In fact, *All in the Family* made its television debut the very day of the Harrisburg indictments, 12 January 1971; by the time the trial and jury selection started, it had been on the air for a year.

Ignoring these false stereotypes paid off. The government put on a month-long, $2 million extravaganza featuring 64 witnesses, including 21 FBI agents and 9 police officers. The defense called no one to the witness stand. After seven days of deliberation, the jury was not able to reach a unanimous decision, and the judge declared a mistrial; but with 10 of the 12 carefully selected jurors arguing for a not-guilty verdict, the government dropped the case.[2]

Blue-collar skeptics? Loyal intellectuals? Was the Harrisburg survey a regional fluke? Look at what the nationwide polls showed at the time. On 15 February 1970 the *New York Times* reported the results of a Gallup poll on the war in Vietnam.[3] Gallup had found that the number of people in sharp disagreement with the government over the war had increased but still constituted a minority. While this increase in opposition was important news, what were particularly intriguing were the data on the opinions of subgroups of the population. These numbers announced with striking clarity that those with the most schooling were the most reluctant to criticize the government's stand in Vietnam. There was a simple correlation (although only in part a cause-and-effect relationship): The further people had gone before leaving school, the less likely they were to break with the government over the war. (See note 3 for the results of the poll.)

During the war in Vietnam, nearly everyone seemed to have one or another gripe about the U.S. government's effort, but few took positions that dissented fundamentally from the government's goals. Some said they were for negotiations, some said they were for an end to the bombing and some simply said they were "for peace." Gallup's survey cut to the bottom line by posing what was always the most incisive question on the war. It asked people whether they would favor or oppose the immediate withdrawal of all U.S. troops from Vietnam.

Age didn't affect the answers much. The ratio of those in favor to those opposed was about the same for young adults as it was for older people. But dramatic differences appeared according to formal education. Those with college educations opposed immediate withdrawal by more than two to one, whereas those not formally schooled beyond the elementary grades were evenly divided on the question. And high school graduates were in between.

Polls taken earlier and later in the Vietnam War,[4] and polls taken during other wars—Korea,[5] for example—show the same correlation with formal education.

Gallup was not the only one to find this connection between attitude and formal education.[6] In a study entitled *A Degree and What Else? Correlates and Consequences of a College Education*, sponsored by the Carnegie Commission on Higher Education, researchers found college graduates to be "more supportive, or 'hawkish,' than the rest of the population." Even in 1968, a year of rising antiwar sentiment and militant actions against the war, people who had been to college remained less likely than others to criticize the U.S. intervention in Vietnam, the Carnegie study found.[7]

People's reluctance to criticize the war was not simply the result of their careful analysis of an isolated issue. Rather, the position people took on the war followed almost mechanically from their overall political outlook (although some had their overall political outlook radicalized by what they experienced when they acted to do something about the war). With Americans being killed every day, almost anything one said about the U.S. intervention in Vietnam was heard as a statement on the U.S. political, economic and social system itself, and rightly so. Thus a narrow statement against the war could elicit a broad response such as "If you don't like it here, go to Russia!" Few now seem to remember that throughout most of the war, those who called for the immediate withdrawal of all U.S. troops were seen as radicals—as critics of a lot more than the war. This explains, in part, the disparity between opposition and activism—why many opponents of the war didn't speak out publicly. More students than workers were antiwar activists, even though workers who had antiwar sentiments far outnumbered students of all persuasions. Workers organizing publicly to get the United States out of Vietnam risked a lot more—namely, their jobs—because their employers were likely to see them as radicals and therefore a threat to the tranquility of the local workforce.

The correlation between attitude and formal education is important for a book about professionals, because professionals typically have large amounts of schooling. Indeed, people in Gallup's occupational category "professional and business workers" have attitudes similar to those of people in the top education category.[8] (Unfortunately, Gallup has no category for professionals alone.)

The relatively uncritical stand of professionals on the issue of war is just the tip of the iceberg, for it is *on the job* that professionals have the greatest number of opportunities to display their ideological caution. Anyone who has ever had a job that involved interacting with professionals, or who has had to deal with doctors, lawyers, bankers or the like, has surely encountered individuals with what we might call the "professional attitude"—confident and assertive individuals who exude the feeling that they are very much at home playing by the rules and that there is no pressing need to question the social structure in which they do their work. In many individuals such identification with the system shows up in the negative: Their confidence immediately melts into fear at any suggestion of *not* playing by the system's rules. (By "the system" I mean the hierarchical organization of production—the system of bosses and employees—and the social, economic and political practices that go along with it. Here and throughout the book my emphasis is on the hierarchical structure: "The system" may be read as "the hierarchy.") And in fewer but more memorable individuals, this conservatism takes the form of elitism or pompousness, seemingly critical postures that cover for personal insecurity but involve no risk, because they compliment the system by implying that it is too egalitarian, too democratic. Whether you are a professional or a nonprofessional, you encounter the professional attitude most frequently at work—and on matters of work—not only because it is in the workplace that you are most often thrust into contact with professionals, but also because it is on the job that professionals are most sure to act like professionals.

Most importantly, it is at work that the attitude of professionals has its greatest impact, both on you as an individual and on society as a whole. Whether a given professional designs buildings, writes newspaper articles, teaches courses or develops investment strategies, she makes important decisions that affect many people. Outside of work, however, the professional's attitude has relatively little effect on society (unless the professional makes a deliberate effort to the contrary). If, for example, you were given the power to dictate the outlook that governs the day-in day-out decision-making of a professional at work, and I were given the power to dictate the outlook that governs what that professional does inside the voting booth once every four years, then your power to shape society would be vastly greater than mine.

(It is worth pausing here to explain exactly what I mean by "society." I use the word not to refer to the collection of individuals who happen to live within the national boundaries, but to denote the set of *relationships* among them. Relationships are indicated by such words as supervisor, employee, capitalist, union member, friend, boss, colleague, representative, housewife, homeboy, chairperson, organization member and so on. Without relationships there is no society. So when I talk about the power to shape society, I mean the power to affect the nature of these relationships. Something's "social significance" is its power to change society, its effect on the relationships among people or among classes of people. Does it strengthen or weaken one group relative to another?)

Public opinion pollsters report that professionals are more liberal than nonprofessionals on many social issues, such as civil liberties, personal morality and cultural issues.[9] Liberal professionals smugly conclude from this that they are a force for social progress and that nonprofessionals are a conservative force in society. But the polls do not justify such a conclusion, for two reasons.

First of all, although professionals may be liberal on this or that question of the day, they tend to be very conservative on a long-standing issue of much greater importance to society: democracy. Discuss politics with a liberal professional and you will not hear a word in favor of a more democratic distribution of power in society, perhaps because in the professional's view ignorant nonprofessionals make up the large majority of the population. Even the most liberal professionals tend toward authoritarianism in their social visions.

The second reason the polls don't demonstrate that professionals are a more progressive force in society than are nonprofessionals is that the surveys focus on broad social questions and not on attitudes in the workplace, where both professionals and nonprofessionals exert their greatest influence on society. The nonprofessional who is conservative off the job is often not at all conservative on workplace issues and therefore is not necessarily a net conservative force in society. Similarly, the professional who is liberal off the job is often very conservative on work issues and therefore is a net conservative force in society.

Indeed, there is an enormous gap between the opinions of professionals and their professional opinions—the opinions that guide their work. When their opinions count, most professionals are conservative. Thus the engineer who believes that corruption is common among politicians in the United States freely offers that opinion. The political scientist, however, fears being quoted as saying any such thing, even though few people would find it shocking.[10] Ask the nuclear engineer whether the nuclear industry influences reactor safety estimates, something that has long been obvious even to nonexperts, and you may get a lecture on the objectivity of mathematical calculations. And the liberal doctor who offers a cocktail party opinion against authoritarian police practices? Go to that doctor's office with a medical problem and see her lean toward the traditional authoritarian doctor–patient relationship. Professionals are liberal on *distant* social issues, issues over which they have no authority at work and no influence outside of work.

Note that developments that raise doubts about the social or economic system itself are never distant issues, even when they are geographically distant and not direct issues at work. As we saw, the Vietnam War, which involved the state's forcing people to make the highest possible sacrifice for debatable reasons, was such a crisis of legitimacy for the system. Such national crises and other anxiety-producing situations or events are immediate issues and so tend to elicit from professionals the same politically timid outlooks that guide their work.

Not surprisingly, while professionals are tolerant of distant social criticism, they have little tolerance for anyone who tries to provoke a debate about the politics that guide their own work. Noam Chomsky, a Massachusetts Institute of Technology professor and an outspoken critic of the state and the intellectuals who serve it, sees this firsthand when he takes a short trip down Massachusetts Avenue to Harvard University. Stepping out of the domain of conservative engineers and into the world of liberal theorists of the state and state policy, Chomsky feels a marked change in the level of tolerance for his radical democratic views. He described this to me in a letter:

> By conventional measures, the Harvard faculty is much more liberal, in fact left-liberal. MIT faculty are very conservative often, even reactionary. I get along fine with the MIT faculty, even when we disagree about everything (which is the usual case). If I show up at the Harvard faculty club, you can feel the chill settle; it's as if Satan himself entered the room.[11]

In this book I want to examine the outlook of professionals where it matters the most, which is on immediate issues—that is, on issues where what professionals do or say affects society directly. All workplace issues are immediate, as are a few outside of work. Thus, when I speak of professionals as uncritical and ideologically obedient, I am referring not to their opinions on distant social issues, but rather to the attitudes they display at work and *in* their work, where their conservatism shows up in its biggest and most socially significant way. And I am referring to their attitudes toward immediate nonworkplace issues, which are issues that raise questions about the merit or strength of the larger system—questions that professionals are usually quick to play down.

I don't mean to imply that *all* professionals are conservative when it counts. Some professionals do make trouble for the establishment. Although relatively few in number, such activist professionals help maintain an influential oppositional subculture in their workplaces, in their disciplines and in society. This subculture provides inspiration, encouragement and a vital safe haven for individuals whose thought deviates from the mainstream. And it gives its members the support they need to challenge their employers and others with power and to push for reform. Oppositional professionals have become increasingly influential since the 1960s, in part because of the battles fought at that time. The civil rights and antiwar movements, by successfully challenging the powers that be, helped make speech freer and the population more skeptical, conditions favorable for the opposition.

However, contrary to common belief, the number of oppositional professionals has remained relatively small. Consider, for example, college professors, who are among the most left-leaning of all professionals. Today, only about 5% of the 550,000 full-time college faculty members in the United States consider themselves to be to the left of the conservative-to-liberal mainstream.[12] This 1-in-20 proportion of leftists hasn't fluctuated much in at least 30 years.[13] If the proportion seems higher than this, that may be because people who break away from the mainstream establish a presence way beyond their numbers and because radicals are speaking out more openly inside and outside of the classroom. Also, in a few disciplines in the humanities, leftists really have increased their proportion significantly—a fact that conservatives have misrepresented to make widely publicized claims that leftists have taken over higher education in the United States. The bottom line is that while the vast majority of professionals continue to share the views of corporate business executives on most basic issues,[14] the important minority that dares to disturb the status quo has grown in influence, if not in size.

For understanding the professional, the concept of "ideology" will emerge as much more useful than that of "skill." But what is ideology, exactly? Ideology is thought that justifies action, including routine day-to-day activity. It is your ideology that determines your gut reaction to something done, say, by the president (you feel it is right or wrong), by protesters (you feel it is justified or unjustified), by your boss (you feel it is fair or unfair), by a coworker (you feel it is reasonable or unreasonable) and so on. More importantly, your ideology justifies your own actions to yourself. Economics may bring you back to your employer day after day, but it is ideology that makes that activity feel like a reasonable or unreasonable way to spend your life.

Work in general is becoming more and more ideological, and so is the workforce that does it. As technology has made production easier, employment has shifted from factories to offices, where work revolves around inherently ideological activities, such as design, analysis, writing, accounting, marketing and other creative tasks. Of course, ideology has been a workplace issue all along: Employers have always scrutinized the attitudes and values of the people they hire, to protect themselves from unionists, radicals and others whose "bad attitude" would undermine workplace discipline. Today, however, for a relatively small but rapidly growing fraction of jobs, employers will carefully assess your attitude for an additional reason: *its crucial role in the work itself.* On these jobs, which are in every field, from journalism and architecture to education and commercial art, your view of the world threatens to affect not only the quantity and quality of what you produce, but also the very nature of the product. These jobs require strict adherence to an assigned point of view, and so a prerequisite for employment is the willingness and ability to exercise what I call ideological discipline.

This book is about the people who get these jobs and become members of the ideological workforce—that is, professionals. My thesis is that the criteria by which individuals are deemed qualified or unqualified to become professionals involve not just technical knowledge as is generally assumed, but also attitude—in particular, attitude toward working within an assigned political and ideological framework. I contend, for example, that all tests of technical knowledge, such as the Graduate Record Examinations (GRE) or the Law School Admission Test (LSAT), are at the same time tests of attitude and that the examinations used to assess professional qualification are no exception. I consider in detail how the neutral-looking technical questions on such examinations probe the candidate's attitude. The qualifying attitude, I find, is an uncritical, subordinate one, which allows professionals to take their ideological lead from their employers and appropriately fine-tune the outlook that they bring to their work. The resulting professional is an obedient thinker, an intellectual property whom employers can trust to experiment, theorize, innovate and create safely within the confines of an assigned ideology. The political and intellectual timidity of today's most highly educated employees is no accident.

TRUSTED CADRE

As attitudes and values have come to play an increasingly important role in the production of goods and services, employers have faced a choice: either hire huge numbers of managers to direct every move of the large number of employees who now do politically sensitive work, or hire employees who can be trusted politically and merely check the results of their work. Employers have pursued both strategies simultaneously. But the first one is limited by its cost, and so today every country in the world, from the United States to China, has a growing cadre of people trusted to do work that requires making decisions based not on detailed instructions but on an assigned ideology.

A long episode of the Cold War drew attention to the Soviet cadre. Beginning in the late 1940s the U.S. government beamed Voice of America radio programs directly to the people of the Soviet Union. These short-wave broadcasts were in English, Russian and a dozen minority languages spoken in the USSR. On and off from 1948 until 1987 the Soviet government operated as many as 3,000 jamming transmitters, at a cost estimated at up to half a billion dollars a year, to drown out these programs—except for the ones in English.

Never in its four decades of jamming did the Soviet government censor English-language propaganda broadcasts aimed at its population. Why? Was it simply because the number of Soviet citizens who understood English was too small to worry about? That is certainly part of the answer, but it cannot be the whole story, because no group was too small for the Soviet government to worry about. English was a standard course in the Soviet schools, and at least some of the students who did well in school and were selected to become professionals eventually learned it. The number of Soviet citizens who could understand English-language broadcasts may have been small, but so was the number who could understand many of the minority languages that were jammed, at least six of which were each spoken by less than 1.5% of the population.

The Soviets never censored the English-language propaganda broadcasts because those who spoke English were a select group of people who were trusted to maintain ideological discipline in their work (even when they were not enthusiastic about the assigned ideology). As Robert C. Tucker, a longtime student of the Soviet Union, told me, "They were more likely to be establishment people, and not dangerous."[15] Many of these people, such as journalists, academics and foreign service professionals, were not only trusted to hear the U.S. government's viewpoint, but were also expected to know it so that they could answer it and not get caught off guard by it. The Soviets apparently treated the English-language broadcasts as if they were an exclusive service for their country's ideological workforce, prepping its members to handle any dangerous viewpoints that made it through the jamming and reached ordinary working people.[16]

As work has become increasingly ideological, professionals have made up a growing fraction of the workforce. In the United States in 1920, only 1 employed person in 20 was a professional. By 1940, this ratio had increased to 1 in 15; by 1960 it was 1 in 12; and by 1980 it had risen to 1 in 8. Today, at the beginning of the 21st century, the ratio is approaching 1 in 6 and growing rapidly. (The year 2000 began with the number of professionals approaching 22 million and total employment approaching 135 million.)[17]

In fact, employment in professional occupations is growing faster than that in any other major occupational group—not only in terms of percentage growth, but also in terms of number of people employed. This was true in the 10-year period ending in 1996 and is expected to be true again in the period 1996–2006, during which the number of professionals is projected to increase 27%, while total employment increases 14%.

The U.S. workforce is splitting into haves and have-nots. Indeed, service occupations are the second fastest growing occupational group numerically and the third fastest in terms of percentage growth. (Technicians are experiencing the second fastest percentage growth but are a small occupational group.) According to the U.S. Department of Labor, "professional specialty occupations and service occupations, which are on opposite ends of the educational attainment and earnings spectrum, are expected to provide nearly half of the total job growth from 1996 to 2006."[18] Such stratification of society has naturally heightened public interest in the people who are eligible for the high-strata jobs. Witness, for example, the media attention paid to *The Bell Curve*'s so-called "cognitive elite" and to Robert Reich's "symbolic analysts."[19]

Who, in more specific terms, are the professionals? In answering this question, one must be careful not to confuse professionals with white-collar workers in general, because white-collar workers, who now make up over one-half of the workforce, are mostly nonprofessionals. Chapter 2 gives a formula for identifying professionals and nonprofessionals by their responsibilities on the job, but a representative listing here will be useful. By any modern definition, the term professional refers to people in a wide variety of fields. The U.S. Census Bureau occupational category "professional specialty" workers includes such people as lawyers; teachers; counselors; social workers; registered nurses; doctors; psychologists; psychic readers; clergypeople; systems analysts; software specialists; engineers; scientists; people working as intellectuals or professors; architects; designers; athletes; entertainers; actors; directors; writers; photographers; artists; musicians; radio and television interviewers, hosts, personalities and newspeople; reporters; editors; censors; public relations specialists; advertising writers; librarians; political scientists; sociologists; urban planners; and economists.[20] My use of the term professional, based on the formula in chapter 2, turns out to be a bit broader. For example, the formula leads me to include not only those in the above-mentioned census category, but certain low-level executives as well. Here I have in mind those people who make up the new corps of salaried MBAs—holders of master's degrees in business administration hired to fill slots in large corporations, financial institutions, advertising agencies and so on.[21] I also include salaried accountants and certain compliance inspectors and law enforcers.

Excluded are those who are above or below professionals in the social pyramid. Thus, among those that neither the Census Bureau nor I include as professionals are, on the one hand, those who hire and fire professionals, and on the other hand, people such as the following: technicians; shopkeepers; "paraprofessionals" such as paralegals, teachers' aides and medical care aides; secretaries and other clerical workers; skilled and unskilled factory, farm, construction and transportation workers; machine operators; craftspeople; repairpeople; sales workers; service workers; and wage workers in general.[22]

The traditional image of the professional as an independent practicing doctor, lawyer or clergyman is misleading not only because of the proliferation of other professions, but also because very few professionals are free practitioners. The overwhelming majority are salaried employees. This has been true for many decades and is increasingly the case today as even the traditionally independent doctors and lawyers are swept into the salariat. Of every 9 professionals today, 8 are salaried employees and 1 is a free practitioner.[23] Hence, when I use the term professional, I have salaried employees in mind.

But not just those in the United States. As my use of an example from the Soviet Union was intended to suggest, the discussion here should be understood to apply to salaried professionals around the world. Whether they are in the United States, Russia or any other industrialized country—or in the developing world, where each country now has a growing modern sector—professionals go through similar training, have similar values and, most importantly, play the same role in the workplace. Perhaps the most striking evidence that professionals worldwide share the same essential features is the way they can fit right in, in dress, attitude and behavior, when hired into the local offices of multinational corporations or when employed abroad.

A system of production that divides its nonmanagement workforce into two distinct components—employees trusted to follow an assigned ideology in their work and employees not trusted to do so—clearly takes ideology very seriously. In fact, this system, now nothing less than a world system, gives questions of ideology *highest* priority. It must do so because of its increasing vulnerability in the face of a more and more politically sophisticated population, and it does so within each and every corporate or governmental division and at all levels of administration within these units. As a result, you cannot make sense of the system as a whole, the organization that employs you, or even your own job, just from a simple list of the goods and services being produced; understanding, now more than ever, means knowing the very carefully constructed ideologies that are guiding the production and that are being advanced through it.

You don't have to be an activist to have a very practical need for such an understanding. Ordinary life as a wage earner, parent, student, consumer, community member or simply resident of the nation inevitably leads to conflicts with powerful organizations: employers, schools, corporations, developers, government agencies and so on. No one responds to every conflict by saying "I'm mad as hell and I'm not going to take this anymore!" Nor does a given individual always back down. Everyone fights back at least some of the time and therefore needs understanding for more than its own sake.

However, to work effectively to change a policy or practice of an organization, or at least to get justice for yourself, understanding the ideology you are up against is not enough. You must also understand the organization's people— first, and most importantly, by understanding the role that each person is assigned to play in applying the ideology to the organization's day-to-day work. This means, in part, understanding the organization's professionals, because they are the people whom executives assign to monitor most closely the goods or services being produced and to maintain in detail the ideology that guides the production and that is carried by the product. Because professionals do this important political work in virtually every institution and workplace—from manufacturing, government and education to the news, advertising, entertainment and culture industries—understanding the political nature of professional work is an important part of understanding society itself. No one working or living in this society, and certainly no one working for social change, can afford to be ignorant of the political role of professionals.

Furthermore, professionals are the role models of the society toward which we are heading, a society in which ideology trumps gender, race and class origin as the biggest factor underlying the individual's success or failure. The victories of the feminist, civil rights and union movements of the past century have moved us closer to such a society. Thus, employers, led by the big corporations, are striving to ensure the survival of their precious hierarchical system of production by making it an equal opportunity system, which means subjecting employees to ideological scrutiny without sexist, racist or elitist discrimination. In the process, the corporations reveal what is most important to them and draw attention to the essential characteristics of the people who pass the strictest version of their scrutiny—professionals.

This book aims to arm people with a sharp understanding of the role of professionals in society. Such an understanding strengthens our collective ability to cope with the social and economic system and to confront it and make changes when we feel that is necessary. It also strengthens us as individuals to handle the daily confrontations that we face, because whether we are professionals or nonprofessionals we must deal with—and sometimes depend upon—professionals at work and elsewhere. If we are to avoid being bewildered, manipulated or even betrayed, it is crucial that we understand the social role of professionals.

HIDDEN CURRICULUM

The book attempts to understand professionals in part by looking at how they are made, from selection to certification, focusing on the role of attitude in the system's decisions about who is and who isn't qualified to become a professional. In short, this book is about the politics of professional qualification and professional practice.

The production of the rank-and-file physicist is the book's main example, although I use examples from many other fields as well. I look at physics, of all fields, because it is the one in which I myself went through professional training; also, physics is especially revealing because of its image as pure science and because its entrance requirements appear to be completely technical and not at all political. The book challenges this apparent neutrality by describing how the system of professional qualification in physics attempts to produce obedient scientists who as employees will give higher priority to carrying out their assignments than to questioning them, and who in any case will be unprepared to second-guess the political and ideological framework that gives rise to their projects and guides their technical work.

I have interviewed many professionals in a wide variety of fields and also many people who went to professional school but did not graduate. Most of these individuals remember their bouts with the qualification system in great detail, almost as if their lives had been at stake, and they usually have some sad stories and some horror stories to tell about conflicts between personal goals and institutional goals, about mistreatment, about broken dreams and about stressed-out fellow students who suffered mental or physical breakdowns. These stories are strikingly similar from field to field, school to school and department to department, yet the people who tell them usually have no idea that

this is the case and hence show none of the insight that would come from recognizing the underlying conflict that the similarity points to. What I find—and
this quickly becomes clear when you probe graduates and dropouts a bit—is
that the qualifying attitude, the way it is favored and the way it is measured are
very much the same across the professions. When someone describes to me
what really goes on in a particular school's professional training program in psychology, law, English, history, economics or any other field, much of what I hear
sounds exactly like professional training in physics, the field I often have in mind
during such discussions. For the same reason, the reader who knows the details
of professional training in any field, even one very different from physics, should
find the politics of professional qualification in physics very familiar.

Serious clashes between university faculty and individual students in professional training are not unusual. As we will see in the story below, these conflicts
are very revealing, and examining them may be the surest way to figure out
what the university's real priorities are in professional training. The confrontations occur over a wide variety of immediate issues, but most boil down to a
struggle over a single underlying issue: subordination. This shouldn't come as a
total surprise, because knowing that the professional's work is ideological—but
ideologically subordinate to management—we might expect to find professional training pushing students to accept an ideologically subordinate role. Indeed, the conflicts students run into as they proceed through the official curriculum expose a parallel, hidden curriculum of subordination.

Look, for example, at what one unusually perceptive student learned from
her conflicts in the graduate psychology program at a very selective, high-rank-
ing midwestern university. I interviewed Elizabeth by e-mail during the summer before the beginning of her fourth year in graduate school, when she was
about half way to the PhD.

> I was in the clinical program. I wanted to work directly with people, helping them
> (as corny as it sounds). I had a philosophy that if I could help children, I could save
> them lots of problems growing up (because the problems would be more difficult
> to treat as an adult). But the strongest reason for going into clinical was that at my
> undergraduate school, we were pretty much told point blank that clinical was the
> best and that the only people who went into other areas of psychology were those
> who couldn't cut it in clinical. Well, I was a good student and I always did well in
> whatever I did, so of course, I wanted to go for the best.
>
> In our program, you start seeing clients your first year. But that's not where the
> problems started. It really started my second year, when I had difficulties with my
> supervisor. I don't know how good a therapist he was, but as a supervisor, unfortu-
> nately, he was horrible.
>
> Basically the problem was that he would tell me I was doing something wrong
> without telling me how to correct it and without being specific enough for me to
> figure out how to correct it on my own.
>
> Sometimes he would tell me I needed to not let the clients get me off track,
> and sometimes he said I needed to go with where the client wanted to go, but he

couldn't help me figure out when. It was very confusing. Sometimes I would do exactly as he suggested in supervision, then after the session, he would tell me it was wrong. I remember once he told me I needed to be sterner, not so sympathetic. So I was. I wasn't mean, but I challenged her [the client's] assumptions instead of just accepting them. I think that was a good thing. Then he listened to the tape and asked where did the change of attitude come from. He said the session was out of character for me and criticized me for it. I couldn't do right. I didn't know what he wanted, and when I thought I did, I still couldn't do it right.

He would tell me sometimes that he didn't know exactly what was wrong, but that there was something. That I didn't seem to get deep enough, but he couldn't tell me what information it was he thought I should have gotten or how to "go deeper." Or the criticism was personal, such as "There's just something about you that prevents clients from feeling confident in you," as opposed to whether it was my speech, my posture, my dress, what I said, etc. Needless to say, constant criticism without direction did a lot for my self-esteem *wry grin*.

After spending a year and a half with this supervisor, and sincere, diligent attempts to improve and to ask for specifics when he didn't give them, I moved to another supervisor. She was much better, but unfortunately, by this time I was far behind in my training, was severely depressed and lethargic, and had self-esteem so low I was having difficulty being effective.

My continued failure (note vicious cycle here) led me to doubt myself in other areas of my life. It spread from feeling like I couldn't be a clinician, to feeling that I didn't belong in grad school, to everyday things like feeling that I was physically unattractive and undesirable, that I was not any good at my job, that I didn't have friends and didn't deserve any—there was literally nothing in my life I felt good about. I also had some physical problems with upset stomach and such, from the depression and not eating right, etc.

I decided I could not resolve the situation in the clinic and I left clinical. [Elizabeth left the PhD program in clinical psychology with a master's degree in clinical child psychology; she switched into the PhD program in experimental psychology, a subfield oriented toward psychology research.]

It had taken me several months to figure out what was going on and to get up the nerve to confront my [previous] supervisor, and unfortunately by that time it was too late. Basically, in a number of ways I didn't play the game. I disagreed with the role they wanted me to play as a therapist, which was very psychodynamic (with that supervisor). I believe in a much more psychoeducational approach, and I was told that I was being too friendly, that I was supposed to be a "blank screen." I felt very uncomfortable with that role and would not take it.

I remember once I was seeing a student who was looking at graduate schools and I was giving her some very practical advice about how to fill out applications and write personal statements (which she asked me for). He told me I was being too friendly with her, that I should not have given her the information, that I should have instead probed about why she was nervous about applying to grad school. Please!

I also openly disagreed with my supervisor and with how the clinic as a system was run. For example, they say they value student input, yet there was a very rigid line between students and staff, staff being very condescending and blatantly ignoring comments and suggestions by students. When confronted with this, they said they had considered our comments and decided they were impractical, yet they did not tell us about this decision until we confronted them, nor would they tell us why.

After talking to other students who had troubles in the clinic, I realized my situation was not unique, nor was it limited to the one supervisor. The clinic has a certain model of what their ideal therapist is. If you do not fit that model and if you do not conform, they make life difficult. The clinic is not open to people with different orientations or perspectives on how to do therapy, though they claim to be eclectic. Their meaning of eclectic is that they have supervisors from different backgrounds, but none who are truly eclectic. If your supervisor is psychodynamic, you'd better give up on any chance to include any behavioral techniques, though the next year you may be under a cognitive supervisor who would scorn the early life history you were taught to take the year before.

When I say "model," I do not mean a theoretical orientation. It's hard to explain exactly. The best way I can think of to describe the students who fit the model student role is to call them brownnosers. (I can think of other terms, but they kinda have to do with how the noses got brown in the first place *grin*.) They do everything they're told with seeming enthusiasm. They boost faculty egos, checking out attitudes and beliefs before writing that paper or giving that presentation. They just kinda go along, and even perhaps go so far as to praise the system. These are, of course, the students despised by the other students who are brave enough (stupid enough?) to stand up for how they feel. I know one of these students who told me it's all an act, just so she will get a traineeship or better recommendations for internships, but others I think really believe it. Overall, students who are most "successful" in the program don't rock the boat, do what they're told, and do what I call "play the game." Perhaps my unwillingness to play has led me, and others, to have difficulty in the program.

With some teachers (not all, to be fair) independent thought is not encouraged. If you bring up opinions, with or without research evidence to back it, you are at least ignored, at most ridiculed. Anyone who disagrees or is an independent thinker is given a hard time. There are actually a lot of independent thinkers in my class. The difference with me was that I don't think I was strong enough to stand up to faculty who tried to conform me. I refused to conform, but I wasn't assertive enough, so my lack of conformity appeared like lack of learning instead of a difference of opinion. I've changed quite a bit as a result of this experience.

Oh, one other thing. Women who get married, or god forbid, have children, are not serious about their careers. Or so the thought in the department goes. This is not even subtle prejudice. Married or pregnant women are given a more difficult time with their research (after all, they're not serious about it, are they?) and are openly told by some faculty that they are making a mistake.

Related to this is a strong gossip network, where your personal life is cut open and scrutinized. Anyone who's smart doesn't let any of their personal life be known to faculty, and are careful about which students they tell. I have a friend who got married over Christmas break and hasn't told anyone but myself and one other person. She's afraid of the repercussions.

I don't want to make [university name] sound like a bad school. There are a lot of very good things, too. And I'm sure the problems I've mentioned are not unique to my school. In fact, based on talking to other students about their training, I feel the training here is a lot better than some programs.[24]

Note that as Elizabeth tries to make sense of her observations, she discovers the subtle but important distinction between ideology and ideological discipline. She witnesses the central role of ideology in professional training ("The clinic is not open to people with different orientations . . ."), and so she knows that the defining characteristic of the faculty's model professional must have something to do with ideology. But she sees many ideologies at work in the clinic, and so she also knows that the defining characteristic isn't just an ideology ("When I say 'model,' I do not mean a theoretical orientation. It's hard to explain exactly."). So she simply lists the defining characteristics, and in doing so paints a clear picture not of a particular ideology but of ideological discipline: The "successful" students are the ones who check out faculty attitudes and beliefs so they can mimic them, the ones who eagerly adopt the current clinical supervisor's outlook, no matter what it happens to be—in general, the ones who subordinate their own beliefs to an assigned ideology.

I could, of course, say a lot more about Elizabeth's story, but my goal in this book is to present a framework that you can use to analyze accounts like hers for yourself.

OVERVIEW

Society's need for professionals leads to its system for producing them, not vice versa, and so the chapters that look at what professionals actually do precede those that look at the way they are educated. Thus chapters 1 to 6 look at the politics of professional work, and chapters 7 to 13 at the way people are selected to be professionals. We will see that the criteria used to select professionals reflect the political nature of professional work.

The first step is to define the professional. Most definitions are simply formalized versions of popular images of the professional. By focusing more on educational requirements than on what professionals actually do, these definitions do more to obscure than to reveal what a professional is. Chapter 2 offers an alternative; it shows how professionals are defined quite naturally by their responsibilities on the job, specifically, by their political responsibilities. Chapters 2 to 6 look at these politics and how they guide the work of professionals.

With chapter 7 we shift emphasis to the selection of professionals. The chapter begins with a look at nonprofessionals, and how their unfulfilling work lives profoundly affect their lives as a whole and lead them to search for ways to escape their situation. It then looks briefly at how historical changes in the economy have directed opportunity-seeking workers and others toward professional work in increasing numbers, exacerbating disputes over the criteria for admission to the professions. I argue that one cannot get to the core of these disputes until one recognizes that there is no set of standards for professional qualification—and, indeed, no professional—that employers and other sectors of society can agree is best. This leads me to argue that despite its seeming political neutrality, the system now used to select professionals is best understood through a political analysis, by which I mean scrutiny of its impact on power in the workplace and on conflicts of interest in society. Finally, I take note of the qualifying examination, which, because it is the keystone of the selection system's claim of neutrality, must be a major focus of any such analysis.

Chapters 8 to 10 look at how the professional is produced. Professional training, like all formal education, tends to make people more conservative. (Lack of formal education, however, does not make people radical.) The process is tumultuous, because students are neither blank slates nor passive raw material. They enter professional training with deeply held feelings about the personal and societal promise of professional work, and during professional training struggle against what often amounts to a brutal attempt to change their very identities. Chapter 8 describes the difference in outlook between those starting and those finishing professional school and looks at the components of the training process that bring about this difference. Chapter 9 illustrates how values are the real bottom line in professional training, and it looks at how the people who oversee the supposedly impartial selection system intervene to enforce their values on the rare occasions when the normal operation of the system fails to do so for them. Chapter 10 analyzes the most crucial and seemingly neutral component of the selection system—the qualifying examination—to uncover its intrinsic politics. These three chapters show how people with political attitudes appropriate for employment as well-behaved salaried professionals emerge from a seemingly neutral selection process that centers on objectively graded examinations on technical material.

Chapter 11 applies this book's analysis to tests used at much earlier stages of selection, specifically, standardized tests. College entrance tests such as the SAT, for example, play a role analogous to that of professional qualifying tests and so are subject to the book's critique. We will see that what appear to be cultural biases in such tests are really more fundamentally political biases.

Chapter 12 looks at how the qualification system handles the large number of people that it rejects. The system cannot simply give the best jobs to those who will serve employers the best. It must also lower the high educational and career expectations of the people that it excludes, so that they will not be insubordinate employees in the jobs that are available to them. We will see how the system uses "neutral" voices to cool out the nonprofessional.

Chapter 13 wraps up the preceding chapters by cataloging some of the self-subordinating behavior that is the hallmark of the prototypical professional—the professional that the training system produces when all of its components, described in the preceding chapters, operate normally.

Chapters 14, 15 and 16 offer some survival and resistance tips for students and professionals. The intellectual boot camp known as graduate or professional school, with its brutal expulsions and remaking of students, is set up to produce highly educated employees who know their place—narrow specialists who do their assigned work without questioning its goals. However, students can thwart the training system's efforts to make them into politically subordinate experts. Excellent techniques for doing this happen to be readily available, because professional training bears an uncanny resemblance to classic systems of indoctrination. Students can simply draw upon the hard-won, proven methods that people have already worked out for resisting indoctrination. Similarly, there are ways in which salaried professionals can maintain and pursue their own agendas.

One of this book's goals is to deconstruct the minimum requirements that make a person a professional. Hence, although much of the analysis here of the professional applies also to managers or administrators, the focus is on rank-and-file professionals, not on those who hire and fire them. Of course, many of those who employ professionals began their own careers as professionals and share many attributes with them. However, employers transcend the professionals they hire in important ways. For example, employers are prepared to review the standards of professional qualification at the training institutions, and they often serve on the committees that do so. They are able to do this because their own hiring work involves assessing the professional's compatibility with the organization. By the very nature of their work, employers must be at least somewhat aware of the politics of professional qualification, an awareness that is not required of professionals in general. Because my focus is on the core attributes required to pass the qualifying examination, when I speak of the professional I refer to the majority who do not employ other professionals.

As professionals become a bigger segment of the forces of production, so the production of professionals becomes a bigger activity in society, heightening public interest in the issue of bias in selection and training. This book's analysis finds the supposed political neutrality of the process of professional qualification a myth: Neither weeding out nor adjustment to the training institution's values are politically neutral processes. Even the qualifying examination—its cold, tough, technical questions supposedly testimony to the objectivity and integrity of the system of professional qualification and to the purity of the moment of personal triumph in every professional's training—does not act neutrally. The ideological obedience that the qualification system requires for success turns out to be identical to the ideological obedience that characterizes the work of the salaried professional.

The analysis that yields this important identity is valid not so much because it gives a self-consistent, unified picture of professionals, connecting their qualifications to what they actually do at work and in society—any theory should do that—but more because it allows one to make sense of real situations, as we will see.

NOTES

1. The phrase comes from an essay title: Harold Rosenberg, "The Herd of Independent Minds," *Commentary*, vol. 6 (September 1948), pp. 244–252.

2. *New York Times*, 13 January 1971, p. 1. Jay Schulman, Phillip Shaver, Robert Colman, Barbara Emrich, Richard Christie, "Recipe for a Jury," *Psychology Today*, May

1973, pp. 37–44, 77–84; reprinted in Lawrence S. Wrightsman, Saul M. Kassin, Cynthia E. Willis, editors, *In the Jury Box*, Sage Publications, Newbury Park, Calif. (1987), pp. 13–47. Jack Nelson, Ronald J. Ostrow, *The FBI and the Berrigans*, Coward, McCann & Geoghegan, New York (1972). William O'Rourke, *The Harrisburg 7 and the New Catholic Left*, Thomas Y. Crowell Company, New York (1972).

3. *New York Times*, 15 February 1970, sec. 1, p. 4; or George Horace Gallup, *The Gallup Poll*, vol. 3, Random House, New York (1972), pp. 2237–2238. The question was worded as follows: "Some U.S. senators are saying that we should withdraw all our troops from Vietnam immediately. Would you favor or oppose this?"

	Favor	Oppose	No opinion
National average	35	55	10
By age group			
21–29 years	39	57	4
30–49 years	36	56	8
50 and over	33	53	14
By extent of education			
College	29	64	7
High school	34	58	8
Grade school	44	41	15

(February 1970 poll of adults in 300 U.S. localities.)

4. Poll released 27 November 1969. George Horace Gallup, *The Gallup Poll*, vol. 3, Random House, New York (1972), pp. 2224–2225. Poll released 31 January 1971. *The Gallup Opinion Index*, Report No. 69, March 1971, p. 11.

5. "Do you think the United States made a mistake in going into the war in Korea, or not?" In this survey, conducted 4 to 9 February 1951, the ratio of those saying "mistake" to those saying "not a mistake" was 0.86 for adults with college educations, 1.2 for adults with high school educations and 1.5 for adults with grade school educations. George Horace Gallup, *The Gallup Poll*, vol. 2, Random House, New York (1972), pp. 968, 973.

6. For further discussion of the landscape of Vietnam War opinion, and references to other studies, see Bruce Andrews, *Public Constraint and American Policy in Vietnam*, Sage, Beverly Hills, Calif. (1976), pp. 33–34, 39–40, 44. For a study of a tiny but elite group of intellectuals, including a description of their pragmatic response to the Vietnam War, see Charles Kadushin, *The American Intellectual Elite*, Little, Brown and Company, Boston (1974). I thank Noam Chomsky for bringing these books to my attention.

7. Elizabeth Keogh Taylor, Arthur C. Wolfe, in Carnegie Commission on Higher Education, Stephen B. Withey, editor, *A Degree and What Else? Correlates and Consequences of a College Education*, McGraw-Hill, New York (1971), p. 125.

8. *The Gallup Opinion Index*, no. 49, July 1969, p. 11; no. 54, December 1969, p. 6; no. 57, March 1970, p. 10; no. 69, March 1971, p. 11. For a more recent example, see *The Gallup Report*, no. 276, September 1988, pp. 5–6.

9. For a summary of many surveys, see Steven Brint, "The Political Attitudes of Professionals," *Annual Review of Sociology*, vol. 11 (1985), pp. 389–414.

10. "Members of Congress are widely perceived by the public to be corrupt." See *New York Times*, 10 October 1991, pp. A1, B17.

11. Letter from Noam Chomsky, 12 October 1992.

12. Only 0.4% consider themselves to be to the right. *Chronicle of Higher Education*, 3 September 1999, pp. A20–21; 27 August 1999, p. 38.

13. Richard F. Hamilton, Lowell L. Hargens, "The Politics of the Professors: Self-Identifications, 1969–1984," *Social Forces*, vol. 71, no. 3 (March 1993), pp. 603–627.

14. See note 9.

15. Telephone conversation with Robert Charles Tucker, 9 September 1991. Tucker was an attaché in the U.S. embassy in Moscow from 1944 to 1953 and a professor of politics at Princeton University in the 1960s, 1970s and 1980s. He edited *The Marx–Engels Reader*, Norton, New York (1972).

16. Kenneth Y. Tomlinson, director of the Voice of America, quoted in *Wall Street Journal*, 2 September 1982, p. 12. (Page numbers in this book's references to the *Wall Street Journal* are generally those in the Eastern edition.) William Whitacre, chief of Voice of America's monitoring branch, told me that to his knowledge the Soviet Union never deliberately jammed VOA broadcasts in English (telephone conversation, 1 November 1989). According to Whitacre's records, the Soviets first jammed VOA (non-English) broadcasts to the USSR in February 1948 and ended their jamming finally at 11:00 UTC, 23 May 1987 (telephone conversation, 20 November 1989). Maury Lisann, *Broadcasting to the Soviet Union*, Praeger, New York (1975), p. 8. Donald R. Browne, *International Radio Broadcasting*, Praeger, New York (1982), p. 18. James L. Tyson, *U.S. International Broadcasting and National Security*, Ramapo Press, New York (1983), p. x. K. R. M. Short, editor, *Western Broadcasting Over the Iron Curtain*, St. Martin's Press, New York (1986), pp. 6 (apparently mistaken on English-language jamming), 99, 104, 113, 128. Mary W. Sowers, Gregory R. Hand, Charles M. Rush, *Monitoring of Harmful Interference to the HF Broadcasting Service: I. Results of the October 1984 and March/April 1985 Coordinated Monitoring Periods*, National Telecommunications and Information Administration, NTIA 85-187, U.S. Department of Commerce, Washington, D.C. (December 1985), p. 67; see also vol. II, on January 1986 monitoring, NTIA 86-206 (October 1986); and vol. III, on June 1986 monitoring, NTIA 87-213 (March 1987). Paul A. Goble, deputy director of research at Radio Liberty, estimates that 10 million of the 50 million Soviets with some kind of English-language training could understand radio broadcasts in English; this would represent about 4% of the Soviet population, or more than understood any but two of the minority languages that were jammed (fax transmission, 28 December 1989). Bernard Comrie, *The Languages of the Soviet Union*, Cambridge University Press, Cambridge, England (1981), pp. 279–281, 302.

17. The numbers given in this paragraph correspond as closely as possible to today's U.S. Census Bureau category "professional specialty occupations." The data for 1920, 1940 and 1960 are from *Historical Statistics of the United States, Colonial Times to 1970*, pt. 1, U.S. Bureau of the Census, Washington, D.C. (1975), pp. 140–145. To extract the number of workers in "professional specialty occupations" from the data on "professional, technical, and kindred workers," I followed *Relationship Between Major Occupation Groups Used in the 1980 and 1970 Census of Population*, Population Division, U.S. Bureau of the Census, Washington, D.C. (October 1982; revised March 1984) and the Census Code list *1970 Census of Population, Occupation Classification*, U.S. Bureau of the Census, Washington, D.C. (December 1973). Beginning with series number 234, I subtracted series numbers 235, 241, 253, 266, 279, 280, 282, 283, 284, 289 and 5% of

255 and added series number 384. (The 5% figure is an estimate for sales engineers, based on 1970 census data.) The datum for 1980 is from 1980 Census of Population, vol. 1, "Characteristics of the Population," *General Social and Economic Characteristics*, pt. 1, United States Summary, PC80-1-C1, U.S. Bureau of the Census, Washington, D.C. (December 1983), p. 1-45. See also 1980 Census of Population, vol. 2, "Subject Reports," *Occupation by Industry*, PC80-2-7C, U.S. Bureau of the Census, Washington, D.C. (May 1984), pp. 295–296. For more recent data and projections on the growth of occupational groups, see George T. Silvestri, "Occupational employment projections to 2006," *Monthly Labor Review*, U.S. Bureau of Labor Statistics, vol. 120, no. 11 (November 1997), pp. 58–83. For the most up-to-date data (current as of the previous month), see the labor force statistics from the Current Population Survey, U.S. Bureau of Labor Statistics, available on the World Wide Web.

18. Ibid., Silvestri, *Monthly Labor Review*.

19. Richard J. Herrnstein, Charles A. Murray, *The Bell Curve: Intelligence and Class Structure in American Life*, Free Press, New York (1994). Robert B. Reich, "Secession of the Successful," *New York Times Magazine*, 20 January 1991, p. 16. Robert B. Reich, *The Work of Nations: Preparing ourselves for 21st-century capitalism*, Knopf, New York (1991).

20. For a fascinating list of 30,000 occupation titles, see 1990 Census of Population and Housing, *Classified Index of Industries and Occupations*, 1990 CPH-R-4, U.S. Bureau of the Census, Washington, D.C. (April 1992).

21. For a detailed, tell-it-like-it-is description of managerial life in the modern corporate power hierarchy, see Robert Jackall, *Moral Mazes: The World of Corporate Managers*, Oxford University Press, New York (1988).

22. See note 20.

23. U.S. Bureau of Labor Statistics, unpublished data on "professional specialty occupations" from *Current Population Survey*, 1997 annual average. I counted as free practitioners not only self-employed professionals (8% of all professionals), but also professionals who are employees of their own corporations (3% of all professionals).

24. Interview by e-mail, 27 July 1992 to 28 August 1992. Elizabeth asked me to withhold the name of her university and her last name.

2

IDEOLOGICAL DISCIPLINE

Doctor, lawyer, teacher, scientist, psychologist, sociologist, economist, engineer, professor: What makes an individual a professional?

Technical knowledge and skill come to mind immediately. But there must be more to it than that, because the worker who picks up technical knowledge and skill on the job does not get reclassified as a professional.

With few exceptions, the professional is a product of the schools. The fact that off-the-job schooling is what makes the difference between the professional and the nonprofessional is curious, because professionals-in-training often complain that much of the prescribed study is "irrelevant" to the technical knowledge and skills they will actually need to do the job.[1] Students feel frustrated by the numerous "extra" requirements that they must fulfill to be allowed to work and that seem to constitute an unnecessary obstacle course.

Nonprofessional workers who feel capable of exercising more authority at work experience the same frustration. Nonprofessionals with years of experience resent being bossed by inexperienced professionals who, in their work, seem to be distinguished not by any greater skill or understanding, but merely by their possession of "paper credentials." Nonprofessionals resent the fact that their suggestions face an extra obstacle to acceptance: their nonprofessional source.[2] The *Wall Street Journal* once reported sympathetically on the plight of disbarred lawyers. One of their examples, Donald Ziglar, was forced by economic necessity to go to work as a shipping clerk in a manufacturing plant:

> When he delivered mail to corporate offices, where executives would be discussing a shipping problem, he yearned to join in. "But I was a nobody, just bringing the mail. It would tear the guts completely out of me."[3]

Should we have more sympathy for this former professional than we have for any of the millions of experienced nonprofessionals who also suffer exclusion from the decision-making process?

Workers throughout the system know the problem. Skilled workers and technicians in industry often have a better idea of what is going on, what the production problems are and what the best solutions might be than do the company engineers and scientists, who often make decisions without taking the views of workers seriously. Educational aides who perform teaching functions in the schools and legal aides who work in law offices are as skilled in many areas as teachers or lawyers, but no one is seriously interested in their views and ideas about education or law. Similarly excluded are nurses and medical technicians—and, often, patients themselves—who are as skilled as doctors in the performance of many diagnostic and treatment procedures, but who are usually allowed only the role of "bit players, while physicians stand at center stage," even though "most medical situations do not require such an arrangement." This is the assessment of Martin Shapiro, a doctor who stopped to take a critical look at medical training immediately after he went through it.[4] He discusses the situation of nurses and relates an incident that illustrates their skills:

> A staff physician was the only one covering the emergency room on a night when someone was brought in with acute pulmonary oedema, a condition in which the lungs are filled up with fluid, usually due to weakness of the heart. The physician-on-duty happened to be out of the emergency department when the patient was brought in.
>
> Pulmonary oedema is a medical emergency. A patient who does not receive prompt treatment can die very quickly. . . .
>
> The nurses recognized the patient's problem instantly. They paged the physician and gave the appropriate supportive care, but they could not give the medications until the doctor came. For ten crucial minutes, the physician did not appear, despite frantic and continued paging throughout the hospital. With the patient seated upright, tourniquets applied and oxygen flowing, the nurses could do little else. . . . They drew up the required medications in appropriate dosages into syringes and stood poised by the patient's bedside. When the physician finally sauntered in, he gave the necessary permission for the potentially life-saving injections.[5]

The tyranny of paper credentials is also well known by countless secretaries and assistants throughout the economy who do much of their bosses' work, and by other workers who are not allowed to exercise their skills independently of one or another of the workplace professionals, who seem to be identifiable mainly by their suits and their "wallpaper."

The system tries to entice dissatisfied nonprofessionals into the individual solution of chasing paper themselves. Thus, while corporations offer to pay their employees' tuition, colleges, in turn, offer academic credit for skills acquired through work experience. Such credit puts workers on the way to obtaining the required paper: Having been granted credit for their skills, they can concentrate more on the "irrelevant" material.

If the seemingly irrelevant material is, in fact, irrelevant, then employers would be foolish to insist on hiring people with paper credentials when they could hire equally skilled nonprofessionals at much lower salaries.

Of course, employers are not being foolish when they insist on credentials. Professionals do something for them that skilled nonprofessionals cannot do. As a look at some examples will illustrate, employers can trust professionals to uphold the right outlook in their creative work.

THE POLITICS OF NOT GETTING POLITICAL

Consider the schoolteacher. Those who employ teachers see them as more than workers who present the official curriculum to the students. A computer or television system could make such a presentation. An important role of the schools is socialization: the promulgation of an outlook, attitudes and values. For example, the schools prepare students for the labor force not just by teaching them arithmetic, English, history and so on, but also by teaching them to follow instructions, adhere to a rigid time schedule, respect authority and tolerate boredom. Lessons in this "hidden curriculum" are taught as much in the numerous school–student interactions not involving the official curriculum as in those interactions that do. The employer trusts the teaching professional to manage these interactions in such a way as to advance the proper values. The professional is one who can be trusted to extrapolate to new situations the ideology inherent in the official school curriculum that she teaches.

As a professional, the teacher is "objective" when presenting the school curriculum: She doesn't "take sides," or "get political." However, the ideology of the status quo is *built into* the curriculum. The professional's objectivity, then, boils down to not challenging this built-in ideology.

It is revealing that teachers who do question the curriculum attract the attention of school administrators, while teachers who are simply incompetent at teaching it tend to be ignored. (Indeed, when teachers are fired it is rarely for not teaching well.) "Legitimate" professional questions for teachers concern not what they should be doing politically in the classroom—the professional has an internalized willingness and ability to be directed in this area—but how best to convey the material in the official curriculum. In this alone, teachers are expected to use their creativity, and the awards of the profession go to those who do best.[6]

Consider the cop. Robots could conceivably enforce the "letter of the law" and keep extremely busy doing so because of the abundance of infractions that occur. However, mindless enforcement would achieve the law's goals only very crudely, if at all, and that is why law enforcers must be professionals. Professionals are hired to enforce the "spirit of the law"—the spirit in which the letter is written. Only the professional is trusted to sense, for example, which of the multitude of minor violations of the "letter" are acts of defiance against the "spirit" and therefore call for a response.

It may not seem very radical to say that the spirit of the law is to defend the status quo. However, the police adamantly deny playing anything but a neutral role in society. Nothing reveals better the actual partisan role of the police and the priority they give to the law's spirit over its letter than do the thousands of "attitude crimes" that draw punishment every day in this country. An attitude crime is behavior that violates the spirit of the law, whether or not it also violates the letter. Maintaining a discourteous or disrespectful manner when pulled over by the police, for example, is not illegal, but it can get you a traffic citation instead of a warning, because the spirit of the law says "respect authority." Similarly, subservience can sometimes get you off with a warning even though you've violated the letter of the law by, say, loitering. But if you talk back to the cops, the very same loitering can lead to handcuffs and a night in jail, especially if you are black or Latino. Surely many of the estimated 20,000 instances of police brutality in the United States each year are "provoked" by the suspect's less-than-deferential attitude.[7]

In 1980, statistics came to light in San Diego County indicating as many as 700 "attitude arrests" there each month. This figure included only cases in which arrestees were released hours or days later with no charges filed. The figure would have been much higher had it included arrests in which the police filed contrived charges as well as arrests for minor violations in which the police filed additional or more serious charges because of the violator's attitude, a practice known as "overbooking."[8]

One San Diegan, Edward Lawson, was repeatedly stopped, frisked and arrested, often violently, solely because of his attitude. Lawson enjoyed walking in pretty residential areas, but as a black man with dreadlocks strolling through wealthy white neighborhoods at odd hours, he would be stopped frequently for questioning by the police. Lawson would demand to know why he was being stopped, but the cops were not interested in giving explanations. When Lawson would press his demand, he often found himself thrown in the back of a squad car with his hands manacled behind him. While Lawson's demand was not illegal, it violated the spirit of the law, which says "know your place."[9]

Punishment for attitude crimes is rampant today. In California alone, police in 1997 made over 85,000 arrests in which they released the arrested individuals without filing charges, mainly because of lack of evidence. An even larger number of cases were thrown out by prosecutors before trial. Sixty-one percent of the individuals given the arrest-and-release treatment by police were minorities.[10]

From employment law to landlord/tenant law to tax law to property law, the spirit of the law is to maintain the privileges of the wealthy. Yet the letter of the law is seemingly neutral on the question. "The law, in its majesty equality," observed Anatole France, "forbids rich and poor alike to sleep under bridges, to beg in the streets and to steal bread."[11] Nevertheless, those who enforce the law tend to see the wealthy as "good guys" and tend to be suspicious of people without property. This is not because police are inherently biased people but because they have to take up the spirit of the law to do a professional job enforcing it. The professional's "objective" enforcement of the law boils down to acting in accord with no ideology *other* than the one built into the law. A cop who challenges the law's built-in bias in favor of the status quo would quickly attract the attention of higher-ups. But this is rarely a problem, because the law enforcement professional is tuned more to following orders than to grappling with moral questions. The police officer's "legitimate" professional questions concern not the nature of the social hierarchy that the law defends, but how best to enforce the law that defends it.

Consider the shrink. Many mental problems originate not in diseases of the brain but in deficiencies of society. The arduousness of living with unfulfilling work, financial insecurity, arbitrary bosses, lack of solidarity and insufficient personal power, together with the anguish caused by racism, sexism, ageism, lookism, ableism and all the other oppressive hierarchies that plague this society, helps explain the fact that more than 10% of the population (and not counting those with substance abuse disorders) suffers from mental or emotional problems. There are enough troubled individuals in the United States to keep busy 100,000 psychiatrists and clinical psychologists and a much larger number of clinically trained social workers and other mental health professionals.[12] People's mental problems often appear as deviations from social or legal norms and therefore are problems for the status quo as well as for the deviant individuals.

The problems of both would be solved if troubled individuals abided by the values of the status quo, and of course the mainstream mental health system more often than not works to alter behavior in that direction.[13] But attempting to adjust people to the unhealthy society that caused their problems in the first place may not always be the healthiest approach for either the individuals or society. A simple alternative would be to help some troubled individuals bring out, clarify and sharpen their implicit critique—to strengthen them for the struggle in which they are engaged instead of removing them from it, because the struggle can be both therapeutic for the individual and beneficial to society. But the institutions of mental health, such as hospitals that employ psychiatrists and clinical psychologists, are institutions of the status quo. They are not about to turn the troubled into troublemakers, no matter how healthful that might be. The mental health professional is someone that such an employer can trust to move confused people away from struggle with social norms and authority and toward a life in which they are "well adjusted" to their place in the socioeconomic hierarchy.

As professionals, psychotherapists are "nonpartisan" in their work: They just help ill people get better. But to declare extreme nonconformity an illness, as psychology professionals often do, is a partisan act because of the down-on-the-victim therapeutic framework it rationalizes: "Treating 'sick' individuals" is a much more politically conservative framework than is "treating individuals troubled by a sick and oppressive society." Evidently it is not the place of the clinicians to question the health of the society to which the patient must be adjusted. Their "legitimate" professional concern is how best to bring about the adjustment. In this alone, they are expected to use their creativity. The few who do raise questions are seen as "getting political," even though it is hard to imagine how they could get any more political than mainstream clinical psychology itself, which often practices conservative social action disguised as medical treatment.

THE EXPERT'S OPINION

As the above examples illustrate, the failure of professionals to question the politics built into their work serves the interests of those who have power in society and helps maintain the social and economic status quo. But refraining from questioning doesn't *look* like a political act, and so professionals give the appearance of being politically neutral in their work.

Nevertheless, the public is becoming increasingly savvy about at least one way in which professionals support the system through their work. People are beginning to understand that the intellectual worker's "professional judgment" or "expert opinion" is not objective as it claims, but rather favors the interest of his or her employer. (Supporting one's employer and supporting the larger system are not the same thing, but because it is basically a corporate system, each boosts the other.) The public most easily recognizes the political tilt of professionals toward their employers when it is blatant. Thus, not many people today are surprised at the Johns-Manville Corporation doctors, whose medical findings for decades helped the asbestos producer suppress information on the deadly health hazard posed by the "miracle mineral."[14] Similarly, many people immediately questioned the scientific opinion of a group of distinguished physicists arguing in favor of nuclear power when it was revealed that the physicists were connected to the nuclear industry and major corporations.[15] And today people may be outraged, but they are no longer surprised, when an HMO medical director—a doctor in a business suit—hustles patients out of the hospital very soon after major surgery, even when common sense indicates further close monitoring.[16]

Expert witnesses in big-money court cases draw further attention to reason's eager subordination to power. Today only the most naive observers are surprised when reputable experts from the same field contradict one another under oath. In high-stakes trials each side can afford the best experts money can buy, and these experts often turn out to be big names in their fields.

Finally, consider the university professors who have received research grants from tobacco companies to study the health effects of cigarettes. These independent medical researchers, whose names are often followed by the letters "MD, PhD," are typically well-respected, highly prolific scientists at prestigious institutions such as Harvard University. Many have served on presidential or other high-level government advisory committees. For decades these scientists have served their sponsors' interests by finding tobacco to be safe and nonaddictive, and by attacking studies that find otherwise. In scientific journals, at scientific conferences, in press releases to the mass media, at congressional hearings and as expert witnesses in court, these doctors have given their professional opinion that cigarettes are not dangerous. Their views fly in the face of estimates, by public health scientists with no connection to the tobacco industry, that smoking kills 1,200 people per day in the United States.

In addition to their grantees, the tobacco companies also have scientists working for them directly. Over the years, a very tiny minority of these researchers have pushed behind the scenes to make public some of their findings critical of tobacco. But they typically did not push very hard[17] and did not leak their findings to warn the public.

It took a socially conscious nonprofessional to show what needed to be done. In 1994 a paralegal who worked for a law firm representing a tobacco company, acting under the name "Mr. Butts" (and in the spirit of chapter 16 of this book), sent 4,000 pages of secret tobacco company documents to an antismoking activist.[18] These revealing "Cigarette Papers" show how embarrassingly easy it is for a well-heeled organization to get what it wants from reputable scientists.[19]

The strategy of the tobacco companies has been to use scientists to make the dangers of cigarettes look controversial. The companies depend upon the fact that many observers hearing the word "scientist" naively think "nonpartisan." Thus the head of the Council for Tobacco Research, which was the major health research organization of the tobacco industry, told Congress, "We are scientists and we seek scientific truth."[20] However, as the public has grown more aware of the need to ask for whom experts are working, the tobacco industry has found it increasingly difficult—but not yet impossible—to use its contrarian scientists to get people to think "controversial" when they hear about research findings that implicate tobacco in disease and death.

WHEN DOES A JOB DEMAND A PROFESSIONAL?

Could you or your boss write a "how-to" manual for your job? The most common answer to this question is yes, because most jobs can be described in unlimited detail. Consider, for example, what a secretary does when the boss scrawls a memo on a piece of paper and says, "Send this to all our salespeople in Texas." The manual might say: Type the memo; let the boss check it; access the sales force database; duplicate the memo; address envelopes; stuff, seal and mail. Any of these steps could in turn be described in as much further detail as desired. Many workers, such as telemarketing salespeople or fast-food order takers, have their very words prescribed: "Would you like fries with that?"

Some jobs, however, involve work that can't be spelled out completely. Here a manual would not be able to say much more than "create": Write a news story; draft a policy; design a product; compose an advertising jingle; draw a cartoon;

tailor a lesson for a class; select a medical test; evaluate someone in need of so-cial services; decide how to proceed in a scientific research project; and so on. Jobs with a creative element can't be completely formularized—a manual could not supply even the first word of a news story, for example.

Beyond a certain point on such a job, the worker faces a blank sheet of paper, and the boss can't tell her exactly what to do. Here employers simply expect their creative workers to act in the corporate interest—the artist drawing a pic-ture for a cigarette ad, for example, is expected to make smoking look good in both specified and unspecified ways. Unlike employees whose actions can be prescribed in unlimited detail, these workers have to understand their employ-ers' interests, because there are moments when that understanding is all they have to go on. Employers designate these special nonmanagement workers "professionals."

Preparing to become a professional is fundamentally different from prepar-ing to become a nonprofessional, because the blank sheet professionals face holds an infinity of possibilities, and there is no way to teach or even list them all. Professional training therefore centers around ideology, because ideology guides the subtle decisions and creative choices that the professional makes as she fills the blank sheet. (The professional's work, in turn, propagates the ide-ology that guides it.) Even those whose range of discretion is humiliatingly in-significant require the special preparation: The system apparently considers ideology to be of paramount importance. Thus, if the work of a particular oc-cupation is in part creative—that is, if the decisions are not *purely* routine or rote—preparing and qualifying for that occupation will include a *major* ideo-logical component involving years of postsecondary schooling, even if the cre-ative work is a *minor* part of the job.

This accounts for the seeming disparity between amount of preparation and authority on the job. ("After all the schooling I went through, they hardly let me make a difference around here.") And it accounts for the seemingly irrelevant part of the schooling required to get the paper credentials that allow one to work as a professional. Despite years of student opposition, these qualifying re-quirements are still imposed, precisely because they are *not* irrelevant. They get the individual used to the kind of political framework within which the skills and techniques of the profession are applied.

When employers designate certain jobs "professional" and insist that em-ployees have professional training—not just the technical skills that seem suffi-cient to do the work—they must have more in mind than efficiency. Hierarchi-cal organizations need professionals, because through professionals those at the top control the political content of what is produced, and because profession-als contribute to the bosses' control of the workforce itself. It is crucial for the functioning and survival of the institution—and the hierarchical system of pro-duction as a whole—that the employees who make decisions do so in the in-terest of the employer. As we will see, the employer's control of the political content of the professional's creative work is assured by the ideological discipline developed during professional training. And the employer's control of the workforce is maintained in part through the professional's elitism and support for hierarchy in the workplace. The preparation process develops, and the qualification process measures, the student's willingness and ability to accept ideological direction from future employers. The one who has met the requirements—the "qualified professional"—can be trusted to do what is "politically correct" when making decisions and creative choices at work.

Professionals sell to their employers more than their ordinary labor power, their ability to carry out instructions. They also sell their ideological labor power, their ability to extend those instructions to new situations. It is this sale that distinguishes them from nonprofessionals, who sell only their ordinary labor power. Those in charge can trust professionals to make some decisions that must be made ideologically; nonprofessionals are trusted to make only decisions that can be made mechanically. Professionals implement their employers' attitudes as well as their employers' lists of instructions; nonprofessionals are only required to implement the instructions.

Nonprofessionals often feel that their employers treat them like unthinking machines, and they long for the more human treatment that they see their professional coworkers receiving. The double standard is inexcusable, but its origin should be no mystery. The root of the bosses' bimodal behavior is structural: In the professional/nonprofessional division of labor, nonprofessionals play a role analogous to that of a machine. Machines are "dead" in the sense that they add to the product no more value than that of the labor that went into building them. In the language of economics, they produce no "surplus value," or profit. (Machines increase productivity, but in a competitive industry they ultimately lead to lower prices rather than higher profits: The first companies to mechanize see higher profits until mechanization in the rest of the industry forces prices down.) Unlike machines, humans, whether professionals or nonprofessionals, add to the product more value than they cost to employ. However, nonprofessionals yield only the ideological work that went into formulating the instructions they follow. Thus, just as machines are dead as compared to human workers, nonprofessionals are dead as compared to professionals in terms of doing *ideological* work. Nonprofessionals do not extend their employers' ideologies through their work, because they do not make ideology-based decisions for their employers, and so the bosses care less about what they think.

Ideological workers are more expensive than non-ideological workers, because they require a greater amount of formal education. The same economic forces that drive employers to replace nonprofessionals with machines (which initially bring higher profits) also drive them to reduce the discretion of professionals by standardizing the work procedure, or even by introducing "expert" computer systems. In each workplace the bosses push for more and more detailed job descriptions and work guidelines, which transform the employee's decision-making into a routine or rote activity and tend to strip the work-result of any imprint of the employee's own thinking.

From The Wall Street Journal, by permission,
Cartoon Features Syndicate

"True, you can't buy loyalty. However, you certainly can lease it."

In fact, nonprofessionals are often *forbidden* to be creative in their work. In many jobs, the more closely the employees follow set workplace procedures and any special instructions for the tasks at hand, the happier the bosses are. Nonprofessionals know that they risk getting in trouble when they innovate to get the job done.

Professionals, on the other hand, are *required* to be creative in their work—but within strict political limits. Their creativity must serve their employers' interests, which often are not the same as their own interests, the interests of clients or customers or the public interest. Thus the corporate PR specialist assigned to field questions about pollution, defective products, the treatment of employees and other sensitive issues creatively uses the truth to paint a pro-company picture. And managed care doctors never forget for whom they are working either. One such doctor, for example, saves his employer $200 by withholding the antiviral drug acyclovir from adult chicken pox patients; without the drug, the severity of the disease and the amount of permanent scarring are greater, but the chance of secondary pneumonia or death increases only slightly.[21] Complications would be costly to the medical care corporation, but the savvy MD intuits correctly that it doesn't make economic sense for the firm to spend so much to insure against them. Employers don't have time to decide every minor issue that affects their political or economic interests, and so they seek to hire others who will do things as if they had done them themselves. Thus, professionals control the technical means but not the social goals of their creative work. The professional's lack of control over the political content of his or her creative work is the hidden root of much career dissatisfaction.

To say that professionals are ideological workers is not to say that they formulate the ideology in the first place, for they do not. Professionals have no more control over the ideology they propagate than nonprofessionals have over the design of the products they produce. Professionals merely have an operational grasp of the ideology inherent in their occupation's actual role in society. Employers trust them to use that ideology to extrapolate policy and handle new problems as they arise, and to do so without constant supervision. Professionals are licensed to think on the job, but they are obedient thinkers.

All professional work is in part creative. However, individuals are selected to do professional work not because they are more creative than others, but because they can be trusted to make sure every detail of what they create is politically correct from their employers' points of view. As human beings, professionals are not more creative than nonprofessionals. In fact, professional training tends to kill off natural creativity. In the corporate headquarters building you can often find more creativity down in the mail room than upstairs in the office of a lawyer, systems engineer or financial analyst, but it is untamed. Employers will hire dull but politically disciplined individuals over those displaying any amount of politically undisciplined creativity.

Just as professionals engage in playpen creativity, innovating within the safe confines of an assigned ideology, so too they engage in playpen critical thinking.

Their work involves judging whether or not the ideas of others are in line with the favored outlook, but does not involve developing their own, independent point of view. Hence professionals tend to be what might be called "book review" critical, which is intellectually and politically safe because it doesn't involve developing or taking a stand for an independent outlook. Professionals generally avoid the risk inherent in real critical thinking and cannot properly be called critical thinkers. They are simply ideologically disciplined thinkers. Real critical thinking means uncovering and questioning social, political and moral assumptions; applying and refining a personally developed worldview; and calling for action that advances a personally created agenda. An approach that backs away from any of these three components lacks the critical spirit.

Ideologically disciplined thinkers, especially the more gung-ho ones, often give the *appearance* of being critical thinkers as they go around deftly applying the official ideology and confidently reporting their judgments. The fact that professionals are usually more well-informed than nonprofessionals contributes to the illusion that they are critical thinkers.

WORKING BETWEEN THE LINES

Professionals look beneath the surface of their technical work and see a world of contending social forces. Where the nonprofessional might see only technical details, the professional sees sides of debates being supported, points of view being advanced and interests being served. Professionals are extremely sensitive to the underlying issues, and little subtext slips by them unnoticed.

But professionals do more than read between the lines. They write between them as well. Like nonprofessionals, professionals spend the bulk of their time doing tedious detail work. However, unlike nonprofessionals, they are expected to make sure that the subtext of each and every detail of their work advances the right interests—or skewers the disfavored ones. If "God is in the details," as the phrase often attributed to architect Ludwig Mies van der Rohe has it, then making sure the details represent the *right* god is the *raison d'être* of professionals. Their assignments typically involve decisions on hundreds of details, and so professionals can't relax their political guard even for a moment. If tedious detail work is mind numbing for the nonprofessional, it is grueling for the professional.

Many people naively think of professionals as nonprofessionals who possess additional technical knowledge or technical skills. Professionals do exercise technical skills, of course, but it is their use of political skills that distinguishes them from nonprofessionals. The product of professional labor is political. It takes sides. The accountant's bookkeeping decision, the journalist's angle on a story, the lawyer's choice of contract language, the historian's depiction of events, the scientist's narrow focus, the minister's sermon, the teacher's lesson, the welfare worker's determination, the comedian's joke[22]—routine professional work tilts one way or the other, and the way it tilts is never an accident.

Nonprofessionals in the workplace often discover the hard way this all-important political component of professional work. In the most common scenario, a seemingly simple problem comes up and a nonprofessional takes the initiative and does what seems reasonable. But nonprofessionals are often oblivious to the forces that are contending beneath the surface of the work, and so their decisions may advance the wrong interests—wrong from their employers' points of view. When this happens they find their initiative rewarded with a bawling out from the boss. "Next time wait and ask somebody what to do." "Somebody," of course, doesn't mean a fellow nonprofessional.

Perhaps no one draws more attention to the political component of professional work than does the lawyer. All professionals give highest priority to making sure the right interests are served. Most professionals do this political work quietly as they much more visibly exercise technical skills that the public sees as nonpolitical: treating illness, informing readers, catching criminals, teaching children how to add and subtract, doing scientific research, developing new technology, designing whatever. For lawyers, however, the perception is reversed, because watching out for the right interests is not only their highest priority but also an unusually large part of what they do. Lawyers exercise the professional's basic ability to sense interests, but, unlike other professionals, they exercise no other skill more prominently.

Indeed, lawyering involves such a high ratio of political work to technical work that technical knowledge is something of an afterthought in the training of lawyers. Yes, law schools do organize instruction around memorizing and applying specific principles of law, but this is done primarily as an exercise to teach proficiency at adopting and working within assigned ideologies. As Talbot D'Alemberte, former president of the American Bar Association and a critic of legal education, told me, in law school the law is just a vehicle to teach a way of thinking.[23] Perhaps the most obvious evidence of this is that students fresh out of law school—even those graduating at the top of their classes—do not feel they have the technical knowledge necessary to pass the bar examination. They must spend a couple thousand dollars to take an intensive six- to eight-week "bar review" course to learn what they need to know to pass the test and get their permit to practice law.

Ironically, the more elite the law school, the more necessary the "bar review," because the professors at the elite institutions emphasize ideological skills. In their words, notes D'Alemberte, "We don't train you to be a lawyer, but only to think like a lawyer."[24] (Getting the student to think like a professional is the top priority in all professional training programs, and so technical skills are of secondary importance not just in law school. Nonetheless, the graduate psychology student, for example, learns more than how to "think like a psychologist" and the graduate history student emerges knowing more than how to "think like a historian.")

This emphasis on ideological skills in law school is precisely what the powerful corporate law firms want, because the high-stakes legal battles they fight defending big business and wealthy clients are paramountly political. The simple ability to recite the law does not qualify one to do this work. Representing powerful clients requires lawyers who can make creative arguments about the intent of the law, who can find ways to argue that the public interest would be served by a favorable ruling, and who can sway public opinion in high-profile cases, where this opinion influences the outcome. Settling losing cases out of court is political work, too. Lawyers for the powerful must know, for example, to give high priority to negotiating clauses that keep the terms of the settlement secret, this to protect the corporation's or rich person's public image and to avoid setting a precedent that would help other wronged parties to obtain justice. Thus the big law firms aren't primarily interested in the technical skills of the law school graduates they hire. Those skills are easily picked up on the job; an ideologically disciplined mind is not. Similarly, the firms don't care much about bar exam scores. In fact, the large firms typically hire law school graduates before they even take the bar exam.

Lawyers have a negative public image because, unlike other professionals, they don't exercise socially redeeming technical skills. For this reason, they are seen as people who take without giving—a nonproductive element of society. Lawyers themselves, especially those at the big firms, make little pretense of doing work that benefits the public at large. Thus, more than other professionals, they feel the need to reserve some of their time to work "pro bono publico"—for the public good. (Most social workers, teachers, journalists, sociologists, scientists and other professionals would feel insulted if you asked them whether they set aside any working time to help make the world a better place.) In the words of Judge Laurence H. Silberman of the U.S. Court of Appeals for the D.C. Circuit, "Lawyers really see pro bono services as the penance they pay for serving a capitalist system."[25]

Perhaps the most widely distributed between-the-lines writing is the handiwork of journalists. The news stories they write for the front page of your daily newspaper are chock full of subtext. This becomes clear when different reporters describe the same event, because then their descriptions differ in substance only by what they have written between the lines.

On 1 March 1993, for example, the lead stories in both the *New York Times* and the *Wall Street Journal* covered the same topic: what had been learned about the World Trade Center bombing, which had occurred three days earlier.[26] The article in the *Times* began with these words: "The bomb that devastated the garage under the World Trade Center in lower Manhattan on Friday apparently was. . . ." The article in the *Journal* began like this: "The bomb blast that drilled a four-story hole in a primary symbol of American commerce was. . . ." Clearly, the words in the *Times* played down the effect of the bomb—it destroyed a garage. Why was the destruction of a garage the top news story in the world, three days after it happened? The *Journal* answers this question up front.

What the *Times* and *Journal* reporters wrote between the lines here was no accident, but adhered closely to each paper's editorial outlook. And in each case that outlook is just what one would expect. The *Times* is written for a readership of professionals, who need ideological direction and reassurance of the system's strength. The *Journal* is written for bosses—business owners and executives—who give direction and do not need to be reminded where their interests lie. Among *Journal* subscribers, managers outnumber professionals more than three to one.[27] Among *Times* readers, professionals outnumber managers three to two.[28]

Let's look at another example of writing between the lines, again from the front page of the *New York Times*. This is the lead sentence of a news report on a 4 July 1992 parade of tall ships: "Majestic in a gray morning mist, the world's largest gathering of tall ships in this century sailed out of the past and up the great amphitheater of New York Harbor yesterday in a stately salute to Independence Day and the 500th anniversary of Christopher Columbus's voyage of discovery to the New World."[29] The reporter's attempt here to write between the lines is rather transparent, despite his flowery language. The phrase that stands out a bit more than it's supposed to is, of course, "voyage of discovery." This clever formulation is modest enough to pass political scrutiny yet still manages to conjure up the old elementary-school-textbook image of Christopher Columbus as the discoverer of America—a European rather than a Native American image. Having planted this point of view in the mind of the reader, the *Times* story then seems perfectly reasonable as it goes ahead and celebrates Columbus in the old-fashioned way, without reservation. It is hard to imagine a nonprofessional coming up with a devious phrase like this—or even wanting to.

NOTES

1. For an example see "Why Are They Cheating?," *Wall Street Journal*, 10 June 1980, p. 20.

2. "Quiet everybody, *Mr. Bill* has an idea! Come on, Mr. Bill, tell us what it is!"

3. "To a Disbarred Lawyer, Much More Than a Job Is Abruptly Shattered," *Wall Street Journal*, 17 June 1980, p. 1. Mr. Ziglar was reinstated as a lawyer after nine years.

4. Martin Shapiro, *Getting Doctored*, Between the Lines, Kitchener, Ontario (1978), pp. 79–80.

5. Ibid., pp. 104–105.

6. Stanley Aronowitz, Henry A. Giroux, *Education Under Siege*, Bergin & Garvey, South Hadley, Mass. (1985), ch. 2.

7. "Conditions at Jail Assailed," *San Diego Union*, 23 July 1979, p. A6. James Ledbetter, "Justice's Delay Is Justice Denied," *Village Voice*, 19 May 1992, p. 8.

8. "System On Trial: Time Behind Bars Without A Crime," *San Diego Union*, 23 November 1980, p. B1.

9. "The California Walkman Wins," *Newsweek*, 16 May 1983, p. 63. "Walking Tall in California," *Time*, 16 May 1983, p. 86. "Edward Lawson speaks out on violence and justice," *Argonaut*, Marina Del Rey (Los Angeles), 6 June 1991, p. 31.

10. All statistics are for adults arrested for misdemeanors or felonies. There were 1.3 million adult arrests in California in 1997, and about ten times that number in the entire United States. Data from State of California, Department of Justice, Criminal Jus-

tice Statistics Center, November 1998. Telephone conversation with Franklin D. Gilliam Jr., UCLA professor of political science, 4 March 1994. U.S. Department of Justice, Bureau of Justice Statistics, *Sourcebook of Criminal Justice Statistics 1997*, accessed online 5 November 1998.

11. Quote adapted from Anatole France (Jacques Anatole François Thibault), *The Red Lily*, John Lane The Bodley Head, London (1927), p. 95 (a translation of *Le Lys Rouge*, Calmann-Lévy, Paris, 1894).

12. *Mental Health, United States, 1998*, DHHS (SMA) 99-3285, Center for Mental Health Services, U.S. Department of Health and Human Services, Washington, D.C. (1998), pp. 116, 117, 154, 216.

13. Isaac Prilleltensky, *The Morals and Politics of Psychology: Psychological Discourse and the Status Quo*, State University of New York Press, Albany (1994).

14. David Kotelchuck, "Asbestos—Science for Sale," *Science for the People*, September 1975, pp. 8–16.

15. See, for example, Charles Schwartz, "Corporate Connections of Notable Scientists," *Science for the People*, May 1975, pp. 30–31.

16. George Anders, *Health Against Wealth: HMOs and the Breakdown of Medical Trust*, Houghton Mifflin, Boston (1996).

17. "How Cigarette Makers Keep Health Question 'Open' Year After Year," *Wall Street Journal*, 11 February 1993, p. A1.

18. "The Insider Who Copied Tobacco Firm's Secrets," *Wall Street Journal*, 20 June 1994, p. B1.

19. Stanton A. Glantz, John Slade, Lisa A. Bero, Peter Hanauer, Deborah E. Barnes, *The Cigarette Papers*, University of California Press, Berkeley (1996), especially ch. 8 and pp. 441–442.

20. "Tobacco Group Draws Criticism in Washington," *Wall Street Journal*, 27 May 1994, p. A4.

21. Teri Murphy, "Managed Care, Managed Misery," *Washington Post*, 16 August 1994, p. A18.

22. Peter Tauber, "Jay Leno: Not Just Another Funny Face," *New York Times*, 26 February 1989, sec. 6, pt. 1, p. 26. For a satire on the extreme scrutiny comedians give their jokes, see Garry Trudeau, "Anatomy of a Joke," *New York Times*, 1 August 1993, sec. 4, p. 15.

23. Telephone conversation with Talbot "Sandy" D'Alemberte, 25 August 1993. D'Alemberte was the 1991–92 ABA president.

24. Ibid.

25. Laurence H. Silberman, *Wall Street Journal*, 31 October 1997, p. A22.

26. "Officials Studying Bomb Clues Seek Several for Questioning," *New York Times*, 1 March 1993, p. A1. "Bombing in New York Bears Some Hallmarks Of Mideast Terrorists," *Wall Street Journal*, 1 March 1993, p. A1.

27. *The Wall Street Journal Subscriber Study*, a 79-page report, Dow Jones, New York (1992), p. 8.

28. *Simmons . . . Study of Media & Markets*, Simmons Market Research Bureau, New York (1993), vol. M-1, p. 25.

29. "A Quiet Majesty Sails the Hudson With Tall Ships," *New York Times*, 5 July 1992, sec. 1, p. 1

3

INSIDERS, GUESTS AND CRASHERS

It was 1984, and journalist Bernard Kalb had been on the State Department beat for eight years. As a veteran of the *New York Times*, CBS News and NBC News, Kalb knew the frustrations of trying to squeeze information out of tight-lipped government officials like State Department spokesman John Hughes, whom Kalb faced almost daily. In his 38 years of reporting, Kalb had dealt with countless government spokespeople, and so when Hughes decided to leave the department and move back home to Cape Cod, Kalb at first anticipated just another routine change of faces. But the change was to be unlike any in Kalb's experience. On 28 November 1984 Secretary of State George Shultz announced that he had recruited someone to replace Hughes as his assistant secretary of state for public affairs. State's new mouthpiece would be—that's right—Bernard Kalb. And so for the next two years Kalb's former colleagues struggled to squeeze information out of *him*—with no greater success, of course, even though they addressed him at press conferences as "Bernie."[1]

How did the Reagan administration know that Kalb, seemingly a longtime adversary as a journalist, could be trusted to speak for its side and routinely tell journalists less than he knew? The answer, put simply, is that Kalb was a professional. At one level, journalism and public relations are conflicting professions, yet the hack and the flack have the same essential qualifying attribute. The administration expects its spokespeople to answer questions at contentious press conferences without making even the slightest ideological slip. Kalb, with his decades of experience maintaining the very strict ideological discipline that is required of *New York Times* and network television news reporters, had the essential skill for the new job. The administration knew that his transition would be an easy one and that they could train him to be a public relations professional in a matter of days; to train a nonprofessional for such a job would take years. Politically, professionals are interchangeable parts.

Ideological discipline is the master key to the professions. Whatever the field, the willingness and ability to maintain "correct" priorities makes the professional. And no matter what the field, the professional's attitudes and values are such that maintaining discipline to an assigned ideology is unproblematic. As a result, in terms of attitudes and values, professionals in very different fields have more in common with one another than with nonprofessionals in their own fields. (The way they relate to the nonprofessionals they work with generally supports this view and shows the attitudes and values in question to be far from democratic.) To the extent that professionals share a common outlook, employers treat them like insiders in society, as if each professional has mastered a crucial part of *every* profession. Thus it is often easier for a professional to move into an entirely new field than for a nonprofessional to become a professional in that field, even if the nonprofessional already works in the field or is a hobbyist with vast knowledge in the field.

Cases such as Bernard Kalb's, in which professionals jump from one field to another virtually overnight, help reveal what it means to be a professional. Revealing, too, are cases in which nonprofessionals skip the usual lengthy requirements and become professionals almost instantly. Here we look at two types of such instant professionals, the first legal but temporary, the second illegal and often long term.

JURORS: PROFESSIONALS FOR A WEEK

Every year, more than a million nonprofessionals get a taste of what it is like to be a professional—when they serve on jury duty.[2] Jury work involves decision-making, and so it should be no surprise that the government gives potential jurors a quick, essentials-only version of the special processing described in the previous chapter. As a result, the juror's courtroom adventure bears an uncanny resemblance to professional selection, training and employment, with the whole process speeded up to such a degree that days represent years. A look at the familiar drill of jury duty reveals what those in charge want most in their decision-makers, and it sets the stage for understanding the conflicts that surround selection for professional school, professional training after selection and professional work itself.

The first order of business in a trial is probing the attitudes and values of potential jurors through questioning and demographic analysis. Based on the results of this ideological assessment, each candidate is either weeded out or selected to serve on the jury. Favored are people who are programmable but not already programmed. (Thus professionals, who are loaded with ideological baggage from their fields and jobs, are often excluded.) Those selected are then subjected to a whirlwind indoctrination in which the judge impresses upon them that they must accept the law as it is given to them and follow that law rather than their own sense of right and wrong. The judge exhorts jurors not to let their views about the merit of the law affect their work. In the most typical words of the court, the guest professionals are told to judge only "the facts of the case, not the law." Jurors who favor decriminalization of marijuana, for example, are expected to vote for conviction anyway if, by their judgment, the defendant really was caught smoking the contraband, as charged. Thus, jurors are expected to exercise judgment, but within an assigned ideological framework that they are forbidden to question—just like professionals. For professionals, of course, their employers' ideologies play the role of the law.

However, there is an important difference between jurors and real employed professionals: Jurors have greater freedom to criticize the assigned framework of values and to act on their own sense of right and wrong. Unlike professional employees, jurors can follow their consciences without worrying about losing their jobs or losing the favor of people who have power over them. If jurors think that justice demands it, they have the right to violate the court's instructions and judge whether the law itself is unjust or misapplied; they are not held in contempt of court for doing that. In fact, such "nullification of the law" by juries has a long and glorious history. Before the Civil War, for example, some northern juries found both slaves and abolitionists "not guilty" of violating the fugitive slave laws, even though their violation of these laws was clear.

Today the government's approach to the "problem" of such independent juries is simply to try to prevent jurors from learning that they have the right to criticize the law. As a result, obedient jurors can sometimes be seen after trials apologizing to defendants whom they didn't really want to convict, saying they had no choice. But not all jurors are obedient. That is because the courthouse system of ideological weeding out and indoctrination doesn't work perfectly, mainly because it is so rushed. Thus, even when prosecutors have an airtight case, juries that are uncomfortable with the law or the way the law is being used don't always convict. Sometimes these juries openly criticize the law. But much more often they choose to convince themselves that there is reasonable doubt in the evidence, because they are ignorant of their right to question the law or timid about asserting that right. Each of these types of juror behavior—ranging from outright obedience to principled dissent, with a kind of place-knowing dissent in between—corresponds to an equivalent type of behavior by professionals.

Members of the Fully Informed Jury Association, a national organization with headquarters in Montana, are dedicated to educating people about their rights and responsibilities as trial jurors. These activists argue that jurors have a moral responsibility to judge the law and the way the law is being used, in the interest of social justice and as a check on those with power. I argue that for the same reasons, all professionals, not just temporary ones, must sit in judgment of the social goals they have been recruited to further.

INADVERTENT SATIRISTS

The values and attitudes that play such an important role in professional work are not quickly or easily learned; more often than not they are conferred—by an upbringing based on middle-class values, as opposed to working-class values. Nor are they easily imitated by nonprofessionals, even by those with technical knowledge. Thus, it should be no surprise that employers take these values and attitudes, and not technical knowledge, as the sign of the professional. People with insight, acting ability and a little knowledge of some profession's technical aspects often take advantage of this fact by using phony credentials or made-up stories about background and training to get and keep professional jobs. For someone hired as a professional in this way—and many are[3]—the job itself serves as a finishing school. Such self-made professionals usually pick fields in which they have worked as nonprofessionals. By combining the knowledge they gained as nonprofessionals with a good imitation of the appropriate attitudes and values, they are often extremely successful as professionals. The well-known tendency of employers to overlook the shortcomings of incompetents who display the proper attitude also works to protect those impostors who have technical deficiencies.

No one knows exactly how many people without the required credentials are now working in professional positions; estimates are high, yet few are caught, indicating that most are never uncovered. Newspapers and magazines carry articles on individual cases, but the coverage is uneven, concentrating on the most prestigious professions—impostor doctors and lawyers are more interesting than impostor accountants and teachers. Judging by these press reports, those crashers who do get caught are typically discovered not because their work arouses suspicion but because some pattern of eccentric behavior or some breach of professional protocol calls attention to them, or they are caught simply because a sharp-eyed bureaucrat in the personnel office notices a discrepancy during routine record keeping. Some are on the job for years before it comes out that they lied about their credentials to get hired.

Individual examples of impostors are interesting because they are so revealing about what is really required of a professional. What the impostor does to master the essence of a profession and gain acceptance by employers and "legitimate" professionals is so different from what the official story says is required, and yet rings so true, that the imitation becomes living satire.

- Instead of going to high school and college, Daniel Morgan simply hung a Phi Beta Kappa key from his watch chain. Rather than take the bar exam, he sprung for subdued, English-cut suits. The black Alabaman, who had studied law in prison, used these props and the name of a legitimate lawyer to operate for seven years as a high-powered trial lawyer in Chicago. As "Edward A. Simmons, counsellor at law," Morgan argued hundreds of cases in court and won acquittals for many people, including some facing serious charges such as murder. He built a thriving law practice and established a law firm with fancy offices in the prestigious downtown area, taking on a legitimate lawyer as an associate and renting desk space to young lawyers. With his impressive record of victories in complicated cases in city, state and federal courts, Morgan was known and respected within his adopted profession. Neither the other lawyers nor the judges had any idea that the high-fee lawyer they were working with was actually a career criminal who had served time in San Quentin, Folsom, Jackson and Marquette prisons.

After he was caught and imprisoned for a few months for "contempt of court" in Chicago, Morgan reopened for business in Washington, D.C. This time he used the name of a lawyer in another state who was licensed to practice in the capital but had never done so. There, as "Lawrence A. Harris," Morgan continued his successful law career, becoming one of the best-known criminal lawyers in Washington and boasting a booming clientele. It was his ability to win in the courtroom that led to his exposure. Morgan branched out from criminal law to the big-money field of personal injury, and when he rejected a large out-of-court settlement in an accident case, he was perceived as a threat. Frightened personal-injury lawyers investigated and exposed him.[4]

- Bob Harris presented impressive credentials to WCBS Radio in New York—a bachelor of science degree from the University of Buffalo, a master of science degree from New York University and a PhD from Columbia University. Soon, millions of people were listening to the weather forecasts of "Doctor Bob Harris," the meteorologist. Although all three of his degrees were fake, his weather forecast record was good. At the peak of his career, "Doctor Bob" was forecasting not only for CBS, but also for the *New York Times* and the Long Island Railroad, taking in a huge total salary. For the *New York Times*, Harris provided the daily metropolitan, regional and national forecasts, as well as captions for satellite photographs and national weather maps. For the railroad, he gave advance warnings of big storms. An anonymous letter to the radio station blew his cover.[5]

- Former Army medic Barry Allan Vinocur was so confident that he could be a good doctor that he was undeterred by the system's judgment to the contrary. When Case Western Reserve University in Cleveland quickly flunked him out as a premed undergraduate, Vinocur "borrowed" his cousin's excellent premed transcripts and got a non-MD surgical research fellowship at Mount Sinai Hospital in Cleveland. At the university, "I couldn't handle the science and math," he remembers. "I was spending all my time reading medical journals. I didn't have the discipline for my classes."[6] But at the hospital, the doctors were impressed with the speed with which Vinocur picked up skills on the job. He learned a lot by accompanying doctors-in-training around the hospital and on rounds, and by watching operations.

After spending much of his time as a research fellow in the hospital's adult critical care unit, Vinocur proposed putting together a basic book on critical care medicine. Thus Vinocur and three doctors edited the *Handbook of Critical Care*,[7] which was printed in many languages and is still used in the field. While at Mount Sinai, Vinocur also authored and coauthored many research papers and medical conference presentations on intensive care medicine.

Vinocur's career at Mount Sinai came to an end not because doctors discovered that he was a college dropout—they didn't find out about that— but because doctors were offended when they found out that Vinocur had put the letters "MD" after his name in a letter to a publisher that he was trying to interest in a monograph.

Determined not to have his medical experience and future work taken less seriously just because of his lack of formal schooling, Vinocur drew again on his cousin's records—this time his medical school transcripts— and declared himself a doctor. He got a position as a resident, first at San Francisco's Mt. Zion Hospital and then, after only a year, at the prestigious University of California Medical Center in San Francisco. He thereby gave some of the state's most well-papered physicians a medical school reject as a colleague. Vinocur worked in one of the most demanding of medical specialties, neonatology, where he won great respect for his skills and techniques in caring for extremely ill premature infants in the medical center's intensive care nursery. Vinocur was considered unusually dedicated to his work. He personally headed an air ambulance service to bring in critically ill infants. He did research and participated in press conferences featuring work in which he was involved. He gained national recognition for his part in a discovery relating to the diagnosis and treatment of hyperammonemia, a rare but life-threatening ailment of newborns.

After three years at the University of California Medical Center, Vinocur was encouraged to apply for a position on the faculty. Routine processing of his application turned up his cousin's records, which, except for the "nickname" Barry, were virtually identical to his. The masquerade ended with an embarrassed University of California and a deal in which Vinocur pleaded no contest to two misdemeanors. He was fined $200, put on 18 months' probation and ordered to provide 100 hours of community service.[8]

- Thousands of American doctors are working on the basis of phony resumes or false credentials.[9] This fact came out in 1984 during the various state and federal investigations that began with the arrest of Pedro de Mesones, who sold about 100 Caribbean medical school degrees to Americans for $5,000 to $50,000 each. The general reexamination of credentials that this case touched off revealed many impostors, but in the process it revealed something that investigators would just as soon have kept quiet: Most of the impostors would never have been exposed by their work as doctors even though they typically worked in situations where medical professionals observed their work daily.

One impostor, found working at a hospital, was described by the hospital administrator as "the brightest resident we have."[10] Similar praise went to Raymond Allard and Barbara Gillon, who worked as interns at Worcester City Hospital in Massachusetts until 17 April 1984, the day hospital administrators learned that the two "doctors" were actually a physician's assistant and a nurse who had bought medical school degrees from de Mesones. "Ray and Barbara are very bright, capable doctors," Dr. James L. McGuire, head of medical education at the hospital, told the *New York Times*. According to the *Times*, doctors on the hospital staff were unanimous in their praise for the performance, capability and motivation of the two. Said Dr. Jack Kelly, a staff physician, "If I had doubts about the backgrounds of any of the interns, they would be the ones I would be least suspicious of."[11]

"REAL WORLD" CREDENTIALS

Unlike these impostors, real professionals go through a crucial part of their training away from the workplace. Seclusion at the university allows time to study the field's technical details, while the social isolation there facilitates indoctrination into the field's culture—the culture that impostors know so well. In spite of the fact that the university plays this important role in society, students often talk of it as not being part of the "real world." It is certainly easy to see things that way. The university world—symbolized by the physically isolated, self-contained, park-like campus with services careful to meet middle-class standards—proclaims itself a community of scholars and students free from the direction and minute-to-minute discipline imposed on persons working elsewhere. The real world, on the other hand, is symbolized by cities like Detroit and New York, centers of production and the control of production, where the hierarchy of power and wealth is clear and no one is surprised to encounter exploitation, alienation and crime. In this real world, employers call the shots. Individuals are hired and fired on the basis of cold judgments of their worth; with a great deal at stake and competitors playing for keeps, employers must renew their no-nonsense attitude every day.

Those who hold to this "two worlds" point of view usually don't think of the realm of the academics as serving the realm of the employers. Indeed, many feel that the university is dysfunctional for the system, that the university makes it easy for students to drift into deviant patterns of thought and to demand change.

Yet the simple fact is that the students the university trains and certifies as professionals *do* go out and function for the system and uphold the status quo. For example, at least 90% of Harvard Law School graduates join corporate law firms. As Calvin Trillin noted in an article in the *New Yorker* about the ongoing struggle between leftist and conservative professors at that school:

> Why, it might be argued, should anyone think it is anything but inevitable that the preëminent law schools of a capitalist society produce lawyers to serve the society's

preëminent capitalists? . . . I suppose it's possible to see Harvard Law School as an institution willing to harbor left-wing professors who are trying to subvert the young, but another way to look at it is as an institution that each fall takes five hundred of our brightest, most idealistic young people and in three years transforms them into Wall Street moneygrubbers.[12]

If the ivory tower in its work as a training institution does indeed serve the system by orienting professionals-in-training to their role in the real world, then how does it do this? My thesis here is that the mechanism involves the qualifying examinations and other requirements[13] for professional credentials that certifying institutions enforce: The requirements for professional standing in a field reflect the social function of professionals in that field—their role in the real world—not just some eternal standards of "excellence" or of proficiency in the tricks of the trade.

To explain in detail the mechanism by which the university produces professionals who will play the desired social role, and to explain the nature of that role, I use the production of physicists as a primary example. The mechanism of selection in physics is the PhD qualifying examination system, which has much in common with systems that other fields use to select professionals. The qualifying examination system is the procedure by which physics graduate students, usually at the beginning of their third year, are told whether or not they will be permitted to continue and complete the work necessary to receive the PhD degree. This examination system gives physics graduate students at most universities an ugly and unforgettable reminder of the real world each and every year as some fellow graduate students are expelled from the university.

I will put off discussing the details of these expulsions because it is impossible to comprehend fully the mechanism by which people are selected to play a particular role in society without first understanding the role they are being selected to play. For the example of physics, one needs to know something about the nature of the work assignments that physicists are prepared to take. Put more generally, a real understanding of the existence and nature of the politics of expert qualification grows out of an understanding of what the expert actually does in society. The typical misunderstanding of the politics of expert qualification—usually a denial of any politics—grows out of an idealized view of what the expert does, a view that fails to reflect the social role of the expert's field. What an expert actually does in society is most accurately determined by asking: What is the social function of the expert's *field* of work?

Many people can tell you the "qualifying" political mentality for an occupation when that mentality is blatantly obvious, as it is in the case of, say, police. Many people can even go on to tell you how that mentality reflects the social order that the occupation helps to maintain. Yet many of these same people accept without question the popular notion that in general the qualifications required to do professional work are *not* ideological. A look at physicists counters this mystification of professional work; specifically, an examination of the social role of the physicist's work helps reveal the politics of professional qualification in physics.

The key to understanding the social role of physicists (and of all professionals) is appreciating the extent to which individuals in the field determine their own work and the extent to which their work is externally directed. The question is, "Who is in charge?" The answer tells us which sector of society the physicist serves.

In the following chapter, I address this question of control by looking first at industrial and governmental physicists and then at the more difficult case of university physicists. The discussion takes advantage of the fact that university physics departments as a group are highly homogeneous in their essential features. The physics department at the University of California, Irvine, where I was trained, has more than one hundred professors, research physicists and graduate students, and is a typical department in terms of research and training. A look at the nature of the research in that department and the handling of graduate students there will tell us a lot about university research and training in physics in the United States.

NOTES

1. "Bernard Kalb Named to Post At State Dept.," *New York Times*, 29 November 1984, p. A25. Kalb switched back to his old profession after the press exposed an administration disinformation program in which the State Department was involved; Kalb felt he had not been hired to be associated with disinformation. However, he refused to confirm that there actually was a disinformation program, for to blow the whistle on official government lying would have been unprofessional. *New York Times*, 9 October 1986, pp. A1, A16, A17.

2. Many millions are summoned, and over one million end up serving on a jury. See Jeffrey Abramson, *We, the Jury*, Basic Books, New York (1994), pp. 251–252.

3. "Deception by Job Applicants Is Called Widespread," *New York Times*, 29 November 1981, sec. 1, p. 32. "Falsified Degrees Growing Problem," *New York Times*, 12 December 1985, p. A21. "As Value of Diplomas Grows, More People Buy Bogus Credentials," *Wall Street Journal*, 2 April 1987, p. 1. Other relevant articles are: "Why Are They Cheating?" *Wall Street Journal*, 10 June 1980, p. 20; "To Boost Pay, More Teachers 'Buy' Degrees," *Wall Street Journal*, 14 October 1980, p. 33; "How Many Impostors Have You Hired?," *U.S. News & World Report*, 13 July 1981, pp. 71–72; "Cracking Down on Sale Of Fraudulent Degrees," *New York Times*, 8 May 1984, p. C9.

4. "King Of The Courtroom Fakers," *Ebony*, October 1958, pp. 71–78. "Supreme Court to Hear Bogus Lawyer," *New York Times*, 10 December 1968, p. 1. "A King's Triumph," *Time*, 20 December 1968, p. 42. "Himself for a Client," *Newsweek*, 23 December 1968, pp. 29–30.

5. "Weather Man for Times and WCBS Is Dismissed Over Credential Claim," *New York Times*, 19 January 1979, p. B8. "WNEW Hires Bob Harris," *New York Times*, 31 January 1979, p. C14. "A Question of Degree," *Time*, 5 February 1979, p. 125. William Flanagan, "Faking Your Way To the Top," *Esquire*, 13 March 1979, pp. 83–84. "Increasingly Sunny," *New York Times*, 29 November 1979, p. B18.

6. "Phony M.D.'s Story," *San Francisco Chronicle*, 8 August 1980, p. 4.

7. James L. Berk, James E. Sampliner, J. Sheldon Artz, Barry Vinocur, editors, *Handbook of Critical Care*, Little, Brown and Company, Boston (1976).

8. "Big Flap Over UC Doctor," *San Francisco Chronicle*, 25 April 1980, p. 17. "UC 'Doctor' Turns In His License," *San Francisco Chronicle*, 26 April 1980, p. 10. "Doctor Impostor Sentenced in S.F.," *San Francisco Chronicle*, 9 July 1980, p. 6.

9. "Investigators Check on Thousands For Falsified Degrees as Doctors," *New York Times*, 4 March 1984, sec. 1, p. 1. "Medical Malady That Resists Cure: One of 50 Doctors Is an Impostor," *Wall Street Journal*, 2 April 1986, p. 21. "28,000 'Doctors' Are Feared Unfit," *New York Times*, 5 May 1986, p. A17. "Up to 20% of Doctors Lied on Resume For Fellowship, Medical School Finds," *Wall Street Journal*, 3 July 1995, p. B2. "Suspicions of False Medical Credentials Ignored, Official Says," *New York Times*, 5 March 1984, p. A13. "Fake M.D. Problem Growing, State Officials Say," *New York Times*, 12 March 1984, p. B6. "Nurse Helped to Expose Medical Degrees Fraud," *New York Times*, 26 March 1984, p. A15. "Credentials of 400 Doctors in State Being Studied," *New York Times*, 1 April 1984, p. 21. "Cheating On Exams For Doctors Causes Alarm," *New York Times*, 3 April 1984, p. C1. "3 Inquiries Open On Bogus Degrees," *New York Times*, 14 April 1984, p. 30. "Two Interns Suspended For Inquiry on Degrees," *New York Times*, 18 April 1984, p. A14. "Dominican Inquiry Points to 2,000 Fraudulent M.D. Degrees in U.S.," *New York Times*, 27 April 1984, p. A28. "Prosecution Is Likely On 100 Fake Degrees," *New York Times*, 8 May 1984, p. B3. "2 Medical Schools Closed In Scandal," *New York Times*, 16 May 1984, p. A17. "Doctors Harmed By Dominican Case," *New York Times*, 20 May 1984, sec. 1, p. 33. "A.M.A. Told of 85% Failure Rate in Basic Test Taken by Foreign Medical Graduates," *New York Times*, 17 June 1984, sec. 1, p. 16. "Medical Association To Evaluate New Licensing Tests for Doctors," *New York Times*, 19 June 1984, p. C4. "Foreign-Trained Doctors In For a Thorough Checkup," *New York Times*, 24 June 1984, sec. 4, p. 24. "6 Arrested for Fake Medical Degrees, Including 3 Known as Doctors," *New York Times*, 13 July 1984, p. A7. "Hospital Dismisses Doctors Tied to Buying of Diplomas," *New York Times*, 5 August 1984, sec. 1, p. 32. "Cuomo Panel Questions Credentials of 6,500 Doctors Practicing in Hospitals," *New York Times*, 8 August 1984, p. B10. "9 Indicted in Inquiry Into Phony Medical Degrees," *New York Times*, 5 October 1984, p. B9. "Thousands Said to Have False Medical Degrees," *New York Times*, 7 December 1984, p. B32.

10. "Investigators Check on Thousands For Falsified Degrees as Doctors," *New York Times*, 4 March 1984, sec. 1, p. 1.

11. "Two Interns Tell Details Of Suspect Degrees," *New York Times*, 17 April 1984, p. C1.

12. Calvin Trillin, "Harvard Law School," *New Yorker*, 26 March 1984, pp. 53–83.

13. "The Graduate Degree: Is It Worth It?," *Los Angeles Times*, 16 August 1979, pt. 4, p. 1. To pre-medical students, the classic example, even the slightest reminder of the competitive medical school admission system has a disciplining effect.

4

ASSIGNABLE CURIOSITY

> Wanted: PhD scientist to work as self-directed seeker of truth. Successful
> candidate will determine own work topics. Excellent laboratory and com-
> puter facilities. Competitive salary and benefits package. EOE/AA, M/F/D/V.

Scientists will tell you in a second that this job ad is fictitious. Yet many of the
same scientists will turn around and tell you that they are self-directed. What is
the reality? Who determines the topics that individual scientists work on?

Answering this question about scientists is important for understanding the
politics of professional work in general, because scientists constitute a kind of
baseline. Salaried doctors, lawyers, accountants, engineers and so on are certainly no freer than scientists in deciding what problems they will take on at
work. So if the scientist's curiosity is externally directed, then whose isn't?

To ask who determines the topics that individual scientists work on is to ask
who in society scientists serve in their work. This is not only a fascinating question in and of itself, but it is also crucial to understanding the politics of professional qualification in science. For only by understanding the actual role that
the rank-and-file scientist plays in society can one make sense of the criteria by
which an individual is deemed qualified to work as a scientist.

To see who determines research topics for physicists, we must look at industry, government and universities, the institutions that each year hire almost all
of the 1,100 to 1,300 people who receive PhD degrees in physics from U.S. universities.[1]

Upon graduation, many of the degree recipients get temporary jobs known
as "postdoctoral fellowships," in order to gain further research experience and
to be in a position to get a good permanent job.[2] These short-term appoint-
ments are usually limited to one, two or three years and are usually at universi-

ties or federally funded research and development centers such as Los Alamos National Laboratory in New Mexico. The "postdoc" typically works extremely long hours assisting in an already-established research project directed by a professor or research group leader. There is little pretense that the postdoc has much of a say in defining the topic of investigation. As a result the experience is often disappointing. One university postdoc wrote the following assessment on an American Physical Society survey questionnaire:

> The postdoc . . . has become a plentiful and captive source of cheap labor for doing the research of and advancing the careers of established academic people while offering little or no opportunities for advancement to the participants and making it more difficult for the participant to later find permanent work in a different field where professional prospects may be more promising.[3]

Graduates who don't become postdocs often go directly into potentially permanent jobs. Most of these jobs are in industry, and the rest are in academic institutions and government.[4] Industrial scientists get their research topics from their employers' programs of research projects. These programs, in turn, grow out of the companies' quests to develop profitable new products and their need to update old products threatened by technological advances elsewhere in the world. Also, industry performs $23 billion worth of research and development annually for the Department of Defense.[5] This lucrative work can add to a corporation's list of topics to assign to its scientists.

A look at the General Electric Company's main research and development facility illustrates how industrial scientists get their research topics. More than 500 PhD scientists and engineers play out their careers at GE's Research and Development Center in Schenectady, New York. The stated purpose of this one-million-square-foot facility, which is one of the world's largest industrial laboratories, is to undertake work that "promises both to advance knowledge and to pay off for General Electric." In practice, however, "pay off for General Electric" takes precedence over the effort "to advance knowledge." In the blunt words of Roland W. Schmitt, speaking when he was GE's senior vice president for research and development and boss of the Schenectady facility, "If it has no payoff for General Electric, it should not be done at all." He added, "I can't truthfully say that all our work advances knowledge."[6]

Most people don't expect corporations to fund unprofitable research. But they may nevertheless think of scientists as people who build their careers by following the dictates of their unfettered curiosities, not by devoting themselves to topics chosen to meet goals like "pay off for General Electric." Those who buy this image of scientists might expect GE to have a hard time getting its scientists to sacrifice their own research interests in favor of the company's research interests.

As it turns out, GE finds it quite easy to circumscribe in this way the careers of its scientists. The company simply makes its technical needs known, and the scientists, through a process of self-adjustment, get interested in the appropriate topics. "You can't select problems for true scientists, much less tell them how to attack the problems. But you can make sure that they are fully informed of the needs of the company businesses that pay the bill," explained the GE research boss.[7]

Industrial scientists who are not content being directed by "the needs of the company businesses," market forces and the goals of contractors can do pitifully little to have more of a say in setting the goals of their own research work. Writing in *Physics Today*, a monthly publication of the American Institute of Physics with a wide circulation among physicists, Alfred H. Sommer shares the tricks he learned while working for over 40 years in five laboratories:

> A frequent problem is that your supervisor wants you to work on a project that you don't believe in or, conversely, does *not* want you to pursue one that you think has potential. There is no simple solution to these problems, but I can make some useful suggestions. In the first case, if you have several projects going, it is often effective to ask the supervisor which of your present projects should be dropped to make time for the new one. In the second case it sometimes pays to work on your project during evenings and weekends or when your supervisor is on vacation or in the hospital.[8]

In light of the powerlessness that this description indicates, it becomes clear why many industrial scientists feel "self-directed" when their employers let them decide for themselves which of *the company's* commercial or military research topics to work on.

Whether or not scientists who work in industry or government feel self-directed, they are not treated as such. Frank von Hippel, a prominent Princeton University physicist, notes that industry and government scientists are not even free enough to question the social value of their own assignments or their institution's work, which may be potentially cataclysmic. Von Hippel has advocated that the American Physical Society help develop legislation that would enable scientists to speak out with less risk:

> It is likely that the protection of the freedom of speech of scientists and engineers in industry and government would have large social benefits. Technology has become so powerful that we can no longer afford to wait to correct a problem until we can count the bodies.

The legislation would

> protect the employee from being *rapidly* "railroaded" out of his livelihood. It means also that he can get an impartial hearing. And finally, if the outside investigator or hearing board finds in his favor, then he has some protection against being "blackballed" in his search for another job.[9]

The more one looks into it, the clearer it becomes that the scientist best suited for harmony in an industrial or governmental position is the one willing to accept direction uncritically in all but the narrow technical aspects of her research work. As a good professional, such a scientist accepts a research problem, tries to see it as an intriguing puzzle of captivating interest, and carries out the research with dedication.

But what about *university* scientists? Unlike their colleagues who work in industry or in government laboratories, university scientists pursue their own intellectual interests—they are certainly not directed to serve profit, technology or the military. Or are they?

DIRECTING THE PROFESSOR'S CURIOSITY

Do university scientists freely set the courses of their own careers, or do outside forces lead them to enter particular subfields within their disciplines and to take up particular topics within those subfields? To ask the same question in a different way, how much freedom do those who fund scientific research give to those who do scientific research?

The federal government sponsors the bulk of the basic science research that goes on in U.S. universities.[10] Most basic physics research at universities, for example, is sponsored by just four government agencies—the Department of Energy (successor of the Atomic Energy Commission), the National Science Foundation, the Department of Defense (through the Army Research Office, the Office of Naval Research, the Air Force Office of Scientific Research and so on) and the National Aeronautics and Space Administration.[11] Ninety-nine percent of the federal funding for basic physics research at universities comes through these four agencies. In 1995 the federal government spent about $590 million on university physics research; about $455 million of that expenditure paid for research characterized as basic.[12] At the University of California, Irvine, my old school, physics professors in 1996 got $8.7 million of their $10.2 million in R&D money from the federal government.[13]

To what extent do the university pipers themselves call the tune when the government pays for their work? The government, like any sponsor, is keenly aware of its influence, and has known the answer to this question since the 1950s, when it began to dominate the funding of basic research in universities in the United States. In 1954, the president of the United States ordered the then four-year-old National Science Foundation to report the effect that federal research money has on educational institutions.[14] The resulting NSF report to the president, *Government–University Relationships in Federally Sponsored Scientific Research and Development*, addresses the question of "direction" explicitly:

> To what extent has the availability of funds from particular agencies given direction to research in the universities? . . . Has the type of work done been determined by the availability of extra-university funds for certain kinds of research?

NSF gives the answer to the president in scientistic language:

> It would be unrealistic to claim that Federal contracts and grants for research at universities have exercised no influence over the types and fields of research un-

dertaken by the institutions. For example, Agency X has funds for support of a given type of work. Professor A at University Y applies for funds to carry on a project in this area although he may be the only one in the school with interests in it, and these interests may have been furthered by the availability of the Federal funds. He employs several research assistants. They are paid for aiding Professor A on the project, and in the process obtain advanced degrees. One of the assistants is very capable. He is taken on the staff as an instructor or even assistant professor. He, too, applies for support for the same type of work and before long University Y has a strong department in the particular area. One cannot conclude that the influence of Agency X was detrimental, but one can say the Agency did influence the direction of research at University Y and perhaps the number of young scientists with the particular research interest.[15]

Clearly, the government understands not only that it influences the content of research at "University Y," but that it also programs new scientists with particular research interests.

Of course, it is already obvious from common sense and simple logic that when a government agency pumps research money into universities for work in areas of its own interest, it affects the kind of research that goes on, so that somewhere university scientists must be taking up topics they would not otherwise investigate.

If, for example, a government agency makes $43.9 million available to universities for basic research in nuclear physics,[16] then university physicists will do $43.9 million worth of basic research in nuclear physics. The government agency, for all practical purposes, will have ordered university physicists to do $43.9 million worth of basic research in nuclear physics. Although this is not the kind of order that names specific researchers, it is an order that individual university professors do end up carrying out.

How aware are academics themselves of the outside influences on the topics that they take up? Are they as aware as their sponsors? As the discussion moves from "Agency X" and "Professor A" and gets closer to home, university scientists show less and less understanding of the influence that others have on the work that they do. They readily agree that the reason university science departments are bigger and do much more research than, say, university philosophy departments has more to do with the priorities of those who sponsor research than with the wishes of scientists and philosophers. With greater difficulty, the university scientist recognizes that much of the research in his or her own field and subfield owes its very existence to the priorities of the sponsors; somehow, the influence of sponsors is easier to recognize in fields and subfields other than one's own. Finally, by asking individual scientists the extent to which they decide for themselves which topics to take up as their own, one often finds that the professors so savor the I-am-my-own-boss self-image that they are unwilling even to consider the possibility that they have less than total control. I have heard academics with defense agency funding put it like this: "I am doing my research because I am interested in it, not because the military directed me to do it. It just so happens that the Defense Department is paying for it."

The National Science Foundation knows better than to believe such claims. It sees the need to look beyond the "usual statement" that university scientists make when they are asked about the origins of their work:

> The distinction between choices made because of genuine interest and curiosity of the staff members and those made because funds were available for a particular field is not easily drawn. Although the usual statement of the research staff is that they are doing work of their choice, that statement is in part offset by the parallel reply to the following question: "If the same funds were available to a department without strings of any kind or interests of sponsoring agencies—except that the money be used for research—would the staff of the department be doing the same research?" The answers are often qualified.[17]

If academics lack a clear understanding of how they are directed toward particular topics, that is in part because they are directed in ways that allow them to see themselves as self-directed. One of the most important of these ways is funding via the "unsolicited proposal." University professors build their careers on research, not teaching. Many professors get the money that they need to do research by writing an outline of the work they propose to do and submitting it to a federal agency that funds research. This is the unsolicited proposal, and using it as a mechanism for funding would seem to give control of research topics to individual scientists, not to sponsors. However, even though writing such a proposal requires a huge amount of time and effort, funding is by no means assured—the National Science Foundation rejects 2 out of 3 proposals, as does the National Institutes of Health—and so professors who want money to do research inevitably have funding agencies' interests in mind as they plan their work and write their proposals. Consciously or unconsciously, they tailor their own interests to match those of the sponsors.[18]

Hence, a scientist's "unsolicited" request for money to work on a particular problem may represent the opposite of what it appears to represent. The scientist's research proposal may actually be an expression of the *sponsor's* desire that the scientist attack the particular problem:

> When academic staff members are asked if they initiated the research now done under contract, the usual answer is "yes." However, further discussion may show that the project arose as a result of conversations or consultations with agencies having specific problems associated with their particular programs and objectives. It is to be expected that an agency having particular interests would consult with scientists who have done work of interest to them, and this consultation may easily result in requests from the university staff members for support in their area of interest.[19]

The professor who is very good at coming up with proposals that get funded is sometimes called a "grantsman," particularly when the professor brings in enough money to hire a large staff of researchers. The name can be derogatory because it suggests a scientist who is concerned more with keeping the money flowing in and building an "empire" than with solving a particular research problem.

With the unsolicited proposal, even university scientists whose research is paid for by the Defense Department can believe they are self-directed and that military need does not determine the content of their work. Even if the military pays for all the research that is being done on a particular topic, it is still practically impossible to prove that the availability of military money is why a particular professor is doing research on that topic.

The federal government's great satisfaction with the work of scientists recruited into large-scale research and development projects during World War II laid the foundation for its heavy participation in basic research after the war. The government channeled much of its post-war financial support for basic science through the Office of Naval Research, which it established for that purpose in 1946.[20] ONR, still very much in business, uses most of its money to back research proposals that it receives unsolicited. This allows academics to decide like perfectly autonomous individuals the topics of the research work that they will do. The Navy need only provide the framework:

> Although these contracts are usually awarded in response to unsolicited proposals, ONR makes every effort to publicize its research needs so that its programs and interests can be taken into account by prospective contractors.[21]

Clearly, a professor's insistence that her services were unsolicited should not lead one to conclude that her financial backers have given no direction to the content of her work.

Like ONR, other major research-funding agencies, such as the Army Research Office, the Air Force Office of Scientific Research, the National Science Foundation and the National Aeronautics and Space Administration, fulfill a lot of their research needs simply by making their interests known and backing unsolicited proposals. Thus the Army Research Office gives professors hints as to where the money is—and thereby allows them to modify their interests accordingly—by publishing its research interests in great detail and quietly mentioning that "ARO receives approximately 700 proposals each year and historically funds approximately 200 new awards."[22] Agencies are often quite specific about their interests: "In Optical Physics, a rapidly growing part of the program, specific current interests include the nonlinear response of isolated atoms to intense, ultrashort electromagnetic fields. . . ." That example is from the National Science Foundation's *Guide to Programs*, which NSF describes as "a compilation of funding opportunities." The guide notes that NSF receives approximately 30,000 proposals each year and makes about 9,000 awards.[23]

Thus, funders find they can arouse the proper research interests in scientists without saying very much. Their money talks—and is brilliantly articulate. However, they choose not to depend completely on this impersonal mechanism. The Office of Naval Research, for example, has a "cadre of 130 Program Officers" who "maintain long-term relationships with investigators, giving ONR an invaluable ability to apply relatively small investments early in the conceptual stages of a project, with great influence on the focus of the work."[24] Indeed, all the funding agencies encourage professors to discuss their ideas with program officers before they submit their proposals. Through these discussions, which are strictly off-the-record, agencies help professors fine-tune their interests. At the Army Research Office, for example, "technical correspondence prior to submission of the proposal" is intended

> to convey to a prospective offeror [one offering to do research] an understanding of the Army's mission and responsibilities relative to the type of effort contemplated. Such correspondence should be handled informally at the working level and is not binding on either party. This type of correspondence should not be referenced in the proposal and will not be considered during evaluation of the proposal nor included in any official contract file.[25]

The Air Force and Navy also use a habeas corpus technique to prime the pump of professorial research interest. Under its Summer Faculty Research Program, for example, the Air Force moves university professors to its laboratories for the summer, where it works quite openly "to develop the basis for continuing research of interest to the Air Force at the faculty member's institution" and "to stimulate continuing relations among faculty members and their professional peers in the Air Force."[26] If by summer's end the trick has been turned and the seed of an appropriate research interest has been planted, then the scientist spreads the Air Force's research interest by carrying the seed back to the university—along with a little fertilizer to ensure its germination: "After completing this program, participants may submit a proposal for continuing research at their own facilities."[27]

Military research agencies have a host of other programs that channel people into military-relevant science. The Air Force's University Resident Research Program, for example, keeps the professor for an entire year, not just for a summer. Its Graduate Student Research Program likewise works "to expose graduate students to potential thesis topics in areas of interest to the Air Force."[28] The Army Research Office's Young Investigator Program aims "to attract to Army research outstanding young university faculty members."[29] The Office of Naval Research "fosters continuing academic interest in naval relevant science from the high school through post-doctoral levels" and beyond.[30] Separate ONR programs target high school students, graduate students, black graduate students, postdocs, young faculty and faculty in general.[31]

At each funding agency, it is the job of the program officers to stay aware of the big picture in research and to make sure that those who receive research money actually do what they promised in their proposals. At the Office of Naval Research, for example, the program officers are active scientists and engineers in their fields. "It is their responsibility to maintain awareness of the progress, trends and accomplishments of science and technology in their particular fields and to maintain contact with potential investigators in those fields. They review proposals submitted by prospective contractors, select those most promising to their program and most relevant to anticipated Navy needs, and monitor progress of contracted work."[32] At the National Science Foundation, each "program director" handles research proposals and is responsible for monitoring the research work of a certain number of NSF grant recipients in a particular subfield. The program directors are the agency's front-line professionals, who keep in close contact with those doing research with NSF grant money.

The much-touted "peer review" process does not usurp the power of the program directors to serve agency goals. Peer review is the process in which an agency asks outside scientists to give their opinions on the scientific feasibility of proposed research; the screening by outsiders leaves the agency with a long list of feasible projects from which it chooses those that best further its goals. Peer review does not reduce the program directors to nonprofessional poll takers: The program directors select the reviewers, decide whose advice to follow in light of the goals of the programs they manage, and monitor the work of the scientists they fund. The program directors are the gatekeepers at the money bin and therefore loom as important figures for researchers, who if not worried about getting a grant, are worried about renewing one. Physicists hoping for National Science Foundation support, for example, are told that "while the advice of all reviewers is taken quite seriously, the final decision for funding is made by the Director and Staff of the Physics Division."[33]

To illustrate how government agencies influence university scientists to take up certain topics in their research work, I have used military agencies as many of my examples. My point is not that military goals motivate most university research, for that is not the case. My point is simply that university scientists adjust their curiosities for their funders—military or civilian. The military agencies are just examples of funders for whom many professors adjust their research interests. I will argue, however, that military agencies are more representative examples than they appear to be at first glance.

A GOVERNMENT AGENCY IS A GOVERNMENT AGENCY

The federal government funds science research through dozens of agencies and subdivisions.[34] The varied names of these federal organizations suggest correctly that the government has a wide variety of research interests. However, if one wants to figure out the government goals that motivate an agency to sponsor a particular research project, it is often very misleading to look to the name of the agency for a hint. For example, the name "Department of Energy" on a research project suggests work motivated by the quest for new or cleaner sources of energy. In fact, much of the research sponsored by the Department of Energy concerns weapons and elementary particles. The name "National

Science Foundation" on a project suggests work motivated by the quest of scientists to understand nature. However, it is misleading to describe NSF as simply a "patron for pure science," because NSF directs much of its money into areas of research with promising technological or military applications. It is the use of the word "Foundation" that makes the name misleading: "National Science Foundation" sounds like the name of an independent organization, not the name of a governmental unit. The National Science Foundation is, in fact, not a foundation. It is a government agency headed by a presidential appointee and funded annually with the tax money that Congress allots it in the federal budget. NSF's 2000 appropriation, for example, was $3.9 billion.

The reason agency names sometimes mislead lies in the overall unity of purpose among the agencies—they are all on the same government team. Each agency sets its research program in light of the government's overall research needs. When an agency considers proposals within its own area of specialization, these government needs provide a guiding framework, helping to define what is "interesting," what is "promising" and what is "useful." Because this framework is the same for all agencies, each government goal can motivate research at many agencies. An example came up in an extensive subfield-by-subfield survey of physics, conducted by the National Academy of Sciences.[35] The Academy's expert panel on atomic, molecular and electron physics, chaired by a leading Harvard physics professor, found government interest in "national security" motivating both the Defense Department and what is now the Department of Energy to fund research in atomic, molecular and electron physics. Specifically, the professor's panel talked about "bomb sighting," "nighttime visual surveillance" and "high-power laser beams."[36] Another example involving the same two agencies is perhaps more familiar: Government interest in the technology of nuclear war motivates research not only by the Department of Defense, but also by the Department of Energy, which funds the nuclear weapons research and development laboratories at Livermore, California, and Los Alamos, New Mexico.

The loyalty of those who run the agencies, and their knowledge of what is in the government's interest, are probably sufficient to ensure that each agency fulfills its role as a good "team player" in the effort to meet government goals. However, the government prefers not to take any chances. According to the National Academy of Sciences study, the executive level of government coordinates the "content and direction" of the research programs in the various agencies.[37] The Academy found that

> well-functioning mechanisms exist, both formal and informal, for political and economic intervention at the technical levels and, to a somewhat lesser extent, for technical input at the political levels.[38]

The Clinton administration, for example, established the National Science and Technology Council to coordinate research and development work and budgets across the various federal agencies "to orient science and technology toward achieving national goals."[39] The president put the secretary of defense and other cabinet members on the council, along with the heads of the National Science Foundation, the Central Intelligence Agency, the National Aeronautics and Space Administration, the National Institutes of Health and a few other agencies. Central to the council's mandate is the belief that "today's problems demand contributions from different fields of study and a team approach from the agencies that make up the Federal R&D enterprise."[40]

Below the executive level, civilian and military agencies such as the National Science Foundation and the Department of Defense work together to enhance their ability to meet the government's science needs. Officials of these agencies meet periodically to divvy up the necessary research work or, as Department of Defense research managers put it, "to apportion research areas in the most appropriate manner."[41] One result is that the National Science Foundation, the Department of Defense and other agencies fund university research in a way that supports one another's special interests.[42] In the words of the Defense Science Board, a senior advisory body to the Department of Defense, "Research and development in universities is supported by many sponsors, each relying on complementary funding from the other sponsors to leverage its own expenditures."[43] The Office of Naval Research, for example, reports that its "programs are heavily leveraged with other Federal and private programs."[44] An example of such reliance is that the Defense Department "depends on other agencies" to do the large amount of nuclear physics research that it needs.[45] In light of this degree of dependence, it is no surprise that the Defense Department worries about "the fate of areas of DoD interest should NSF budgets fail to maintain appropriate funding levels."[46]

Another way in which government agencies show that they have common goals is by taking over the funding of one another's university research projects when bureaucratic convenience makes it desirable to do so. This is common practice, as is the joint funding of research projects by agencies with names that suggest different missions. Because military-motivated research is an area of much activity, one finds "outright transfers"[47] of university research projects from the Department of Defense to the National Science Foundation as well as the less direct process of NSF "picking up"[48] projects when Defense Department funding runs out, and vice versa. I saw an example of this at the University of California, Irvine, when the National Science Foundation[49] took over from the Navy[50] the funding of a long-standing physics research project on effects that occur at the surfaces of solids. NSF spent over $500,000 to keep this project going.

The ease with which a research project's funding can bounce between a military agency and a civilian agency is just one more indication that agencies of both types are part of a team working to meet the government's research goals. Because government agencies do not divide up research strictly on the basis of the social goals that motivate it, it would be a serious mistake to think of agencies such as the National Science Foundation, the Department of Energy and the National Aeronautics and Space Administration as strictly nonmilitary.

University researchers know or at least sense this. They don't say openly that in a military and industrial superpower like the United States, government agencies must and do serve military and industrial goals. Rather, they reveal their awareness of the system's power over them by the lengths to which they go to avoid appearing to themselves and to others as the servants of the system that they are. Thus, often when one asks individual scientists what practical applications their work might have, they deliberately think narrowly enough to answer that it has none, and they give this answer quite proudly! I am always puzzled at first when a scientist stretches the truth to this strange end, until I realize that the question touches on the extremely sensitive issue of whom the scientist serves. This strange response from scientists is aimed above all else at leaving the impression that they are not servants of anybody but themselves.

Whenever a question has any bearing on this sensitive issue, scientists choose their words very carefully. For example, when one puts the question, "Who supports your work?" to professors with Navy funding, they are likely to answer quietly, "ONR." They are very unlikely to say, "the Office of Naval Research," because of the nasty words "naval research," and they are even more unlikely to say simply, "the Navy," because that sounds downright military. On the other hand, professors with NSF money will answer the same question proudly, "NSF," or just as likely, "the National Science Foundation." They are delighted to answer the question, especially if their work looks as if it might be motivated by military or marketplace goals, because the "Foundation's" name and image ring of pure science, the quest for truth and, above all, the individual scientist's own agenda. Perhaps the least deceptive and most informative answer that a university scientist can give to the question, "Who supports your work?" is simply, "The government."

Although the freedom of scientists to set their own work agendas is severely limited, professionals in many other fields enjoy even less freedom. For example, those in the so-called subprofessions—teachers, social workers, nurses and librarians—have their work prescribed almost completely. Employers trust them less. By contrast, the freedom of salaried professionals in a number of fields is comparable to that of scientists. Examples range from columnists and staff writers at newspapers and magazines to producers and entertainers employed by television networks, and include other salaried professionals, such as architects, museum curators, faculty members in all subjects at universities, commentators and critics, designers and so on. Professionals who are often thought of as completely self-directed, such as some filmmakers and artists, are not typical professionals in that they are generally independent, unlike the great majority of professionals, who are salaried staff members.

NOTES

1. *Enrollments and Degrees Report*, AIP R-151.35, American Institute of Physics, College Park, Md. (March 1999), figure 7 and table A2.

2. *1997 Initial Employment Report: Follow-Up of 1996 Physics Degree Recipients*, AIP R-282.20, American Institute of Physics, College Park, Md. (July 1998).

3. Beverly Fearn Porter, *Transition—A Follow-Up Study of 1973 Postdoctorals*, in Report of the Physics Manpower Panel of the American Physical Society, Milan D. Fiske, chairman, *The Transition in Physics Doctoral Employment 1960–1990*, American Physical Society, New York (August 1979), pp. 17–23, 113–192, and especially p. 184.

4. See note 2, figure 4.

5. Estimate for fiscal year 1997. *Federal Funds for Research and Development: Fiscal Years 1995, 1996, and 1997*, vol. 45, detailed statistical tables, NSF 97-327, National Science Foundation, Arlington, Va. (1997), pp. 57–60 (table C-10).

6. Roland W. Schmitt, "Research at General Electric," *Physics Today*, June 1980, p. 9.

7. Ibid.

8. Alfred H. Sommer, "How to succeed in industrial research," *Physics Today*, September 1976, p. 9, emphasis in original.

9. Frank von Hippel, "Protecting the whistle blowers," *Physics Today*, October 1977, p. 9.

10. In 1996, for example, the federal government sponsored about $10 billion worth of basic research in academic institutions; other sponsors brought the total to $15 billion. See Data Brief, NSF 98-303, National Science Foundation, Arlington, Va. (3 March 1998).

11. *Federal Funds for Research and Development: Fiscal Years 1995, 1996, and 1997*, vol. 45, detailed statistical tables, NSF 97-327, National Science Foundation, Arlington, Va. (1997), p. 161 (table C-61) and p. 169 (table C-69). *Academic Research and Development Expenditures: Fiscal Year 1996*, detailed statistical tables, NSF 98-304, National Science Foundation, Arlington, Va. (1998), pp. 151–152 (table B-53).

12. Ibid., NSF 97-327.

13. Ibid., NSF 98-304.

14. Executive Order 10521, sec. 5, 17 March 1954.

15. *Government–University Relationships in Federally Sponsored Scientific Research and Development*, NSF 58-10, National Science Foundation, Washington, D.C. (April 1958), pp. 17–18.

16. "Clinton's R&D Budget Defers Pain to Unkindest Cuts By Republicans," *Physics Today*, April 1995, pp. 65–71.

17. See note 15, p. 17.

18. William H. Whyte Jr. discusses this in his classic book *The Organization Man*, Simon and Schuster, New York (1956); see his three chapters on "the organization scientist," and pp. 234–235 in particular.

19. See note 15, p. 18.

20. For a concise history and description of the military's large and influential role in university science since World War II, see Stanton A. Glantz, "How the Department of Defense shaped academic research and graduate education," in Martin L. Perl, editor, *Physics Careers, Employment and Education*, AIP conference proceedings no. 39, American Institute of Physics, New York (1978), pp. 109–122. See also Bruce S. Old and The Bird Dogs, "The evolution of the Office of Naval Research," *Physics Today*, August

1961, pp. 30–35. When the National Science Foundation was created in 1950, the Navy's chief scientist, Alan T. Waterman, was named its first director.

21. *Contract Research & Technology Program*, ONR-1, Office of Naval Research, Department of the Navy, Arlington, Va. (April 1982), p. 3.

22. *Broad Agency Announcement*, FY 1999–2001, DAAD19-99-R-BAA1, U.S. Army Research Office, Research Triangle Park, N.C. (October 1998), quote on p. 1, "ARO Research Interests" on pp. 3–59.

23. *Guide to Programs, Fiscal Year 1998*, NSF 97-150, National Science Foundation, Arlington, Va. (1997), pp. ii, iv, x, 6-11.

24. *Guide to Programs*, Fiscal Year 1996, Office of Naval Research, Arlington, Va. (January 1996), p. 1.

25. *Guide for Unsolicited Research Proposals*, ARO-P 70-1, U.S. Army Research Office, Research Triangle Park, N.C. (November 1983), p. 2.

26. *Research Interests and Broad Agency Announcement 97-1 of the Air Force Office of Scientific Research*, AFOSR pamphlet 64-1, Air Force Office of Scientific Research, Bolling Air Force Base, D.C. (1 October 1996), pp. 51–52. The Air Force programs that I mentioned were not funded in the most recent fiscal year, and their future is unclear. Equivalent programs run by the Office of Naval Research continue.

27. Ibid.

28. Ibid.

29. See note 22, pp. 67–68.

30. "About ONR," page on the World Wide Web, Office of Naval Research, Arlington, Va. (posting of 9 September 1998).

31. ONR Corporate Programs Division, pages on the World Wide Web, Office of Naval Research, Arlington, Va. (posting of 29 April 1998). The graduate student program is a joint program of the Army, Navy and Air Force.

32. *Contract Research & Technology Program*, ONR-1, Office of Naval Research, Department of the Navy, Arlington, Va. (April 1982), p. 7, "investigations" corrected to "investigators" by private communication.

33. National Science Foundation, Division of Physics, pages on the World Wide Web, update of 26 June 1998. For more details about NSF grant proposals and how they are evaluated, see *Grant Proposal Guide*, NSF 99-2, National Science Foundation, Arlington, Va. (October 1998).

34. See note 11, NSF 97-327, pp. 83–85 (table C-22).

35. Physics Survey Committee, *Physics in Perspective*, National Academy of Sciences–National Research Council, Washington, D.C. (June 1972).

36. Nicolaas Bloembergen headed the subfield panel. Ibid., vol. 2A, pp. 419–420.

37. Ibid., vol. 1, pp. 654–655, 658–659.

38. Ibid., vol. 1, p. 652.

39. *National Science and Technology Council*, a folded brochure, National Science and Technology Council, Executive Office of the President, Washington, D.C. (1994).

40. Ibid.

41. See Stanton A. Glantz, Norm V. Albers, "Department of Defense R & D in the University," *Science*, vol. 186 (22 November 1974), pp. 706–711, especially p. 710.

42. Charles Schwartz, "Physics and the military," *Physics Today*, October 1984, pp. 9, 122–124; correction, December 1984, p. 94.

43. *Report of the Defense Science Board Task Force on University Responsiveness to National Security Requirements*, Office of the Under Secretary of Defense for Research

and Engineering, Department of Defense, Washington, D.C. (January 1982), p. 3-5. Report reprinted in *Hearings on Military Posture*, House Armed Services Committee, document number 97-33, pt. 5, U.S. Government Printing Office, Washington, D.C. (1982), pp. 256–327, especially p. 294.

44. See note 24.

45. See note 35, vol. 1, p. 694.

46. See note 43, p. 5-2 (p. 316 in House reprint).

47. See note 35, vol. 1, pp. 687–688.

48. Ibid.

49. National Science Foundation grant NSF/DMR-78-09430, "Theoretical Investigations of Surface Effects in Solids and the Properties of Semiconductors." Principal investigators: Richard F. Wallis and Alexei A. Maradudin. NSF spent $208,500 to sponsor this project from 1 December 1978 through 30 November 1982. Pleased with the results, NSF continued its sponsorship through grant NSF/DMR-82-14214, "Theoretical Investigations of Surface Effects in Solids, Nonlinear Phenomena and the Properties of Semiconductors." NSF gave Wallis and Maradudin $209,300 for the period 15 December 1982 through 31 May 1986, and paid about $131,000 to the Boeing Computer Services Company, a division of the Boeing Company, to give Wallis and Maradudin (or, more accurately, their postdocs and graduate students) eighty hours of CPU time on a Cray supercomputer.

50. Office of Naval Research contracts N00014-69-A-0200-9003 and N00014-76-C-0121 and renewals thereof, "Theoretical Investigations of Surface Effects in Solids and Optical Properties of Solids." Principal investigators: Richard F. Wallis and Alexei A. Maradudin. The Navy funding covered the period 1969 through 1978.

5

THE SOCIAL SIGNIFICANCE
CONCEALMENT GAME

From the General Electric Company to the National Science Foundation, the scientist's curiosity is directed. The previous chapter suggests that university scientists adjust their curiosities for their funders in much the same way that industrial scientists adjust theirs for their employers. But was it really necessary to look at all the national studies and official statements to show this? Aren't the social goals of scientists' work obvious once the scientists have adjusted their curiosity and secured their funding? Couldn't one simply walk into a sampling of labs and offices, look at what the scientists are doing and say, "Aha, adjusted curiosity!"? Sometimes it *is* that easy, but more often the social goals of a scientist's work are not at all obvious, as a look at some examples of adjusted curiosity in action will show.

For the examples, I turn to the sizable physics research programs at the University of California, Irvine. UCI is among the top 20 universities in the United States when ranked according to federal research and development funds received annually for work in physics.[1]

Physics research at UCI is typical of physics research in the United States:

- Most of it is sponsored by the federal government. In 1996, for example, the federal government paid for 77% of the physics R&D done at American universities, and 85% of that done at UCI.[2] Physics research at UCI is also typical in that a significant portion of this federal funding comes through military agencies.
- The three physics subfields that receive the heaviest research funding at UCI—condensed matter physics, plasma physics and particle physics—are subfields that receive heavy funding nationally. The federal government channels much of its basic physics research money into these

subfields.[3] Thus, in the UCI physics department these three subfields account for the work of 30 of the 39 professors, all 17 of the nonfaculty PhD research physicists, 18 of the 20 postdoctoral researchers and (therefore) 33 of the 39 graduate students who have chosen a research specialty. (The department has 74 graduate students in all.) Of the 77 doctorates granted by the department in the five-year period 1993 to 1998, 74 were in the three subfields.[4] A similar narrowing of research focus is found in departments nationwide. Even though condensed matter physics, for example, is just one of more than two dozen physics subfields, it alone accounts for the work of more than one-fifth of the physics graduate students in the United States.[5]

• Finally, physics research at UCI, when categorized by level of investigation—basic or applied—is either typical of university physics research in each subfield or leans toward the basic. (Basic research determines physical mechanisms; applied research puts known mechanisms to use.)

The UCI program of research in physics, being typical in degree of federal sponsorship, subfields of concentration and level of investigation, can tell us a lot about the nature of university physics in the United States.

It is easy to pinpoint whose needs the UCI physics research programs serve: Simply "follow the money" back to its source—in this case the government. However, even though this does, in my opinion, identify whose interests that determine the content of the research, it is evidently not sufficient to cause very many people to question their belief that university professors are self-directed. Therefore, in giving examples of adjusted curiosity in UCI physics research, I will go beyond merely identifying the sponsors. I will identify in detail the particular social goals that motivate the sponsors, and I will show that physics research at UCI addresses specific technological needs that arise from those social goals. The point of looking at some of the technical details of physics research at UCI is not to become knowledgeable in the technological needs of the funders, useful as that may be; rather, it is to see more fully how funders' interests set the direction of research and to get a more complete understanding of adjusted curiosity.

The way research is described, funded and carried out conceals its social origins. The titles that scientists give their research projects (and publications) usually make their work look very abstract and esoteric. These titles, and the technical descriptions that accompany them, make no mention of underlying technological goals. This practice lends prestige to the work by making it look more basic and more like a pursuit of truth for its own sake. Someone who takes a look at the titles and abstracts of research projects and sees no hint of the work's social origins usually comes away marveling about how far from practicality scientists' free-running curiosities have led them.

Outside observers aren't the only ones to make this mistake. It is sad but common for a graduate student to work her dissertation problem through to completion while never knowing its social origin. (Later I will show how the qualifying examination selects people who are comfortable working with this kind of ignorance.)

Grant proposals make the motivating interests no more explicit. In these applications for research money, the customary pretense is that the researcher is simply pursuing her curiosity about the mysteries of nature, and that the funder is simply looking to support "excellence" or "good science."

In fact, it is very difficult to get information on the social goals that underlie the government's funding of individual scientists' research projects. Even though a research project typically consumes hundreds of thousands of tax dollars, the crucial information on government goals spreads mainly by word of mouth. A government funding agency's description of its particular interest in a research project—its reasons for funding it—is usually not made public. The researcher's description of the project is usually available, but this turns out to be nothing more than a nuts-and-bolts description of the work—the narrowest possible view. Such descriptions, already uninformative, are presented in technical language that is almost impossible for a nonspecialist to understand. However, when the sponsors' descriptions are available—and I have obtained a few funding agency descriptions of UCI research projects in condensed matter physics and plasma physics—it is fascinating to compare them with the researchers' descriptions. The striking contrast makes it clear that the usual descriptions, from the scientists themselves, conceal the social origins and political significance of the work.[6]

CONDENSED MATTER PHYSICS

Condensed matter physicists, also known as solid-state physicists, specialize in studying the mechanical, thermal, electrical, magnetic and optical properties of metals, semiconductors and insulators. They examine, for example, how materials conduct electricity and heat and interact with light and sound. They discuss the properties of solids in terms of simple models that specify the arrangement of a material's molecules and that assume certain interactions between the molecules. A starting point for the solid-state physicist's description of complicated systems is the perfect crystal—such as a single crystal of table salt—whose periodic molecular arrangement makes it quite amenable to mathematical representation.

At the University of California, Irvine, solid-state theorists Alexei Maradudin and Douglas Mills headed a federally funded research project, "The Interaction of Electromagnetic Radiation with Solid Materials." In their application for Air Force funding, the two physicists described the objectives of their work:

> The objective of the proposed program of theoretical research is an increased understanding of the interactions of electromagnetic radiation, particularly in the infrared, with matter. To be studied are the consequences of the inelastic scattering

of electrons from ionized impurities in a doped semiconductor on infrared absorption in the Drude tail; the additional structure introduced into the infrared absorption spectrum of a p-type semiconductor of the zincblende structure when this absorption band overlaps the transverse optical phonon absorption line; the line shape for infrared absorption by localized vibration modes (due to H⁻ ion impurities) in alkali–halide crystals; and the determination of the contribution of electron–electron scattering to the real part of the conductivity of a metal in the infrared. The effects of impurities on interband absorption in solids, and the inelastic scattering of light from a plasmon coupled to localized vibration modes in semiconductors will also be investigated. Finally, theories of the refraction and reflection of surface polaritons in the infrared at interfaces they encounter, and of the Brillouin scattering of light from an opaque solid will be constructed. The solution of these problems will require sophisticated theoretical and computational techniques, some of which remain to be developed.

Far from shedding light on whose interests the research serves, this description leaves one wondering whether the search for such political significance is perhaps absurd. Can't research exist for purely "scientific" reasons and seek understanding for understanding's sake?

A look at the Air Force's description of professors Maradudin and Mills's $578,000 project is most revealing:

> Aerospace communications surveillance and detection systems require electro-optical devices which exploit the special properties and interactions of infrared radiation with solid state materials. Infrared materials research has high potential for airborne and satellite applications.
>
> This is a theoretical research effort to investigate the interaction of electromagnetic radiation with solid materials, to investigate fundamental processes and elementary excitations that occur mainly in the infrared region of the electromagnetic spectrum, and to study bulk and surface optical properties as well as nonlinear optical phenomena in solids.
>
> The infrared optical properties of these materials are important to the development of infrared detectors and coherent sources, integrated optics and electro-optical techniques, and high energy infrared laser windows and mirrors as well as interactions of materials subjected to laser beams.[7]

Here the nature of the social foundation of this fundamental theoretical physics research becomes clear: "surveillance and detection," "infrared [heat] detectors," "windows and mirrors" for high-energy lasers, "materials subjected to laser beams"—in a word, weapons.

Before they started on this project, Maradudin and Mills did similar work for the same sponsor under the title, "Theoretical and Experimental Investigation of Material Properties of Crystals and Crystal Surfaces." Here's how the government described this work:

> High energy laser technology is finding wide application in future Air Force systems. Both in the production of intense radiation and in the hardening of certain

critical components to this radiation, the interactions of photons with matter is of extreme importance. Rather than trial-and-error testing of a wide variety of materials this research seeks a fundamental understanding of the quantum interactions in and on crystalline solids.[8]

Maradudin later worked with UCI physics professor Richard Wallis on another research project, "The enhanced backscattering of light from random surfaces and related phenomena." According to the U.S. Army, which funded the $300,000 project,

> The [Maradudin–Wallis] work is highly relevant to the Army and to DOD at large for the generation of signatures for IFF [identification of friend or foe]. Other applications will include camouflage. . . .[9]

The various research projects given as examples here sound very arcane in the professors' descriptions, but, as the funders' descriptions show, all are clearly connected to the funders' technological needs.

Among the federal agencies that have sponsored condensed matter physics research at UCI are the National Science Foundation, the Army Research Office, the Office of Naval Research, the Air Force Office of Scientific Research, the Department of Energy and the National Aeronautics and Space Administration. Interestingly, at UCI the military agencies have directed almost all of their money to theorists, leaving the National Science Foundation to pick up most of the tab for the experimental work.

PLASMA PHYSICS

Plasma physicists specialize in studying ionized gases. Such gases are so hot that electrons become detached from gas atoms, resulting in a glowing, electrically conducting mixture of negative electrons and positive ions, which is called a plasma. Examples of plasmas are readily found outside of the laboratory: in neon signs, metal-vapor street lights, flames and nuclear explosions, and in and around the sun and the stars. Plasma physicists investigate mechanisms of ionization and the properties of plasmas over a wide range of temperatures and pressures. They study plasmas' interactions with electric and magnetic fields, particle beams and solid surfaces; they study the characteristic motion of the particles that make up plasmas, the propagation of waves in plasmas, and the various kinds of instabilities that develop when one tries to arrange magnetic fields so that they will act as "magnetic bottles" capable of confining the hot plasmas. Many plasma physics research projects are part of an effort to achieve controlled thermonuclear fusion, in which the nuclei of light atoms, such as the hydrogen isotopes deuterium and tritium, merge and release large quantities of energy. Both military and civilian applications motivate work on controlled fusion; one heavily funded approach is to compress fuel pellets until they explode like tiny hydrogen bombs.[10]

UCI physics professors Norman Rostoker and Nathan Rynn ran a plasma physics research project titled "Electron Beam Switching Experiment." In their proposal to work on the project under government contract, they described what they had been doing and what they planned to do:

> We are evaluating energy storage devices that involve accumulation of electrons in a magnetic trap and rapid release of the energy by magnetic switching. We have obtained significant results with a small scale experiment involving a thermionic injector and fast magnetic compression. . . . In addition, the use of a pulse line and diode for injection into static fields will be evaluated. We also plan to study several other methods to produce short intense radiation pulses.

Nowhere do the researchers say why anyone would want to produce short intense radiation pulses. The funding agency is, by contrast, straightforward:

> Objective: Develop ultra high power sources for simulating nuclear weapon effects and having energy storage capabilities significantly exceeding present simulators.[11]

Simulation allows the development of real-world systems in the laboratory. In the words of a report from a major Army weapons research and development laboratory in Adelphi, Maryland, which coordinated much of the government's effort in nuclear weapons effects simulation:

> Since at this time tests cannot be conducted in a real nuclear weapon environment, simulators are the only available link to reality.[12]

The ability to simulate the effects of nuclear weapons allows the U.S. government to get around some of the obstacles that nuclear test ban treaties place in the way of preparation for nuclear war. Professors Rostoker and Rynn, by contributing to the government's "link to reality," helped it violate one of the hopes people had for the test ban—an end to the further development of nuclear war technology—without actually violating the letter of the treaties.

Irvine physics professor Gregory Benford described his research project, "Coherent Radiation from Relativistic Beam-Plasma Instabilities," in his application for the $130,000 U.S. Army grant that he received to do the work. He proposed to undertake

> detailed studies of the coherent curvature spectrum, to verify the theory in detail and discover how the mechanism can be scaled to higher frequencies and higher power levels. Improving measurements of the dependence of output power on ω_p, B and γ, using the spectrometer, will aid in this. Elaboration of the coherent curvature scheme, by injecting the rotating beam into a magnetic field which increases in z, will identify further the resonance condition ($\omega_p \lesssim \gamma^2 \omega_c$) necessary for emission.

The Army describes this project as an experimental and theoretical effort

> to obtain high power mm and sub-mm radiation based on the electromagnetic emission from plasmas in which instabilities are excited by a relativistic electron beam.

This program is relevant to the mm and sub-mm program that is underway at HDL [an Army laboratory] as well as programs at other DOD laboratories. HDL is also interested in this research as a source of X-ray radiation for their radiation damage studies.[13]

It doesn't take much technical knowledge to understand why the government is interested in electromagnetic radiation with wavelength around one millimeter: The military can use a coherent source of this radiation to build devices capable of identifying targets that are obscured by battlefield smoke, dust or fog. In the words of a *Physics Today* report on the Department of Defense budget for basic research, "the region of approximately 1 mm wavelength appears to be best for detecting targets and guiding weapons under conditions of poor visibility."[14] The Army explains:

Current efforts in the near-millimeter-wave portion of the spectrum (100 to 1000 GHz) are directed toward providing the Army with the capability for operating under all visibility conditions. Near-millimeter-wave systems can operate in realistic battlefield environments where there are obscurants such as fog, smoke, and dust; the performance of electro-optic and infrared systems, in contrast, degrades under similar circumstances. In addition, near-millimeter-wave systems provide improved resolution, smaller size, and better electronic-countermeasure protection than most microwave systems.[15]

The Naval Research Laboratory, which also works on millimeter-wavelength radiation, is motivated by

interesting applications in such diverse fields as surveillance radars, electronic warfare, tactical battlefield target designators, and plasma heating devices for fusion.[16]

And yes, the Air Force, too, sponsors research in this area, saying this about its plasma physics program:

Our primary areas of interest encompass novel concepts for the electron-beam-driven generation of high-power microwave and millimeter-wave radiation. . . .
The high power microwave research to be sponsored will . . . look to primary applications in future directed energy weapons and electronics countermeasure systems. Possible applications for large area surveillance systems are also of interest.[17]

Obviously pleased by the results of Benford's work on the initial grant, the Army contracted with him to do another $220,000 worth of such work, foreseeing "payoff in terms of a new mm wave source."[18]

The Air Force contracted with solar plasma physicist Gerard Van Hoven, when he was at UCI, to run a $742,000 research project titled "3-D MHD modelling of solar activity." According to a restricted Air Force report on the professor's work, Van Hoven's

effort is directed towards development of computer generated solar activity forecasts that can serve as inputs for warnings and alerts of solar driven "space weather."[19]

"Space weather" refers to conditions in Earth's ionosphere and magnetosphere. The Air Force funds research on it because bad space weather

> can degrade the performance of Air Force spacecraft and systems. Both the nominal and disturbed space environment can disrupt the detection and tracking of missiles and satellites, distort communications and navigation, and interfere with global surveillance operations.[20]

The Navy, too, does space weather research, anticipating that

> geomagnetic disturbances will become an increasingly important concern for the Navy's Command, Control, Communication, and Computer Intelligence (C⁴I) and Command and Control Warfare (C²W) systems.[21]

Finally, UCI physics professor Norman Rostoker and adjunct professor Amnon Fisher received a government contract for a project titled "Plasma Controlled Collective Ion Acceleration." Here's why the government contracted for this work:

> The Navy needs quantitative information on methods to generate intense ion beams with energies up to 1 GeV for directed energy applications, sources of intense radiation through impact with targets, new sources of energy via interaction with pellets, etc. The electron beam front collective acceleration of ions to be carried out in this contract has the scaling characteristics which are necessary to fulfill the requirement stated above.[22]

The professors do this research because "the Navy needs. . . ." In fact, one can say that the entire UCI program of basic research in plasma physics—and the condensed matter research program as well—exists precisely because of the short-term and long-term technological needs of the dominant sectors of society. The financial backers of plasma physics at UCI have included the National Science Foundation, the Army Research Office, the Office of Naval Research, the Air Force Office of Scientific Research, the Department of Energy, the National Aeronautics and Space Administration and the Defense Nuclear Agency (recently renamed the Defense Special Weapons Agency and then absorbed into the Defense Threat Reduction Agency).

In light of the intimate intellectual relationship between many university faculty members and the military, and the large sums of money involved, one could argue that these professors are in essence part of the military, despite the fact that at university ceremonies they wear academic robes rather than Army, Navy or Air Force uniforms. Indeed, many of the professors I have mentioned could leave the university and take jobs at military laboratories, such as the Army Research Laboratory or the Naval Research Laboratory, without affecting the social or scientific significance of their work. Moving to a military laboratory would, however, take a big toll on any university professor's public image. The public image of researchers at military laboratories is poor compared to that of university professors, who are generally seen as intelligent, open-minded, objective intellectuals—even when their research work is exactly the same as that of researchers at military laboratories. This positive image is part of the mystique that university academic employees exploit and propagate.

Professors doing military research often use the university mystique to mislead people about the social significance of their work. Benford, the UCI mm-wave researcher, is a good example. He finds the university setting to be particularly useful because his part-time work as a science fiction writer brings him more than the average scientist's share of attention from the media—including the media's inevitable curiosity and inquiries about the nature of his own research work. When the media interview turns to the potential uses of his research, Benford honestly enough talks about portable, high-resolution radar units. However, on the question of how such radar units would be used, the professor tells the naive reporter, "When you're fighting a forest fire, for instance, you can't see what you're dropping the water on because of the smoke."[23]

It is not my purpose to show that many ivory-tower scientists are the social equivalent of military scientists, true as that is. I set out to make a narrower point: that fundamental theoretical and experimental physics research at UCI and other universities in large part owes its existence to society's demand for technology, not to scientists' desire to increase humanity's understanding of nature. If a funding agency decides it no longer needs the work it is sponsoring at UCI and decides to spend its money on something else, and if the government does not make a corresponding increase in the budget of another agency, then that work at UCI would be finis. The end would be visible in the plunge in person-hours spent on the work, publications produced, graduate students "taken on," postdocs hired, computer time used, and so on. Remaining in great abundance would be most of the necessary conditions for the research: professors trained and willing to do it, computer time available for purchase, office space in the proper environment, graduate students, hordes of postdoc applicants and so on. Gone would be what is, for all practical purposes, the determining or sufficient condition for the research: commercial or military–governmental need.

IT TAKES A PROFESSIONAL

Ninety-five percent of the more than $220 billion worth of research and development done each year in the United States is sponsored by industry or government.[24] If, as we have seen, scientists serve their sponsors, then it would be fair to conclude that most scientists serve industry or government interests. The exceptions get much of the publicity, but they are not relevant to understanding the professional training system, the primary function of which is to produce the tens of thousands of rank-and-file scientists needed to staff the country's public and private laboratories. But do scientists really have to be professionals to do their jobs?

Great technical knowledge is not sufficient to get and keep a job as a scientist. Every small step in scientific research opens up a virtually unlimited number of directions, all of which lead to new scientific truth, but not all of which lead to scientific truth of interest to those who employ the scientists or sponsor their research. Scientists must therefore make many small but important decisions as they go about their work. I asked the manager of a basic research program with a budget of $2 million per year to describe this decision-making process, which lies at the heart of basic research. Kristl Hathaway manages a magnetic materials research program at the Office of Naval Research. She selects mainly university professors to receive the basic research grants that she gives out:

> There's a model of curiosity-based research that is sort of like just following your nose. It goes on this little wandering path, like if you took a pencil and just made scribbles on a board. But the truth is, from anything you do, there are always lots of puzzles. You say, "Gee, look, I stumbled on this new material" or "I see this new phenomenon." When you find something new, you don't just have one direction you can go from there. You generally have choices. You can always push it in several different directions. And often they are of equal scientific interest, or curiosity. You say, "Well, I can't go five different directions at once, but they all look interesting."
>
> The impact, or the strategic stuff, you overlay on top of that. It seems to me that if you want your life to be meaningful, you want to push the research in the direction that's going to have an impact and be meaningful to other humans. Otherwise it is just going to kind of fold back on itself and solve this little puzzle and then solve some other little puzzle. So you pick to do first those things that'll have the largest impact, to move the field forward the most rapidly.
>
> And that's a good filter to use for research proposals. Often I'll get five proposals when I can fund only one, and they're all good science. Very few people do bad science, you know.[25]

Employers understand this and have given much thought to the question of how to get what they want from their scientists. Harvey Brooks, an influential Harvard physicist who served on science policy-setting bodies such as the President's Science Advisory Committee (for Presidents Eisenhower, Kennedy and Johnson) and the National Science Board, noted that "scientific work involves a multiplicity of choices of direction, many of which depend on very small influences in the mind of the investigator." Furthermore, said Brooks, "the cumulative effect of the small biases placed in the mind of the investigator by his sponsor can have a profound effect on the direction and impact of his research."[26] By transferring their biases to the scientists whom they employ, employers can ensure that these scientists maintain the right direction in their day-to-day work. In fact, employers have no stricter or more direct way of controlling employees who make lots of small but important decisions in their work; making decisions for such employees would defeat the purpose of hiring scientists rather than technicians in the first place.

However, an outfit can't have a "profound effect" on its scientists' work un-less it hires scientists who are willing and able to take up the "small biases" of those who employ them. Thus, an institution that is considering hiring (or fir-ing) a particular scientist looks beyond the individual's technical knowledge. It tries to determine whether the scientist is one who exercises "good judgment" in her work or is one who tends to go in directions not in her employer's inter-ests—that is, it looks for someone willing and able to pick up its "small biases." To George Pake, who was a member of the President's Science Advisory Com-mittee (for Presidents Johnson and Nixon) and then commander of Xerox Cor-poration's 600 research scientists and engineers, this calls for "creative profes-sionals"—scientists who understand their bosses' needs and adjust their curiosities accordingly:

> There is little success likely to come from showing researchers to a laboratory, de-scribing in detail a desired technology or process not now existent, and com-manding: "Thou shalt invent!" Instead, the enterprise seems to go better if some overall goals or needs are generally described and understood and proposals for research projects or areas of investigation are solicited from the creative profes-sionals.[27]

Xerox and other employers want and get scientists who work from an un-derstanding of their sponsors' interests, not from detailed instructions. To do their jobs, these scientists have to be sufficiently aware of their employers' in-terests to adjust their own thinking about what is interesting, about what to pursue and what to drop at the many decision points in their work. This is one way in which employers' interests are extrapolated into the day-to-day detail of scientific work. To do work that meets their employers' expectations, the scientists must have the "right" priorities, the "right" values and the "right" sense of what is important.

When the bosses simply announce their interests and stop short of translat-ing them into detailed marching orders, they are demanding that profession-als act like professionals. They expect those closest to the work to watch for and find new ways of serving those closest to the purse strings. Kristl Hath-away, the Navy program officer who funds basic research, told me how it works in practice:

> We get a lot of researchers, many of whom are university professors, who call up and say, "I'm available. What would you like me to work on?" The truth is, we're waiting for the research community to tell us what they should do. They are the ones who see the directions in which they can go. They are the ones sitting in the lab with a problem and saying, "Oh, from this I see I could do this experiment or this other experiment or this calculation." Then they should be thinking, "Well, which of these has some impact? And which agency would be interested in that kind of impact?" Then they can call up and you can kind of iterate [go back and forth] with them. But they have to know enough about the impact of what they are thinking of doing to know which agency to talk to.[28]

We should note that in a sense employers need only fine-tune the direction of their scientists' work. Scientists already have the proper general orientation because mainstream scientific thinking, as much today as throughout history, is connected to establishment social interests. The scientific ideologies, or "paradigms," that scientists internalize during their training guide their thinking in every important area of their work, determining, for example, the particular abstractions or models they use, the procedures they consider valid and even their notion of what constitutes progress and understanding. But how are the paradigms chosen? As philosopher of science Thomas Kuhn observed, paradigms are incommensurable—that is, there is no transcendent scientific framework in which one can compare paradigms and choose the best, and so such choices are made on the basis of values, or social factors. Since no two paradigms solve the same problems, the choice between them involves deciding which problems it is most important to solve—clearly a question of values.[29] In any historical era the values of those at the top of the social hierarchy dominate; as a result the paradigms that emerge from the scientific competition have a built-in tilt toward establishment priorities. Through the paradigms, then, social forces direct scientific work even in the rare cases when employers or funding agencies do not.

Because they internalize both the paradigms and their employers' priorities and values, scientists, at least in their own eyes, are completely nonpartisan in their work: They don't "get political." They don't think about, let alone challenge, the ideology built into their techniques. Contrary to popular images of scientists as challengers of established beliefs (like Galileo or Einstein), the vast majority of scientists never seek to test their paradigms and do not participate in paradigm disputes. They don't waste their employers' coin by getting caught up in efforts to overthrow existing worldviews or to establish new ones. Instead, they tend to treat the accepted models of reality as reality itself.

A large fraction of these scientists are employed by one or another institution of the military–industrial complex, but they do not raise questions about the social function of their work. And they can't plead ignorance either, because as we have seen, to do what is expected of them they have to be at least somewhat aware of their employers' or funders' interests. They don't challenge their employers' goals; they don't question the social structure that they bolster; they don't offer an alternate view of what scientists should be doing on the job. They have an internalized willingness and ability to be directed in the most important areas. They concentrate on how best to carry out their assignments—only here do they use their creativity, and then only within the limits of the dominant paradigms. In short, these scientists are professionals.

Like all professionals, scientists maintain ideological discipline in their work: They adhere to the dominant paradigms, and they work as if their employers' priorities were their own—that is, they work uncritically toward assigned social goals.

Professional scientists do not necessarily agree with their bosses' every decision. However, the professional who does disagree with a decision typically goes along with it anyway, griping harmlessly to coworkers that the decision was "political" rather than "scientific." Such gripes are harmless to the power structure because they naively suggest an impossible "science for science's sake," rather than an alternative laboratory politics.

Those who become rank-and-file scientists are certainly not born with a desire to devote their working lives to solving problems for big business or the military–industrial complex. In fact, like others living in corporate America, those headed for training as scientists are likely to think of such interests as "the other side" in an ongoing struggle for power in society. Yet the message here is that trained rank-and-file scientists are willing and able, if not eager, to adjust their curiosities for those with the most power in society. How does this come to be? How do people come to be intellectual workers who are so at home working on the other side of the fence? We will see how professional training works to produce such people.

NOTES

1. *Academic Research and Development Expenditures: Fiscal Year 1996*, detailed statistical tables, NSF 98-304, National Science Foundation, Arlington, Va. (1998), pp. 151–152 (table B-53).

2. Ibid.

3. Much federal money goes into nuclear physics as well. National Research Council, *Physics Through the 1990s: An Overview*, National Academy Press, Washington, D.C. (1986), pp. 129–130 (table S3.6).

4. *1999 Graduate Programs in Physics, Astronomy, and Related Fields*, AIP R-205.24, American Institute of Physics, Woodbury, N.Y. (1998), pp. 69–71. Postdoc data from physics department chair, 26 March 1996.

5. *1996 Graduate Student Report*, AIP R-207.29, American Institute of Physics, College Park, Md. (September 1997), table 5 and unpublished source data for that table. I counted surface physics as part of condensed matter physics. Almost 90% of physics graduate students are working in the following subfields: condensed-matter physics; particles and fields; astronomy and astrophysics; nuclear physics; atomic and molecular physics; optics and photonics; atmospheric, space physics and cosmic rays; materials science; plasma physics and fusion; biophysics; relativity and gravitation; low-temperature physics; applied physics.

6. For pioneering work on such comparisons, see Stanton A. Glantz, Carol A. Farlow, Richard A. Simpson, Norm V. Albers, Dennis E. Pocekay, William E. Holley, Michael F. Becker, Stephen S. Ashley, Michael R. Headrick, *DOD Sponsored Research at Stanford, vol. 1, Two Perceptions: The Investigator's and the Sponsor's*, Stanford Workshops on Political and Social Issues, Stanford University (1971). Norm V. Albers, Stephen S. Ashley, Michael F. Becker, Carol A. Farlow, Stanton A. Glantz, Richard A. Simpson, *DOD Sponsored Research at Stanford, vol. 2, Its Impact on the University*, Stanford Workshops on Political and Social Issues, Stanford University (1971). "Defense Research: The Names Are Changed to Protect the Innocent," *Science*, vol. 175 (25 February 1972), pp. 866–868. Stanton A. Glantz, Norm V. Albers, "Department of Defense R & D in the University," *Science*, vol. 186 (22 November 1974), pp. 706–711.

7. Air Force Office of Scientific Research contract F49620-78-C-0019, as described in Work Unit Summaries filed at the Defense Technical Information Center, dated 26 October 1978 and 29 August 1985 (final report), accession no. DF041700. The Defense Technical Information Center (DTIC), located at Fort Belvoir, Va., was formerly known as the Defense Documentation Center (DDC).

8. Air Force Office of Scientific Research grant AFOSR-71-2018, as described in DTIC Work Unit Summary of 22 May 1978, accession no. DF031200.

9. Army Research Office grant DAAL03-92-G-0239, as described in DTIC Work Unit Summary of 23 May 1995, accession no. DA322612.

10. Ross Flewelling, "Laser fusion: image and reality of a military program," *Science for the People*, July–August 1981, pp. 28–31. William D. Metz, "Ambitious Energy Project Loses Luster," *Science*, vol. 212 (1 May 1981), pp. 517–519. National Research Council, *Plasma Science*, National Academy Press, Washington, D.C. (1995), pp. 21, 60, 69, 70, 157 and ch. 5.

11. Defense Nuclear Agency contract DNA001-74-C-0056, as described in DDC Work Unit Summary of 14 May 1976, accession no. DH001582. The work continued under contracts DNA001-77-C-0003 and DNA001-79-C-0046.

12. *Laboratory Review*, Fiscal Year 1981, Harry Diamond Laboratories, U.S. Army Electronics Research and Development Command, Adelphi, Md., p. 63. The Army Research Laboratory was established in 1992 and subsumed Harry Diamond Laboratories.

13. Army Research Office grant DAAG29-78-G-0020, as described in DTIC Work Unit Summary of 16 November 1979, accession no. DA0F9122.

14. *Physics Today*, June 1980, p. 84.

15. *Laboratory Review*, Fiscal Year 1979, Harry Diamond Laboratories, U.S. Army Electronics Research and Development Command, Adelphi, Md. (1980), p. 133. See also *Broad Agency Announcement*, FY 1996–FY 1997, DAAH04-96-R-BAA1, U.S. Army Research Office, Research Triangle Park, N.C. (October 1995), p. 66. *Broad Agency Announcement*, FY 1999–2001, DAAD19-99-R-BAA1, U.S. Army Research Office, Research Triangle Park, N.C. (October 1998), pp. 15–24.

16. *1978 Review*, Naval Research Laboratory, Washington, D.C., p. 17. See also *1998 NRL Review*, Naval Research Laboratory, Washington, D.C. (April 1998), p. 55.

17. *Research Interests of the Air Force Office of Scientific Research and Broad Agency Announcement 99-1*, AFOSR pamphlet 64-1, Air Force Office of Scientific Research, Arlington, Va. (October 1998), pp. 23–24.

18. Army Research Office contract DAAG29-80-C-0013, as described in DTIC Work Unit Summary of 12 December 1979, accession no. DA0G0642.

19. Air Force contract F19628-93-C-0136, as described in DTIC Work Unit Summary of 24 November 1995, accession no. DF594616. I had to pose as a defense contractor to obtain this report on Professor Van Hoven's work. It is stamped: "RELEASE TO U.S. GOV'T AND THEIR CONTRACTORS ONLY. FURTHER DISTRIBUTION IS NOT AUTHORIZED WITHOUT PERMISSION OF OUSD(A+T)DDR+E." These letters refer, of course, to the Office of the Under Secretary of Defense (Acquisition and Technology), Director of Defense Research and Engineering.

20. See note 17, p. 45.

21. *1995 NRL Review*, Naval Research Laboratory, Washington, D.C. (May 1995), p. 209.

22. Office of Naval Research contract N00014-79-C-0560, as described in DTIC Work Unit Summary of 23 July 1980, accession no. DN975487.

23. Gary Taubes, "Science in his lab, science in his fiction," *Discover*, August 1983, pp. 66–72.

24. Data Brief, NSF 99-302, National Science Foundation, Arlington, Va. (16 October 1998).

25. Telephone conversation with Kristl Hathaway, 14 October 1994. Hathaway asked me to note that her views are not necessarily those of the Office of Naval Research or the Department of the Navy.

26. Harvey Brooks, *The Government of Science*, M.I.T. Press, Cambridge, Mass. (1968), pp. 112–113.

27. George E. Pake, "R & D Management," text of speech delivered 9 October 1984 to the Institute of Electrical and Electronics Engineers—Franklin Institute Centennial Technical Convocation. At the time of this speech Pake was Xerox's group vice president for corporate research, and Xerox was spending about $600 million per year on research and development. Pake left Xerox in 1986.

28. See note 25.

29. Thomas S. Kuhn, *The Structure of Scientific Revolutions*, third edition, University of Chicago Press, Chicago (1996), p. 110.

6

THE DIVISION OF LABOR

The gibes usually come in the course of normal conversation: "It's a very tricky experiment, and I don't think the preliminary result will hold up for long. But hey, I'm sure that by the time it's retracted you theorists will have already explained why it just *has* to be right." The rivalry between experimental and theoretical physicists is often carried on with humor, but the underlying issue of occupational respect is a serious one, and every remark is noted.

Anyone who works around physicists quickly realizes that theorists, the people who work with symbols, are more respected within the profession than experimenters, the people who work with things. All theorists, not just an elite group of "Einsteins," receive special respect within the field, and so there is a hierarchy of status between the thousands of rank-and-file theorists and the thousands of rank-and-file experimenters who are employed in universities, government laboratories and industry. As a student, teacher and observer of physics for the past 25 years, I have often wondered about the source of this disparity in status, yet I have never been able to find anything within the practice of physics that accounts for it. (It is worth noting that many other fields are stratified in the same way. Within economics, linguistics, sociology and so on, theorists are looked up to more than individuals who collect and analyze data. Similarly, within the humanities, philosophy is more prestigious than other fields.)

The hierarchy has parallels far back in history. In the Dark Ages, the social status of priests was higher than that of craftsmen. The justifying mythology was that the priests were closer to God, but of course the widespread belief in this mythology had a material basis—the power of the Church. This example suggests what I consider to be the most incisive question that one can ask about the hierarchy of status within physics: What is the material basis for its persistence?

Physicists working in the United States number anywhere from 50,000 to 100,000, depending on your definition. Experimenters outnumber theorists two to one, but this ratio is not high enough to make theorists seem at all uncommon within the field or scarce within the job market.[1] Employers put both theorists and experimenters on the same salary scale, and it is often the experimenters who control the biggest research budgets. So money, while definitely a source of status among physicists, does not account for the unequal distribution of respect between theorists and experimenters.

What about intellectual freedom? Within any field, the highest status usually goes to those whose work is most independent of views set down by others. Among these individuals are those who help formulate the models that guide the work of others in the field. In physics, these are the researchers who challenge the field's paradigms or who develop new paradigms (that is, new ideologies, or ways of viewing the world). These physicists, who are mostly theorists, do indeed enjoy high status within the field. However, only a handful of theorists exercise this kind of intellectual freedom in their work; most theorists, like most experimenters, merely *use* the established paradigms. While intellectual freedom distinguishes an elite group of theorists, it does not explain the hierarchy that divides the rank-and-file theorists, who use the paradigms to do their calculations, from the rank-and-file experimenters, who use the paradigms to make their measurements and construct their devices.

The work of these theorists and experimenters adheres with great discipline to the accepted views in their field, the paradigms. Rank-and-file scientists are ideological in their work, then, not because they produce ideology like the elite, but because they confine themselves to the given ideology without deviation. This ideological discipline is characteristic of all rank-and-file professionals, who, unlike the nonprofessionals below them in status, are trusted to understand and use the ideology, but who, unlike the elite above them, are not employed to formulate or question the ideology. If this relationship between professionals and the ideology of their fields seems familiar, that is probably because it is the same as the relationship between professionals and the outlook of their employers, discussed at the end of the previous chapter.

A relatively small number of physicists go beyond merely using the paradigms and instead work to fine-tune them. Much of today's particle physics research—both theory and experiment—is such "middle range" work. This work aims to refine what is known as the "standard model," which is the prevailing theory of the properties and interactions of quarks, electrons and the other elementary particles. Many particle theorists work to extend the standard model to more phenomena, make predictions that test various parts of the theory, and reconcile the theory with experimental findings. At the same time, many particle experimenters search for new phenomena in specific areas where the theory might be extended, work to confirm or contradict parts of the theory, and measure parameters that are needed to do calculations based on the theory. This sort of middle-range work is directed by the paradigms it serves to refine, making it almost as intellectually circumscribed as the work done by the majority of physicists, which merely uses the paradigms. In any case, fine-tuning of paradigms is as likely to be done by experimenters as by theorists and therefore cannot contribute to the difference in status between the two groups.

If neither financial nor intellectual freedom is the material basis for the hierarchy that divides rank-and-file theorists and experimenters, then what is? What about the importance of the work? A conductor on a train, objecting to the engineer's greater prestige (and salary), once asked me rhetorically, "Who is more important in an orchestra, the conductor or someone who plays an instrument?" Many workers, like this train conductor, feel they don't get the respect they deserve. They find that no matter how hard they work, their status in society stays about the same, for it is tied more to the type of work they do than to how well they do it. Hence, from conductors and teachers to nurses and secretaries, workers wanting greater respect (or salaries) tend to center their arguments on the unrecognized importance of their work. Within physics, however, everyone seems to agree that the field cannot advance without both theoretical and experimental work, and the notion that the work of rank-and-file theorists is more important than that of their colleagues in the lab is only infrequently put forward.

Finally, consider intellectual difficulty. Of course, the intellectual difficulty of any job is largely a matter of opinion. Nevertheless, a job's reputed intellectual difficulty is an important source of social status. In a research laboratory, a physicist or even a graduate student has higher social status than a machinist, glassblower or electronics technician, even though the skilled worker may have a higher salary because of greater seniority. The physicist is simply thought to do the more intellectually difficult work.

And by design, the physicist generally does. However, the opposite is frequently true on important components of a project, because it is often intellectually easier to figure out what needs to be done than actually to do it. It may not tax the physicist's mind to say "An ultrasensitive picosecond-pulse counter would certainly do the job here," or "Make a large circular flange and find its center to within half a thousandth of an inch," but designing the needed components, building them and making them work, which may be the technician's assignment, can involve much difficult problem solving.

If physicists have higher status than technicians because in most cases their work is genuinely more intellectually difficult, then is there also a genuine imbalance of intellectual difficulty between theory and experiment that accounts for the hierarchy among the physicists themselves? Indeed, the work of the rank-and-file theorist is generally thought to be more intellectually difficult than that of the rank-and-file experimenter. But experimental work, like theoretical work, is mainly intellectual labor, and coming up with a strategy to attack a theoretical problem is not necessarily more intellectually difficult than coming up with a strategy to attack an experimental one. Actually carrying out the experimental approach involves both intellectual and manual work, just as carrying out the theoretical approach involves both intellectual and clerical work. The clerical work—tedious algebraic manipulations, computer programming and debugging, looking up mathematical relations, and so on—severely limits the pace of the research, and theorists cannot claim to spend a larger fraction of their time on creative work than do experimenters. (An advertisement in *Physics Today* for computer software that does algebra and other symbolic manipulation invites frustrated theorists to "Imagine having more time to ponder the abstract, rather than having to derive the solution."[2])

In any case—and this is the problem—the reality doesn't seem to matter much. Even though making nature behave in the laboratory is clearly as intellectually difficult as making models of nature behave on paper, people simply do not associate the former with intelligence to the same extent. Good measurements require as much cleverness as good calculations, but there is a tendency to see them as requiring less. Feeling at home in the physical world, the world of apparatus, is just as much an intellectual achievement as feeling at home in the symbolic world, the world of equations, but people generally consider it a lesser accomplishment. Theorists have higher social status not because their work is any more intellectually difficult, but because people *perceive* it to be.

What accounts for this false perception? To most people, theory's greater intellectual difficulty is simply a matter of common sense. What, then, is the source of this mistaken common sense about work in science?

The answer can be found in the structure of work in the larger society, beginning with the separation of mental and manual work, of conception and execution. This division of labor is inherently hierarchical and makes possible a hierarchical system of production in which nonlaborers control the products of the work of laborers. (I use the term "nonlaborers" here in a very narrow sense, to refer specifically to those at the top of the hierarchy of production, in any of the world's hierarchical economic systems: Nonlaborers are those who control the employing institutions, whether through the party, as in Communist countries; through the government, as in Socialist countries; or through ownership, as in capitalist countries.)

The hierarchical system of production looms large in the lives of people throughout society, and every individual is keenly aware of where he or she stands in it. Those who control the employing institutions and who enjoy the right to treat the products of labor as their own have great power both in the workplace and in the larger society, and have higher social status than laborers. This basic arrangement sets the tone for the culture, which mediates the assignment of status to people throughout the society. In the culture, work gains social status if it resembles in form the activity of those at the top, and loses status if it resembles the work of laborers. Thus the manipulation of symbols has a higher social status than the manipulation of things. The culture makes a fetish of this hierarchy of mental over manual work, carrying it way beyond the immediate needs of the system of production. So if your job requires "getting your hands dirty" you automatically have one strike against you as far as social status goes, whereas if your job is extremely intellectual, your work is seen as semidivine, glowing with the radiance of disembodied thought.

This explains, finally, the higher social status of rank-and-file theorists over rank-and-file experimenters. These scientists have equal financial and intellectual freedom and do work of equal importance and intellectual difficulty, making them technically equal performers within the hierarchical system of production itself. However, in the fetishizing culture associated with that system of production, the work of the experimenter is tainted by its manual component. As such, it is seen as less intellectually difficult and less deserving of status. Hence, while the dominance of nonlaborers over laborers in the larger society is the material basis for the higher social status of rank-and-file theorists over rank-and-file experimenters, it is the companion culture that actually hands the theorists their higher status. This culture is the source of the common sense that the work of theorists is more intellectually difficult than that of experimenters. The ranking of respect within physics comes from outside of physics.

WEAKENING THE INDIVIDUAL

The culprit—the hierarchical division of labor—has another dimension relevant to physics: It leads to extreme specialization. In particle physics, for example, it is not unusual now for several hundred physicists from several dozen institutions to collaborate on a single experiment at an accelerator laboratory. Thus one routine paper in *Physics Letters*, reporting results from a standard-model experiment at the European particle accelerator laboratory CERN, has 562 authors from 39 universities and government laboratories.[3] (The names under the title consume three of the article's nine pages.) Each institutional group of physicists contributes a component of the experiment, and individual physicists within each group specialize even further. A professor might be occupied with budgets, production schedules or purchasing decisions. A research associate or postdoc might work on an electronics system, part of a particle detector or a computer program for receiving data. One might find a graduate student calibrating photomultiplier tubes, soldering the hundreds of wires in a wire-chamber particle detector, tracing pulses through an electronics system or sitting in front of a computer terminal debugging a program. In any case, the typical physicist in the collaboration does work in which no amount of creativity could significantly influence the overall course of the experiment. And with narrow work assignments, individual initiative is more likely to cross boundaries and to be seen as intrusive, even if it makes sense scientifically.[4]

The division of labor within research projects is often so hierarchical that the distribution of authority is more like that of the military than that of a democracy. Professors are at the top, and are themselves organized in a strict hierarchy. (You can usually tell who's at the apex by looking at who is getting publicity, because the professors who have the most power within a physics project usually designate themselves "spokesmen" and forbid the other professors to speak to the press.) Next in line are "research physicists," who are PhDs whom professors hire with their federal contract or grant money; research physicists get professorial wages but do not get tenure or a vote at meetings of their university physics department. Postdocs follow, and graduate students are at the bottom. There is not even a pretense of democracy among these scientists. The professors at the top of the hierarchy have total creative control over the experiment. If a physicist below the top has a real say in what is done, that is not because a democratic structure ensures it, but because an individual at the top happens to be a "good boss" and allows it.

Those who are troubled by such practices within any field should examine the larger society within which the field operates. A critical and somewhat detailed examination of the division of labor outside of physics, for example, is necessary for anyone concerned about the practice of physics. First, this type of examination provides a deeper understanding of the external source of the hierarchy within physics, and thereby allows one to judge for oneself how amenable to change that source might be. Second, it alerts us to practices to watch out for in physics, for no field is immune to the increasing division of labor and the problems that come with it. While these problems may be most noticeable in large physics projects, they are certainly not confined to big physics. So, having traced the higher status of theorists to the hierarchical division of labor outside of physics, let us take a closer look at the role the division of labor plays in work as it is usually organized in the larger society.

No matter what the product is, employers divide the work into many parts and assign each employee to one type of activity. Narrowly focused individuals can work in a more machine-like way and get more work done per hour. Moreover, people who exercise fewer skills or simpler skills can be paid less. Hence, employers label the division of labor "efficient." But it is efficient only if one ignores the social cost of organizing production in a way in which jobs tend to be monotonous and unsatisfying. Such jobs, instead of allowing individuals to develop their mental and physical faculties by exercising them freely and fully (that is, instead of being fun), numb the mind and the body and retard the personal development of those employed to do them. A system of production that works efficiently toward the goals of employers does not necessarily work efficiently toward the goals of employees or toward the goals of society in general.

More important to employers than the economic benefits, however, are the political benefits of the division of labor—benefits that help management maintain its authority in the workplace. Confined to a range of activity that is limited both horizontally and vertically, employees do not gain firsthand knowledge of the overall organization, strategy or goals of the institution that employs them. Those who work within this division of labor see the consequent ignorance in themselves and in their coworkers and feel a need to be directed by people who comprehend the whole operation. Management has the broadest view of what is going on, and this helps make its supreme authority in the workplace seem natural and justified.

We should note, however, that even as employees feel the need for managers, they don't like actually being "managed." Least accepting of management's authority are those who imagine greater self-management, at least for themselves. When employee resentment of management authority becomes sufficiently deep and widespread, the "efficient" system of production becomes inefficient even from management's selfish point of view, because disaffected employees engage in what amount to silent, personal strikes. Thus employee absenteeism, sloppy work, hostile attitudes and so on have forced some companies to ease up on the strict, know-your-place division of labor and try systems of production that are more personally empowering and engaging. These systems of greater self-management do require a less rigid division of labor so that employees can gain a broad understanding of the organization they are a part of, not through rumors and company newsletters, but through real participation in a wide range of activity at all levels.

Discouraging employees from thinking about self-management is not the only political function of the division of labor. By making employees easier to replace and by deflating their feeling of accomplishment in their work, the division of labor strips workers of their sense of power in the workplace, discouraging them from challenging management on the way the work is organized. And the division of work into narrow tasks (most of which are the same even when the product is different) denies workers a feeling for what they are producing, thereby discouraging them from challenging management on the nature or design of the product or service. Hence the division of labor, by making self-management seem impossible and by strengthening management's control over the workforce and over the content of the work, helps make the hierarchical system of production more secure.

The historical trend is toward an increasingly fine division of labor and an increasingly strict confinement of individual employees to their assigned areas of work. This trend affects professionals and nonprofessionals alike, distancing all employees from decision-making on the overarching moral and political issues. Professionals are forced into increasingly narrow specialization during training, and more than ever must specialize even further once on the job, especially when they are employed in large organizations, as is increasingly the case. So even the employees whom management trusts politically to use relatively broad technical and organizational knowledge of the production process find management confining them to work on smaller and smaller pieces of the big picture. No professionals are immune. Even philosophers, who at one time struggled to develop thought that encompassed all human endeavors, are now hired on the basis of their willingness and ability to carry out the minutely specialized work of analytical philosophy. Consequently, they increasingly identify themselves as masters of the associated specialized tools and methods, rather than as independent moral and political thinkers.

Scientists, who are this chapter's main example and whose specialization is typical of salaried professionals in all fields, should look critically at the division

From *The Wall Street Journal*, by permission, Cartoon Features Syndicate

"My vacation was so-so, but I really am enjoying the boss's vacation."

of labor and the problems that come with it. Social hierarchies are sources of social friction, and those in science are no exception. Reducing the divisions of labor within science, and doing what we can to chip away at the external ones, will help break down social hierarchies in science and can only help make scientific work more fruitful, more socially beneficial and more fun.

NOTES

1. Sample survey of AIP society membership, work subfield versus theoretical/experimental focus for full-time PhD workers, for overall membership and for American Physical Society subset, unpublished 1998 data, American Institute of Physics, College Park, Md. (1998). *1997 Graduate Student Report*, AIP R-207.30, American Institute of Physics, College Park, Md. (July 1999), p. 2.

2. Advertisement by the Macsyma division of Symbolics Inc., *Physics Today*, February 1991, p. 43.

3. P. Aarnio et al., "Measurement of the mass and width of the Z^0-particle from multihadronic final states produced in e^+e^- annihilations," *Physics Letters B*, vol. 231 (16 November 1989), pp. 539–547.

4. For further discussion of some of the issues that this paragraph deals with, see the following article, which I have drawn upon: Andrew R. Pickering, W. Peter Trower, "Sociological problems of high-energy physics," *Nature*, vol. 318 (21 November 1985), pp. 243–245.

PART TWO

SELECTION

OPPORTUNITY

Phew! That sales clerk sure had an attitude.

—Common complaint

Nonprofessionals often seem to resent their place in the social order. Even when they take home more money than their professional coworkers—as when a newspaper editor's secretary, for example, is paid more than entry-level reporters—nonprofessionals remain much less excited about the status quo. And if nonprofessionals find society less than inspiring, society is hardly agog about nonprofessionals. The research assistant on Wall Street, the junior copywriter on Madison Avenue, the international licensing assistant on Fashion Avenue— any of these $25K professional-track beginners have more social status than does the $30K secretary or even the $40K administrative assistant.

If pay rates don't account for the nonprofessional's greater dissatisfaction and lower social status, then what does? The culprit becomes clear when nonprofessionals reveal their inner thoughts: It's the nature of nonprofessional work itself.

The typical nonprofessional today is a white-collar worker, not a blue-collar worker. But while the nonprofessional workforce may have adopted more fashionable dress, discomfort with the hierarchy remains widespread. Here is Christopher Winks, an insightful office worker, with thoughts stimulated by his first day on a new assignment. He makes clear his dissatisfaction with the very nature of the work, and by doing so hints at the appeal of professional work.

> The office in which I was to be working for the next few weeks was a franchising operation that contracted out secretarial services to clients, among other things. But I only found that out a few hours after I had begun work; immediately after I walked in, introduced myself to the supervisor, and found an empty desk, I was put

to work transcribing a tedious legal document, dictated by a disembodied individual who sounded as if he made it a habit to speak with pebbles in his mouth.

What struck me about this was that my supervisor had tacitly assumed that what counted in this job—as, no doubt, with hers—was the *what* and not the *why*. You had a job to do and you did it. And since that unwritten rule obtained in every other corporation, regardless of whether this firm did management consulting, real estate speculation, or constructing nuclear power plants—what difference did it make if the purpose of it all was known? It came down to the same thing no matter where you worked. This attitude of passive cynicism has always seemed to me to be the most pervasive feeling in offices.

The uniformity of the work process has another consequence that hit home as I struggled to keep up with the unending flow of legal babble: No matter what job you do, you can learn everything there is to know about it in a matter of minutes. After that, there are only details—sometimes perverse, sometimes complicated, but always insignificant in comparison to the basic structure of the tasks performed. About an hour after I had walked in, I felt that I had been working there for months, and I still didn't know what the company did in the first place!

The office consisted of a series of cubicles with tall dividers. To speak to anybody, I had to stand up and peer over the partition. Each cubicle was unbelievably cramped; there were no windows; the ceilings were claustrophobically low; and fans spread the stale air around equitably and democratically.

After a few minutes of dictaphone transcription, I gazed at the crabbed, stilted words that seemed to be flowing from my fingers even though they had nothing to do with me, and was uncertain whether I felt contempt, amusement or utter amazement at what I saw.

As the day wore on, I felt recurrent pains in my lower back. The typed material in front of me would become blurred from time to time as my eyes had to strain more and more under the harsh glare of the fluorescent lights. My head pounded. I craved a stiff drink, or perhaps two or three. I thought I would weep for sheer frustration and rage at having to sit down in a tiny cubbyhole and transcribe bullshit—useless, pointless bullshit. The split between mind and body that even "easy" work demands—and which I was diligently reinforcing despite my better instincts (which in any case were all locked in a little compartment of my brain lest they interfere with the pace)—was breaking down. The inhumanity of wage labor can only really be experienced when its effects permeate your entire being.[1]

When you ask nonprofessionals why they go to work, most don't talk about building a career, being creative or making a meaningful contribution to society. They talk about making money. Yet people whose jobs represent little more than an exchange of time for money are only momentarily satisfied when they get their paychecks. As the preceding testimony makes clear, the problem is not the amount of compensation for the work, but lack of satisfaction from the work itself. Even at twice the salary, office worker Christopher Winks would still find it hard to keep his mind from questioning his body as his fingers type out "useless, pointless bullshit."

An unsatisfying work life is much more than a 40-hour-per-week problem, because of its profound effect on your morale while you are off the job. You may be pained to think of it as such, but your job is probably the biggest project of your life. It is probably the only activity to which you will ever devote the most alert of your waking hours with such disciplined regularity, day after day after day. During no other period of comparable length in your life will you make an effort of this magnitude on any project of your own. Thus, for all practical purposes, your life's work is at stake, and so it is understandable that your most serious struggles are to control it, not to sell it at a higher price.

A work life controlled by others has severe and inevitable consequences, and accounts for much of the stress that individuals suffer. Powerlessness at work can mean many things, all of which are stressful: difficulty getting assigned to work that is interesting and creative, lack of control over (or even sight of) the end result of your work, lack of control over how to do your work and when to do it, close supervision, lack of control over the work environment, lack of privacy, vulnerability to sexual harassment, lack of respect, and job insecurity. This attractive package comes with the worry (although you try not to think about it) that your blood, sweat and tears are going into work of questionable social value, work whose bottom line is enriching some corporation, serving the military or bolstering some elite. People stuck with such unfulfilling work often find themselves engaging compulsively in any of a variety of escapes. The escapes themselves are a reliable sign of someone who lacks intrinsically satisfying work: anxiety eating, alcohol and drug use, compulsive buying, vegetating in front of the TV, total scheduling and extreme busyness—anything to avoid the pain of reflecting on your situation.

DREAMS OF ESCAPE

Nonprofessionals want some creative control over whatever they are helping to produce, and they want to feel the interaction between that product and society. That is, they want to experience both the technical totality and the social totality of their work. They want a sense of accomplishment from their lifework, not merely survival. And, of course, they want jobs where they don't have to jump when the boss speaks, where they can control their schedule and where they are not driven by boring work to live for the next weekend or vacation.

Professional jobs are seen as offering such work. Professionals influence what is done and the way it is done, and they get more than money for their efforts; they get recognition as a matter of course, even for the work of their assistants. Professionals are not ignored when decisions are made at work; their opinions are routinely solicited. And professionals are not "bossed" like nonprofessionals; they are allowed some control over how they go about doing their work.

One conspicuous manifestation of workers' desire for such dignity is the fact that many white-collar and even some blue-collar nonprofessionals consider themselves to be professionals even though their employers, who have the ultimate say, do not.

Employment agencies understand and cynically exploit the desire of workers to get more out of their work than a paycheck. Every Sunday, through thousands of misleading or even contrived help-wanted advertisements in newspapers across the country, these job agencies compete to lure white-collar nonprofessionals to register with their offices. The advertisements offer not jobs, but "careers"; they hold out the false promise of the kind of work and status that is usually reserved for professionals. The agencies know that ads emphasizing career have greater appeal than those emphasizing money: For workers eager to have some creative control over their work, the prospect of a job that gives even a degradingly small taste of professional activity is a powerful lure. The actual jobs behind these advertisements usually turn out to involve little more than tedious shitwork such as typing.

Various "career training institutes" and "academies" also take advantage of the dissatisfaction of nonprofessionals. Although these businesses don't train people for real professional jobs any more than the job agencies place people in such jobs, their advertisements on daytime TV, buses and matchbook covers also make heavy use of the word career as a code for professional work. These rip-off schools often aim their advertisements explicitly at those "stuck in dead-end jobs," knowing that this will not significantly limit their audience.

Becoming a professional has not always figured so prominently as an answer to the frustrations of the worker. More typical has been the strategy touted by 19th-century writer Horatio Alger, whose rags-to-riches stories hyped the notion of the "self-made man." Seeking to realize the dreams made to look more feasible by such tales, countless workers saved their hard-earned wages toward the day when they would start their own businesses, become their own bosses and make their escape from working-class life. Even today, many base their hope on this classic version of the American Dream. While the dream does come true for a very few, most who try to make it work lose their life's savings in the attempt. Nevertheless, as in a lottery,[2] the mere existence of success stories, few as they may be, is enough to attract keen interest in playing the generally tragic game. The odds don't matter much when it is your only perceived chance of escape.[3]

OPPORTUNITY TO ESCAPE

However, as the large corporations and conglomerates have grown and extended their tentacles into virtually every neighborhood, all but the very least profitable areas of economic life have been removed from the game, and ever fewer workers see real opportunity in their freedom to enter the competition and become their own bosses. This diminished sense of opportunity is an important side effect of corporate expansion. If not offset by new sources of perceived opportunity, it would soon lead to serious trouble for the corporations themselves, because the perception of opportunity is key in selling the undemocratic workplace to those at the bottom—the workers—whose cooperation

BAM!

the corporations need. Opportunity is held up as something that makes up for the hierarchical nature of the system of production. People would resent more strongly and oppose with greater unity a setup that they felt not only deprived them of dignity but also denied them any opportunity to achieve it.

Widespread belief in individual opportunity protects the system from potentially devastating attack—it protects a backward setup in which a minute number of people exercise control over the nation's huge amount of capital in industry, agriculture and transportation, while vast numbers of people work that capital and get nothing more than monetary compensation for their time. Individual opportunity is a powerful component of American ideology, powerful enough to elicit support for the system from all quarters, even from many exploited and unorganized workers who are at their bosses' mercy.[4] If workers destined to be used up and discarded by employers cling nevertheless to "the American Way," it is not because they are ignorant of their destiny, but because they sense it. They feel that their only ray of hope for a satisfying life emanates from the "opportunity" the American system offers. Ironically, the more agonizing the position of such individuals in the hierarchy, and the more desperate their craving for a way out, the more emotional may be their defense of the system. Thus, through the ideology of individual opportunity, the system can keep the majority of workers in stressful and alienating jobs, and even get some enthusiastic support, just by maintaining the opportunity for a few workers to escape their survival-oriented work lives.

How do the corporations keep the crucial ideology of opportunity alive now that they no longer pretend that you have any real chance of entering into competition with them? Through a simple shift in the mechanism: Now your vehicle for escape is propelled not by your opportunity to compete *with* the corporations, but by your opportunity to compete *within* them.

The classic strategy, of course, is to "start at the bottom and work your way up" on the job. However, work is increasingly organized in ways that obstruct or completely block this pathway. With the ever-finer division of job tasks, for example, employees learn fewer skills doing their jobs, so that their work does not naturally broaden their knowledge and prepare them for advancement. Their narrow assignments typecast them and keep them playing the same specialized job roles even when they change employers. Workers who manage to overcome this problem face increasingly strict barriers that prevent them from advancing beyond nonprofessional jobs unless they have the right paper credentials, which they cannot get at work.

Hence today's model strategy for positioning yourself within the employing institutions, which have no compunction about hiring people to start at the bottom and stay there, is to start (or start over) at the professional level. The opportunity to "start your own business and be your own boss" has in large part been replaced by the opportunity to "become a professional and have some autonomy" within somebody else's organization. We will see, though, that this coveted autonomy is restricted in the most fundamental way.

Today's emphasis on finding your opportunity within the corporations keeps alive the ideology of opportunity—an ideology that serves the corporations *indirectly* by generating support for the hierarchical setup as a whole, as mentioned above. But the shift in the location of opportunity does something extra for the employers. It channels your efforts to escape into the *direct* service of the corporations: To become eligible for the better jobs within the corporations, you work to develop the skills that the corporations value. Thus the name of the biggest game in the land of opportunity today is making yourself more valuable to the bosses. And because the employers assess your value mainly by examining your credentials, the paper chase is on. A few generations ago, what worker would have sought college credit for work experience, an advertising point for colleges today? Who would have cared much about mail-order term papers and degrees? Today, more than ever, workers see their great opportunity for escape from unsatisfying working lives in terms of further schooling, professional training, degrees, credentials, licenses and certificates. Local college parking lots fill up after 5 p.m. Employers eagerly pay the tuition, even though worker turnover is high and few of the workers who do stick around will be reassigned to more productive jobs based on their evening studies. The company springs for the course fees less to upgrade its workforce than to sustain the ideology of opportunity and keep employees oriented toward individual rather than collective solutions.

Wage workers are not the only ones forced to adopt new career strategies because of the large corporations' tightening grip on the economy. As C. Wright Mills notes in *White Collar*, his classic study of the new "little man": "Rather than carry on his father's business, many a boy has been trained, at his parents' sacrifice, to help man some unit of the big-business system that has destroyed his father's business."[5]

But there is a rub: The number of openings for professional positions is limited, and no one is guaranteed a slot. For those forced to defect from family business to big business, having to actually *compete* for a position as a subordinate employee adds insult to injury. For workers, the limitation on openings is simply a reminder that, for them, the more the system evolves, the more it stays the same. As those who shift out of family businesses enter into competition with the children of professionals for the limited number of professional jobs, workers without either of these advantageous backgrounds find that, once again, as with their right to compete with the corporations, only relatively few workers can benefit from the opportunity to compete within them. The fact that so many workers are actively pursuing at least some long-term program of officially recognized "self-improvement"—almost to the point that it is a national mania—does not mean that a large number of higher-level positions are waiting for people to fill them. It simply means a large number of people are not satisfied with their positions, and a rather narrow path to better ones has been laid out. Each step along the path has been specified in detail, effectively standardizing and circumscribing workers' efforts toward advancement. The pursuit of opportunity has been rationalized and institutionalized.

A LIFE-AND-DEATH MATTER

The stakes are high for anyone who asks, "Will I be able to go to school and become a professional?" Riding on the answer to that simple yes-or-no question are the individual's education, occupation and income—three of the four most common measures of social class (social origin is the fourth). It is no wonder, then, that issues of opportunity in a hierarchical society arouse as much emotion as do questions of war, capital punishment and other life-or-death matters. Ironically, this strong reaction to issues of opportunity makes more sense than those who display it realize, because social class literally *is* a life-and-death issue.

People experience big differences in rates of sickness and death according to the amount of education they have, the type of work they do and the amount of money they make. These disparities between socioeconomic groups have been increasing, yet the public is only vaguely aware of them, because the mass media rarely mentions them and because until recently academics have conducted almost no studies to document them.[6] (The sponsors of social science research evidently have not been interested in drawing attention to the lethal nature of the hierarchical social structure.[7]) However, actuaries and the insurance companies and pension plans that employ them have made it their business to know about such disparities.[8] "Earn More, Live Longer" is the blunt title of an article written by a senior actuary at the U.S. Office of Personnel Management and published by the Society of Actuaries. The article, which professional schools could use as a recruiting tool, reports the results of a study that grouped over a million retired federal employees by their final salaries. The study found that people who worked in the lower salary ranges, where nonprofessionals are most likely to be, are dying at a much faster rate than are people who worked in the upper salary ranges, where professionals would be. Consider, for example, the implications for 57-year-old males who are receiving annuities today: Those whose salaries were less than $30,000 (1994 dollars) are twice as likely to die within the next 12 months as are those who made $60,000 to $80,000.[9]

The people who have the best jobs enjoy lower death rates across a wide spectrum of diseases and other threats to life. The Metropolitan Life Insurance Company documented this by releasing mortality statistics on male employees of two large companies. Employees with low-paying positions were over 30% more likely to die during any given year than were their better-paid coworkers. Those with the better jobs were less likely to suffer fatal cancer, diabetes, cerebrovascular disease, heart disease, influenza, pneumonia, accidents or suicide—every cause of death studied.[10]

According to the Centers for Disease Control and Prevention,[11] professionals are more likely to be in excellent health than are workers in any other major occupational group, whether white-collar or blue-collar. And they are only half as likely as other employees to be in fair or poor health.[12] They experience fewer hospitalizations and shorter hospital stays than do their nonprofessional coworkers, such as clerical and other administrative support employees.[13]

The professional's higher income is not the underlying factor. The CDC found that even when professionals and nonprofessionals have the same incomes, the professionals enjoy markedly better health.[14] Thus the individual who fails to become a professional, but nevertheless manages to achieve a professional-level income, will be significantly less well off.

The stress caused by social hierarchy is what produces the excess sickness and death, studies find.[15] People in higher social classes experience less stress, and therefore live healthier and longer lives—but so do people in less hierarchical environments. Thus, the less income inequality there is within a country, state or community, the better the health and the greater the longevity of *middle-income* individuals.

Of all the measures of social class, level of education turns out to be superior as a predictor of physical and psychological well-being. Of all the occupational groups, professionals have the highest level of education.[16] So it would be hard to make the stakes in professional training any higher for the individual.

UGLY SCENE AT THE NARROW GATE

As workers have had less and less choice in how to get ahead, they have focused more and more attention on the question of who gets to take the key steps to advancement. Their sensitivity to this issue of opportunity is heightened further by their own personal histories, which often contain painful compromises, and by every reminder that some people do have creative and fulfilling working lives. The touchy topics include affirmative action in university admissions, in admissions to professional school, in hiring and in promotions. A system that promises unlimited opportunity while actually rationing it puts the worker in a sore spot, ready to strike out at anything that seems to limit the chance of escape.

The disputes that have arisen within the resulting explosive climate are evidence of the gross mismatch between aspiration and the amount of opportunity available to fulfill it. Perhaps the most publicized example was a claim in 1974 that affirmative action programs discriminate against whites. In that year Allan Bakke sued the University of California for admission to its Davis medical school after he failed to secure one of the 100 annual openings there. At the time of the Bakke case, the UC Davis medical school was rejecting about 2,000 applicants annually, the large majority of them white (the number has since risen above 4,000). The school had changed its admission system so that 16 of each year's 100 students would be admitted according to criteria that took into account certain background factors. In effect, this program admitted 16 students—almost always minorities—with lower grades and test scores than were otherwise required. Even though some minorities met and were admitted by the "normal" criteria—that is, as part of the 84—the use of "changed" criteria was the only way to get the desired minority student population.

Because his grades and test scores were higher than those of the 16 minorities, Bakke claimed he was more qualified to become a doctor and should be admitted. The media play given this case was intense enough to legitimize and popularize a notion that was new to most Americans, "reverse discrimination." Within the explosive climate described above, focusing national attention on a claim of "reverse discrimination" could send only one message to the opportunity-starved worker: The minorities are taking your opportunity, and that is one big reason why you are still where you are.

Such racism takes the anger that springs from the frustrations of a life of limited opportunity and aims it at other victims—the minorities—thus taking the heat off the hierarchical system that by its very nature restricts the number of openings. And so we have ludicrous situations like the one at UC Davis, where almost 2,000 rejected whites could think of 16 minorities as stealing their opportunity to become doctors. Those suckered into the racist diversion reveal themselves in a variety of ways: as they try to cover their attacks on affirmative action by emphasizing how they are so very much in favor of "equal opportunity"; as they make little jokes about how, for a particular job opening, it would have been an "advantage to be black or female . . . or a black female, ha ha ha"; or as they more openly cry "reverse discrimination!"

The worst thing about victim blaming is not that it does nothing to increase opportunity, but that it works against such an increase. The pyramid-shaped socioeconomic hierarchy, and the power elite at the top of it, will be secure as long as those at the lower levels blame one another for their lack of access to jobs with greater decision-making power—and as long as they fail to question the system that makes the decision-making power scarce in the first place by holding so much of it at the top.

When those who have failed to break out of unchallenging jobs do not blame minorities or women for their plight, they usually blame themselves. They become targets of their own anger to the extent that they believe that the competition in which they are failing is both proper and fair. Self-blame is another form of victim blaming, and through it the hierarchical system that limits opportunity is once again spared criticism.

A STRATEGY FOR UNDERSTANDING

While those who blame themselves for not getting ahead focus on their failure to meet the qualifying standards for training or advancement, those who blame minorities and women focus on the fact that those groups have not been held to the standards. Neither type of victim blamer dares to question the standards themselves. Apparently without even thinking about it, they go along with the generally accepted belief that there is a universal notion of individual merit, one that is politically neutral and that can therefore be agreed upon even by people who otherwise disagree in the most fundamental ways because of their conflicting interests. Upon such a notion of merit one could base standards for qualification that are fair and for the good of all sectors of society. Victim blamers believe such standards are possible, and they measure today's standards against a notion of merit that they think is above partisan politics.

However, conflicts of interest within society (this is not a classless society, after all), and conflicting visions of the way society should be, lead to conflicting standards for qualification, and for professional qualification in particular. The first step in judging today's standards for professional qualification, then, must be to state a point of view, because no one can honestly claim to judge them on behalf of universal interests. Ironically, supposedly universal definitions of merit or excellence have historically represented the interests of only a small segment of the population. Working people, minorities and women, who together make up the large majority of the population, have had a difficult time becoming professionals, except when they have been the children of professionals or, in times of economic expansion, the children of upper-strata workers. I will evaluate today's standards for professional qualification from the point of view of this underrepresented majority.

We can uncover what the criteria are all about by asking what they do for us as individuals and as a society (see the definition of society on page 13):

- Do the qualification criteria give members of the underrepresented majority much opportunity to become professionals?
- Do the qualification criteria help produce professionals who will best serve society?

A detailed look at particular examples will help us answer these questions for the qualification criteria of the professions in general. Because the peculiarities of medical training bring into public view some criteria for professional qualification that are more hidden in other fields, I will continue in this chapter the discussion of medicine that I began with the Bakke case.

To be certified as a professional in any field, you must demonstrate that you are "qualified." You do this mainly by completing professional school. However, you are not allowed to *enter* professional school unless you already possess some of the qualifications that are in the end required for certification as a professional. Exactly what portion of the professional qualifications you must have in advance varies from profession to profession.

In some professions, training programs give applicants relatively good odds of being admitted, but relatively poor odds of completing the training. Others are just the opposite. Medical schools, most notably, require extremely high grades and test scores, extensive interviews, recommendations and other documentation just for the chance to try to learn medicine, but once a student is admitted to medical school, completion is almost assured. Astoundingly, more than 96% finish.[17] By way of comparison, fewer than half of engineering school freshmen ever get their engineering degrees. The determination that one is qualified to become a medical doctor is made more *before* medical school than during or upon completion.

The existence of an early and clearly defined point of decision on careers in medicine works to stimulate the controversy in medical school admissions. Unlike training programs that admit a group of students and then weed out individuals at points along the way, medical schools do the selection just once, in advance, so that whether they like it or not, the results are easy for all to see. This makes any inequality in the selection of doctors more obvious to the public than would be the case in professions with training programs that make greater use of weeding out as a method of selection, where the bias is more hidden in the day-to-day training process.

Because medicine demands that the student fulfill so many of its expectations in advance, just for admission to training, it is a field where an examination of the training school admission criteria should reveal a lot about the nature of the criteria for professional qualification. With this in mind, let's use the two questions posed above to evaluate today's criteria for professional qualification in medicine—both the standard criteria and the special criteria used in affirmative action programs.

Benefit to Individuals

Do the qualification criteria give members of the underrepresented majority much opportunity to become professionals? The standard criteria for medical school admissions make fewer doctors of working-class, minority and women students than the proportions of these groups in the population would dictate. The standard criteria tend to fill medical school openings with students from middle-class families, often the children of doctors.

By contrast, special admissions programs increase the opportunity of the underrepresented majority. Even those working-class whites who see opportunity as a zero-sum game and who do not understand the overriding importance of fighting racism should agree that this is true and not a problem. In the affirmative action program at the UC Davis medical school, for example, few of the 16 spots set aside would otherwise have gone to working-class whites.

However, nationwide there is only one opening per year in medical school for every 17,000 Americans, and so the total amount of individual opportunity at stake in medical school admissions is relatively small. But there is more at stake here than opportunity. The existence of working-class, minority and women doctors helps counter at least the form of classism, racism and sexism that questions the capabilities of members of these groups. Special admissions criteria, then, benefit not only the few working-class, minority and female individuals that they make into doctors, but all members of the underrepresented majority, because the special criteria help counter ideologies that put down and divide the groups that make up this majority. The standard criteria benefit neither the individuals nor the groups.

Benefit to Society

Do the qualification criteria help produce professionals who will best serve society? This is by far the more important of the two questions. Most people are, with good reason, more concerned about the nature of the medical care available to them than about whether they themselves can go to medical school. From the point of view of the working class, for example, the kind of medical care one doctor gives workers over the course of a career is far more important than the opportunity for one worker to become a doctor. Analogous statements are true for other professions. In general we must judge criteria for professional qualification most of all by their effect on the way the resulting professionals will function in society.

If workers want the best possible doctors—best, that is, from a working-class point of view—then charges that special admissions programs "lower the standards" must be taken very seriously. Unfortunately, people who think of themselves as being on the political left generally do not face the question of standards squarely, and so they argue for affirmative action solely in terms of our first question—increasing opportunity for the underrepresented. Those on the political right who equate affirmative action and lower standards know that our second question—producing professionals who best serve society—is indeed more important than our first,[18] and so they have an advantage in the debate. However, when they use terms like "most qualified" or "best possible professional," they show their failure to understand that a professional is more than someone with technical knowledge.

In the case of doctors, most people do recognize that it takes more than just technical skill to make the professional a "good" one. People routinely judge a doctor to a great extent on his attitude. This is not because people don't understand anything in medicine beyond bedside manner—obviously they know it doesn't matter much if the doctor is unpleasant to be with, as long as he otherwise gives the best possible treatment. The reason people pay attention to a doctor's attitude is that it indicates how much he cares—that is, how concerned he will be that his diagnosis is correct, and how meticulous he will be in his treatment. People worry, quite justifiably, that a doctor may care more about the outcome when treating a rich or influential patient than when treating them. People have learned from their own experience, and from the horror stories of others, that they can judge a doctor even though they have not gone to medical school themselves. They know that there are many ways in which the doctor reveals how much he cares. Does he take time to listen, or does he act rushed? Does he explain what he knows, solicit and answer questions, discuss his reasoning and present various courses of action and their advantages and disadvantages? Or does he present only his conclusions—or just a prescription? Is he authoritarian? Condescending? People recognize that the quality of a doctor's professional work is a function of attitude, not just technical skill.

Doctors who treat patients like machines, focusing on their malfunctioning parts in isolation from one another, patching them up and sending them out the

door and back to work, are not that different from the notorious "company doctors" in their attitudes and values. They function harmoniously with a system
that measures human ailment and injury in terms of "man-hours lost" to production. Such doctors do not help workers identify and fight the social causes
of their illnesses. They assign responsibility for illness narrowly to the physical
agents that are involved, such as germs, without even mentioning the social
causes, such as stressful working conditions, pollution and unfair wages. The
overall outlook of these doctors, as expressed through their work, has more in
common with the outlook of employers than with that of workers. The compe-
tency of a doctor in his professional work, then, as seen from a working-class
point of view, involves questions of attitudes, values and outlook—in short, political questions.

Politically, most doctors present textbook cases of the conservative pathology:
They are arrogant toward those below them in the social hierarchy and submissive to those above. They know their place—and expect you to know yours.
Thus the typical doctor works year after year with a narrow focus on patching
people up, content never to take a stand against the social inequities that gen-
erate so much stress and disease. Such service work is necessary, of course. But
that work, whether prescribing antibiotics or tranquilizers or operating on people's wrists to relieve carpal tunnel syndrome, is part of the status quo, not a
contribution to social progress.

Tilting in the conservative direction along with the doctors are the medical
students, who typically show a version of the doctor's conservatism that is socially acceptable among youth. Where does this tilt come from? No apparent
political test is used in selecting people to enter medical school. Rather, individuals are selected as "most qualified." Nevertheless, the results, which are
consistent year after year, demonstrate that the qualification system is not politically neutral—if not in its design, then certainly in its effect. The final result
is doctors who are oriented toward the establishment rather than toward the
underrepresented majority, so from that majority's point of view the standard
criteria now being used to determine professional qualification in medicine do
not help produce doctors who will best serve society. The standard criteria do
not pass the test of our second question.

What about the *special* criteria, the norms that medical schools use to select
students for the positions set aside under affirmative action programs? Do
these criteria fare better on our second question? If special admissions result in
doctors who are even slightly less conservative (but otherwise equal), then the
underrepresented majority does benefit when the standard criteria for admission are suspended, as was done for the 16 positions at UC Davis. Because of
their experiences as victims of discrimination, minorities as a group are clearly
to the left of center on the American political spectrum and, on the average, are
less conservative as doctors.[19] Thus, as far as our second question is concerned,
to the extent that special admission criteria play a role in producing the less
conservative doctors, special criteria are indeed better than standard criteria.

It is crucial to note that the underrepresented majority is not necessarily better served merely by selecting working-class, minority or women students instead of middle-class white males; it is possible to do that in a way that produces doctors who are no more oriented toward the underrepresented majority than are the traditional lot. In fact, when the standard criteria do admit members of the underrepresented majority, they do so in just that way. For example, students from lower-class families who are selected for admission *by the same criteria* as others do not make less conservative doctors. In the words of Columbia University medical sociologist John L. Colombotos,

> the socioeconomic background of physicians has little effect on their political attitudes. The reason for this is not that physicians from lower-class backgrounds have become less liberal than they were before they entered medicine, but that they were no more liberal than physicians from upper-class backgrounds to begin with.[20]

Colombotos told me that apparently there is "differential selection" somewhere along the way.[21]

What all this means is that the standard criteria at their best—that is, when equal opportunity is enforced—select more carefully for political orientation than for socioeconomic background. The result is that professionals with working-class backgrounds are no more likely than others to maintain a working-class orientation in their work. Affirmative action, on the other hand, does benefit workers, minorities and women, because it admits them *on a different basis*—through a relaxed version of the standard criteria—leading to graduates who are more likely to be oriented toward serving the underrepresented majority through their work.

SELECTION AS A POLITICAL PROCESS

The professional's watchword seems to be extreme political caution, and indeed radicals are rare at the professional level in any field. Is the political subservience of those who are deemed most qualified just a coincidence? I maintain that there is no coincidence; being positioned to serve the establishment is an important component of qualification—at least from the establishment's point of view. And because the establishment runs the game, the criteria for qualification embody its point of view. I hold that political discipline is a necessary requirement for one to be deemed a qualified professional. Of course, this discipline alone is not sufficient for qualification, but it is by far the most socially significant requirement in that it distinguishes the professional from the skilled nonprofessional.

From the point of view that qualification criteria favor one or another political orientation, the affirmative action criteria used for the 16 positions at the UC

Davis medical school represent not lower standards, but *politically different* standards. Opponents of affirmative action would have us view the 16 positions as "political" and the other 84 as going "according to merit." We will see that the 84 are no less political than the 16. In general, we will find that the system demands a high price—a political price—of all those it allows to work as professionals.

The important issue in choosing professionals, then, is political orientation. To say this is not to advocate the selection of professionals on a political basis but simply to recognize that the system of training and employment already does so. My goal isn't to "inject" politics into the process of professional qualification but to uncover and fight the bias already in operation—the bias against the underrepresented majority.

To fight this bias will require an uphill battle all the way. Cultural and news media ranging from newspapers and novels to television and movies describe a society that selects its professionals according to "merit." The only time the selection of professionals is treated as a political issue is in discussions of the allocation of scarce opportunity, usually professional school admissions. Even then, it is taken for granted that any politics end after admission, and that the ultimate certification to work as a professional is given or denied on the basis of a straightforward evaluation of the individual's technical skills. The notion that the individual's attitude, values and orientation toward the underrepresented majority should play an important role in this evaluation (as the example of doctors might suggest) is rarely discussed in the media. When it is, the discussion is usually limited to special cases, such as the question of whether or not producing more black doctors will increase the number of doctors working in poor black neighborhoods. The notion that professional qualification is inherently political does not even enjoy a refutation. That political considerations *already* play a crucial role is simply kept outside the universe of debate.

Recent history saw the issue of the attitudes and values of professionals break into the open most dramatically in China. During the Cultural Revolution there in the 1960s, nonprofessionals turned the tables on professionals by joining the ongoing "red versus expert" debate in large numbers. The issue was what to emphasize in evaluating professionals—their politics or their expertise? For people in socially influential positions—university professors, for example—this was a period of intense scrutiny, and many were driven from their privileged spots, at least temporarily.

To this day, the U.S. press uses an openly denunciatory tone whenever it mentions these events. By using this tone within reports that are intended to be taken as objective, the media proclaim that Americans are unanimous in their outrage over the way the intellectuals were treated in China. This outrage is certainly characteristic of American intellectuals, who at the slightest reminder still hotly denounce the treatment that their counterparts in China received at the hands of the masses. As has been well publicized, some of the Chinese youth brigades went beyond militant but nonviolent means. However, the comfortable American intellectuals who denounce them show little understanding of the rage that fueled the violence. But even the nonviolent aspects of the Cultural Revolution rile up American intellectuals. They talk about the sending of professionals to do manual work on farms or in factories for a few years as if it were a crime against nature, the work itself a living nightmare. And they ridicule the notion that professionals can "learn from the peasants." American nonprofessionals, on the other hand, many of whom have been known to spend their entire lives doing farm or factory work, don't get so worked up about the dissing of the experts in China. Perhaps they are intrigued by the idea of challenging the role of professionals in our own society.

Despite their strong feelings about it, American intellectuals generally misunderstand the red versus expert debate. Most see it as part of an attempt by leftists to *introduce* politics into the work of professionals. (If this seems familiar, it is because we saw the same misunderstanding before, in those who argue against affirmative action by saying they want professional school admissions to remain "nonpolitical.") We will see that the red versus expert debate arises from a *recognition* that the work of the professional is already political in nature; the move to discuss professional qualification in openly political terms represents a rebellion against the conservatism that pervades the professional's work. One can truly understand the red versus expert debate only by coming to understand these politics. That means identifying the particular values and attitudes that "coincidentally" accompany the expert's technical qualifications and seeing how these values and attitudes make it possible for the individual to be employed as a professional. To have a complete picture, one should also understand how professionals are political in their very origins—how the requirements the system imposes for certification as a qualified professional are political in nature, and by what *mechanism* the favored political orientation is imposed.

THE INSTRUMENT OF SELECTION

Anyone skeptical about a professional training system that claims to be politically neutral should examine that system most carefully at the point where it examines the would-be professional most closely. Training programs in almost every field make sure they have a well-defined point somewhere along the path to professional qualification at which they subject the candidate to intense scrutiny. The candidate usually encounters this as a very formidable and highly technical (and thus seemingly neutral) examination that he or she must pass to be allowed to continue. This professional qualifying examination is a hurdle that a significant fraction of candidates never pass.

A professional qualifying examination is a long test that few aspiring professionals can escape. It is not an exaggeration to say that it is much easier to dodge the draft during a war than it is to dodge this test and become a professional. In both cases the stakes are high. With the exam, the candidate's entire future working life is at stake; anyone who is not passed is either kicked out of the professional training program or barred from entering it, depending on the profession. Candidates so failed have virtually no chance for careers as professionals in their chosen fields. The large institutional employers require professional certification, and it is becoming more and more difficult to pursue a career outside the large institutions. Careers in science are particularly restricted in this way. Almost all positions for scientists are within universities, government and large corporations. The PhD degree is increasingly required for the interesting jobs, especially in the fields most centered in research universities and government laboratories. Thus most people hired to do basic research in biology or physics have PhDs, whereas research employment in engineering or computer science is less exclusionary.[22]

Would-be geologists, economists, chemists, historians, mathematicians, psychologists, biologists, political scientists, physicists and so on—that is, students in fields where the advanced degree plays the role of a professional license—must take the professional qualifying examination after they have been in graduate school one to three years, depending on the field and the training institution. Graduate students know the test by various names: the "qualifier" (qualifying examination), "comps" (comprehensive examination), "orals" (oral examination) or "prelims" (preliminary examination), to mention a few. The ordeal typically consists of multiple written tests administered over a number of days, followed by an oral test.

In other fields, as explained earlier, one must formally demonstrate some of the final set of professional qualifications just to be permitted to enter the professional training program. Thus, even though he or she is probably a college graduate, the aspiring doctor, lawyer, dentist, optometrist, veterinarian or corporate manager, for example, agonizes over taking the MCAT (New Medical College Admission Test), LSAT (Law School Admission Test), DAT (Dental Admission Test), OCAT (Optometry College Admission Test), VAT (Veterinary Aptitude Test) or GMAT (Graduate Management Admission Test). In other fields the GRE (Graduate Record Examination) plays a similar role.

Whether the examinations are given after a few years of graduate school or before professional training begins, they are a crucial part of the mechanism that opens or closes the gate to a career as a professional. I consider all of them to be professional qualifying examinations.

Professional qualifying examinations should not be confused with licensing examinations, which are taken upon *completion* of professional training. The latter tests play a much smaller role in deciding who will be a professional and who will not. Few students emerge from professional training only to find themselves barred from practicing their profession due to failure on a licensing test. Even the student who has low MCAT scores, for example, but qualifies for admission to medical school anyway because of family influence or donations, is almost assuredly going to get through medical school and pass the licensing examination—the "National Medical Boards"—and become a doctor. The hard part is getting into medical school.

Investigations in the 1980s found quite a few people skipping medical school altogether by buying bogus foreign medical school degrees and using them to go directly into hospital training programs in the United States. (Two such "graduates" were described in chapter 3.) Even these people—from what they learn in the clinical training—pass the licensing exams and get permits to work as doctors.[23]

The significance of the licensing test as a gatekeeper varies from field to field, although it is never as significant as the qualifying examination. The licensing test is possibly most significant in law (the fabled bar exam) or architecture, and least significant in the very large number of fields where the qualifying examination is given during graduate school. In fact, in these latter fields the examination given to award the license—the advanced degree—is rarely more than a ritual. The "defense of dissertation," as it is called, is a ceremonial examination that almost no one fails. The crucial juncture is qualification, not licensing.

Qualifying examinations themselves are very revealing documents. Because of their major role in the very serious business of selection, qualifying tests must contain information on the central goals of all the study that leads up to them. In fact, those who set the goals often do so through qualifying examinations. Although these exams come immediately after many years of schooling, their purpose is not to document how much was learned; rather, they are administered to measure the skills that are considered important in the professional. The difference is more than a matter of labels or interpretation. While an achievement test and a selection exam may look the same, they have opposite power relationships to the curriculum. The former, like a glorified final exam, is defined by the curriculum. The latter, like an admissions examination, caters to the needs of the institutions for which it selects, and ends up defining the curriculum that leads up to it. Through this "backwash" effect, qualifying examinations have more influence over the curriculum than do teachers themselves. By simply analyzing these exams, one can learn a lot about the goals of the years of training that precede them.

Those who write qualifying examinations have tremendous influence over the curriculum. If they impose a ridiculous examination, an equally ridiculous curriculum will appear immediately to prepare students for it. One striking example of this is well-known to people in the many developing countries with British- or French-style educational systems. Even after national independence, admission to and awarding of degrees from local secondary schools and local and foreign universities were governed by examinations with questions not even pretending to reflect local concerns.[24] Thus, in the British colonies and former British colonies of Africa, for example, students could be found studying the geography of the English Lowlands, English literature and European history. Some advanced students had to study such topics as the social and economic history of Tudor England.[25] African graduates had to know about Charles Dickens, the succession of ruling monarchs and the Battle of Waterloo. They studied all this instead of learning about African ecology, culture, language and history, in order to pass the all-important examinations. (The schools served the interests of business owners in the developed world by helping to prepare a class of locals with whom the colonists could comfortably do business.)

In recent years, alternative topics have replaced some of the most obviously elitist sections of these selection examinations. However, examinations still reign supreme, dictating the curricula in primary schools, secondary schools and colleges in much of the developing world. Progressive teachers in these countries have had little power as individuals to reform the curriculum—even in their own classrooms—because to do so would leave their students less well prepared for the all-important measure. Such teachers must content themselves with stealing a few minutes here and there to teach what they think is important.

The World Bank, from its headquarters in Washington, wields great power in the developing world's educational systems. With education projects under way in 87 countries, the bank is the world's largest single source of education policy advice and external funds for education.[26] One thing the bank wants to do is to take advantage of the influence of examinations to support curricula of its own liking. It apparently wants developing countries to select students for secondary and higher education—and, therefore, for the highest positions in their countries—on the basis of the students' ability to answer questions that look a lot like those that appear on American aptitude tests such as the SAT. I will not analyze why the bank wants to staff underdeveloped countries with such people, except to note that the tests favor technocrats over visionaries—that is, people who tend to innovate safely within assigned systems over people who tend to question assigned systems. Interestingly, the bank's education division claims that in the developing countries, unlike in the industrialized countries, such tests do not favor the children of the wealthy.[27] In any case, the bank knows that you can control the school curriculum of an entire nation simply by controlling the crucial qualifying examinations. According to a report published by the World Bank on an experiment in Kenya,

> in the schools, examinations are never neglected. For the last two years leading up to any selection examination, the effective curriculum of the class is defined not by the official syllabus or the official textbooks, nor by what the teachers were taught during their last in-service course; but by the content of the most recent selection examination papers. . . . The topics which teachers choose to teach and the methods by which they teach them are determined more by the nature of the terminating examination than by the specifications of the formal curriculum. The aim has been to harness the backwash effects of the examination to constructive purposes, so that the aims of the curriculum developers are buttressed and not sabotaged.[28]

So, too, in professional training programs, the qualifying examination is the cold bottom line. Analyzing qualifying examinations is not easy, but by looking directly at the bottom line you can cut through the myths and popular images that surround and mystify a profession, and in this way get the least distorted picture of what the years of study are all about.

NOTES

1. Christopher Winks, "Manuscript Found in a Typewriter," *Processed World*, no. 1, San Francisco (Spring 1981), pp. 2–7. I edited the quote mainly for length. See also Barbara Garson, *The Electronic Sweatshop: How Computers Are Transforming the Office of the Future Into the Factory of the Past*, Simon and Schuster, New York (1988). For a graphic and incisive description of the situation of a blue-collar nonprofessional, see Studs Terkel, *Working*, Random House, New York (1974), pp. xxxi–xxxviii. See also Barbara Garson, *All the Livelong Day*, Doubleday, Garden City, N.Y. (1975).

2. People buy lottery tickets with only the prize in mind, even though the value of a ticket is the product of prize and probability, which is usually far less than the ticket's cost. For example, while a 1-in-10,000,000 chance at a million-dollar prize is worth only a dime, it is easily sold for more. The average $1 New York Lotto ticket is worth 40 cents.

3. For example, despite 2,000-to-1 odds that virtually guarantee failure, large numbers of African American high school athletes believe that they will be able to earn a living playing professional sports. "Improbable Dreams," *U.S. News & World Report*, 24 March 1997, p. 46.

4. The ideology of opportunity goes to work on individuals long before they get jobs. For a vivid description, see Jay MacLeod, *Ain't No Makin' It*, Westview Press, Boulder, Colo. (1987 and 1995), pp. 125–129 in 1987 edition or pp. 124–128 in 1995 edition.

5. C. Wright Mills, *White Collar*, Oxford University Press, New York (1951), p. 268.

6. Gregory Pappas, Susan Queen, Wilbur Hadden, Gail Fisher, "The Increasing Disparity in Mortality between Socioeconomic Groups in the United States, 1960 and 1986," *New England Journal of Medicine*, vol. 329, no. 2 (8 July 1993), pp. 103–109.

7. Vicente Navarro, "Race *or* Class or Race *and* Class: Growing Mortality Differentials in the United States," *International Journal of Health Services*, vol. 21, no. 2 (1991), pp. 229–235. James Lardner, "Deadly Disparities," *Washington Post*, 16 August 1998, p. C1.

8. For a survey of old but still relevant studies, mainly by researchers outside of the insurance industry, see Edward A. Lew, Jerzy Gajewski, editors, *Medical Risks: Trends in mortality by age and time elapsed* ("A reference volume sponsored by the Association of Life Insurance Medical Directors of America and the Society of Actuaries"), two vols., Praeger, New York (1990), chap. 3 and pp. 4-21 and 4-22.

9. Michael R. Virga, "Earn More, Live Longer—Variation in Mortality by Income Level," *Pension Section News*, no. 28, Society of Actuaries, Schaumburg, Ill. (March 1996), pp. 1, 7–10.

10. "Socioeconomic Mortality Differentials," *Statistical Bulletin*, vol. 56, Metropolitan Life Insurance Company, New York (January 1975), pp. 2–5. Note 8, p. 3-38. "Socioeconomic Mortality Differentials by Leading Causes of Death," *Statistical Bulletin*, vol. 58 (January 1977), pp. 5–8. See also *California Occupational Mortality, 1979–1981*, California Department of Health Services, Sacramento, Calif. (March 1987).

11. *Health Characteristics by Occupation and Industry: United States, 1983–85*, Vital and Health Statistics series 10, no. 170, DHHS publication no. (PHS) 90-1598, U.S. De-

partment of Health and Human Services, Public Health Service, Centers for Disease Control, National Center for Health Statistics, Hyattsville, Md. (December 1989).

12. Ibid., p. 40 (table 3). *Health Characteristics by Occupation and Industry of Longest Employment*, Vital and Health Statistics series 10, no. 168, DHHS publication no. (PHS) 89-1596, U.S. Department of Health and Human Services, Public Health Service, Centers for Disease Control, National Center for Health Statistics, Hyattsville, Md. (June 1989), pp. 39–40 (table 17).

13. See note 11, p. 21 (table M).

14. See note 11, p. 44 (table 6).

15. James Lardner, "Deadly Disparities," *Washington Post*, 16 August 1998, p. C1. Abigail Trafford, "Health and the Wealth Gap," *Washington Post*, Health section, 18 May 1999, p. 6. "For Good Health, It Helps To Be Rich and Important," *New York Times*, 1 June 1999, p. F1.

16. John R. Reynolds, Catherine E. Ross, "Social Stratification and Health: Education's Benefit Beyond Economic Status and Social Origins," *Social Problems*, vol. 45, no. 2 (May 1998), pp. 221–247.

17. The graduation rate has held steady over the years. Data from the Association of American Medical Colleges, Section for Student Services, Washington, D.C. (December 1997). The classic study is Davis G. Johnson, Edwin B. Hutchins, "Doctor or Dropout? A Study of Medical Student Attrition," *Journal of Medical Education*, vol. 41, no. 12 (December 1966), pp. 1097–1269. See also Davis G. Johnson, William E. Sedlacek, "Retention by Sex and Race of U.S. Medical School Entrants," *Journal of Medical Education*, vol. 50, no. 10 (October 1975), pp. 925–933.

18. See, for example, Larry Miller, Herb Schreier, Jon Beckwith, "Racist Outbreak at Harvard Medical School," *Science for the People*, July 1976, pp. 20–25.

19. See, for example, John L. Colombotos, "Social Origins and Ideology of Physicians: A Study of the Effects of Early Socialization," *Journal of Health and Social Behavior*, vol. 10, no. 1 (March 1969), pp. 16–29, especially p. 27.

20. Ibid., p. 25.

21. Telephone conversation with John L. Colombotos, 7 July 1983.

22. National Science Foundation, Division of Science Resources Studies, unpublished table created from SESTAT (science and engineering workforce) database, showing individuals whose primary work activity is basic research by occupation and highest degree level, National Science Foundation, Arlington, Va. (12 April 1996).

23. See notes 9 and 11 at the end of chapter 3.

24. For a description and defense of the British examination system in the developing world, see John Cameron, *The Development of Education in East Africa*, Teachers College Press, Columbia University, New York (1970), ch. 10, "Selection and Examination."

25. Michael Omolewa, "London University's Earliest Examinations in Nigeria, 1887–1931," *West African Journal of Education*, vol. 20, no. 2 (June 1976), pp. 347–360.

26. *The World Bank and Education*, World Bank, Washington, D.C. (September 1998). *Primary Education*, a World Bank policy paper, World Bank, Washington, D.C. (1990), p. 6.

27. See, for example, the following articles from members of the World Bank's education department: Stephen P. Heyneman, "A brief note on the relationship between socioeconomic status and test performance among Ugandan primary school children," *Comparative Education Review*, vol. 20, no. 1 (February 1976), pp. 42–47. Stephen P.

Heyneman, "Why Impoverished Children do well in Ugandan Schools," *Comparative Education*, vol. 15, no. 2 (June 1979), pp. 175–185 (reprinted in World Bank Reprint Series, number 111). Stephen P. Heyneman, William A. Loxley, "The Effect of Primary-School Quality on Academic Achievement across Twenty-nine High- and Low-Income Countries," *American Journal of Sociology*, vol. 88, no. 6 (May 1983), pp. 1162–1194.

28. H. C. Anthony Somerset, *Examination Reform in Kenya*, report no. EDT64, World Bank, Washington, D.C. (February 1987), pp. 15–16, 31.

NARROWING THE
POLITICAL SPECTRUM

"All I want to do now is make some big bucks," a physics graduate student told me as he neared completion of his PhD and was starting to look for a job. He knew this simple statement said a lot about how his goals had changed during graduate school. While he may not have even clearly remembered his original intellectual interests or his original degree of determination that his work be of benefit to society, he did realize that somewhere along the way he had become very flexible in these personal and social goals. Listening to him I could see that he sought "big bucks" not as payment for valuable skills that he would put at his employer's disposal, but as compensation for intellectual interests and social goals abandoned.

Once the student abandons his own agenda, his course is set, and before long he is working like the physicists described in chapters 4 and 5: as if the agenda of the dominant sector of society were his own. How does the professional physicist come to abandon his own agenda and adopt an outlook that is appropriate for what physicists actually do in this society? This chapter looks at the steps.

Most people, including leftists, do not think of professional training as changing people; they think of it as simply teaching people facts and skills. Anyone holding this static view of the individual will not be able to explain why professional education is the way it is or why professionals are the way they are. Those who run professional training programs certainly take a dynamic view of the individual, and we should, too, if we want to understand how they make professionals.

BEFORE THE NARROWING

The outlook of students completing professional training programs is markedly different from that of students entering them. (By professional training programs I mean traditional professional school as well as graduate PhD programs.) While the new professionals emerge from training somewhat more conservative on average than they were when they entered, the most striking difference is that they show less diversity in their attitudes—their views of the world, the nature of their intellectual interests, the roles they see for themselves in society, the roles they think their chosen field should play in society, and their goals for society itself.

The student beginning professional training is usually highly optimistic about the opportunity for an intellectually rewarding and socially beneficial career. This is certainly the case in physics, where the beginning graduate student sees "the kind of work physicists do" as research on intriguing fundamental questions aimed at furthering human understanding of the universe, leading sooner or later to socially beneficial technology. The student enthusiastically anticipates doing creative work in this quest for seemingly eternal truth. Moreover, both the economy and the culture respect the scientist and uphold the notion that the good scientist's professional work is objective, politically neutral and universal in content. Thus the beginning student sees the possibility for a rare combination: career work that is intellectually, materially and socially rewarding, and that is free of political direction or interference. (The expectation of political freedom follows from the student's faith that the search for truth transcends even the most serious earthly struggles for social power.) The student outside the sciences anticipates the same rewards and freedom, expecting that professional status will bring autonomy in the workplace and a career free from domination by any powerful hierarchy.

If students are overly upbeat about what becoming a professional can do for the individual and for society, that is not because they are naive, although naivete makes this possible. Rather, they are searching with some urgency to find a way to achieve their personal and social goals. Students are well aware that in a hierarchical society one does not automatically get to live a life with any significant independence from management and its monitoring and control of the details of work and even of some leisure activity. Students beginning professional training are not properly aware, however, that there is a price to pay for any independence gained by becoming a professional. A look at those who have paid the price—students emerging from professional training—gives a hint as to what the price is.

Students finishing the ordeal of professional training often appear to be pressured and troubled, as if under some sort of unrelenting duress whose source they can't pinpoint. Anyone who has been around a university graduate department or other professional school has undoubtedly seen many such students. These students end up doing much of their work while in a state of physical and mental fatigue, precluding the creativity and enjoyment that were once their priority. They are no longer the upbeat students who entered the professional training program. Students who were adamant in not wanting to become cogs in the machine, students who would join the system only on their own terms, students who stood solidly behind their own goals for society—many of these students now have a tired, defeated look about them, and an outlook to match. Many are now quite willing to incorporate themselves into one or another hierarchy, and to put up no resistance there, overt or covert, as they help do the work that furthers their new employers' goals.

The willingness shown by the new graduate to function harmoniously with the system is usually not the disingenuous kind shown by people who have fundamental reservations but who are reluctantly going along with the only choice available. The new graduate often feigns reluctance so as to maintain appearances, but it is usually painfully obvious that deep down something has changed. The individual has taken a step toward adopting the worldview of the system and goals compatible with the system. Students who once spoke critically of the system are now either silent or fearfully "fair and responsible" in their criticism. They are careful not to be provocative—not to do or say anything that might displease individuals in authority. Any opposition is now sufficiently abstract and theoretical to not be provocative. (Don't assume that behavior motivated by fear is disingenuous. It usually isn't, because the safest way to behave in a way that will please the powerful is to do so genuinely. The most blatant examples are cases of the "Stockholm Syndrome," named for a 1973 incident in which hostages taken during a bank robbery in Sweden grew to identify with their captors.)

Although the professional has sidelined his original goals, he usually retains some memory of them. Any such memory inevitably points to the compromises he has made and therefore can be an unrecognized source of unease in the professional's life.

None of this is to imply that new professionals are left without goals. Ironically, however, the primary goal for many becomes, in essence, getting compensated sufficiently for sidelining their original goals. Robert H. Frank, a Cornell University professor of economics, tried to find out exactly how much compensation people deem sufficient for making this sacrifice. He surveyed graduating seniors at his university and found, for example, that the typical student would rather work as an advertising copywriter for the American Cancer Society than as an advertising copywriter for Camel cigarettes, and would want a salary 50% higher to do it for the cigarette company. The typical student would want conscience money amounting to a 17% salary boost to work as an accountant for a large petrochemical company instead of doing the same job for a large art museum. Indeed, employers that are seen as less socially responsible do have to pay a "moral reservation premium" to get the workers they want. Frank found that men are more likely than women to sell out, and this accounts for at least part of the gap in average salaries between equal men and women.[1]

Once the professional adopts this new, quantitative measure of success, the system has him in the palm of its hand, for he maximizes his compensation by working hard to further the goals of his employer, and thus the system. And work hard he does—12-hour or longer workdays are standard for many young

Doonesbury © 1991 G. B. Trudeau. Reprinted with permission of Universal Press Syndicate. All rights reserved.

Doonesbury by Garry Trudeau

professionals. According to the *Wall Street Journal*, "in some investment-banking and law firms, seven-day, 100-hour work-weeks aren't uncommon." At First Boston Corporation, a large international investment banking firm headquartered in New York City, "Young associates stay late about three nights a week. The other nights they're out by eight or nine," the chairman of the corporation's recruiting committee tells the *Journal*.[2]

Moreover, in spite of his marathon effort and to his employer's further delight, the young professional feels that he must not be working hard enough, because the compensation never quite seems to satisfy him; the feeling of "having it all" eludes him. In fact, his efforts are futile, for no amount of income or status can make whole a social being who has abandoned his own intellectual and political goals. The situation tends to be self-perpetuating. The professional's priority on compensation inhibits him from developing and pursuing his own intellectual and political goals, because the independent thinking necessary to do that is incompatible with the mind-set necessary to do best for his employers and therefore to do best in the rat race. Furthermore, the rat race is an all-encompassing effort: The young professional works the week like a sprint and is left with only a few hours of leisure time out of the week's 168 hours. To prepare his mind adequately for the professional work ahead, he must spend his hard-won free time "working at relaxation," certainly not reflecting.[3] Until the professional assigns highest importance to developing and advancing his own political goals, serving the system will be not just his job, but his life.

METAMORPHOSIS AND UNNATURAL SELECTION

There are only two conceivable mechanisms by which those completing professional training can come to be different in outlook from those beginning it: ideological weeding out and ideological transformation. Both mechanisms—elimination and assimilation—operate at every step in the production of the professional.

In physics, about half of the students who enter PhD programs leave without the degree,[4] many due to outright expulsion. This massive elimination allows the political biases in the weeding out process to have a strong effect on the overall political nature of the graduating class. Adjustment works hand in glove with this elimination in forming the class politically: Many of those who survive the weeding do so by "shaping up" under the threat of being culled, and in the process undergo attitudinal transformations that make them politically compatible with the others who are not weeded out.

Professional physicists are produced in five steps: admission, courses, "qualification," research and employment. The weeding out and transformation at each step shape the character of the final product, the annual crop of new physicists. In admission there is a small amount of weeding out and very little transformation: The large majority of applicants to physics PhD programs gain admission, and they don't have to go through many changes to do so. In courses there is further weeding out, and transformation gains in importance. Qualification is the step at which the system decides officially whether or not the student may, in principle, become a professional in his chosen field; it is around this stage that most of the elimination and adjustment occurs. In the student research project there is further transformation but only a small amount of weeding out, as a few leave the field. Finally, in employment a small amount of adjustment is often necessary, and there is also further weeding out, as some graduates never get jobs in the field.

This series of steps is fairly standard for all professions whose members are a product of graduate training. The amount of weeding out and transformation at each stage of training varies from field to field and from school to school, but the basic program is the same. Although training for the traditional professions is structured somewhat differently, qualification remains the crucial step. As I discussed in the previous chapter, qualification in medicine is early, at admission to medical school; accordingly, both transformation and weeding out operate at full force: The admission process engenders the infamous self-centered, competitive outlook of the premed student and involves a high percentage of rejections. Because my main example is physics, I focus on the elements of professional training in graduate school, which is where physicists are trained, and I leave it to the interested reader to identify the corresponding elements of training in traditional professional school.

Critics of education and the professions have paid very little attention to the step of qualification, even though this is where students either get the green light for careers in their chosen professions or have their hopes for such careers reduced to fantasies. The critics evidently do not see the heart of the selection system as favoring students with particular attitudes and outlooks. The critics' silence on the issue reveals the unspoken assumptions they share with the system: Qualifying is mainly a matter of meeting basic standards; the qualification process is a nonpartisan evaluation of whether or not the student is good enough to become a professional in a particular field; the question of whether or not the student qualifies is prior to any question of ideology; all questions of ideology aside, some candidates (and in some fields, evidently, most of the candidates) just don't have the right stuff to be professionals, so qualifying is more a personal matter than a political one.

Even leftist critics of education and the professions can often be heard using the rhetoric of personal merit in informal conversation. Consider the difference between asking a student who recently took the qualifying examination "Did you pass?" and asking that student "Did they pass you?" These two questions reflect vastly different outlooks. People often say, "Congratulations on passing," in a way that implies "You've shown that you've got what it takes." Or they say, "I'm sorry you didn't make it," while resolving to themselves never again to mention what they consider to be a personal failure. They make the subject awkward and embarrassing by viewing it as a question of individual merit. Their focus on the student, not on the examiners, announces their general acceptance of the examiners' criteria for selection. When the issue is how "good" the student is, there is no criticism of what the examiners are looking for and nothing is exposed about the true nature of the field that the selection system functions to reproduce.

Every professional training program reinforces the unspoken assumptions listed above by presenting its process of qualification as an unbiased assessment of the student's aptitude in the field. The central element of this assessment is the qualifying examination. This examination, which I maintain is far from neutral politically, is the centerpiece of the selection system because, ironically, as a technical test, it gives the selection system its image of neutrality. But the qualifying examination is part of the selection system not just to give that system an ideologically unbiased look; the examination is also an important part of the *mechanism* by which the selection system imposes its ideology. In fact, the qualifying examination is the keystone of the ideologically biased process of weeding and transformation. It serves simultaneously as an imposed objective, disciplining student goals toward the norm, and as a measure, revealing the student's degree of orientation toward that norm.

I will discuss each step in the production of the professional physicist, focusing on qualification. Disillusionment can strike the student at any step in the process. In the example here, it hits late in the game, during research.

ADMISSION

Just about anyone with a bachelor's degree in physics (4,000 are issued each year in the United States) or a related subject can, without much difficulty, apply and gain admission to a graduate program at a "reputable" university physics department. Nevertheless, two-thirds of the students receiving bachelor's degrees in physics do not continue toward the professional degree in physics. In fact, about half of the physics bachelor's degree recipients do not go to graduate or professional school in any subject, and so there is clearly a good deal of selection at the transition from undergraduate school to graduate school.[5]

The student's socioeconomic status is an important factor in this "self-selection" for graduate school. The working-class student, particularly the graduate of the public four-year college, tends to be either shut out socially, recognizing in advance that professional training is "not for the likes of me," or shut out economically, being unable to enjoy the luxury of five or more years of freedom from the job market, usually because of family financial obligations. To get a PhD in physics requires an average of more than six years of graduate work.

PhD-granting universities do not have the working-class atmosphere that exists at community colleges and at many public four-year colleges, where students often hold part-time or even full-time jobs. Universities are usually park-like and located in areas where rent is high and where working-class culture and lifestyles are out of place. UCLA, where I was an undergraduate, is typical of many such universities with large graduate departments. Located in the high-priced Westwood area of Los Angeles, the campus is a middle-class camp, a place where students with middle-class values can feel comfortable as they play and study. Campus facilities help maintain the middle-class atmosphere. For example, more than a dozen eating establishments, each with "its own distinctive personality, decor, and menu,"[6] operate on the campus, offering more than 800 menu items.[7] Health and indulgence are their two most prominent themes, as evidenced by their annual consumption of over 100 tons of lettuce, 54 tons of mozzarella cheese and 27 tons of coffee beans.[8] Thus a yuppie-in-training can lunch at an outlet featuring a baked potato bar or a 70-item salad bar, and then, just a short walk away, relax at a campus facility featuring gourmet cheesecake and fresh baked goods, "gourmet coffees" and "custom" smoothies containing fresh fruit juice blended with "your choice of 12 fruit options."[9]

Of course, not all campus facilities and services correspond to middle-class culture, but even those that do not are often vehicles for what any worker coming upon the campus scene would probably see as indulging in class privilege: Only middle-class students would have the time and money. While working-class youth are spending their days at boring jobs or at high school–like two-year or four-year colleges, their middle-class age-mates are off enjoying themselves at universities, which many fraternity and sorority members and other middle-class students treat as amusement parks, only with lecture halls instead of rides. A daytime walk across the UCLA campus, which is built on a plot of land more than four times the size of Disneyland,[10] finds students crowding into a large pinball and video game arcade, shooting pool in a room devoted to the activity, eating made-to-order pizza and hot German pretzels, buying fudge and 130 types of candy by the ounce, lining up for frozen yogurt sundaes and banana splits, keeping the attendant at an ice cream parlor busy scooping to fill their orders (busy enough, in fact, to make it one of the largest outlets of Baskin–Robbins ice cream on the West Coast) and choosing from ten varieties of "fresh baked, hot from the oven" cookies, ranging from chocolate chip and peanut butter to chocolate mint and macadamia nut. Nor are the student's academic responsibilities forgotten in all the fun: Lecture notes for more than one hundred large classes at UCLA are published weekly and sold at an often-crowded office on campus, supposedly to allow the student to go to class and "concentrate entirely on the lecturer's words."[11]

Even though graduate students are unable to spend as much time as undergraduates participating in all this, the activity does illustrate the middle-class orientation of the institutional culture in which all students and faculty work. A visitor to the UCLA campus senses almost immediately how working-class students—particularly working-class minority students—might feel out of place at the university. The discomfort that such students feel is similar to that felt by middle-class white students who wander into one of the campus's small enclaves of other cultures, such as the hallway, offices and minority studies libraries near the office of equal opportunity programs. The affluent student is at home at the university; the working-class student is a visitor there. Thus it is no surprise that a study of undergraduates at the University of California, Santa Barbara, found that the upscale institution's reputation as a "party school" stems from the practices of affluent white students only. These economically secure students "are more likely to drink, use drugs, and party frequently, and are less likely to spend time studying," than are minority students and working-class white students, the study found.[12] Clearly, working-class students at working-class four-year colleges cannot casually make the transition to a university graduate school. This helps to explain why even though admission to physics graduate school is easy for all, students with physics bachelor's degrees from four-year colleges are much less likely than their university counterparts to become physics graduate students.[13]

Physics majors who work their way through college as undergraduates may find it difficult to continue on to the professional degree as part-time students. The University of California, Irvine, is quite open about this: "In general," warns the university catalog, "graduate study in the physics Ph.D. program is expected to be a full-time activity. Other proposed arrangements should be approved by the Graduate Committee."[14] The application backs this up; individuals seeking admission must answer the question, "Do you intend to pursue a full-time academic program at UCI?"[15] About 96% of the 10,000 physics graduate students in U.S. PhD-granting departments are full-time students.[16]

The university discourages part-time physics graduate study not to reduce the number of working-class students, but rather to maintain the conditions that are necessary for professional training. Professional schools are not in business simply to teach college graduates more facts and skills, but to teach values as well, to produce a particular kind of individual, the professional. To do this, the university must have its graduate students' undivided attention. The student most easily trained is the one whose body and mind are on campus, who has no mental foothold, point of reference or source of critical distance outside his or her university department, and is therefore free to drift in the proper direction under the influence of the world of values maintained by that department. Jobs per se are not the issue for the university; indeed, the university itself gives half-time jobs in the physics department to most of the physics graduate students that it admits. The university's policy against part-time physics graduate students is really a policy against physics graduate students with *off-campus* jobs, students whose lives do not center on the campus.

Whatever its primary purpose, discouraging part-time graduate study in physics does lower the number of working-class students who make the transition from undergraduate school to graduate school. And as I will explain below, the half-time physics department jobs are not used to make up for this class bias in the selection of graduate students.

Beginning graduate students who are given departmental employment are usually hired as teaching assistants, who do teaching and grading tasks that research-oriented faculty consider to be academic drudgework. Advanced graduate students are hired as research assistants. Physics departments can offer employment to most of the students they admit because military and industrial goals motivate large federal research budgets for physics, and the resulting contracts and grants have made physics departments among the richest on university campuses. Departments in the humanities and social sciences give financial support to fewer students and give less money to those that they do support, often by giving them fractional teaching assistant jobs.

Even though the university pays graduate students only a fraction of what it pays faculty to do the same work, graduate students of all socioeconomic backgrounds who are offered these jobs take them eagerly. They do so either to save their parents' money or to relieve themselves of the heavy burden of hustling money off campus while struggling in an academic program that demands total immersion for any reasonable chance of success. These jobs can mean the difference between success and failure as a graduate student. (The fact that the jobs are clearly exploitative, but too important to give up, has helped to spur graduate student employees at many universities to unionize and strike.) Physics departments and prospective physics graduate students know the importance of the jobs and think in terms of two fundamentally different kinds of admission to graduate school: admission with and without an offer of employment.

Employment is usually bestowed on the basis of academic achievement. It is thus most likely to go to those who didn't have a job or a cultural conflict interfering with their undergraduate studies—students from the higher socioeconomic groups. Departments use the offers of employment to attract the students they think are the best and who might otherwise go elsewhere. The academically average working-class student who gets no offer of employment, but who tries to attend graduate school anyway, is at a tremendous disadvantage with respect to a similar student from a middle-class family with financial resources. The extra burden of having to leave the department to earn money goes to the working-class student, helping to perpetuate that student's relatively low academic standing. This is an example of what the French sociologist Pierre Bourdieu describes as the university's tendency to transmute social hierarchies into academic hierarchies—to guide students to academic slots that correspond to the socioeconomic slots from which they come.[17]

Whether the class bias in admission to PhD programs is deliberate or merely a side effect of the university's efforts to maintain the conditions necessary for effective professional training, the university needs the bias if it is to operate at anywhere near its present efficiency. Middle-class students are simply easier than working-class students to train as professionals. They are not smarter; their attitudes and outlook simply need less adjustment to meet the system's demands.

COURSES

Beginning physics graduate students must devote an entire year or two of their lives to homework. Indeed, the first part of physics graduate school is well described as a boot camp based on homework. One characteristic of any boot camp is that the subject matter the instructors present in their day-to-day work is not really the main thing they are teaching. Teaching the subject matter is certainly one goal, but it is not the main one. In military boot camp, for example, drill instructors make recruits spend large amounts of time learning to dress to regulation, march in precise formation, chant ditties, disassemble and reassemble rifles, carry heavy backpacks, and so on, yet the main goal of all this is something much more profound: to create soldiers who will follow orders, even to their deaths. Similarly, the most apparent goal of graduate physics courses is to indoctrinate the students into the dominant paradigms, or theoretical frameworks, of physics. But the primary goal is to train physicists who will maintain tremendous discipline on assigned problems.

During their first two years in physics graduate school, students take a fairly standard set of courses. These courses, which are each up to a year in length, include the following:

- *Classical mechanics.* Here students use principles such as Newton's second law ($\mathbf{F} = m\mathbf{a}$) and conservation of energy and momentum to calculate the motion of objects subjected to gravity, friction, torque and other forces. The course usually includes special relativity as a topic.
- *Electricity and magnetism.* Here students study general equations derived from experiments with static and moving electric charges. They use these equations to calculate the electric and magnetic fields and forces associated with various distributions of charge and current. This course also covers the electric and magnetic properties of matter and the propagation of light in matter.
- *Quantum mechanics.* In this course students study phenomena on an atomic or subatomic size scale in terms of probabilities. They calculate in great detail the energy levels of electrons in atoms.
- *Mathematical physics.* It seems that at the heart of each physics course is a theory that has one clear-cut success, or elegant application—the explanation of the hydrogen atom in quantum mechanics, for example. This theory has any number of significantly messier applications, in which the clear-cut success serves as a prototype. The mathematical physics course focuses on the mathematics used to do and to extend the prototype calculations that are presented in the other courses. A few differential equations and their "special function" solutions receive much attention.
- *Thermodynamics and statistical physics.* Here students study statistical models of the behavior of molecules and use these models to calculate the bulk properties of gases, solids and other systems.

The same textbooks are used in universities throughout the United States for most of these courses. Fashion changes so slowly that professors often teach from the same texts that they used as students. A year-long graduate physics course typically uses a single textbook, and so the student's entire col-lection of graduate-level textbooks may take up only a couple of feet of shelf space. As familiar as the faculty and students are with these books, they might not be able to tell you their titles, because they almost always refer to the books by the authors' last names: "That's in Jackson," "Let's look in Sakurai," "Does anybody here have Goldstein?" Here physicists are referring to the texts *Classical Electrodynamics*, *Modern Quantum Mechanics* and *Classical Me-chanics*, respectively.

The typical course features three 50-minute lectures per week. A pattern is usually quickly established in which the professor repeatedly fills the black-board with equations, copying from handwritten notes, while the students try to copy each boardful into their own notes before it is erased to make room for the next. Professors usually tell their classes to feel free to ask questions, but their rushed answers quickly convey a different message—that questions im-pede their race to present their voluminous notes in the allotted time. Hence, after the first two or three lectures, students ask few questions, and those are usually minor points of clarification: "Shouldn't that be a minus sign?" or "Is that a theta squared in the numerator?"

To the amusement of people passing by the classroom and glancing in, pro-fessors stick to this formal lecture pattern even when there are only one or two students enrolled in or attending the class. Students eager to develop their physical intuition see such small-group lectures as missed opportunities for truly educational discussions. On the other hand, members of the cult of fact and formula see no absurdity in even the one-on-one lecture: Like any other lecture, it supplies the listener with an uninterrupted flow of valuable facts and figures.

The homework usually consists of the professor's selection of problems from those appearing at the end of the chapters in the textbook. The assignments are made every week or two in each class and can be very demanding. On nights before class meetings at which homework is due, problem-solving sessions often run into the early morning or even predawn hours, the only break being a "food run" to a nearby candy machine or junk-food outlet. It is not unusual for students to miss the class itself while finishing up the assignment or to fall asleep during the lecture.

A final exam in every course marks the end of each semester. The exams are like the homework: more problems to solve. In fact, the exam problems are often very similar to or even identical to homework problems. The exam is typ-ically either a two-hour in-class test or a take-home test for which students may have up to a few days. While the take-home test may be pedagogically superior, it is nevertheless a grueling experience for the student. From the minute the test is handed out until the minute it is due, the student is engaged in a marathon-style effort. The fact that near-perfect papers will be competing against each other keeps the pressure high and adds to the repulsiveness of the experience.

Finally, the professor assigns each student a grade, usually an A or B. By graduate school convention, anything less indicates failure.

QUALIFICATION

A bachelor's degree in physics, admission to physics graduate school and A's and B's in the graduate physics courses do not qualify a student to complete the work for the professional degree in physics. About half of those admitted will be eliminated before PhDs are handed out, and most of this weeding out occurs around a formal process of qualification, in which the student is either passed on a special test or is expelled from the university. In chapter 2 I discussed the reason the system takes professional qualification so seriously, seriously enough in this case to expel many advanced students. Professional work is politically sensitive, and so requires an individual who has not just a working knowledge of the dominant paradigms of the field, but also a willingness and ability to hold to the attitude deemed proper for the position. This attitudinal discipline is measured in part by the discipline the student is willing to bring to assigned work, for such discipline is ultimately ideological.

Courses are not sufficiently reliable as a measure of this discipline. They can succeed in their most obvious goal—giving students a working knowledge of the dominant paradigms of a field—yet leave incomplete their goal of producing people who will maintain the desired discipline on assigned work. Moreover, a course grade can sometimes be no more than what it claims to be—a measure of subject matter learned—and is therefore not a reliable measure of properly disciplined work style. This creates the need to take the students who have already passed the courses and examine them again, with the qualifying examination. This massive test to end all tests is not primarily concerned with measuring the basic subject matter learned in the courses—the courses themselves have already measured that. It functions more as a measure of commitment to a particular work style.

At the University of California, Irvine, the physics department administers its Physics Qualifying Examination once a year, just before classes begin in the fall. The rules limit the student to only two attempts, and the faculty may discourage particular students from even trying it a second time. The student is "free" to choose what year to take the test, but he must weigh his level of preparation against the increasing number of years he is gambling on his attempt to pass. Most take the test after spending at least two years as a graduate student.

The prospect of failing the qualifying test frightens the student, even the student who is the best at answering the kind of questions used on the test. The student is frightened because his desired future as a professional in his field of interest is at stake. But he is also frightened because society does not guarantee his material security (except at a life-shortening subsistence level).[18] It seems possible for the individual, if suddenly of no value to employers, to go overnight from a job to walking the streets, from being somebody to being nobody, from living in the suburbs to living on skid row, left to suffer and struggle for survival among the desperate at the bottom of society. It doesn't matter that such individual downfall is very unlikely; by simply featuring the possibility, the system announces the fundamental insecurity of the individual. This insecurity unrelentingly haunts the student studying for the qualifying test. The student sees professional training as his chance for a secure future, with status and nonalienating work, his chance for a life free from the threat of a nightmarish trip to the bottom of the heap. An important chunk of his past is also riding on the qualifying test, because no matter how many years he has invested in preparation, coming close to passing is worth nothing in terms of attaining professional status. The years of preparation go down the drain along with the hoped-for career.

The qualification system is especially terrorizing for the working-class student, whose security depends so strongly on his value to employers. The working-class student who sees himself as upwardly mobile feels that he has farther to fall, with opportunity unlikely to knock a second time. This disparity in pressure is fine with the system, because working-class students need more adjustment anyway. If the student acts like the qualifying exam is a life-and-death issue, he does so to the extent that he feels that his ultimate socioeconomic status is at stake.

One consistently finds the most terrorized students doing the most work in research lab jobs, working the longest hours. What others consider shitwork, they have to see as great opportunity, and so they are the ones who end up doing it. This is another example of the university's tendency to transmute social hierarchies into academic hierarchies.

The graduate student who isn't passed on the qualifying test is barred from registering for classes and is fired from his job as a teaching assistant, regardless of his job performance. His office and desk are quickly assigned to someone else. Overnight, he has become a mere visitor in the place where he had been spending most of his waking hours working and studying. His presence is suddenly very awkward, a downbeat reminder of what can be done to anyone. He gets the same kind of overly nice and overly cold treatment that people give to cancer victims. Very soon he goes away. His name itself strikes an unhappy note and so isn't mentioned much by those with whom he spent so much time. He is a nonperson.

The possibility of being failed on the test scares the student for another reason: humiliation in front of family and friends. What can the student say after literally flunking out of a subject after studying it for 6 or 7 years or more?

The threat of missing out on a career as a professional in his field of interest, of losing the years he has wagered on such a career, of immediate unemployment and nonperson status, of humiliation as a flunk-out—these threats terrorize the student. If the student is not part of an independent organization that can analyze what is going on and raise a defense if necessary, then he may adjust his ideology to that of those with power over him when he senses that doing so will increase his chances of survival. He would make this adjustment not because he is a weak individual, but because individuals are weak. The unorganized student, like the victim of cult indoctrination or a "deprogramming" attempt, is caught alone.

Studying for the qualifying test is an intense process, consisting almost entirely of working problems. Students get the bulk of their practice problems from old qualifying exams. These problems and their solutions are like catechisms in that they are fairly well known but not easily learned.

Beginning with the student's first day in graduate school, the fraction of his effort in physics that he devotes specifically to passing the examination increases. For most students this fraction reaches 100% months before the exam. However, the intensity of the studying usually increases beyond this measure: Test preparation, having become 100% of the student's effort in physics, expands even further, until it constitutes 100% of the student's *life* effort. Except during the valuable hours, minutes and seconds reluctantly rationed out to such necessities as sleeping, eating and defecating, the student anxiously readies himself for the test.

Although study schedules vary, the student typically awakens in the morning, eats a quick breakfast and resumes his problem-solving work. Twelve hours later, that night, we find him still studying, having taken breaks only to eat and only when he could not concentrate. Late at night, if he is physically incapable of further concentration, he "crashes." If, however, he *can* continue, he may feel that he *must*, in which case he may work far into the early morning hours. He is keenly aware that these are not "extra" hours—he will get a later start the next day. Weekends are merely another 48 hours to study.

The intensity of the work during this period is ominous: It sets a precedent for later work on a professional job. Indeed, any accommodation that the student makes in attitude or ideology while preparing for the test will be in the direction of those who command the large amount of social power necessary to extract such a marathon effort from the student.

One indication of the pressure on the student is the physical and mental toll that the preparation process takes. While I was at UCI, for example, a physics graduate student suffered permanent loss of most sight in one eye after he went through the stress of weeks of intense study for his second bout with the test. He paid a high price to be passed. Another student "freaked out" in the weeks before his second encounter with the test. He was not passed. Such effects go beyond the students themselves to their families; students have no choice but to in effect cut themselves off from their partners and children for some months before the test. Those who are failed on the test, of course, have their problems exacerbated and have the hardest time convincing themselves that it was worth it.

The test itself is typically a week-long ordeal of examinations. On Monday, Tuesday and Wednesday of test week at UCI, for example, the physics graduate student goes through a gauntlet of morning and afternoon sessions of written examinations on various physics subtopics. One year it went like this:

Monday	10 a.m. to noon	Electricity and magnetism
	2 p.m. to 4 p.m.	Math physics
Tuesday	9 a.m. to noon	Quantum mechanics I
	3 p.m. to 5 p.m.	Statistical mechanics
Wednesday	9 a.m. to 11 a.m.	Classical mechanics
	1 p.m. to 2 p.m.	Quantum mechanics II
	3 p.m. to 4 p.m.	General physics

After this barrage of seven written examinations the student stands alone before a committee of three faculty members for a two-hour oral examination. This takes place on Thursday or Friday, and each student is assigned a different committee. Members of the committee typically ask problem-type questions and the student answers using the blackboard.

At the end of the week the entire physics faculty gathers in a closed meeting to decide the fate of the students. Strange as it may seem, in most physics departments a student's score on the test is only one factor in the faculty's decision as to whether or not that student has passed the test. Students are not usually told their scores; this gives faculty members the option of deciding that a student has failed the test even if that student has outscored someone they are going to pass. In arriving at their personal opinions on whether to pass or fail a student, individual faculty members consider anything and everything they know or think they know about that student, including impressions carried away from informal discussions with the student and with others around the department.

A faculty member who talks informally with a student in the hallway or at the weekly after-colloquium reception inevitably comes away with a feeling about whether or not that student "thinks like a physicist." The student's political outlook can easily make a difference in the faculty member's assessment. For example, in the usual informal discussion of an issue in the news, the student who rails against technical incompetence and confines his thoughts to the search for technical solutions within the given political framework builds a much more credible image as a professional physicist than does the student who emphasizes the need to alter the political framework as part of the solution. Indeed, the latter approach falls outside the work assignments given to professional physicists in industry and academe and so represents thinking unlike a physicist's.

When everything else is equal, the student who is known around the department has the advantage of personal relationships with faculty members. Disadvantaged once again is the part-time student or the student who must work off campus; these students are not seen much in the halls, in the student and faculty offices, at the colloquia or at the teas. The image of these students as part of the "physics community" is apt to be weak when the faculty decides on qualification.

Anxiety runs high at the faculty meeting. Most faculty are perfectly comfortable with an authoritarian system that dictates who passes and who fails, especially a rationalized authoritarian system in which "the scores," not the professors, do the dictating. However, with its consideration and evaluation of all aspects of the candidate's life, the authoritarian system has its totalitarian moment, and in that moment it passes final judgment on the career plans of the individual. Some faculty feel overexposed taking such a direct hand in the process. Sometimes the result is much discussion and debate about who to pass and who to fail, especially if the test scores don't match the preferences of all the faculty members. The magic of the test, though, is that such conflict usually doesn't arise: The decision indicated to the faculty by "nonphysics" considerations such as attitude almost always agrees with the decision that would have been reached by consideration of the test score alone. That is, the student who has an outlook that the faculty doesn't like and whom the faculty does not want to pass usually, but not always, gets lower test scores than those the faculty wants to pass.

A master's degree is almost always given to those who are not passed on the exam. This degree is not highly regarded by faculty or students at PhD-granting institutions and is readily tossed out as "a consolation prize for those who are to be discouraged from going on," to use the words of the National Academy of Sciences.[19] The master's degree, and sometimes the offer to let the student take the test another time, is given to "cool out" the student. It also serves to console the consciences of the faculty who kick the student out. (Chapter 12 looks at cooling out in greater detail.)

Those who are not passed on their second encounter with the test don't get a second booby prize, just a kick in the butt. It is hard to forget scenes involving these victims of the qualification system: Bill E. near his desk, packing his books and papers into boxes after freezing up during the test; Tom B.'s wife rushing down the hall behind her husband to a professor's office in outraged disbelief that Tom had been failed for the last time, as if it must be some sort of horrible mistake, running as if toward murderers standing over her husband's body.

The qualification system clearly has a permanent effect on the lives of those it weeds out. But does the process of qualification have a permanent effect on students who qualify? The answer to this question is no for some students and yes for others. The student who is detached from the subject in which he is majoring—for example, the student who has chosen his major mainly because it is the subject offering the highest income and status potential of all the subjects in which he thinks he could succeed—sees qualification as just another hurdle to be vaulted, just some more prescribed alienated labor, and is little affected by doing this work. (By "alienated labor" I mean work that the individual wouldn't do if he didn't have to. Such work is not intrinsically satisfying but serves the interests of someone else—today the educator, who is producing trained people, and tomorrow the employer, who owns the product of the laborer's work. The sign of non-alienated labor is the disappearance of the distinction between work and play for the individual doing it. Non-alienated labor is usually more intense than alienated labor.)

However, the student who loves the subject and is not alienated from it is profoundly affected by the qualification process. The process of preparing for the qualifying test, because of the kind of questions on the test and the way they must be answered, tragically alienates this student from his or her own field of interest. The test emphasizes quick recall, memorized tricks, work on problem fragments, work under time pressure, endurance, quantitative results, comfort with confinement to details, comfort with a particular social framework, comfort with the hierarchical division of labor, and so on, and it de-emphasizes physical insight, qualitative discussion, exploration, curiosity, creativity, history, philosophy and so on. This forces the student who wants to be passed to adopt an industrial view of the subject, to view it as an instrument of production, to use it in an alienated way. The next two chapters look in greater detail at how the test's format and questions alienate the student from the subject.

Because few careers in physics can be pursued outside one or another institution, students who for love or money want careers in physics must obtain the credentials that the employing institutions demand. Students in this bind have little choice but to plunge into the intense and protracted test-preparation process. The lovers of physics insist to themselves that the alienated labor involved is just temporary, that it is just to get over a hurdle beyond which lies the opportunity to do physics the way it is supposed to be done.

Everyone has had the experience of being motivated by interest to work on a hobby or project with great dedication and perseverance. To prepare adequately for the qualifying test, the individual must maintain this kind of discipline on the practice problems for a seemingly unending period of time—motivated, however, not by his interest in old exam problems, but by his desire to be allowed to pursue his interests in the subject. Hence, even if the student finds some of the practice problems interesting, the preparation process sets the stage for his alienation from the subject, for he labors on the practice problems because he is under the threat of expulsion, and he labors on them not in a satisfying way, but hurriedly, because of the large number of problems he must cover.

The exam ends not only hundreds of hours of explicit preparation, but also thousands of hours of indirect preparation—courses taken, work done and problems discussed with the test in the back of the student's mind. Students should not cavalierly label their alienated labor as merely temporary, as instrumental to get the degree but easily reversed afterwards. Performing intense alienated labor for an extended period of time changes the student. It dampens his creativity and curiosity, clouds his memory of his original interests and ideas and weakens his resolve to pursue them, while getting him used to doing protracted, disciplined labor on assigned problems.[20] It is empty rhetoric to tell the student who has gone through the qualification process that he is free now to pursue in his career his original goals, for he is now a different person.

What the student thought was a temporary concession to the system—"I'll play along just enough so that I can get what *I* want from the system"—turns out to be the beginning of a forced, permanent adjustment to the system. The alienated work that the student did to prepare for the qualifying exam, work that was merely to assure his future, *is* his future.

It may seem strange that the student has to demonstrate his willingness and ability to perform alienated labor in his subject of interest to be allowed a career in that subject. However, from one point of view this requirement is appropriate, because a certain amount of alienation makes the student better able to stomach most jobs in his field, which require disciplined work on assigned problems. The qualifying exam measures the student's willingness and ability to lead such an employer-oriented work life. Being passed on the qualifying test is less a politically neutral mark of intellectual achievement or self-discipline than it is a demonstration to future employers of a readiness to play by the rules at work.

In practical terms, being passed on the professional qualifying exam means being permitted to begin a kind of apprenticeship, the nature of which depends upon the field. During this apprenticeship, the professional-to-be learns more technical skills, but the main lessons are on the protocols, communication skills and organizational skills that the professional uses to practice the tricks of the trade. Although these skills vary from one profession to another, they typically include how to organize a work project, deal with clients, write reports, make presentations at professional meetings and delegate work to assistants and secretaries.

The student who has been passed on the qualifying examination is a bit like the son of the chairman of the board of a corporation who is given a job in the mailroom. The son differs from the other workers in the mailroom in that he is on the track to an executive position, as everyone in the company knows without being told. Similarly, those passed on a qualifying examination are not yet professionals, but there is little doubt that it is just a matter of time before they will be. The institution that examined them has agreed in principle to make them professionals. There is usually no doubt that the student can learn the technical and nontechnical skills that he or she is expected to pick up after the qualifying exam, even though doing so may require many hours of hard work. The student already has the most crucial qualities of the professional. Those who staff the training institutions certainly act in accord with this view. Students who are passed on the exam often report an abrupt and bewildering improvement in the way they are treated by faculty members and others. As professionals-in-principle, they are already junior members of the club.

RESEARCH

The graduate student who qualifies must do one more thing to get the degree: work on a multiyear research project under the supervision of a faculty member. Whether the student works on a self-contained research problem or on a problem that is just one part of a large research project, the years of work serve

From *The Wall Street Journal*, by permission, Cartoon Features Syndicate

"To tell you the truth, I don't keep up much with the old crowd."

to induct him into a particular subfield and get him accustomed to doing research in the standard way.

The nature of the student's research problem, the way the student gets the problem and the way the student works on the problem are all reminiscent of industrial research. First, the problem is usually narrow and of little general intellectual interest. Second, the student rarely develops the problem himself. Instead, he "chooses" his research topic from the problems that faculty members are planning to work on. The professor who supplies the problem, which is usually very similar to problems on which the professor and his previous graduate students have done extensive work, becomes the student's dissertation adviser. Third, the student will toil on this problem 50 or 60 hours per week for four, five, six or more years,[21] doing work that is more often tedious than not. Much of the creative part of the work is done by the student's adviser (who is often the student's employer as well) during meetings with the student. At these meetings, which are often weekly (but which may be daily if the professor-employer is the "slave driver" type), the student gets instructions on what to do next, usually called "suggestions." In scientific fields, these are typically ideas about what to modify in a calculation, a computer program, an electronics system or whatever. The student goes off, tries to get it to work and reports the results at the next meeting.

The choice of a research topic is particularly important for students headed for university jobs. More often than those who get jobs in industry, these students end up spending their entire careers working in the same subfield that their graduate student research topic came from, and often on closely related topics within that subfield.

Even when every professor and research group in the department is willing to take on a particular student to work on an available problem, that student is far from free to choose one of the available problems. Subfields vary widely in the financial support available for graduate students, in job prospects after graduation, in the number of years it takes to get the degree and in the general intellectual interest of the problems addressed. Because of these differences, the student's socioeconomic class and cultural background play an important role in his choice of subfield and topic within that subfield. Students from more secure backgrounds exercise freer choices, and students from less secure backgrounds are more subject to the channeling of curiosity and career that was described in chapters 4 and 5.

The less secure students are driven into subfields that offer immediate and continuing financial support. This support usually takes the form of a "research assistantship," in which the student's adviser or group leader hires the student to assist in a research project, using money from a federal contract or grant issued for that work. The research problem that the student has been given is part of that work, so from the student's point of view the student is hired to work on his own research project. Most students would rather be an RA than a TA (teaching assistant), so as to devote more time to their research and thereby graduate sooner.

Well-funded subfields offer more—and more secure—research assistant-ships. Secure assistantships are not going to expire after a year or two when a one-time grant runs out; they come from groups with ongoing government re-search contracts or multiple research grants that are regularly renewed. Hence students tend to develop a special intellectual interest in well-funded subfields. In fact, students find the research problems in these subfields doubly interest-ing because subfields that are well funded at the university are usually the ones that offer the best job prospects after graduation: University research in these subfields is funded so heavily because the subfields are areas of heavy com-mercial or military activity. Students know that job prospects vary greatly by subfield and are well aware of which subfields the marketplace has deemed "hot." Thus 27 physics graduate students take an interest in condensed matter physics (the basis of electronic devices) for every one who takes an interest in acoustics, and 30 take an interest in nuclear physics for every one who takes an interest in geophysics.[22]

Also, at a given school it often takes many more years to get a PhD in some subfields than in others. Students from less secure backgrounds are more likely to choose one of the quicker subfields, or at least one of the surer research problems, even though such a problem is also certain to be more routine and of less general intellectual interest.

A significant number of graduate students now get their research training by participating in large research projects in which the work is organized in a way that matches the industrial model even more closely. As industrial research has become more and more specialized, university research too has tended toward a focus on narrower problems and an increasing division of labor in the pursuit of those problems (see chapter 6). The ever-finer division of labor is particularly apparent in subfields where experiments are undertaken by large university re-search groups or by collaborations of research groups from many institutions. In particle physics, for example, accelerator laboratories such as CERN (near Geneva, Switzerland), the Fermi National Accelerator Laboratory (in Batavia, Illinois, near Chicago) and the Stanford Linear Accelerator Center (in Stan-ford, California) now play host to collaborations that bring together hundreds of physicists for a single experiment. Such experiments can span a decade from the overall planning and the design, construction and testing of the particle de-tectors to the collection and analysis of data and the publication of all the re-sults. A graduate student working on such an experiment typically gets to know just one of the many pieces of apparatus involved. After collecting the data, the various groups in the collaboration typically divvy it up for analysis at their home institutions. Graduate students usually analyze some of it as part of their work for their degrees.

Whether the graduate student has worked in a large group or alone, when at long last he completes what he understood to be the agreed-upon work, typi-cally he is dismayed to find that his adviser sees things differently. The adviser seems never to stop asking for another measurement or another calculation.

When the adviser finally relents, the student writes a lengthy description of his research, the dissertation. He gives a talk and answers questions about his work before a small audience at a "defense of dissertation" ritual, and then receives the PhD degree.

Disillusionment

"Are we having fun yet?" This would be a cruel question to ask graduate students during the research phase of their training. It would rub in the fact that the "temporary" compromises they made to get past the qualifying examination are still very much in effect and are going to remain so at least until the end of graduate school, which may be years away. This predicament, and the way the student gets into it, was the subject of an insightful satirical article published anonymously during the Vietnam War. The article appeared in a truly underground newspaper. The *Physics Free Press* was a short-lived, tell-it-like-it-is publication, produced secretly and distributed nationally by graduate students and postdoctoral research fellows who had to remain anonymous for their own protection. The article, apparently written by a solid-state physicist, is in part a response to the shortage of physics jobs at the time. However, it is mainly a response to a training system in which students expecting to do exciting, important work find themselves instead confined to narrow technical problems that have been detached from the larger goals that engender them—or worse, that are situated in a socially reactionary context such as that of the military or the powerful corporations. Here is the article in its entirety:

Steps to *Disillusion* a Young Physicist

I

As you walk into Dr. Fartsworth's office, you timidly wonder, "Why would the world's distinguished expert on low-temperature thermal conductivity of doped CaF_2 ever agree to take *me* as a graduate research assistant? *Me*—with my B+ in Solid State—and him—with his Nat. Acad. Sci. membership, consultantship with ITT, 150 published works and well-chewed pipe. I was in his course, but I wonder if he ever saw me."

II

As he puffs pipe smoke in your face, he tells you his research group is large, but yes, he can "take on" one more student in the fall. He gives you a stack of his most recent works for you to read. You're in the group!

III

Let's see—what are Fartsworth's articles?

Refinement of Pariser–Parr–Pople Calculations on Praseodymium Crystals.

Low-Temperature Thermal Conductivity of Lanthanum Fluorides: Deviation from Debye Approximation.

Splitting of Metastable $4f^6 5d$ Excited Configuration in Crystalline Gd–CaF$_2$ at Low Temperatures.

A twinge of boredom and frustration touches down, but you chase it away with the thought that you are reading *real* science.

Pariser–Parr–Pople Methods Applied to Gd-Doped CaF$_2$.

Does Fartsworth really *like* this shit?

IV

Well, there you are, fixing the leak in the vacuum system which insulates the liquid helium which cools the neodymium strontium chloride crystal which needs to have a splitting in its absorption spectrum looked at, for some reason.

V

Fartsworth gets the funds to take you to the Gordon Solid-State Conference in Boulder, Colorado, with him. He invites you; you say yes as you think, "Wow! Near the Rockies! I can get in some hiking!" Apparently, Fartsworth wants to keep up with new developments in calcium fluoride. Sure he does, right?

VI

The lobby and conference rooms of the Boulder Hilton are filled with well-dressed Dr. Fartsworths from all over the country, a debutante's ball of physicists, a veritable mutual admiration society for the peacocks of physics, all circulating from clump to clump, talking and building their reputations.

VII

Fartsworth advises you, "Don't talk about your neodymium experiment with Jim Weiss over there; he's in the same field." "Gee, I hope his vacuum system is busted too, or he'll publish first!" you think. It's OK, you talk to Jim Weiss about the weather in Colorado and he slyly doesn't mention neodymium either.

Hey, there's Stan, one of Fartsworth's former students. "Hiya Stan, watcha doin' here?" Stan looks grim. He tells you how he can't find a job after two years as a postdoc, so now he's scavenging around the big shots in the lobby hoping to discover a tentative job offer. He can't talk long, 'cause there are hundreds of young physicists around the lobby looking for the same dough and he must resume the hunt.

VIII

The travel grant paid for plane fare and hotel for this conference, $815, enough to pay a postdoc one month, but now Fartsworth is using it up in his ten-minute talk on lanthanum-doped CaF$_2$. (That's $81.50 per minute.) You think, "Is ten minutes nearly long enough to summarize two years of research? Or maybe it's ten minutes *too* long."

But you learn fast in those ten minutes. Fartsworth's goal is to glibly mention ideas it took both of you two months to fully grasp; to be both confusing and smooth, bored and witty; and above all, to *impress*. And the audience *is* impressed;

a few wise guys make attempts to steal away the victory with irrelevant and puzzling questions, but Fartsworth can handle them. He's a real pro. Everyone is properly bamboozled and Fartsworth is smiling.

Ten minutes later, after the next talk, no one in the room remembers anything about lanthanum-doped CaF_2, but they do remember Dr. Fartsworth. Mission accomplished.

IX

You finally complete your first paper, but even its appearance in a "highly respected" and thick biweekly journal sandwiched between two other equally dull and opaque articles fails to alleviate your growing boredom and disillusionment with a career in physics, a career that once seemed to promise excitement, glamor and importance.

Are you going to spend your whole life in a mad, cutthroat ego trip just to see your name in print every six months? Or is the real pleasure in seeing your name referenced in someone else's useless article?

X

The morning *Tribune* headline grabs your throat:

Campus Anti-War Crazies Invade Computer Center

Bastards! (They sure have balls, though.) Don't they have any respect for anything? (Maybe they're not so crazy.) Those punks screwed up some professor's military-contracted programs! (Far trucking out!)

You don't like violence, but the computer takeover looks more relevant to you than anything that's sat on your lab bench for the last two years.

XI

The University Faculty Meeting is discussing how to preserve its academic chastity in the face of the computer's rape by anti-war demonstrators and other crazy hoods. One professor, highly respected for his public spiritedness as indicated by his association with the Institute for Defense Analysis and "defense-related problems," sobs that two years of his work on simulated bombing missions has been destroyed by anti-war violence. A poli-sci professor indignantly declares that his files on "Elites and Leadership in Anti-Communist Cambodians," prepared for the State Department, have been stolen and published in a local underground newspaper, a clear violation of his academic freedom.

Then Prof. Fartsworth gets up to denounce the freaks, saying that computers and electronics are the greatest advance for civilization since the TV, therefore to attack a computer is an uncivilized act.

Of course, he doesn't mention the untold advantages of electronic, computerized warfare to the civilization of Vietnam.

The professors are now finished farting in unison against the threat to their collective existence, and return to their offices to individually resume slitting each other's professional throats, perhaps to emerge again if their academic freedom is again touched by the turmoil of the real world.

XII

By now, your irrelevant research project, the ego-based seminars and conferences, the race to publish, the social hypocrisy of your professors, all these are bringing you to unexpected conclusions about the world of physics. It is a world full of corrupting contradictions, just like any other big business: mutual cooperation is only a route to personal advancement; communication is meant to confuse; progress is measured in published papers per year, quantitatively, just like the GNP; and just like the economy, Big Physics thrives via hypocrisy, competition, deception, waste and irrelevancy.

The startling similarity between Big Physics and private big business is no accident, either. Consultantships, research for industry, and technological aids to imperialist wars, all put physics in the service of big business, sometimes directly but often indirectly through the government. Both physics and business are based on the "every man for himself" principle. Although there are a few "winners"—the Seaborgs and Tellers in physics and the DuPonts and Rockefellers in business—most everyone else loses through disillusionment, mental anguish and the threat, now real, of imminent unemployment.[23]

EMPLOYMENT

The student who by some malfunction of the system graduates without having gotten used to performing disciplined labor on assigned problems—that is, the student who has not developed an assignable curiosity and has not accommodated to being a "top flunky" in someone's hierarchy—even this student is not home free. As he seeks career work it becomes clear that although he may remember his original goals, he is not trained to pursue them, having spent his time working in the prescribed direction, maintaining the prescribed attitude. However, his demonstrated ability to do disciplined intellectual work in his field upon command, to "temporarily" suspend his prerogative to shape the world in his own way through his intellectual work, and to perform alienated intellectual labor—this skill, however it is phrased and no matter how much he dislikes exercising it, is valuable in the marketplace. Thus he soon finds himself employed, doing work all too familiar, work similar to what he previously accepted only because it was to be temporary, only to get the degree. This is not to say that even the product of a malfunctioning training system is doomed to work as a complete ideological servant of the very status quo that he wants to change; he can remain a force for change, but only by joining with like-minded professionals and non-professionals to act on issues involving the content of his work.

When the professional training system does not malfunction, it selects and produces people who are comfortable surrendering political control over their work, people who are not deeply troubled by the status quo and are willing and able to do work that supports it. Nevertheless, some jobs subject the graduate to further scrutiny and conditioning. For example, in a university job, which must lead to either tenure or dismissal, the graduate finds himself in a new multiyear qualification struggle, with all the attendant conservatizing effects. To qualify for tenure the assistant professor must get as much published as possible, and so he pursues the work that he knows best: topics closely related to his dissertation. And he does this work in the way most likely to meet the approval of journal referees, namely, conservatively, being careful not to raise any controversy.

Whether the young professional has surrendered political control through the normal process of qualification or by somehow slipping through the qualification system but then failing to conspire with like-minded people, he turns his efforts toward achieving along more traditional lines. Thus the yuppie finds himself running in the conventional rat race. He follows the course of this race obediently and aggressively, with all his energy. He measures his progress *quantitatively* now, in tender valued throughout the system: bucks pulled down, possessions accumulated, position attained. Scientists are no less likely than other professionals to follow this course. The university scientist gets recognition, status, promotions and raises by publishing papers. The industrial scientist keeps score by publishing papers and also by getting patents.[24] Thus, the scientist whose bottom line is defined by the market is likely to view a research project in terms of the papers or patents that can be mined from it. There must be many such scientists, as scientific journals are filled with papers on narrow topics of little interest that have obviously been published more to advance careers than to advance knowledge.

Nothing reveals more clearly the degree to which employed professionals are alienated from their subjects than does the sharply contrasting behavior of the hobbyists or "buffs" in their fields. When hobbyists encounter one another at a social gathering, before long you will find them talking eagerly about the content of their subject of common interest, showing an excitement, enthusiasm, wonder and curiosity that is reminiscent of beginning professional students. This rarely happens when professionals talk casually with their colleagues. Unlike the amateurs, the professionals don't talk much about the work itself; they often appear detached from their subject, as if they don't derive much satisfaction from it. Yes, they "talk shop," but their focus is so far from the content of the work itself that you would have a hard time if you had to guess what kind of "shop" they work in. A commercial bank? A junior high school? A government agency? A university department? Casual conversation among professionals tends to focus on the actions and personalities of employers and powerful figures within their fields—the standard gossip topics of the powerless. Their gossip is by no means idle, however, for the politics are central to their work as professionals.

Thus, at the wine-and-cheese reception after an English department colloquium, a first-year graduate student musters the courage to approach the speaker, a well-known professor from another university, and ask a question about literature. But before the conversation has gotten very far, a local faculty member walks up and derails it with the question that *he* has been waiting to ask: "Is Jones really planning to leave Yale? I heard a rumor." Soon the two professors are engrossed in a wide-ranging discussion about job openings around the country, research grants, book contracts, journal editors and who's jockeying for power in the field. The graduate student, realizing that the conversation is not going to return to the evidently less important topic of literature, retreats back into the crowd. Versions of this generic scene occur frequently in every field.

The professors here symbolize the tragedy of all employed professionals who started out as students loving their subjects. Such students submit themselves to the process of professional training in an effort to be free of the marketplace, but instead of being strengthened by the process they are crippled by it. Deprived of political control over their own work, they become alienated from their subjects and measure their lives by success in the marketplace.

NOTES

1. Robert H. Frank, "Can Socially Responsible Firms Survive in a Competitive Environment?" in David M. Messick, Ann E. Tenbrunsel, editors, *Codes of Conduct: Behavioral Research into Business Ethics*, Russell Sage Foundation, New York (1996), ch. 4 (pp. 86–103). *Chronicle of Higher Education*, 21 February 1997, p. A37.

2. "Some Business Grads Learn to Hate Their Glamorous Wall Street Jobs," *Wall Street Journal*, 18 December 1985, p. 31.

3. Most Americans have less than three hours per day of leisure time. *The Harris Poll, 1998, #35*, demographic details on questions 801 and 805, Louis Harris & Associates, New York (8 July 1998). "Working at Relaxation," *Wall Street Journal*, 21 April 1986, sec. 4, pp. 1–2.

4. *Enrollments and Degrees Report*, AIP R-151.35, American Institute of Physics, College Park, Md. (March 1999), table A3.

5. *1997 Bachelor's Degree Recipients Report*, AIP R-211.29, American Institute of Physics, College Park, Md. (September 1998), figure 6. For an analysis of the enormous amount of "self-elimination" that takes place at the transitions between educational levels, see Pierre Bourdieu, Jean-Claude Passeron, *Reproduction in Education, Society and Culture*, Sage, Beverly Hills, Calif. (1977), pp. 152–164.

6. *A purpose of its own, ASUCLA*, a 16-page booklet, Associated Students, University of California, Los Angeles (1983).

7. *Associated Students UCLA*, a 16-page booklet, Associated Students, University of California, Los Angeles (March 1992). For details on each eatery, see the ASUCLA site on the World Wide Web.

8. Ibid.

9. ASUCLA site on the World Wide Web, Tropix eatery, update of 26 October 1995.

10. In estimating the ratio of areas of UCLA and Disneyland, I did not count land used for parking. Disneyland occupies 85 acres of land, with additional area for parking. UCLA covers a total of 419 acres, 10% of which is occupied by parking lots and parking structures.

11. See note 6.

12. Richard Flacks, Scott L. Thomas, "Among Affluent Students, a Culture of Disengagement," *Chronicle of Higher Education*, 27 November 1998, p. A48.

13. See note 5, AIP R-211.29, figure 5.

14. *1998–99 UCI General Catalogue*, University of California, Irvine (July 1998).

15. *Electronic Application for Admission to Graduate Study*, University of California, Irvine (accessed on World Wide Web, 1 November 1998).

16. See note 4; unpublished data from the 1997 AIP Graduate Student Survey.

17. Pierre Bourdieu, Jean-Claude Passeron, *Reproduction in Education, Society and Culture*, Sage, Beverly Hills, Calif. (1977), pp. 152–153.

18. Among urban white Americans, for example, those receiving relatively low incomes have life spans 10% to 13% shorter than those receiving relatively high incomes. Evelyn M. Kitagawa, Philip M. Hauser, *Differential Mortality in the United States: A Study in Socioeconomic Epidemiology*, Harvard University Press, Cambridge, Mass. (1973), p. 71.

19. Physics Survey Committee, *Physics in Perspective*, National Academy of Sciences, Washington, D.C. (1973), vol. 2B, p. 1213.

20. Some students perform the alienated labor well but fail to accommodate to it adequately. Thus, it is not unusual to see a few students emerge from the mindless frenzy of preparation, pass the exam and then quit graduate school. Only after it is all over do these students have the luxury of a moment to reflect on the alienated work they are being prepared to do. Students who can't imagine themselves doing such work for a lifetime, students upset with the degree to which they are diverging from their original conception of what it would be like to do physics—these students often quit.

21. *1996 Graduate Student Report*, AIP R-207.29, American Institute of Physics, College Park, Md. (September 1997), figure 3.

22. Ibid., table 5 and unpublished source data for that table. I counted surface physics as part of condensed matter physics.

23. "Steps to *Disillusion* a Young Physicist," *Physics Free Press*, vol. 1, no. 3 (November–December 1972), pp. 13–14. This is the only issue I have; I would appreciate any help in finding the others, and I'd love to meet anyone who was involved in putting them out.

24. Most patents have no commercial value. Even a patent that is worth something does not necessarily benefit the industrial scientist more directly than the publication of a paper benefits the university scientist: although the patent is issued in the scientist's name, he must assign ownership to his employer.

9

THE PRIMACY OF ATTITUDE

Being a good civics student and learning to recite the right ideology won't get you a job where ideology is important, a professional job. An institution is not going to trust someone to make decisions in its interest and in its name unless that person shows an almost instinctive feeling for the right ideology. To become a person whose instincts employers can trust, the aspiring professional must not only be willing and able to accept from the system the ideological direction of his professional work, he must also *internalize* the assigned ideology, or at least act convincingly as if he has done so.[1] (As a practical matter, employers usually make no explicit ideological "assignment" but merely fine-tune the ideology inherent in the status quo.) Internalizing an ideology means more than becoming very good at following its dictates. It means adopting it as one's own. Only that earns the trust of employers. The result is a reliable servant who sees himself as self-directed, for in his work his employers let him make most decisions according to what he feels is right.

The actual social role of the professional is usually vastly different from the one anticipated by the student who has even the slightest idealism. Thus, the process by which the professional-in-training comes to accept the ideological direction of his work is neither smooth nor easy. Much difficult psychological, cultural and political adjustment is required.

Indeed, the most difficult part about becoming a professional is adopting the professional attitude and learning to be comfortable adhering to the given ideological framework, which some students find quite alien. When students fail to complete professional training programs, they almost always do so because they have problems adjusting their attitude, not because they are unable to learn the technical tricks of the trade. That is, people who drop out of school usually do so not because they lack the ability to go farther, but because they

148

are consciously or unconsciously unwilling to become the type of person the system demands. The greater the adjustment an individual has to make to behave in the expected way, the less likely it is that that individual will do so.

A good example of the type of adjustment that turns students into dropouts involved an unusual case at the New York State Police Academy—unusual because the exact nature of the adjustment was clear for all to see. The state ran a 22-week training program, involving the equivalent of 27 credit hours of college work, to make police out of recruits. Half of the 74 black and Hispanic males in the 1981 class dropped out before graduating, while the dropout rate among the 97 white males was only 6%. Why the big difference?

The superintendent of the state police blamed a federal court, which had found the state police guilty of practicing discrimination in hiring, and he blamed the recruits: "We had to go so far down in the list to meet the requirements of a court that some of them could not meet the academic standards of the academy."[2] But, according to the *New York Times* and Justice Department documents,[3] some of the 37 minorities who dropped out "said that academic problems had been the least of their troubles at the academy." They described a hidden curriculum and a hidden system of evaluation, taking the form of a program of subtle and not-so-subtle provocation that included after-hours practical jokes drawing attention to race; racist comments and jokes during class; assignment of minorities to "work detail" and other forms of punishment imposed arbitrarily or imposed for conduct for which whites were not disciplined; encouragement of white recruits to harass minority recruits and to rate them lower on peer evaluations; the "tearing apart" of minorities' rooms, and so on.

These special mini-ordeals for minorities were organized or encouraged by the academy instructors and staff. They were evidently the academy's unsophisticated way of asking the minorities to either drop out or give assurance—through their responses—that they were willing to live with the dominant attitudes in the police force. Indeed, this kind of incessant testing of attitude divides its victims into two groups: those who respond to it as harassment and usually drop out discouraged because of it, and those who are willing to accommodate to the terms the system sets down for survival. Accommodation to the racist atmosphere was evidently no problem for the particular whites recruited, but for the particular minorities it was quite difficult. Playing along with the jokes and other tests required the minorities to hold tenaciously to the role of people who above all want to live in harmony with the system. Learning to play along meant learning to see yourself the way the system sees you.

Ronald Dutes, a black recruit, entered the academy after completing three years and 81 credit hours toward a bachelor's degree at the City University of New York's John Jay College of Criminal Justice, in Manhattan. He dropped out of the academy just three weeks before graduation. Interviewed on graduation day, Dutes told the *New York Times*, "A lot of the black guys who graduated today had to smile, fake it and take it to make it through. They are not looking for good troopers but for people they can direct and mold. They don't want to deal with your blackness and your background, and can't accept you being proud of what you are."[4]

It is difficult to imagine a U.S. police force with no mechanism for dropping those who are unwilling to tolerate the dominant attitudes in hierarchical society. Given the racist nature of those attitudes, it is no surprise that minorities, unless they are very carefully selected, drop out at a higher rate. The New York State Police Academy stood out not because of its hidden criteria for success—turning the unwilling into dropouts is universal—but because its mechanism for creating the dropouts was so crude and transparent.

Because professional work is ideological, to be deemed qualified to do it you must in essence assure future employers of their control over the most important part of your social existence—the ideological direction of your work. You give this assurance by conforming to the assigned ideology during training. The police academy simply would not have been doing its job if it had not, in one way or another, offered the minority recruits the choice: Demonstrate conformity or drop out. Certainly, those who refuse to get with the program when they are students are the least likely to embrace assigned ideologies when they are employees. These "problem people" do not look like budding professionals to the faculty, and so the faculty tries to deny them the professional credential for which they came.

For an example of how similar the screening process can be in a more academic profession, let's move from the police academy to the chemistry department of a 40,000-student "Big Ten" university. The liberal professors who run the PhD program here would be insulted to see their setup likened to that of a police academy. Yet the two training programs share an essential feature: an environment that some students find to be perfectly friendly but that, at the same time, is very hostile to students whose attitudes and values don't conform to the dominant ones. And here in academe, just like at the police academy, "good" students not only adopt the faculty's values as their own, but also go after students who fail to do so. Such attacks should come as no surprise, because nonconformity, no matter how quiet, stands out as a challenge to the dominant values, which form the core of professional training. Although students are often the ones who do the dirty work of answering challenges to the faculty's values, the faculty is ultimately responsible for the attacks, because the gung-ho students who launch them are simply carrying the faculty's values to their logical conclusion.

Nan, a Quaker who has made serving others her life's focus, learned this the hard way when she entered graduate school and found herself in the often viciously competitive culture typical of a research university. Nan's schooling had been interrupted after high school by an illness that lasted for a number of years, during which time she decided what she considered to be important in life. In spite of a chronic metabolic disability that reduced her stamina, Nan flourished in the friendly environment of her undergraduate school, a 5,500-student state college in New England. She was the first person that the state's

vocational rehabilitation commission had ever sent to a four-year college. There
she developed a strong interest in teaching and a dream of doing so at a four-
year college, for which she would need a PhD. When Nan entered graduate
school and was assigned to teach an undergraduate organic chemistry laboratory class mainly for premed students, she had her own ideas about how to do
so: Unlike all the other teaching assistants, she didn't focus narrowly on technical material, but took up relevant social issues as well, and she didn't grade in
the usual adversarial way. So, of the 240 chemistry graduate students in the
huge department, Nan was atypical in many ways—because of her sex, age, disability, religion and humanitarian priorities—each of which was a potential
point of vulnerability in the competitive environment.

I interviewed Nan (whose real name I have withheld at her request) during
her third year in graduate school. Here's her story, edited mainly for length.

> As soon as I applied to chemistry graduate schools, they started actively recruiting
> me, because I had a phenomenal undergraduate record. I graduated summa with
> a double major in chemistry and biology. I also had departmental honors in chem-
> istry. Once you're accepted in a graduate department, they will fly you out and put
> you up and wine you and dine you and say, "Why don't you come here?" That's the
> usual recruiting in the physical sciences. I turned down a four-year fellowship at [a
> better-known Big Ten university] to come here. Their recruiting wasn't as person-
> alized, and I felt I wouldn't really fit in there.
>
> When you get here you find that there are some serious problems that they
> didn't tell you about. There is quite a bit of sexual harassment, but not as much as
> there is gender harassment—you know, the things that they would not do to you if
> you were a man. I immediately started having harassment problems, mostly from
> other graduate students. But it's very weird here: A lot of my friends—women in
> physical chemistry—have no trouble at all and are very happy.
>
> The department favors the middle-class white males and people who are very
> aggressive in personality—at least the organic division does, anyway. The favored
> students are aggressive both in and out of class. They're the ones who peck the
> other students, you know. [Laughs.] *Not nice people.* Generally they are also
> rather bigoted.
>
> The department puts all the first-year students—50 people—in one big room
> with cubicles. That room, of course, is a pressure cooker. People there don't get
> along with other people. One woman from my class declared who her adviser would
> be after one month, just so she could get out of that damn place. Then she got some
> lab space with a desk and lived happily ever after [laughs]. I took a lot of flack in
> that room—about my age and my quiet lifestyle and my disability and things like
> that. Some of it was pretty rotten. It's like being pecked to death by ducks.
>
> The attitude of some of these people really comes out when they have to be TAs
> [teaching assistants]. Then they're in the lab, and you see the way they treat the
> undergraduates—it's just horrendous. They are disrespectful in manner, speech
> and teaching style, and tend to grade very unfairly. I got in trouble with the course
> instructor for supposedly being too lenient with my students. I help students when
> they're supposed to be helped. I visit each student individually in the lab and help
> them think out things and reason them. And I help them with their writing.

Also, I think there are important ethical aspects of teaching pre-meds, and so I teach to their ethical and social science backgrounds as well as to their chemistry background. I wrote a paper on this and presented it at a chemistry educational conference this summer. When the experiment is going in an organic lab, a lot of times something will have to cook for a couple of hours. Then you have time to talk. We would talk about ethical things—scientific honesty, peer pressure, discrimination, or, like, why do you want to be a doctor, or why do you want to be a pediatrician and not some other kind of doctor who could make more money. It was very interesting. We run five simultaneous organic sections in this big huge lab, and I used to have students from other sections in the lab come over and hang around on the periphery and eavesdrop. The other grad students thought I was a nut, but I was consistently in the top three when the students did TA evaluations at the end of the quarter.

I had one really bad harassment incident while I was teaching in the undergraduate organic lab. The TA in the next teaching station decided to come over and start getting on me about my grades, my choice of adviser, my research project and how dumb it was and everything—right in front of my class. He totally disrupted things and my students ended up a week behind the other sections. I was just incensed that he would disrupt a class, so I filed a complaint.

Now, every year the faculty sponsors a big, kind of formal dinner party that about 100 people in the department attend. It's held in a big banquet room of a restaurant, and the students perform skits as a kind of payback. One tradition at the party was the first-year class giving a "Horse's Ass Award" to the professor who, like, abused them the most or whatever. Well, I very stupidly accepted my adviser's invitation to go to the party my first year, and they broke with tradition and gave the Horse's Ass Award to me. I was all dressed up and everything—wearing my only dress—and I'm sitting next to my adviser, and they announce this award. And, you know, it's just devastating. I was pretty unhappy, because I felt I was nailed for complaining about harassment. I did manage to get that award stopped, though, and this year they didn't have it.

I had never had any problems getting along with people before I came to this aggressive place. I was one of the most well-respected people on campus at my old school, because I used to tutor everybody and help out and stuff. But that's, of course, the kind of behavior that's punished here. It's extremely competitive here; stepping on people is rewarded. All my best friends here are people on the service staff.

One of my most serious problems my first year was getting people to understand that I can do chemistry, but that I do it just a little slower. My undergraduate work took five years. With my stamina problem, I can only put in like 40 hours a week, which is much less than what faculty members expect from graduate students. The advising committee that I had before I chose an adviser told me to take too many classes. They don't understand the "reasonable accommodation" clause of the Rehabilitation Act of 1973 even when it is explained to them. The law specifically mentions workload adjustments and time extension for completion of educational programs. I knew I couldn't handle that workload. My second quarter I got shingles [a painful, stress-induced sensory nerve infection] and went over to the health services, and the first thing the doctor said to me was, "Are you a graduate student?" I said, "How can you tell?" She said, "Oh, they always get shingles."

With my workload way too high, and dealing with crap every day from the hostile environment, I got two C's in my first year. I have now completed all 36 units required for the PhD; I got the two C's and the rest are B's. But because of the C's, at the end of my first year the graduate committee sent me a letter saying that I hadn't met all the requirements for staying in the PhD program. I was put down into the terminal master's degree program. After I got that letter I went to the director of graduate studies and said, "You know this isn't fair. What gives?" He said I can always try to get back into the PhD program. You have to reapply. But I found out last week that getting back into the PhD program is not common at all.

I think two kinds of women survive. The ones who don't take any crap from anybody make it. They swear and drink and carouse, and they basically do what I think is acting like a man. And also, I think the women who are better accepted, in another way, are ones who are traditionally feminine. But if you're somewhere in between, you may be running a risk. And I'm one of those kind of 'tweeners. There's a women in my research group who is very traditionally feminine, and she has never had any problems. They're the right size, shape, hair style. Kind of stylish and kind of pretty. As a matter of fact, the prettier you are here, the less people bother you. And they're a little more submissive. In a research group meeting, for example, although not in the cooperative group I am in, people often start sniping at each other. First about chemistry and then about personal things. Women who are traditionally feminine will take that in the group meeting and then go home and cry about it, rather than say, "Hey, I don't like that." I'm one of the ones who'll say, "Hey, I don't like that." [Laughs.] But when you say that, the pushing and shoving starts. The people on the other side push a little harder, and then you have to push back a little harder. It can escalate into anything.

There are people here who are trying to do something, but they're kind of scared. I could transfer to another university, but if I did that, I would not only be leaving behind the people who are still here, but I would not be able to make changes for the future people. I am the only one left who has been treated this badly, and I have decided to stay and kick back. I thought I came here to do really good science, but it's turning out I am needed here for a very different reason.[5]

The general point of these examples from the schooling of police and scientists is that students in professional training run into trouble not because they are incapable of comprehending more advanced concepts, but because consciously or unconsciously they refuse to make peace with the dominant attitudes and values. This holds true even when there is no extracurricular harassment to blame, in which case students who have problems often end up questioning their own intellectual adequacy, not realizing that they are contending with a hidden curriculum of attitudes and values in their classes and examinations.

THE CONVERGENCE OF PREJUDGMENT AND SCORE

"The good is the well-adapted," wrote social critic Max Horkheimer in 1946, explaining the way popular Darwinism would have us judge one another.[6] Today this spooky formula for evaluation is so widely accepted and so rarely challenged that many people judge even their own worth by how the job market judges them. Their salaries, for example, are often a more sensitive, more personal, more private, more hush-hush topic than even the intimate details of their sex lives.

Students seeking credentials that they can use to get professional jobs face judgment long before they get to the job market, as the professional and graduate schools they attend decide who may stay and get the credentials and who must leave without them. These institutions are very much in the business of making value judgments about students—but do they use the popular Darwinist formula to do so?

The university professors who do the screening would deny using the formula. Even professors who boast about how "marketable" their graduates are would not say that the goal of their screening is to select the well adapted, to choose the individuals who have the values, attitudes and skills suitable for productive service to employers. Most faculty members would say they screen for technical ability, not for a particular outlook. They would say they simply measure technical skill with a technical examination—the qualifying examination given in graduate school, for example. If individuals who pass this examination are marketable, it is simply because they are "good at the subject."

But what does it mean to be good at the subject? One way to answer this question is to look at the definition of good inherent in the technical examination itself, inherent in what exam-takers are called upon to do to demonstrate that they are good. I argue that the candidate can learn the particular skills necessary to be deemed good by the exam only by maintaining a particular narrow focus within the subject over a long period of time, and that the candidate can maintain this narrow focus for the necessary time only by adopting particular values and attitudes. These values and attitudes are precisely the ones that make an individual useful to employers as a professional with assignable curiosity and ideological discipline, and are in fact the fundamental qualifying attributes—it is the individual's outlook that is actually being examined by the qualifying examination. The result is graduates who are willing and able to serve the status quo through their assigned work on the job, but whose uncritical outlook and alienated relationship to the subject matter leave them unprepared to use their knowledge to formulate an independent understanding of the world, let alone to change it.

Here I offer an example that illustrates the priority of values and attitude over technical skill as the qualifying attribute. The example is an anomalous student—a student who displayed the qualifying values and attitude but not much of the technical skill emphasized on the exam. This student was passed. I maintain that a student with identical technical skill but with a "bad attitude" would have been failed; I will look briefly at one such student. I go on in the next chapter to analyze the qualifying examination itself to uncover the values that it favors and to see why it is so rarely necessary for the faculty to overrule the scores and pass and fail students out of numerical order, as happened in the case of the anomalous student.

Long before they give the qualifying examination, faculty members develop strong private opinions about which of their students have the attributes of a professional and which do not. They give the qualifying examination less to discover which of their students are qualified to receive professional credentials than to enforce the judgments they have already made. The results of the technical examination usually parallel the faculty's judgments but are much less obviously connected to values and attitudes, allowing individual faculty members to describe the decisions on qualification as purely technical and to hide their personal thinking and their personal role in the career screening. A professor can put on a "test-grader" hat and act like a reluctant agent of the exam. Instead of having to say, "I'm sorry, you don't fit our image of a professional in this field, so *we didn't pass you*," the professor can simply say, "I'm sorry, you didn't do well on the test; *you didn't pass*." We are expected to believe that the exam bosses the faculty, dictating its decision on each student—that the dummy decides what the ventriloquist says.

The magic of the test is that it allows this fiction to be maintained by the faculty and accepted by its innocent victims (and by otherwise critical outside observers, as we saw in the previous chapter). In spite of its completely technical form, the test is usually an excellent measure of the student's outlook, and so there is usually no overlap between the scores of the students that the faculty wants to pass and the scores of the students that the faculty wants to eliminate. All the faculty does is put the scores in numerical order and draw the pass–fail line. But what happens when the examination fails to do its job? What happens when the examination does not divide the students as the faculty would divide them?

In some departments the faculty abides by the scores as a matter of policy. Going strictly by the scores makes it easier for individual faculty members to convince themselves and others that technical skill is the fundamental qualifying attribute, and makes it easier for these professors to play down their personal role in the career screening and to rationalize away any feelings of guilt that surface. However, the professors pay a price for these advantages when the order of the scores does not fit their preferences. Then their policy of abiding by the scores leaves them with no option that they consider to be satisfactory, and they must pick their poison when they draw the pass–fail line. If they draw the line low enough to pass every student that they want to pass, then they will also pass one or more students to whom they do not want to give professional credentials. If they draw the line high enough to fail every student that they want to fail, then they will also fail one or more students to whom they want to give professional credentials. Departments that go strictly by the scores are willing to pay this price because they don't have to pay it very often: the test does its job well and produces few students with anomalous scores.

Even so, most departments find this too high a price. They see professional credentials as too important ever to award or deny against their better judgment. How do these departments go against what the examination says without destroying the image that the technical skill emphasized on the test is the fundamental qualifying attribute? The key is secrecy—they simply don't tell students their scores. The faculty tells students whether or not they were passed, and sometimes gives them a qualitative indication of their performance on the various parts of the test, but does not give them enough information to figure out, for example, that the faculty failed a student who outscored a student who was passed. Revealing the numbers in such cases would obviously provoke students to ask what the actual qualifying attributes are and would touch off an open political discussion about the propriety of these attributes. The secrecy, like the neutral image of the test itself, has a single purpose: to avoid open discussion of the actual qualifying attributes. Opposition to the simple reform of letting students know their test scores is nothing more than opposition to an open political discussion of the actual qualifying attributes. Such a discussion would be political because every statement, every suggestion for change, would imply support for or criticism of the way the faculty does career screening, the way it exercises social power.

Secrecy is the modus operandi of the physics department at the University of California, Irvine, but one year while I was a student there an instructor sympathetic to my critical investigations into the qualification system gave me a copy of the scores. About a week before the examination I had interviewed each of the eight students taking the test, and after the test I spoke with a few faculty members about the basis for the decisions that had been made at the post-test faculty meeting. There had been disagreement at that meeting, and this increased the willingness of faculty members to talk.

Of the eight students who submitted to the ordeal, two—I'll call them Dave and Nick—were told that they failed the test. Dave and Nick had each completed three years of physics graduate work and were beginning their fourth. This was the second time they had taken the examination, so they were cut short and kicked out of physics graduate school.

The faculty always feels more comfortable when there is a noticeable gap between the scores of the students they pass and the scores of the students they fail. Indeed, in this case Dave and Nick did form a rather distinct "low group" at the bottom of the curve. The problem, however, was that there was a third student in that group. And that student, call him Gary, was passed.

Dave, Gary and Nick were the only students whose scores were below the average, and their scores were closely grouped. To faculty members who didn't know these students well, this was an open-and-shut case. Passing Gary seemed particularly hard to defend because his total score on the sections of the test that he took was lower than Dave's total score on those sections, and no one was arguing that Dave should be passed. (Gary, too, was taking the test for the second time but, unlike Dave and Nick, was directed to take only particular sections of the test; of course, he was required to pass those sections.) In spite of Gary's low scores, the faculty declared that he had passed the test. Why?

Two things should be obvious, even to an outsider. First, the qualification system apparently saw in Gary the crucial qualities that suit one to work as a professional in physics. Second, the weeding out instrument, for whatever reason, failed to indicate the presence of these crucial qualities.

The answer to the question of why the faculty passed Gary lies in the image that he projected to them. Gary was a hard worker. For example, he worked extremely long hours in a professor's plasma physics research laboratory where he was employed. The respect Gary showed for authority, to those above him in the hierarchy, was palpable. His fellow students noted that while there was nothing unusual in the way he would receive their explanation of a question of physics, he would receive the identical explanation from a professor as if it were particularly enlightening. Gary was willingly obedient to the whims of power. Practices and dictates of the system that others at least griped about, he would try to talk of as opportunities.

Gary was not notably praising of the system, but he was strikingly uncritical of it. At first this seemed peculiar, because even the most ardent supporters of the system have complaints about it. But it soon became clear that Gary's unwavering speak-no-evil behavior was less a reflection of his support for the system than a reflection of his fear of its power. His fear was not irrational, but stemmed from an understanding of the system and of his position in it. Gary knew what he was doing: He recognized the fundamental importance of attitude in qualification, made an accurate estimate of the attitude the system wants and then made a conscious effort to project that attitude. After he was passed on the qualifying examination Gary evidently felt it safe to relax a bit in his efforts to maintain the proper image, and he moderated his intense laboratory work schedule. The faculty must have known all along that Gary did not believe completely in the image that he was trying to project. But the professional training system requires mainly that the student play the game; it counts on the fact that the "temporary" tends to become permanent, that one cannot avoid becoming, at least in part, the image that one maintains.

If Gary's attitude was good, then Nick's was not. The most immediate manifestation of Nick's attitude problem was a refusal: During the months of intensive preparation before the test, Nick studied books, refusing to study the old tests like all the other students. He loved physics and could not bring himself to alienate himself from his subject by adopting the narrow focus of the test. In light of the way Nick studied, he scored well on the test—in the low group with Gary, but not way below that group as one might have expected. This outcome is consistent with my own estimate, based on having known both of these graduate students, that Nick's general knowledge of physics was greater than Gary's. The overlap between Nick's broad understanding and the narrowly focused test allowed him at least to score in the low group. But unlike Gary, Nick was in the low group without a redeeming attitude. More to the point, he was in the low group in large part *because* of his attitude. The exam had done its job well, and all the faculty had to do was follow the dictates of the score.

Nick's focus on texts rather than tests appeared foolish to his fellow graduate students. Indeed it was foolish from the point of view that puts highest priority on obtaining a professional credential. But Nick wanted to believe in the work he was doing to prepare for the examination, not only because that work itself was very intense and protracted, but also because he wanted to believe in the professional credential that he thought he would receive because of it. Thus, his quiet refusal to study the old tests was both an act of self-preservation—preservation of the unalienated self—and an act of "civic courage"—where one simply behaves as if the system really is as it says it is or really is as it should be. By studying books Nick behaved as if the examination that qualifies one to get professional credentials really is a test of one's overall understanding of the subject.

When the faculty met to decide the fates of the students who had taken the qualifying examination, the professor who headed the plasma physics lab in which Gary worked argued in favor of passing Gary, while the professor who headed the condensed matter physics lab in which both Nick and Dave worked had nothing to say. Some faculty members did not want to pass Gary, but in the end they went along with Norman Rostoker, the professor arguing that Gary deserved to be passed. When I learned that there had been disagreement at the meeting, I asked Rostoker why he had argued in favor of passing Gary. "I consider him a gifted person who is not good at exams," explained Rostoker. "There has to be enough flexibility in the system to permit gifted people who don't do well on exams to get a PhD."

However, when the faculty applied this fair-sounding system to Nick and Dave, who evidently are "not good at exams" either, the result was quite different, presumably because no one perceived either of these low scorers as "gifted." But why not? How does the system define gifted? What did Gary have that was more important, that was more fundamentally qualifying, than the technical skills measured by the examination? I questioned Rostoker further. Because of the unique circumstances—it having just become public knowledge that the faculty passed someone who did poorly on the examination—Rostoker was in no position to maintain the usual pretense that the technical examination itself is the bottom line, that technical skill is the fundamental qualifying attribute and the highest priority in the university's program for producing professionals. What, then, is the operating definition of gifted, if not good performance on the technical examination? The "extremely important" qualities in a physicist, explained Rostoker, are "discipline in work and tenacity to stick to problems. Mostly, that is what you learn in the university. You learn that, and values. The other stuff [technical knowledge] you pick up on your own."

The decision to overrule the examination scores left many people shocked and disillusioned. The dismayed ones were not tenured members of the faculty, but students and untenured faculty, the people with the least understanding of the politics of professional qualification. From the point of view of these people, Nick and Dave were at least as good at physics as Gary. However, the examination's failure to do its job and the faculty's failure to maintain secrecy (and, for those who heard it, Rostoker's explanation) revealed that from the point of view of professional qualification an important part of being good at physics is being well

Calvin and Hobbes © 1992 Watterson. Reprinted with permission of Universal Press Syndicate. All rights reserved.

Calvin and Hobbes by Bill Watterson

adapted. What was disillusioning about this incident was its implication that there is no value-free definition of what it means to be "good at physics."

Score always reflects attitude, but the mechanism by which it does so is rarely as obvious as it was in Nick's case. The next chapter aims to uncover the more usual but much less obvious mechanisms: how the qualifying examination selects people with particular values even though it focuses not on values, but on "the other stuff," to use Rostoker's words for the technical material. At the same time, the chapter aims to identify the political significance of the values that are required for certification as a professional. We will see how the test is objective but not neutral: objective in that different graders will come up with more or less the same scores, but not neutral, for it tends to favor the students who will make the most manageable employees—students with a subordinate attitude and mainstream values.[7]

NOTES

1. The meaning of "internalization" is illustrated by the "Universal Soldier," whose battlefield actions are to his government's liking even though "His orders come from far away no more" (line from the song "Universal Soldier," Buffy Sainte-Marie, Gypsy Boy Music, Inc., used by permission). Fortunately, the soldier described in the song is not really universal. He is more accurately the "professional soldier." The Vietnam War gave us many examples of the antithesis of such professionalism: troops who couldn't be trusted with weapons because they might turn them on officers when they thought they could get away with it, open questioning of national policy, and so on.

2. "Half of Minorities Drop From Class For State Police," New York Times, 18 July 1981, p. 25.

3. Ibid. U.S. Department of Justice press release, 22 February 1984. United States of America, plaintiff, v. State of New York, et al., defendants, "Motion of the plaintiff United States for an order enforcing the final decree and granting supplemental relief" and "Memorandum of the plaintiff United States in support of its motion for an order enforcing the final decree and granting supplemental relief," civil action number 77-CV-343, filed 22 February 1984 in U.S. District Court, Albany, N.Y. "U.S. Sees Bias at State Police Academy," New York Times, 23 February 1984, p. B3. "Racial Bias Denied By State Police," New York Times, 24 February 1984, p. B5.

4. See note 2.

5. Telephone interview, 25 October 1992; e-mail messages, 26 September 1992, 16 October 1992, 22 October 1992 and 28 December 1992.

6. Max Horkheimer, Eclipse of Reason, Oxford University Press, New York (1947), p. 126. "In popular Darwinism, the good is the well-adapted, and the value of that to which the organism adapts itself is unquestioned or is measured only in terms of further adaptation."

7. People's tendency to confuse objectivity and neutrality, and to take the former as a sign of the latter, bolsters the test's image of legitimacy. Here the test works just like the discipline it serves, for physicists themselves are objective but not neutral: Different physicists come up with the same scientific results within the uncertainties of their measurements, but their work generally advances the social interests of the institutions that sponsor it. See Robert N. Proctor, Value-Free Science? Purity and power in modern knowledge, Harvard University Press, Cambridge, Mass. (1991).

10

EXAMINING THE EXAMINATION

A qualifying examination is a statement as well as a test. It is a training institution's official declaration of the type of knowledge that is at the heart of "knowing the subject." If enough students accept the official line that the examination tests the most important skills in the subject, then the training institution can maintain an intimidating atmosphere in which any dissatisfaction with the narrow focus required to prepare for the examination is seen to reflect a possible lack of dedication to the subject. The institution can equate dedication to the subject, which students see as a legitimate qualification requirement, and dedication to a particular focus within the subject, which is the actual qualification requirement that the institution enforces through the examination.

Students who don't automatically accept the examination's priorities have to go along with them and adjust the focus of their study anyway, if not because of the intimidating atmosphere of general acceptance of the exam's priorities, then because of the threat of expulsion, which the atmosphere of acceptance works to legitimate. Because the qualifying examination carries the threat of expulsion, it compels the student's attention and dictates, at least "temporarily," the student's orientation. Students judge much of what they do in part on its usefulness as preparation for the looming assessment. Under the threat of expulsion any independent notion of what constitutes learning the subject dissolves into studying for the test, and students make this change quietly out of fear that any objection would be misinterpreted as a lack of dedication to learning the subject—legitimate justification for expulsion.

Training institutions don't hide their narrowing of what counts as learning the subject. They often give the beginning graduate student a stack of tests from previous years. The student quickly learns that questions often repeat in similar or even identical form, making it even more imperative to study the exams. With official encouragement, then, learning the subject collapses into studying for the test, and studying for the test in turn quickly degenerates into studying the test itself.

Because the qualifying examination plays a very serious role in the production and selection of professionals, being actively imposed as both a model and a measure—a model of the type of knowledge that the training institution deems of primary importance in the professional and a measure that is usually accurate in picking individuals with the attitudes that the training institution favors—a close look at the examination itself should reveal most accurately what the system seeks in professionals.

IMPOSING A SOCIAL FRAMEWORK

Most people see the professional's skill, in and of itself, as nonpartisan: It is no more applicable to work that perpetuates the social order than it is to work that challenges it. Even most leftists think of such skill as politically neutral, though widely misapplied. But does the technical skill that makes the newly graduated professional so well suited to fill a slot in the corporate–governmental complex—so well suited to serve the status quo in an institution of the status quo— really suit the individual equally well to work for social change? A close look here at the process by which an individual is certified as an employable technical expert will reveal that it is impossible to separate the required skills from the political context in which they are used in the workplace: The skills required for certification as a professional reflect the political situation in which the employers' need for professional workers arises. The professional's skills themselves are indeed partisan, because the practices and attitude that make professionals valuable workers for furthering the goals of the hierarchies that employ them are incompatible with the critical skills and independent thinking that would be required to challenge those goals and hierarchies.

The student's level of enthusiasm for the test-preparation work is of vital importance. It seals the student's future, because to be passed on the test and allowed to have a career in the field, the student must study with great intensity. The degree to which a student is able to maintain the necessary protracted concentration on the test-preparation problems reflects the student's feelings of interest. A student is not automatically interested in a set of problems just because the problems are in his or her field of study. For example, many students who are very interested in a subject and who put in much time in a dedicated way learning it are quite unenthusiastic about studying qualifying examination problems in the subject. Nick, the student who refused to study the old test problems, worked day and night on problems from the books that he studied. "They're very good problems, although they may not help in passing the qualifying exam," he told me.

Nick's behavior was just an extreme case of a common phenomenon, which one can understand only by recognizing that all problems signify human activity and that students react, consciously or unconsciously, to the particular activity that the problems connote. A student's interest in a set of problems depends strongly on the student's reaction to the human activity associated with the problems—that is, on his comfort or discomfort with the "social framework" of the problems. The student's comfort with the social framework of the problems is, in turn, determined by the student's outlook. Any conflict between the student's outlook and the social framework of the examination causes a conscious or unconscious unease that sabotages the student's effort to prepare. The qualifying examination score, then, is a good measure of the student's willingness and ability to work within the examination's social framework. In this sense it is a political score.

What social framework does the qualifying examination impose? What do these problems say socially? The obvious place to look for the answer to this question is in the problems themselves. At first glance, however, it appears that the answer is not there, for all we see are isolated technical puzzles that seem to be value free, that seem to stand above social activity. Ironically, it is the very fact that the problems are presented as pure technical puzzles, stripped of any obvious reference to social goals, that reveals the unstated social framework of the qualifying examination, for only one social framework can impose itself by remaining hidden (and perpetuate itself better that way than by being stated openly): the social framework of the status quo. By the social framework of the status quo I mean work or other activity serving hierarchies, propagating the dominant ideology and perpetuating the social structure.

The qualifying examination reeks of the social framework of the status quo. This framework emanates from the test on three levels. The social framework of the status quo is announced by:

1. The test as a whole, independent of the field that the test serves.
2. The test as a collection of problems in a particular field, independent of the content of the questions.
3. The structure of the test and the nature of the questions.

- 1. *The test as a whole.* As a set of questions that form a qualifying examination, the test represents gatekeeping itself, and so imposes the social framework of gatekeeping. Prior to the role of the field in society or the details of the individual questions, this booklet of problems represents passing or failing; it signifies the important social activity of selecting and rejecting people who want a career in a particular field. Hence the competitive examination would not stand apart from social relations even if its questions did. The examination is a socially innocent collection of technical puzzles only in the same narrow-minded sense that a gun is a socially innocent collection of metal parts.

    Because of the special role of the professions—especially the sciences—in the economy, the ability to do professional work has come to be closely associated with intelligence. As a result, qualifying tests—especially in the sciences—carry the additional social framework of intelligence testing. This causes disproportional anxiety in nonconformist students, who are likely to feel that their intelligence isn't detected fully by intelligence tests. And it causes disproportional anxiety in minority and female students, who secretly fear that there may be some truth to the racist and sexist theories that they aren't as smart as whites or males. The fact that studies have proven such theories to be false doesn't completely eliminate the "stereotype threat" felt by these students.[1]

Student recognition of the social framework imposed by the exam as a whole, particularly the making and breaking of careers, accounts for the fact that students whose main goal is a career in the subject assign greater importance to the qualification problems than do students who are primarily pursuing their curiosity in the subject or are interested in using the subject in nontraditional ways.

- 2. *The test as a collection of problems in a field.* As a set of questions from a specific field, the qualifying examination symbolizes the problems that the field addresses in the real world and imposes the social framework in which these problems arise. What images are invoked by a collection of technical puzzles drawn from a particular field of work? If no other context is specified, isolated technical puzzles will situate themselves in their historical and contemporary context, where they will serve as reminders of the discipline's past and present role in society and as reminders of the social structure and ideology in whose service such puzzles have arisen. In this way isolated technical puzzles invoke images of the social hierarchy and the dominant ideology—the framework of the status quo. (Even if isolated technical puzzles did not invoke images of the work of the status quo, they would still impose that framework because the paradigms of the field, in terms of which the technical puzzles and their solutions are framed, reflect the dominant values of the historical period.) As a general rule, when isolated technical puzzles are imposed in a course or examination, by default the framework of the status quo is imposed as well.

What, for example, is the social framework of physics? The day-to-day work of the 50,000–100,000 physicists employed in the United States defines better than any other measure the role of physics in this society. Most of this work is problem solving motivated directly by corporate and military interests, and much of the rest is connected indirectly to the same interests, as discussed in chapters 4 and 5. Only an extremely small fraction of physicists do work that is difficult to trace to these interests, and only a fraction of that fraction do work that challenges the dominant paradigms.

The military–industrial social framework of physics touches the individual through the psychological environment, or atmosphere, that it fosters. An atmosphere is a prevailing attitude. At the heart of every atmosphere is a key issue, which is usually unstated, and a "normal" approach to that issue. This approach serves as an example of the "normal" way to deal with

other issues that come up, and so defines an attitude. For example, the unstated issue at the heart of the tense atmosphere of the workplace staff
meeting is the boss's authority, and deference is the normal approach; this
puts strong pressure on each employee to maintain a subordinate attitude.
The unstated issue at the heart of the macho atmosphere of the men's
locker room is women, and domination is considered the normal approach; this puts strong pressure on each man to project a macho attitude.

I give this second example because it is analogous to institutional
physics not only in form, but also in content: The unstated issue at the
heart of the military–industrial atmosphere of institutional physics is nature, and domination is the normal approach; this puts strong pressure on
each scientific employee to adopt a military–industrial attitude. Playing
with nature, getting to know nature, understanding nature, cooperating
with nature—in the military–industrial atmosphere such activities are not
justified as ends in themselves, but only as the means to an end. And that
end, in a word, is power. Power is the normal motivation within the military–industrial atmosphere. The normal physicist is the one who, deep
down, finds the work with nature exciting in large part because of its potential contribution to social power; this physicist works to dominate nature either to contribute to military or economic power or to contribute to
the cultural power of physics. The down-to-business military–industrial atmosphere pervades all the institutions of physics. Thus the typical basic-
physics research project at a university is carried out no more playfully and
no more democratically than a military or industrial work project.

The cultural power of physics is its influence on the way people view the
world. What physicists say about the nature of the world is taken seriously
in large part because physics plays an important role in military and economic power and in the way people work and live. The cultural power of
physics is not simply a by-product of its military and economic power but
is important to the maintenance of that power. The cultural power of
physics lends legitimacy to the political actions of the institutions that use
physics; thus, for example, corporate and governmental spokespeople are
taken seriously even when they defy common sense with statements about
the necessity of a new weapons system or the safety of radioactive waste.

Despite the physicist's reputed lack of interest in things social, and despite the fact that many physicists do spend much of their time working
alone on technical problems, it is normal for physicists in the military–industrial atmosphere to see their work as having great social import. The
source of their feeling that their work is important is largely social: the past
and potential importance of such work to military and economic power
and to the way people view the world. The social importance of television,
lasers, nuclear weapons, satellites, computers, men on the moon, quarks,
black holes and other physics-based technologies and notions hangs heavily in the air in the physics workplace without being mentioned. In the mil-

itary–industrial atmosphere the physicist seeks to do socially significant work through nonsocial activity, and the prospect of success stirs a sense of power in the individual researcher. Even the epitome of the nonsocial worker, the "nerd," is largely a socially motivated animal.

The military–economic and cultural power of physics leads people to view any set of physics problems with reverence. People's sense of the role of physics in society—its historical and contemporary service to technology and its influence on the way people view the world—confers social status not only on those who work on physics problems, but also on the physics problems themselves. In this way the isolated technical puzzles of the qualifying examination become a celebration of the field's social role, a reminder of its contribution to power.

Not all students are equally comfortable in the military–industrial atmosphere carried by the problems of the qualifying examination. Some students are fans of the status quo; others seek change and want to take no part in the status quo. The former will be quite comfortable in the atmosphere that surrounds the qualifying examination. The latter will feel like outsiders and may have trouble making the commitment necessary to pass the test.

- 3. *The structure of the test and the nature of the questions.* The remainder of this chapter explains how at this level the qualifying examination serves the corporations and other employers.

TURNING TRICKS

Questions on qualifying examinations often penalize the creative student while rewarding the student who mindlessly applies memorized "tricks." To solve a typical math or science problem, you manipulate symbols in a sequence of steps, each of which takes you closer to the solution in a way that is apparent. However, it is possible to contrive problems whose solutions require a step that appears to be arbitrary or even counterproductive, the logic of that step becoming clear only later in the problem. This crucial step is the trick. The student who doesn't know in advance the trick required to solve a test problem is extremely unlikely to discover it while working on the problem, especially if no time is allotted for that purpose, and so problems based on tricks favor the memorizer over even the creative individual who has a good overall understanding of the subject.

Some problems that can be solved without tricks are nevertheless made easier by tricks, as two examples from mathematics will illustrate. Because tricks often seem simple and obvious *after* they are explained, readers will better appreciate their nature by attempting the two problems now, before reading the discussion below:

1. Multiply 503 by 497.
2. The cube root of 64 is 4, because $4 \times 4 \times 4$ is 64. What is the cube root of 1,728?

Problems that are made easier by tricks can be put into two groups. The first, represented by problem 1, are problems simplified by tricks that are useful in many situations. To multiply 503 by 497 quickly and with little chance of error, you can write the factors as $(500 + 3)$ and $(500 - 3)$, whose product is $250{,}000 - 9$, or 249,991. This trick is based on the algebraic equation $(a + b)(a - b) = a^2 - b^2$ and is useful for multiplying any numbers that are equally spaced around a number whose square is easy to compute. The second group, exemplified by problem 2, are problems made easier by tricks that are useful in essentially just one problem. For example, to solve the cube root problem above,[2] you can simply recognize 1,728 as the number of cubic inches in a cubic foot, which is 12 inches by 12 inches by 12 inches, and so the answer is 12.

In either case the tricks are optional—you can do the multiplication the long way and the cube root by trial and error. However, with a slight change—say, a stringent time limit on the problems—the tricks become mandatory. Under this condition the questions would still look like tests of arithmetic skills, but they would really be disguised tests of memory and of the ability to "psych out" the questions.

One often finds that a qualifying examination problem is impossible to solve without a special trick that is good for only that one problem. This kind of problem is usually constructed by starting with the trick and working backwards. The student who attacks such a problem with creativity, with an understanding of the subject, with insight and with the standard tricks of the trade gets absolutely nowhere. The special trick is the only approach to the problem that works. The unwitting student who uses the "wrong" approach, as logical as that approach may be and as effective as that approach may be in general, sinks deeper and deeper into increasingly complicated calculations—a frustrating "mess," as it is often called—in an ultimately futile effort to get an answer. Because only the special trick works, only the student who has seen the problem before—and memorized it—can solve it. And because the student's creativity, understanding, insight and experience do not lead to the trick, they contribute nothing to the student's score.

Students are eager to learn the standard tricks of the trade for the field they are preparing to enter. A symbol-manipulation routine that is good for only one problem will be part of this standard bag of tricks only if the problem is particularly important in the field. Otherwise the routine will remain just another obscure entry in the reference books. Qualifying examination problems that require *special* tricks are not likely to be particularly important problems in the field, because, like the cube root problem above, they are typically written around the tricks rather than around something important in the field. Hence even the student who knows the standard tricks used by people working in the field cannot necessarily solve the qualifying examination problems that are based on obscure tricks.

What is the aim of examination problems that reward the memorization, quick recall and mechanical application of obscure symbol-manipulation routines? Problems that are disguised requests to give performances of memorized obscure routines clearly do not test the student's creativity, understanding, insight or knowledge of the standard tricks of the trade. However, they do an excellent job of revealing whether the student is willing and able to do disciplined, alienated work on assigned problems—the assigned problems in this case being the test preparation problems, which include problems based on obscure tricks.

I present here as an example a "quantum mechanics" problem from a physics PhD qualifying examination that was given at the University of California, Irvine. My argument doesn't depend on this example, and so readers not familiar with the technical details of quantum mechanics can skim the next few paragraphs without missing an essential part of the discussion. The problem, as it was stated:

Consider a 1 dimensional harmonic oscillator.

$$H = -\frac{\hbar^2}{2m}\frac{d^2}{dx^2} + \frac{k}{2}x^2$$

Minimize the energy for a triangular trial wave function.

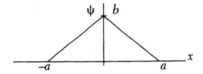

Compare your calculated value to the true ground state energy for H.

The reader wishing to appreciate this example fully should stop here for a minute or two and just list the steps to solve the problem.

The curtness of the statement of the problem—"minimize the energy"—ensures that many students will not even know what they are being asked to do. The problem is an example of a technique for calculating an upper bound on the ground-state energy of a system, but few students are likely to recognize it as such, because the technique is not central to quantum mechanics and is often not part of the curriculum. Hence, most students will not be able to decode the phrase "minimize the energy"; they will not realize that the problem is asking them to compute the energy associated with the pictured wave function and then to adjust a and b so that the energy is minimum.

Students who do decipher the question can begin to show some quantum mechanics skill by computing $H\psi$ and integrating $\psi^*H\psi$ over all x to get the expression for the energy. However, there is a catch. In most problems involving a function that has two parts that meet at a sharp point (the diagonal lines that meet at point b in this problem), physicists handle each part separately. In this problem, however, separately applying the Hamiltonian H to each part of the wave function ψ leads to the wrong answer. The trick here is to treat what appear to be two linear functions as a single, absolute-value function—that is, as a single binomial with an absolute value–function term; the second derivative of the absolute-value function is twice the Dirac delta function, which will contribute to the energy integral.[3]

This crucial mathematical trick is so obscure that the only students likely to have learned it are those who have worked this particular physics problem before. The few students who somehow know the obscure mathematics from somewhere else are not much better off than those who don't know it at all, for they are unlikely to know that its use is required in this physics problem. Simple as the solution seems *after* it has been explained, it is certainly not something a student is likely to discover while under examination.

The trick that solves a problem may reflect a principle of the subject, but use of the trick certainly does not imply an understanding or even a recognition of the principle. Due to the peculiar function used in the problem discussed here, the single point where the two diagonal lines meet actually contributes one-half of the energy. The mathematical trick that leads to the right answer accounts for this energy, but students who use the trick do so because they have memorized the need to do so, not because they recognize the need to account for the energy associated with the one point, and certainly not because they understand the quantum mechanical reasons why the one point contributes so much to the energy.

It is unlikely that the people who use this problem on a qualifying examination expect the student to understand the quantum mechanics of sharp points in wave functions; such quantum mechanics is obscure—sharp points in wave functions do not occur in nature and do not play much of a role in the quantum mechanics curriculum. Anyone interested in simply measuring understanding would know better than to try to do so with this problem. Those who use this problem are not troubled by the fact that the typical student who gets credit for it probably does not really understand it, because a problem based on an obscure trick does not aim to test any such understanding; it aims to see if the student saw the problem, and memorized it, while preparing for the examination. By revealing what the student did specifically to prepare for the examination, problems like this are an excellent measure of the student's willingness and ability to do disciplined, alienated work, the work that characterizes the preparation process. It is this willingness and ability, not knowledge of obscure tricks, that employers value most. Hence, the examination serves employers well even if students quickly forget the obscure tricks that they must memorize to pass. It is understandable that such forgetting, which is a big worry of naive students, does not trouble professional training institutions or employers. (The examination's emphasis on tricks also is part of its emphasis on speed, which favors a narrow-minded approach to problems, as I discuss in the next section.)

Standardized professional and preprofessional qualifying examinations, just like the faculty-written tests that I have been discussing, also measure the student's willingness and ability to memorize the obscure and to "psych out" the test writer's intentions. Consider the Graduate Record Examination, a multiple-choice verbal, quantitative and analytical test given to college graduates seeking admission to programs for higher degrees, and the SAT, a mainly multiple-choice verbal and mathematical examination given to high school seniors who are seeking admission to the colleges of their choice. The verbal sections of these standardized tests feature rarely used words that students typically encounter only on such tests and in test-preparation books. The analogy, antonym, sentence-completion and reading-comprehension questions that make up these verbal sections frequently offer more than one correct answer, only one of which gives credit. (The same is true of questions on standardized science achievement tests used in admission decisions, as Albert Einstein's collaborator Banesh Hoffmann shows in very simple language in his 1962 book, *The Tyranny of Testing*.[4]) The tests' instruction to pick the "best" answer means that the successful student is the one who either shares the testers' values or senses those values and adopts them for the examination. In general, students who simply look for the answer that they think is best don't do as well as those who look for the answer that they think the test makers favor. The unconscious ideological discipline that the latter approach represents is the preprofessional's first step toward the more developed ideological discipline that characterizes the professional.

TIME PRESSURE AND PROBLEM FRAGMENTS

What about examination problems that do not require tricks? Do these problems, too, favor the memorizer over the individual whose primary tools are creativity and insight? The answer is yes, and the reason is the structure of the examination, in particular its time pressure and the fragmentary nature of its problems.

Work done under time pressure—be it craft work, service work or intellectual work—is easy to spot, because people under time pressure don't simply do faster work. They do different work. (It is of lower quality.) Similarly, time pressure on an examination calls for—and rewards—a particular approach to problems. The timed examination favors students who are comfortable grinding out answers to problems without taking the time to develop insight into the situations described in the problems. (Coming up with correct answers, which many students do by mechanically following similar test-preparation problems that they have memorized, certainly does not imply understanding.[5]) Students who are comfortable only when they proceed on the basis of a comprehensive understanding—for example, physical science students who can work with confidence on a problem only by developing a feeling for the physical situation described in the problem, or biological science students who require a feeling for the organism, or social science students who cannot work without a feeling for the social situation—these students are at a disadvantage on a timed test. Such students gain their insight into a problem by looking at special cases, by exploring interesting blind alleys (most of which turn out to be dead ends), by thinking about analogous situations and so on, all of which take valuable time from other problems on the test, resulting in lower scores. The qualifying examination favors students who take a conservative approach to problems, a narrow, mission-oriented approach based on the memorization of large numbers of test-preparation problems; disfavored are students who take a broad, exploratory approach based on developing a feeling for what is going on in the problems.

The typical qualifying examination problem is actually only a fragment of a real problem. It is a technical part of a problem, or part of a technical part of a problem. That the social or even physical context in which the problem arises is rarely specified hurts some students and helps others. It saps the motivation of people for whom a problem is more than a puzzle, people for whom the "solution" to a problem is not the last line in a calculation but is a statement about the situation in which the problem arises (that statement, of course, may be based on a calculation). These people, who want to explore the problem in its context, who get satisfaction from the impact of their work within the context, who often do their best work solving whole problems, where one must sort out relevant and irrelevant information in disorderly and confusing situations— these people are judged to be qualified or unqualified in their profession by their response to the problem fragments that the examination throws at them. For those who have adopted a rote, mechanistic approach, however, the narrowness of assigned problems is not an obstacle. In fact, these people are often more comfortable with technical subproblems than they are with whole problems, where the context is a distraction or source of anxiety.

The qualifying examination's time restrictions and context restrictions both select for students who take a narrow approach to problems. Such restrictions make the examination much like a game, a high-stakes game in which it is imperative that you take a narrow approach if you want to be a serious contender, a game in which winning simply means that you are good at the narrow approach.

These restrictions are similar to those under which most scientists and other professionals employed throughout the corporate–governmental–university complex do their assigned work. Hence, by rewarding the narrow approach, the seemingly objective examination puts the label "most qualified" on those who are best suited to serve employing institutions as narrow problem solvers. Time pressure and fragmented problems on a qualifying examination may appear to be testing for some politically transcendent "speed skill" or "technical skill," but are actually testing for the narrow approach that institutions demand of their professional employees. In this sense these skills themselves are political. The inextricable connection between skill and approach blows the cover of political neutrality on skill.

I should emphasize that this kind of discussion about people who take a narrow-minded approach to problems is necessarily a discussion of professionals rather than nonprofessionals, because nonprofessionals are not trusted to extrapolate memorized solutions and apply them to new situations even in a narrow-minded way. Nonprofessionals are expected, in essence, to approach problems with a closed mind: to follow carefully instructions that specify in detail how to handle routine problems, and to refer deviant problems to professional employees in the organization.

BOREDOM AND ENDURANCE

Examinations that span many hours or many days test something that shorter examinations do not: endurance. Does this feature of qualifying examinations act neutrally? That is, does the endurance obstacle merely work to weed out those who are not genuinely interested in the subject? Or does it favor some types of interest in the subject over others? The answer to this question follows from a look at the potential mismatch between a student's interest in a profession and the profession's primary role in society.

I have described how professional qualifying examinations are indirect in the way they test for the values that characterize the professional. Such examinations work largely through their structure, and could be built around any aspect of the relevant professions and still end up selecting and rejecting more or less the same people. Nevertheless, the aspect emphasized on a qualifying examination is not arbitrary, and it serves to fine-tune the selection process. Although people within a profession work at a variety of jobs, each emphasizing a different set of skills, the profession's qualifying examination is often based on just one set of skills: the skills needed to do the type of work that the profession does as its main social function. This is the case for professions whose qualifying examinations are given after a couple of years of graduate school, as in the natural and social sciences, as well as for professions whose qualifying examinations are given just before admission to professional training, as in the medical professions.

Today's typical physicist, for example, is employed to solve technical problems for industry or government, and so it is no surprise that the examination given to students wishing to enter physics emphasizes calculations, making it in part a test of the student's ability (and, because of the commitment required, willingness) to attack such problems. In fact, the examination consists almost exclusively of calculations, as if calculations are all there is to the subject. Even students who want to enter the field to pursue philosophical issues, to challenge the direction of the field, to demystify the field for the benefit of the general public, or simply, as an end in and of itself, to comprehend the field's insights into the world—even these students must as a condition of admission demonstrate through the calculational examination their ability to serve the military–industrial complex. The physics student who wants a career designing missile guidance systems is not required to know much about the philosophical foundations of physics, but the physics student who wants to pursue the philosophical issues *is* required to demonstrate employability by the aerospace industry. The field admits new members on this basis not because the calculations are more basic than the philosophical foundations, and not for any other technical reason, but because the field is an integral part of the larger social and economic system. In general, the particular set of technical skills that you would need in order to help carry out a field's primary role in serving the system comes to define what people in the field speak of as "the basic skills that everyone entering the field should have."

A short examination would not be able to distinguish reliably between students who have these skills and students who are merely familiar with them. Students taking a qualifying examination are likely to have at least some interest in every facet of the profession they are seeking to enter, including some interest in the profession's primary function in the system, and the skills deriving from this interest might be enough to get them through a short test.

It takes a long examination to separate the men from the boys (to use a repulsive metaphor made appropriate by the competitive, male-gendered atmosphere in most fields). Students with a deviant interest in the subject have a common reaction to a protracted examination that is oriented not toward their interest in the field but toward the field's main function in the system; it is the same reaction that they have to the months-long process of preparing for such a test: They find it a bore, an agonizing chore. In contrast, students who feel at home with the examination's orientation find the weeklong test an exciting challenge; the marathon test is *their* game. Those with a deviant interest in the subject can play this game too because it is one aspect of their field, but the endurance test exposes their limited tolerance for it. As the ordeal drags on and on, hour after hour, day after day, the mind of the student with a deviant interest wanders. This student has an increasingly difficult time concentrating and at some point during the examination is likely to resign mentally.

Clearly, an endurance obstacle does not act neutrally in a test. On a typical qualifying examination it acts to weed out students who are merely interested in their field's primary role in the system, and to select students who are comfortable with and committed to the kind of work involved in playing that role.

TECHNICAL DETAILS, NAKED FORMULAS AND "USEFULNESS"

When outsiders thumb through the pages of a qualifying examination, they often comment that the test looks "very advanced." Indeed, the test is advanced—but not necessarily along the lines they have in mind. Some naive observers, knowing that they are looking at an examination for admission to a profession, assume they are looking at questions that test the candidate's ability to assess the underlying principles of the subject, to critique the foundations upon which the subject is built. What they are actually looking at, however, are questions that are advanced down the road to narrow specialization, questions that avoid critical examination of the fundamentals through their burial in the technical details of specialized applications.

The skills required for decoration with the mantle of qualification—the advanced degree—indicate clearly the kind of work the individual is being prepared to do. The ability to examine critically the ideological and social framework of the field is, of course, a prerequisite for anyone challenging the field's view of the world or role in the world. Those hired by corporations or the government to do research or development work or by universities to do normal paradigm work[6] need no such critical ability, and in fact will work more harmoniously without it. The qualifying examination's narrow focus on technical detail makes it an appropriate test for these rank-and-file experts, who will be employed to work uncritically within an assigned ideological and social framework, and who will therefore live in a world where only technical detail remains. It is no surprise, then, that developing a critical view of the field is an extracurricular activity, one that the training institution discourages not only through the test's exclusive focus on the technical details of specialized applications, but also through its coverage of a large number of such applications. (One reason students are reluctant to look into critical views of their field is that the time diverted to do so would leave them that much less "technically expert.") As a result, the students who are the most likely to pass the test and get professional credentials are often the ones prepared to do little more than render technical service to employers within the given ideological and social framework.

One common feature of the many characteristics of the qualifying examination discussed in this chapter is that they all place a higher value on unexamined production than on understanding. These characteristics of the exam include its emphasis on memorized tricks, a mechanistic approach, work under time pressure, problem fragments, endurance, confinement to technical detail and comfort with the separation of theory and experiment. Another way the test shows its orientation toward uncritical production is by the type of answer it deems valid. Almost all questions on physics examinations, for example, are designed to have answers that are formulas rather than explanations or discussions of meaning or significance. The formula is seen not as a tool to help with an explanation, but as "the answer." The supposition is that the formula answers, which often are approximations that bear little resemblance to more exact formula answers, "say it all," and so students usually are not even asked to interpret them. That the formula, not the explanation or discussion of significance, is the final answer reveals values embedded in the examination. Valued is the concise instrumentalistic summary of nature, the naked formula—a recipe sufficient for manipulating nature but sorely insufficient for understanding nature.

Even something as simple as a weight hanging on a string illustrates the point. Why does the weight swing back and forth after you give it a push? What can you say about its motion in terms of forces, velocities and accelerations? Is the acceleration ever horizontal? Where is it zero? Most physicists would have trouble answering these questions, yet they can perform a mathematical derivation routine that yields, for example, an approximate formula for the time that the pendulum takes to swing back and forth. The qualification system's values, which reflect the larger system's need for people who will engage in unexamined production, tell students that by obtaining formula "answers" such as $T = 2\pi\sqrt{l/g}$ they have done the most important work of the physicist, and so students are only slightly embarrassed when questions like those above expose their lack of feeling for what is going on.[7] Their embarrassment is much greater when they forget a routine for deriving a formula. For simple and complex problems alike, it is very common for students to obtain the "right answer" somewhat mindlessly, without grasping what is going on, or even with a fundamental misunderstanding.

On the very last line of an exam answer that gets 100% credit one often sees a formula with a rectangle drawn around it. In the culture of science, the box says not only "This is the answer," but also "This is what is of value." Whether one is inclined to box a formula or an explanation or statement about meaning is a question of values; the examination announces its values and priorities for the subject by making the formula the goal and the end of the problem, the bottom line in every sense of the word. In this value system, anything that follows the formula is seen more as commentary than substance. It is no accident that the bottom line on questions used to select scientists today is the formula, the recipe that science gives to engineering. The formula answer is simply another way in which the values of a society dominated by a powerful military–corporate–university complex show up in questions that are supposedly "pure science." Selecting new scientists with a test that places higher value on recipes than on explanations or discussions of meaning is one of the many ways in which university scientists serve the needs of employers. The examination's values help adjust students for employment in the military–corporate–university complex, where much of the work even dispenses with formula results and uses numerical (computer) methods to go directly to the most quantitative form of all—arrays of numbers. For students who seek to grasp the understanding of the world offered by the field, but not as a way of preparing to serve the technical needs of the military–corporate–university complex, the adjustment of priorities from explanations to uninterpreted formulas represents a greater loss than the final adjustment from formulas to numbers.

Without developing an intuitive feeling for the subject, the scientist cannot critically examine the paradigms that he or she uses, does not have a sense of what the field can and cannot do and is less able than the hobbyist to use the field independently, outside of workplace assignments. Hence the qualifying examination's priority on recipes over understanding (or, equivalently, its use of recipes as the *measure* of understanding) produces scientists whose only real ability is to serve the system. The system protects itself by producing people with "know-how" rather than people with "know-why."

The system is set up to produce servants, not critics, and it succeeds at this in part by propagating a culture of science that is fundamentally uncritical. The uncritical nature of this culture is revealed clearly by the values of those who are in it, by the kind of activity that they feel is most worthwhile. In this culture, physicists who take care of technical details but who do not question the ideological and social framework in which they are working, or who come up with formulas or numbers but do not develop an intuitive feeling for the physics of the problems on which they are working—such physicists do not see themselves as technical servants uncritically meeting the needs of the military–corporate–university complex, but simply as physicists doing work that is "useful." In this culture, the rare physicist who engages in critical examination of the field and its role in society is seen as doing work that is at best less useful and at worst not even a legitimate part of the field. Thus, at the University of California, Berkeley, physics professor Charles Schwartz was denied a pay-step advance after he switched the focus of his research and publishing from theoretical atomic and elementary-particle physics to the critical examination of the social role of physics. A university dean explained the denial to the chairman of the physics department in a letter marked "STRICTLY CONFIDENTIAL":

> I am sorry to tell you that the proposed merit increase for Charles L. Schwartz to Professor III effective July 1, 1976 has not been approved. Dr. Schwartz is a good undergraduate classroom teacher and a successful PhD director. Reviewers [other members of the physics faculty] and I do not, however, believe that his work since 1970 can be considered scholarship in Physics. Although every department gives its faculty wide latitude in choosing an area for research, this latitude is not infinite. If Professor Schwartz were doing scholarly work in a field unrelated to physics, this work should not and could not be used as the basis for a merit increase in the Physics Department. His contributions in all other areas are sufficiently satisfactory that, should he produce first-rate research in physics as he has done in the past, advancement would seem assured.[8]

The culture of science encourages students to feel a sense of accomplishment when they complete assignments, even when they do so uncritically and without developing an intuitive feeling for the work. After all, such work is "useful." Indeed uncritical, unintuitive work *is* useful—to individual employers and to the system as a whole, because it gets the job done without challenging the ideology and social agenda that it advances. But for the same reason, it is not useful to those who want to make such a challenge or even to those who just want to have a say in the ideology or social role of their own work. An examination favors people who feel a sense of accomplishment when they do the type of work that it rewards. People who are comfortable with the established order feel a sense of accomplishment when they complete uncritical, unintuitive work that the order deems useful, and are therefore favored by the qualifying examination, whose emphasis on taking care of technical details within an unquestioned ideological and social framework and de-emphasis on explanations rewards an uncritical, unintuitive approach. The uncritical culture is powerful, so that even people who oppose the present order intellectually, if they haven't internalized their opposition, may too feel a sense of accomplishment when they serve the system well. Workers who are not critics—that is, workers who don't ask themselves whose social agenda a particular work assignment advances, and who thereby fail to determine for themselves whether the work is worthwhile and whether a personal sense of accomplishment is in order—are doomed to serve the system whose culture determines these things for them.

Albert Einstein never took a physics qualifying examination. If he were going through professional training today, however, he would be judged at some point by such a test. One can imagine an examiner seating Einstein in a cubicle, handing him a set of questions about the technical details of specialized problems, looking at the clock and announcing, "You've got two hours, show us what you're worth." An Einstein would not stand out on such a test, but his score would be meaningful nonetheless. It would be a good measure of his ability to serve the military–corporate–university complex, that is, to do "useful" work, not his ability to look critically at the field's role in the world or view of the world. The system measures human beings, and the field itself, by their ability to serve the established order.

THE ELITIST'S ADVANTAGE

Qualifying examinations hold theory in higher regard than experiment and thereby favor students who do the same. An examination is a statement as well as a measure, and those who agree with the values that a test proclaims have the advantage of feeling at home during the months of arduous study that lead up to it.

In physics, qualifying examinations declare their higher regard for theoretical work over experimental work both through their content and through their form. The simple fact that the test that determines who is qualified to go on to work in the field concentrates on how to do things with theory, almost to the complete exclusion of how to do things with real materials, is a strong statement about what the examiners think is most important in the professional physicist (see chapter 6). Also, the examination takes a primarily written form. Even the relatively short oral section is held in a classroom rather than a lab, and a material object is rarely brought in to serve as the object of discussion. A student's insight, creativity and intuition regarding the "nature of nature," derived from experience in the garage workshop or lab or simply from the experience that follows from a general interest in working with physical objects, go almost completely undetected by the examination. The test is more sensitive to knowledge about the "nature of models of nature," derived from textbook practice with the dominant paradigms and from a general orientation toward theory.

To those who feel that the hierarchy of social status associated with the theorist/experimenter division of labor is proper, it makes perfect sense that the test emphasize the "pure thought" that stands above the grime of the laboratory. Students with such elitist beliefs are often happy never to have contact with the actual objects of the theory that they are studying. These students naturally study the subject in just the way the examination presents it, and therefore end up having an advantage on the test. On the other hand, students who are less taken by the status of theory, or who simply seek a more complete knowledge of physics, will not see the examination's version of their subject as glamorous, because for them work with symbols out of the context of work with things is simply dry and boring. These people, whose interest, development, skill and very understanding of physics derive from their encounters with the interplay between experiment and theory (a totality that professional physicists have experienced less and less over the years) will be at a distinct disadvantage in trying to prepare for the qualifying examination. Thus, the qualification test favors those who support the hierarchical division of labor—those with elitist beliefs. The fact that a system of professional qualification favors elitists should come as no big surprise. After all, employers typically trust professionals to help maintain hierarchy in the workplace and, through their work, elsewhere in society.

One result of a selection system that ranks theory higher than experiment, and that by implication accepts the separation of the two, is the creation of specialists who have little ability to deal with theory and experiment in an integrated or even connected manner. These people—and I have encountered many over the years—perform well on the tests but flounder (or give answers that are embarrassingly unrealistic) when asked to explain one or another of the many physical phenomena that appear in everyday life. Clearly, the division of labor is a problem not only for physicists, but for physics as well. Other fields suffer from the same problem.

We have seen in this chapter how the distinct lack of enthusiasm that many otherwise enthusiastic students show for qualifying examination problems is understandable in terms of the student's sensitivity to the examination's unstated social framework, that of the status quo. That framework is imposed by identification of the isolated technical puzzles first with career tracking and intelligence testing, second with the field's past and present service to the system, and third with alienated and unsatisfying work performed under authoritarian social conditions.

The qualifying examination favors those most willing and able to work within the social framework of the status quo. Those comfortable with the status quo are the ones whose enthusiasm for performing intellectual labor is least likely to be dampened by a lack of knowledge of and control over the social goals of their work assignments, the ones least troubled by surrendering this key element of the creative control of their work to those who see and oversee the big picture. Similarly, those who favor the qualifying examination system often turn out to be the least critical of the social hierarchy and the dominant ideology, that is, the least critical of existing power relationships and therefore the least progressive politically.

The social framework imposed by the examination problems and by the rest of the qualification system maps out a domain of allowed activity that ultimately becomes the playpen of the nonradical credentialed expert and the cage of the individual working for progress in the social structure. To have any chance of success, the latter must step outside the confines of professional work.

NOTES

1. Claude M. Steele, Joshua Aronson, "Stereotype Threat and the Intellectual Test Performance of African Americans," *Journal of Personality and Social Psychology*, vol. 69, no. 5 (1995), pp. 797–811. "Test Scores and Stereotypes," *Chronicle of Higher Education*, 18 August 1995, p. A31. "Can Racial Stereotypes Psych Out Students?" *Los Angeles Times*, 11 December 1995, p. A1.

2. See Richard P. Feynman, *Surely You're Joking, Mr. Feynman!*, Norton, New York (1985), pp. 192–198.

3. After calculating the energy, find b in terms of a by normalizing the wave function, and then find the minimum energy. The minimum energy for a triangular wave function is $\sqrt{3/10}\,\hbar\omega$, or $0.55\,\hbar\omega$, where ω is $\sqrt{k/m}$. The actual ground-state energy is $\frac{1}{2}\hbar\omega$.

4. Hoffmann's critique of multiple-choice testing is not at all outdated. Banesh Hoffmann, *The Tyranny of Testing*, Crowell-Collier, New York (1962).

5. John S. Rigden, "Problem-solving skill: What does it mean?" *American Journal of Physics*, vol. 55 (October 1987), p. 877.

6. For a detailed description of "normal paradigm work," see Thomas S. Kuhn, *The Structure of Scientific Revolutions*, third edition, University of Chicago Press, Chicago (1996).

7. When the weight is at either end of its swing, its acceleration points back along its trajectory; when the weight is at the lowest point of its swing, its acceleration is vertical, up along the string; at some point in between, its acceleration must be horizontal. Nowhere is the acceleration zero. The formula is most accurate for swings of small amplitude. T, the period of the pendulum, is the time it takes the weight to swing back and forth once; l is the length of the string; g, the strength of gravity, is 32 feet/second^2, or 9.8 meters/second^2.

8. Letter from Calvin C. Moore, dean of physical sciences at the University of California, Berkeley, to Geoffrey F. Chew, chairman of the physics department, 24 May 1976.

⓫

GRATUITOUS BIAS

Standardized, multiple-choice tests should not escape scrutiny in a book about the production of professionals. Some such tests are nothing less than professional qualifying examinations—the Medical College Admission Test, for example. Others, such as the Graduate Record Examination, serve as graduate school admission tests for fields that do their professional training in graduate school. Still others, such as the Scholastic Assessment Tests (formerly known as the Scholastic Aptitude Test), make an early cut, at the point of college admission. Extending this book's approach to these objectively graded qualifying tests exposes the political origin of their cultural bias and shows the bias to be less superficial than most critics of standardized tests realize.

Critics of standardized examinations say that the tests favor middle-class, white and male students over working-class, minority and female students. Their main target is the Educational Testing Service, the company that produces the SAT, which each year assesses the college qualifications of two million high school students, and the GRE, which each year assesses the graduate school qualifications of nearly 400,000 college students and others. The critics have embarrassed ETS and other test makers by publicizing examination questions whose biases with respect to class, race or gender are obvious: questions requiring familiarity with activities such as polo, sailing, horseback riding, tennis and golf and with words such as regatta, pirouette and minuet; questions based on reading passages that never mention minorities; questions that refer to men more than women.[1]

Test makers have responded by changing the look of their tests. Today tests such as the SAT and the GRE may still look difficult in places, but they do not look biased. In fact, the tests look very liberal, seeming to bend over backward for the disadvantaged student. References to middle-class recreational activities have disappeared, as have disproportionate references to men. Students now read passages about poor minority women. (One SAT, for example, featured a reading passage on the role of women in the changing lifestyles of migrant Mexican-American families.[2]) ETS makes sure that every edition of the SAT has a reading question about minorities. Thus, students have read about African American artisans in preindustrial America, African American artists today, the civil rights movement, blacks reclaiming their ancestry, Chinese scientific achievements, the worldview of the Navajo, industry in Puerto Rico, black soldiers in the Union Army and the Black Art movement.[3] ETS now subjects each question to a "sensitivity review"[4] to eliminate terminology that would offend any ethnic or gender group, and a "differential item functioning"[5] review to make sure that minorities and whites (and women and men) whose scores match on the test as a whole also score equally well on the question under scrutiny. This ensures that no question is more biased or differently biased than the test as a whole.

These changes are not evidence of substantial bias, say the testers, just "fine-tuning." The test makers take the position that the tests weren't biased in the first place and obviously aren't biased now. This position is consistent with the fact that the changes have had no substantial effect on the scores of women, minorities, low-income students or any other group. Lower scores reflect deficiencies in education, say the testers, not bias in testing.

Despite the reforms and the arguments of the test makers, the critics have a gut feeling that the tests are still unfair. They see disadvantaged students who are clearly capable of learning but who are barred from many colleges and scholarships because of low test scores. Common sense tells the critics that the tests are not neutral in this process. In the absence of a fundamental understanding of the problem, some critics have adopted the strategy of finding and exposing as many imperfections in testing as possible. But until the critics offer a clear, sharp analysis of *why* the selection examinations are biased and *where* the bias resides in the examinations, the enterprise of selecting and rejecting people through standardized examinations will continue to be seen as a legitimate social practice. The key to the required analysis is to see the tests not as a flaw in a nonpartisan system of college admission, but as a logical part of a larger system of college admission, college education and employment that itself needs to be criticized. Those who dare to do this will be labeled radicals, but their broader perspective will quickly give them clear insight into long-standing testing issues that are otherwise impossible to resolve. Here I will look at the tests as part of a larger system and use that view to explain why test questions that are biased on their face appeared on the examinations in the first place, why their removal has not affected scores and where the bias resides in the tests.

BIAS—NECESSARY AND UNNECESSARY,
HIDDEN AND SUPERFICIAL

The advertised goal of college admissions examinations is to estimate how well individuals will do in college. While some critics argue that the tests should be abolished because they often fail to meet this goal, I argue that they should be abolished because they often *succeed*. Admissions examinations are an instrument of bias even when they accurately estimate the degree to which individuals have what it takes to succeed in college, because the colleges themselves are biased. The mainstream educational institutions are biased toward reproducing the current social structure, so that middle-class, white and male-gendered attitudes, values, outlooks and approaches to problems spell success in college, while working-class, minority and female-gendered perspectives do not.

The main educational mission of the colleges in any country is to produce people to staff and perpetuate that country's social and economic system, and so it is no accident that the same attitude and values that are the key to success in college are the key to success in jobs that require a college degree. The student whose middle-class values make college something of a party is likely to advance faster on the job after graduation than the student whose working-class values make college an arduous experience in an alien world, even though the latter student works harder than the former. The favored outlook, which best serves the interests of the establishment, is by no means universal or easy to teach. Colleges can fine-tune the values and attitudes of students, but as large, impersonal institutions with thousands or tens of thousands of students, they cannot give enough individual attention to carry out major transformations. They fulfill their mission mainly by admitting those with the right attitude and values and by rejecting those who would require a major reorientation to become good servants of the system. The colleges deal with "incorrect admissions" less through the difficult and costly process of transforming attitudes and values than through simple disposal—the college dropout rate is about 50%.

To minimize their mistakes, colleges use admissions tests that favor students who have the attitude and values that are the key to success in college and in jobs that require a college degree. Because of the orientation of the colleges and the nature of the larger social hierarchy, these attitudes and values are more likely to be held by middle-class students than by working-class students, by whites more than by minorities, by men more than by women. Hence, any test that works at predicting success in college necessarily favors middle-class, white and male students, because those students are more likely to have the attitude and values that spell success. Such favoritism is not the purpose of the tests; it is just a sign that the tests are doing a good job of selecting the people best suited to staff and perpetuate the social and economic system. With this understanding one need not make a special argument to explain why the tests, the colleges and the system as a whole also welcome those working-class, minority and female students who, through cultural self-denial, the assumption of

From *The Wall Street Journal*, by permission, Cartoon Features Syndicate

"These days we don't give them aptitude tests;
we give them attitude tests."

alien values or other adjustments, have the attitude and values, the style of thinking and approach to problems, the general orientation and outlook that allow them to serve the system well.

If the job of college entrance examinations is to select the people who will best serve the system, then these tests have no need for questions on which middle-class, white or male students do better than working-class, minority or female students who are equally prepared to help maintain the social structure. Nevertheless, a few questions with such gratuitous biases have appeared on college admissions examinations. To understand why, one must first understand the kinds of bias that an examination can carry and the ways in which it can carry that bias:

- An examination can carry basically two kinds of bias: unnecessary bias, which the examination does not need to achieve its actual social goal, and necessary bias, which the examination must have to achieve its actual social goal. A test that aims to rate people according to their knowledge of grammar, for example, needs a bias in favor of those who know grammar and against those who do not, but does not need a special bias against, say, people who vote for Democrats, people who don't know how an oscilloscope works, or any other group. The test has no need for, say, northeasterners to outscore residents of Appalachia who know grammar equally well. Similarly, to achieve their goal, college entrance examinations need a bias in favor of those who are likely to serve the system well and against those who are unlikely to do so, but these tests do not need a special bias against working-class, minority or female students. The necessary bias by itself screens out those working-class, minority and female students who are unlikely to become good servants of the system.
- An examination can carry bias in basically two ways: in its superficial content, which includes the topics of the questions and the vocabulary used, and in its hidden content, which includes the context, form or structure of the examination and its questions.

A look at some examples will help clarify the crucial distinction between a question's superficial content and its hidden content and will illustrate how these two levels of content carry unnecessary and necessary biases. Here are a couple of questions from the SAT.[6]

BRIDLE:HORSE::   PIROUETTE:DANCER::

(A) bone:dog   (A) touchdown:referee
(B) olive branch:dove   (B) motivation:coach
(C) valor:soldier   (C) somersault:acrobat
(D) precept:conduct   (D) model:sculptor
(E) devotion:duty   (E) rink:skater

An examination's superficial content can produce both necessary and unnecessary bias. Here the words "bridle" and "pirouette," which are part of the superficial content of the questions, help produce the test's necessary bias to the extent (if any) that students familiar with them are more willing and able than others to serve the system, and therefore are more likely than others to do well in college; sorting out students in this way is a goal of the test. The same two words produce an unnecessary bias to the extent (if any) that they are not equally familiar to students who are from different social groups but who nevertheless are equally willing and able to serve the system, and who therefore are equally likely to do well in college; sorting out students in this way is not a goal of the test.

The rest of the bias in an examination comes from the hidden content of the test and its questions. Consider the examples above: They are isolated word puzzles; they must be answered quickly; they test aptitude; they exist within the social framework of the status quo; and so on. As the previous chapter explains, this sort of hidden content is biased in favor of those willing and able to carry out assignments for the system and against those whose orientation leaves them unprepared to serve. Here the hidden content produces necessary bias—that is, bias that helps the examination achieve its goal.

Test makers such as ETS check each examination question for biases by using a mathematical technique known as the Mantel–Haenszel method for the measurement of differential item functioning.[7] This technique does not identify a college admissions test question as biased just because, say, a much smaller percentage of black students than white students picks the wanted answer, for black students on the average might not be equally prepared to do well in college. A test item is said to function differently for blacks and whites only if blacks and whites whose scores match on the test as a whole do not score equally well on the item. The underlying philosophy is that blacks who would do as well in college as whites—as indicated by their identical scores on the test as a whole—should score as well as whites on the question. Hence, this method flags only questions that have an unusual amount of unnecessary bias or that have a bias against different social groups than those the test as a whole is biased against. More precisely, the method can identify particular questions that have more (or less) than the average amount of unnecessary bias against a particular group, but it cannot detect bias that pervades the test.

What the test makers find when they use the Mantel–Haenszel method to check for biases against particular social groups tells us something about how large a role such unnecessary biases play in college entrance examinations. A test's superficial content varies a lot from question to question as words and topics change, but the test's hidden content stays more or less the same from one question to the next. Therefore, if the test is biased against a particular social group, and if the questions carry much of this bias in their superficial content, then one would expect to see a lot of question-to-question variation in the amount of bias against the group. It is just such a variation that the Mantel–Haenszel method is capable of detecting (and the only thing the method is capable of detecting). However, the test makers' application of the method to various social groups has shown that there is, in fact, not much question-to-question variation in the unnecessary biases. This implies that there is not much unnecessary bias in the superficial content of the questions. And the previous chapter's detailed analysis of the hidden content of test questions found only necessary bias. So the test simply does not have much unnecessary bias. The test's bias is mainly what is necessary for it to accomplish its goals.

In the case of the SAT, this necessary bias favors those who are the most promising from the establishment's point of view: the most promising college students, the most promising future staffers of the system. This bias accounts for the low test scores of various social groups, whose members clearly have the aptitude for further learning but not the attitude and values that would make them good servants of the current social structure. The SAT would more properly be called the Scholastic Attitude Test and is little more than a system service examination.

The small amount of unnecessary bias that standardized college entrance examinations do have tends to be quite visible: Through their application of the Mantel–Haenszel method, test makers have in a sense proved mathematically that any unnecessary biases in these tests reside in the superficial content of the questions. According to an ETS spokesman, when you look at the questions that this technique consigns to the trash heap, the source of the bias is usually quite obvious,[8] meaning that the unnecessary bias is in the superficial content of the questions. This doesn't imply that all the bias in the superficial content is unnecessary, just that all the unnecessary bias is in the superficial content.

Meanwhile, the test's necessary bias is carried more in its hidden content than in its superficial content, in the form rather than the face of its questions. Even if the test were made up exclusively of questions whose superficial topics were working people, minorities and women, middle-class white males would still get the highest scores, as they do now on such questions. In any case, an admissions or qualifying examination's necessary bias in favor of those who would best serve the system is certainly its main bias, and as such it accounts almost completely for the score differentials that are often thought to be the result of class, race and gender biases.

Although questions with unnecessary biases play an insignificant role in producing these score differentials, they have received a great deal of attention because they are so easy to spot. One can understand the origin of these questions and the reason that their unnecessary, very visible biases usually favor the same groups that the tests' necessary bias favors—middle-class, white and male students—by looking at how examination questions are written.

FREUDIAN SLIPS

There are mathematical methods for determining how well a college admissions examination does its job of predicting success in college; one can compare test scores and college grades, for example. But there is no formula for writing the examination that will do the best job. The most that question writers can do is maintain a mental image of a student who does well in college and dream up questions that will be more difficult for other students than for this student. The more accurate the writers' mental image of the kind of student that their clients, the colleges, want, the better they will do at writing questions that favor such students. The goal of today's liberal admissions or qualifying examination is to offer all students, rich and poor, majority and minority, male and female, an equal opportunity to serve the system, but the question writer's image of the student set for success in college is probably that of a middle-class white male, not because the question writer is prejudiced, but because such a student *is* the most likely to succeed. It is inevitable that question writers working with this mental image will from time to time take a cheap shot and write a question whose superficial content gives an unnecessary advantage to middle-class, white or male students. However, the resulting scattered gratuitous biases against poor, minority and female students cannot account for the significantly lower scores of these students on the test as a whole; it is the systematic bias in favor of those best prepared to serve the status quo that accounts for the scores. If the cheap shots are important, it is because they are Freudian slips by question writers, and like such slips in general, are embarrassing because they are revealing—in this case, revealing of the testers' mental image of the typical student that the colleges seek.

The Educational Testing Service inadvertently drew my attention to one of their Freudian slips—one showing that they consciously adjust which groups of people their tests favor. They must make such adjustments, of course, to meet the changing recruitment priorities of their clients, the colleges. The example illustrates the historic change from the old recruitment regime, which (among its other biases) simply favored men, to the present regime, which favors anyone with male-gendered values. When I phoned the giant gatekeeping organization to see what they would tell me about test bias, they put me in touch with one of their principal measurement specialists, Michael J. Zieky. Yes, Zieky said, ETS often finds bias in proposed test items and does its best to root it out. The example he chose to give me was that women get lower scores than men on questions about war and on questions about geometry.[9] A few days after I spoke with Zieky, a couple of ETS booklets he had promised to send arrived in the mail. As I read about the testing behemoth's "sensitivity" to women, I was startled to come across this:

> Where a question in a mathematics test might once have mentioned Mary Smith's calculations for roasting a turkey, a similar question today might mention her calculations for establishing missile trajectories.[10]

Missile trajectories—a masterful combination of war and geometry! This choice of context, surely made unknowingly, blurts out the testers' male-gendered view of expanded opportunity for women. As suggested by the question's original formulation in terms of turkey roasting, which put the woman in a stereotypical kitchen role, question writers of the old regime favored men. As suggested by the question's new context, today's question writers favor anyone who has a male-gendered orientation and who is therefore advantageously positioned to succeed in college today.

The actions of the test makers show that they understand thoroughly the different kinds of bias and different levels of content discussed here. They know full well that the visible biases, which in the past proved very costly in terms of public relations and threatened the entire testing enterprise, are in fact unnecessary and can be dropped—or better yet, freely manipulated to make the test appear to favor the disadvantaged—without affecting scores. The resulting questions that appear to favor working people, minorities and women are most easily answered by middle-class white males because these questions have a more fundamental bias, a bias toward those with the attitude and values that the system seeks. By reversing the unnecessary biases in the superficial content of the tests, liberal psychometricians have done little more than put an egalitarian face on an instrument of pro-system bias. They have worked hard to make this superficial change, but they have worked even harder to prevent examination reform from going beyond it.

Professional question writers certainly know which social groups are most likely to do well on the tests that they help construct, but that is not what makes them good question writers. They are good at their job of coming up with just the right questions because they have an intuitive feeling for the values, attitude, outlook and approach that the tests favor—they have internalized the spirit of the tests. Because they have made the spirit of the tests their own, they are likely on occasion to "gild the lily" and come up with questions whose superficial content carries the very same bias that the test as a whole carries. A look at some examples is informative and entertaining, but one must remember not to overestimate the importance of biases that are visible in the superficial content of test questions. Apparently whoever wrote the following GRE "analytical ability" questions understands, perhaps subconsciously, that one characteristic of students who are promising from the system's point of view is a willingness and ability to comply with bureaucracies rather than fight them. (As with all the examples that I present, to understand the argument fully the reader should actually write down answers before proceeding. The official answers are in note 11.)

Questions 40–42

To apply to college a student must see the school counselor, obtain a transcript at the transcript office, and obtain a recommendation from Teacher A or Teacher B.

A student must see the counselor before obtaining a transcript.

The counselor is available only Friday mornings and Tuesday, Wednesday, and Thursday afternoons.

The transcript office is open only Tuesday and Wednesday mornings, Thursday afternoons, and Friday mornings.

Teacher A is available only Monday and Wednesday mornings.

Teacher B is available only Monday afternoons and Friday mornings.

40. Maria, a student, has already seen the counselor and does not care from which teacher she obtains her recommendation. Which of the following is a complete and accurate list of those days when she could possibly complete the application process in one day?

   (A) Friday
   (B) Monday, Wednesday
   (C) Monday, Friday
   (D) Wednesday, Friday
   (E) Monday, Wednesday, Friday

41. John, a student, completed his application procedure in one day. Which of the following statements must be true?

   I. He obtained his recommendation from Teacher A.
   II. He obtained his recommendation from Teacher B.
   III. He completed the procedure in the morning.

   (A) I only
   (B) II only
   (C) III only
   (D) I and III only
   (E) II and III only

42. Anne, a student, has already obtained her transcript and does not care from which teacher she obtains her recommendation. Which of the following is a complete and accurate list of those days when she could possibly complete the application process?

   (A) Friday
   (B) Monday, Wednesday
   (C) Monday, Friday
   (D) Wednesday, Friday
   (E) Monday, Wednesday, Friday

Questions 25–26

(1) You cannot enter unless you have a red ticket.
(2) If you present a blue form signed by the director, you will receive a red ticket.
(3) The director will sign and give you a blue form if and only if you surrender your yellow pass to him.
(4) If you have a green slip, you can exchange it for a yellow pass, but you can do so only if you also have a blue form signed by the director.

(5) In order to get a red ticket, a person who does not have a driver's license must have a blue form signed by the director.
(6) You can get a yellow pass on request, but you can do so only if you have never had a green slip.

25. The above procedures fail to specify

    (A) whether anything besides a red ticket is required for entrance
    (B) whether you can exchange a green slip for a yellow pass
    (C) the condition under which the director will sign the blue form
    (D) how to get a red ticket if you have a yellow pass
    (E) whether it is possible to obtain a red ticket if you do not have a driver's license

26. Which of the following people can, under the rules given, eventually obtain a red ticket?

    I. A person who has no driver's license and who has only a green slip
    II. A person who has no driver's license and who has only a yellow pass
    III. A person who has both a driver's license and a blue form signed by the director

    (A) I only
    (B) II only
    (C) I and II only
    (D) II and III only
    (E) I, II, and III

Anyone attempting to impose an admissions system like the one in the above question at, say, a rock concert, would discover very quickly that different individuals respond in different ways to systems of bureaucratic control. Yes, some people would spend their time focused on the rules, analyzing and reanalyzing them, trying to figure out what they are "supposed to do." Others, however, would simply present whatever documents they have and demand to be let in. Yet others would take a glance at the rules and storm the gate. An individual's tendency to submit to bureaucratic control or to fight it, or to do some of each, reflects the individual's attitude about how to deal with power—a political attitude.

To many of us a decision to storm the gate would show more analytical ability than would a decision to submit to an oppressive level of bureaucratic control, but the test works to give *lower* analytical ability scores, not higher scores, to those who would resist. Those whose political orientation leads them to comply with schemes for bureaucratic control feel at home working within systems of rules like the ones in the above questions, and typically have a lifetime of experience with such an approach to draw upon in answering this type of question. On the other hand, those whose political orientation would lead them to choose resistance as the answer to the broad problem of what to do are not likely to do their best work when restricted to the narrow problem of how to do what you are supposed to do. Yet this is the problem that serves as the official measure of analytical ability. When all else is equal, then, the test will give higher analytical ability scores to individuals whose tendency is to comply than to individuals whose tendency is to resist.

The test as a whole tilts toward those who feel comfortable working within arbitrary rules, who are used to working out technical details within a dictated framework, who make their way in the world through careful attention to the rules. These individuals do not require motivation from or even knowledge of the social origin of their assigned problems; as soon as the rules are revealed, they jump right into the detail work, without the mental reservations that disturb and distract others. The test favors these cooperative objects of bureaucratic control, and as the examples above indicate, sometimes does so blatantly.

We have seen that what appear to be cultural biases in selection examinations are actually political biases at root. The tests serve the interests of employers and help reproduce the current social structure by favoring individuals who are most likely to fit in well in hierarchical organizations. The tests' success at doing this is cause for their abolition. Without the benefit of test scores, an educational institution's ranking of applicants would be less of a ranking by attitudes and values and would therefore result in a more politically diverse student body. Ultimately, employers would have to contend with, and make concessions to, a segment of the workforce (at the higher educational levels) that is more politically diverse and therefore less politically subordinate.

NOTES

1. "Biggest Testing Service Faces Critical Scrutiny As Its Influence Grows," *Wall Street Journal*, 28 February 1978, p. 1. "College Entrance Tests Discriminate, Expert Says," *Los Angeles Times*, 18 November 1978, p. 18. "Educator Wages War on 'Biased' Tests," *Los Angeles Times*, 17 December 1978, pt. X, p. 10. "Groups Charge Bias in Merit Scholarship Testing," *New York Times*, 29 June 1988, p. B6. See also David Owen, *None of the Above*, Houghton Mifflin, Boston (1985).

2. Educational Testing Service, *10 SATs*, College Entrance Examination Board, New York (1986).

3. Ibid.

4. *The ETS Sensitivity Review Process: An Overview*, Educational Testing Service, Princeton, N.J. (1987). Paul A. Ramsey, "Sensitivity Review: The ETS Experience as a Case Study," in Paul W. Holland, Howard Wainer, editors, *Differential Item Functioning*, Lawrence Erlbaum Associates, Hillsdale, N.J. (1993), ch. 19 (pp. 367–388).

5. "Testing Service to Use New Method to Find Biased Questions," *Chronicle of Higher Education*, 28 May 1986, p. 1 and accompanying articles on p. 13. Paul W. Holland, Howard Wainer, editors, *Differential Item Functioning*, Lawrence Erlbaum Associates, Hillsdale, N.J. (1993). Michael Zieky, *Differential Item Difficulty in Test Development at Educational Testing Service*, a five-page typewritten paper, Educational Testing Service, Princeton, N.J. (April 1988). Alicia P. Schmitt, Neil J. Dorans, *Differential Item Functioning for Minority Examinees on the SAT*, research report RR-88-32, Educational Testing Service, Princeton, N.J. (May 1988).

6. The official answer to the bridle question is d; see "Groups Charge Bias in Merit Scholarship Testing," *New York Times*, 29 June 1988, p. B6. The official answer to the pirouette question is c; see Educational Testing Service, *10 SATs*, College Entrance Examination Board, New York (1986), pp. 240, 249.

7. See note 5.

8. Telephone conversation with Michael J. Zieky, a principal measurement specialist at the Educational Testing Service, Princeton, N.J., 24 August 1988.

9. Ibid.

10. See note 4, *ETS Sensitivity Review Process*.

11. Questions 40 to 42 are from *GRE: Practicing to Take the General Test*, 9th ed., Educational Testing Service, Princeton, N.J. (1994), pp. 37–39. Questions 25 and 26 are from *GRE Information Bulletin, 1980–81*, Educational Testing Service, Princeton, N.J. (1980), pp. 28–29. Here are the official answers: 40–D, 41–E, 42–E, 25–A, 26–D.

"NEUTRAL" VOICES

"Where's the red one? Who can tell me where it is for sixty?" The operator of an illegal street hustle known as Three-Card Monte tries to engage someone in the crowd. But none of the midtown Manhattan pedestrians who have stopped to watch the action responds.

"Here," he says, turning over the card that everyone knew was the red one. "Watch it now!" He turns the card facedown again and slowly interchanges it with the other two cards on his makeshift table, fashioned from a couple of discarded cardboard boxes.

"Where is it now? Tell me for sixty," he says, peeling off three twenties from a wad of bills. "Who saw it? Anybody?"

"You. Do you know where it is?" he asks a man in the crowd.

The man hesitates.

"Just point to it. Just point to it, for free. Go ahead," urges the dealer, trying to hook the mark.

The man points to a card. There is little doubt that it is the red one, because the dealer, openly frustrated with the crowd's reticence, had moved the cards at baby speed this time, just to get people to start playing the game.

"Show me sixty and you're a winner," says the dealer to the man, offering him the opportunity to fill in the skipped step of betting by simply displaying the $60 that he would have bet. The man need not actually hand over the money, because the winner always gets his bet back anyway, along with his winnings. The game's rules, it seems, are bigger than both the dealer and the player, and so the dealer must ask the player to at least go through the motions of placing a bet.

"Show me sixty," repeats the dealer, in the tone of someone obliged to walk a beginner through the steps of the game.

"Show it to him, show it to him," advise two knowledgeable-sounding people in the crowd in excited whispers, encouraging the mark to seize the opportunity and win $60.

The mark is a bit bewildered; everything seems to be happening so fast. But he tries to appear like he knows what he's doing. He pulls out his wallet, removes $60 and shows it to the dealer.

The dealer reaches out to receive the money, as if it were being handed to him, but the mark hesitates. "I have to hold it," says the dealer.

The mark doesn't want to disrupt things now that he is just moments away from collecting his winnings. With his mind on the $60 that he is going to get, he decides to view the dealer's request as just another rule. It's only for a few seconds anyway, he thinks, as he hands his $60 to the dealer.

"Turn over the red one," invites the dealer, gesturing toward the cards.

The mark slides the red card to the edge of the table and flips it face up—but wait a minute, it's black!

"Aw, damn!" yell the mark's two self-appointed advisers, showing sympathy—but in the process implying that this is a legitimate outcome.

Stunned and disoriented, the mark is struggling to figure out what's been going on.

"You took my money," he says quietly, apparently thinking out loud. And then, with greater confidence: "You took my money!"

"A bet is a bet . . ." the dealer starts to explain.

"You took my money! Give it back!" interrupts the stung mark, who now appears to be on the verge of using force.

A heated exchange of words ensues, and there seems to be no way that one man or the other can prevail through talk alone.

But then someone in the crowd says, "You lost, man."

These words seem to work a kind of magic on the mark, who suddenly appears to have lost full confidence in his own position. For the first time he allows himself to consider accepting the situation as it stands, perhaps by viewing it as the words from the crowd suggest: as his loss of a fair game rather than as his victimization by the dealer. The same words—"You lost, man"—had they come from the dealer himself, might have been further provocation. But coming from a nonpartisan, neutral, disinterested source, they are persuasive.

To finish cooling out the mark, the dealer offers a consolation prize that actually has some value, but he links this offer explicitly to the mark getting on with his day. "I'll give you a free chance to win twenty so you can have a nice day," says the dealer.

The mark, no longer making any demands, watches the dealer deploy the cards and interchange them a few times.[1]

At the dealer's signal, the mark reaches out and turns over what should be the red card, but isn't.

"Ooooh!" exclaim the two vocal people in the crowd.

And the mark walks away, disappearing quickly into the busy pedestrian traffic.

The dealer resumes his work immediately, giving himself the professional look of a casino employee who doesn't stop to react emotionally to the outcome of the game. But before he can hook another mark, a lookout stationed up the block spots a cop and motions back to the table. In an instant the dealer is a pedestrian, floating inconspicuously down the street. The boxes and cards that he has abandoned suddenly look like ordinary trash left out on the sidewalk for collection, and the people in the crowd go on their way.

But look! Look who the dealer is walking with. You guessed it—it's the two people who advised the mark. In fact they are the ones whose flamboyant winning and losing had attracted the crowd in the first place. (They always won in a way that made you think "That was easy; I could have done that," and lost in a way that made you think "That was stupid; I could have won that one easily.") And they are the ones who spoke up at the con game's three critical junctures. At the hook: encouraging the mark to go ahead and "show sixty." At the sting: saying "Damn!" at the black card to frame the operation as a fair game rather than as trickery. And at the cool-out: encouraging the mark to view the outcome as his own failure by saying "You lost" instead of "He misled you."

I witnessed this scene during my lunch hour one day and have tried to recount it here as accurately as possible. (Yes, the streetwise hustler really did say "so you can have a nice day.") In fact, I've seen this game—a variation on the age-old shell game—many times on New York City sidewalks, and it is pretty much the same every time.

I watch these games in part because the people who operate them often display extremely impressive insight into the way people think and show great sophistication in their use of psychology. Surely their intuition and skill would make the typical professional psychologist look dull in a comparison. Watching the shills is especially instructive. The dealer could certainly engage some marks without the shills' help, but he wouldn't survive for very long without their protection. It is easier to get a person to believe a false promise than it is to get the person to accept a loss, and when the game moves from the former stage to the latter the operator's personal authority by itself is no longer sufficient to manipulate the mark. Thus, the operator has his neutral voices. For the operator of the game, getting the mark to go peacefully is a necessity, not an option, and so cooling out is not something that happens "after" the game. Cooling out is an integral part of the game.

There are lessons here that go far beyond the game itself. In 1952 sociologist Erving Goffman wrote a paper in the journal *Psychiatry* showing that many institutions, authority figures and ordinary individuals in "legitimate" society engage in activity that is essentially the same as that of the con artist cooling out the mark.[2] In fact, as educational sociologist Burton R. Clark later showed, cooling out is one of the main social functions of institutions of higher education in the United States.[3]

The U.S. socioeconomic system, like the hustler, makes false promises, the principal one being that social mobility is available to all who work hard. By its very nature, a hierarchical system cannot possibly keep such a promise. The number of positions at successively higher levels decreases very quickly and is always less than the number of hardworking people who want the positions. This structure sets many ambitious workers on a collision course with the reality of limited opportunity. When they are finally hit with the tragic disappointment, they may become angry or resentful, and so the hierarchical system must engage in widespread cooling out. It does this not only to protect its agents who stand at the gate and do the dirty work of exclusion, but also to make sure that those who have been disappointed do not become opponents of the hierarchical system itself and enemies of its power elite. It is vital to the system that the losers serve the hierarchy respectfully, and not sabotage it, when they find themselves with jobs that have lower social status than the society of "unlimited opportunity" had led them to expect. Cooling out is therefore an integral part of the socioeconomic system.

Those who say "That's life" should understand that there is nothing natural about a system that kills the spirit of large numbers of people by first putting them in a position where they need opportunity, then promising them virtually unlimited opportunity and finally making them losers.

The hierarchical system itself does create much of the need for opportunity in the first place. Its hierarchical division of labor, in which the interesting and creative parts of work are separated out and reserved for a few, while the tedious and mind-dulling parts are heaped on the many, has a lot of people wishing for better jobs. And its hierarchy of authority, in which decision-making power is concentrated at the top, has a lot of people wishing for jobs where they have some say—or, at the very least, insulation from those above them (autonomy). If jobs were designed in a way that did not force people to specialize in the uninspiring parts of work, and if decisions in the workplace were made democratically rather than by a hierarchy of bosses, two of the main goals that drive individuals to seek opportunity would already be met: more fulfilling work and a fair share of power.

As the avenues for getting ahead in this country have narrowed, the route of formal education has become dominant, so that today the pursuit of opportunity in the United States is to a large extent institutionalized in the colleges. As a result, the colleges have become one of the pyramidal system's main tools for cooling out people's "unrealistic" career ambitions. They do it on a massive scale, yet by necessity conceal the fact that that is what they are doing.

The process of cooling out students' high educational and career expectations begins, of course, long before college. Grades from high school teachers and advice from counselors have an effect, but it is easy to base your hopes and plans on the thought that these people are underestimating you. Their reactions to you have always been very subjective, after all, and so perhaps their professional assessments, too, contain errors of judgment due to misimpressions, personality conflicts, personal prejudices and so on. But then comes the big aptitude test, and a few weeks later when you open the envelope and look at your scores you feel like you really are looking at a true picture of yourself. SAT and ACT scores have a powerful impact on the self-images of students, and those whose self-images are hit hard lower their expectations. They may not even apply to the colleges that they most want to attend.

For most students, college itself means further cooling out. The lower the social status of the college, the greater its orientation toward wrapping up the formal education of its students. In fact, cooling out competes with remedial instruction to be the *raison d'être* of the community or junior college. These two-year institutions, which take in two-thirds of a million graduating high school seniors every year,[4] allow large numbers of people to "go to college"—and to get it over with posthaste. Today "we're playing more of that winnowing function," says George Prather, an official in the 100,000-student Los Angeles Community College District.[5] Nationwide, most students going from high school into two-year colleges plan to transfer to four-year colleges or universities, where they can earn bachelor's degrees.[6] In the end, however, a large majority of "transfer program" students either switch to a terminal program or leave college altogether. Each year, only about 5% of those enrolled in two-year colleges transfer to bachelor's-granting institutions, an astoundingly small fraction.[7] For example, Los Angeles City College in the 1997–98 school year managed to transfer only 481 of its 15,000 students to the California State University system, and just 73 students to the more-prestigious University of California system. Statewide, California's 106 community colleges, which constitute the largest system of higher education in the world, opened the year with 1,143,000 students. By year's end 56,000 (4.9%) had transferred to the California State University or University of California systems—and 1,087,000 had not.[8]

Clark analyzed the process by which junior colleges change transfer students into terminal students. He considers as an example a student who wants to be an engineer but who is destined not to be one. What might be the sequence of experiences that cools him out? At many junior colleges these experiences start even before classes do, in the form of testing and counseling. Thus, after an enrollment examination in English and mathematics, our would-be engineer may find himself in remedial classes, which delay his eventual transfer to a four-year college and, more importantly, shake his self-image as a future engineer. At a required advising session, a counselor looks over his "counseling folder," which contains transcripts from other schools, test scores, recommendations from teachers and so on. Although his file is thin, the counselor observes that high school grades and test scores such as these usually suggest a less ambitious program—"but of course you are free to go ahead and try the pre-engineering program if you want—just remember that we have a lot of really good vocational programs here, too."

The student will face this folder again and again as the months go by and as grades and "need for improvement" notices from instructors accumulate. The file of impersonal, objective-looking data shadows him and, when it grows sufficiently strong, will stalk him. The counselors, skilled in handling the "over-ambitious" student, use the growing file to justify becoming more persistent with their advice. Advice given at previous counseling sessions is in the student's folder and is now cited impersonally as part of the accumulating "evidence." The counselors edge the student toward a vocational program, but they never countermand his choices, for the whole point of the protracted exercise is to avoid a personal, hard "No," and to have the student make the "correct" choice on his own.

Finally, the student is put on academic probation for receiving below-average grades and must now submit to more than the usual amount of counseling. Students are allowed to stay on probation for a number of semesters or indefinitely, depending on the school, so probation does not force many students out of junior college. Rather, it is designed to get the student to think about himself and admit to his thinking the possibility of reclassifying himself as a terminal student. Reclassification would allow him to receive the college's two-year degree, Associate in Arts, by putting him in classes in which he would get grades high enough to bring his average up to the required level.

He relents, at last, and reclassifies himself, marking a big change in his life. The college expedites changes of this sort by making them appear as small as possible: Our student will be an "engineering aide" instead of an "engineer." There is a world of difference, of course, but on the surface things appear pretty much the same: He continues as a student (at least for the time being) and tells family and friends that he has decided to "start out" as an engineering aide.

The junior college's cooling-out work, like all cooling-out work, is *necessarily* hidden. When it isn't hidden, there is no cooling out. In fact, when attempts to cool people out become apparent, they backfire badly: Seen as attempts at manipulation, they provoke anger and heat things up. The junior colleges, in spite of their actual function, are widely thought of as transfer stations for students on their way to bachelor's degrees. If these institutions were to get a reputation among high school students and their families as dead-end side tracks for losers in the paper chase, many students would refuse to go to them. The pyramidal system, which uses formal education to allocate scarce opportunity, would have to find some other way of cooling out the "excessive" number of students who want bachelor's degrees. The four-year institutions themselves, with their dropout rate already at 50%, would be reluctant to help by increasing their share of the cooling-out action.

Many students who do get bachelor's degrees want to work toward a professional credential, such as a law degree, medical degree or PhD. As we have seen, the criteria that determine who is permitted to do this include attitude, and in particular favor individuals who have the kind of uncritical attitude, or narrow focus, that makes them easy to direct. But it is not enough for the qualification system to give the best positions to those who will do the best job from the point of view of employers. It must also cool out the high educational and career expectations of those who are excluded, including those who would do the best job from other points of view, such as that of clients and the public. Professional qualifying examinations help to do both: Not only do they help identify those who would serve employers best, but they also help cool out the "failures."

Failures are not a waste product of the educational system, but are carefully "produced." At every level of the paper chase, those who don't get credentials are comparable in number to those who do,[9] and so the losers cannot simply be given the brush-off. The system must shut them out without turning them into enemies, because they are to become a large part of the workforce. To get them to work hard, if not enthusiastically, on jobs with lower-than-hoped-for social status (and to get them to do so without having to give them more control over the content of the work and over the workplace), the system must make sure that those weeded out feel they have been treated fairly. Those who fail, just like those who pass, must feel well matched to their station in the social hierarchy of production, and an impersonal, objective-looking examination is a very persuasive matchmaker.

A good example of such a matchmaker is the big qualifying examination that sends graduate students either on to the PhD or out of graduate school. Although the rest of this chapter focuses exclusively on this faculty-written professional qualifying examination, most of the discussion applies to qualifying examinations in general, including standardized preprofessional qualifying tests, such as the SAT and ACT, and standardized professional qualifying tests, such as the LSAT, MCAT and GRE.

The examination's cooling-out power, like the cooling-out power of the voice in the crowd and the material in the counseling folder, comes from its nonpartisan image. The fact that the exam strongly favors particular values and attitudes must, like the affiliation of the shill and the socioeconomic goals of the junior college, remain hidden. The nature of the test must appear to be dictated purely by the subject itself, and not at all by consideration of the kind of obedience that employers want in a specialist. Students faced with dismissal will seize upon any point in the evaluation system that they find unfair. Clearly, the qualification system would not work very well if students saw the exam in part as a probe of their attitudes and values. If students perceived the political element, the test would be no more persuasive than a faculty member saying "We don't like you." Accusations of bias would certainly follow, making a public issue of the system's notion of what kind of person makes the best professional, and forcing the educational institution to debate its notion openly—and in the process to reveal not only its politics, but also, and more importantly, the very fact that it *has* politics. As it is, students generally do not perceive the political element and therefore are led to confront themselves instead of the institution. The exam's squeaky-clean image makes the crucial difference between the messy kicking out and the peaceful cooling out of those not wanted by the system.

The test's nonpartisan look transforms it from a tool of the institution into an independent third party, allowing the institution to maintain a purely positive image: The institution is set up to produce successes; it is the test that forces denial. ("Modern personnel record-keeping, in general, has the function of documenting [for] denial," notes Clark.[10]) When faculty members judge a student negatively and crush the student's hopes of becoming a professional in the field, they use the test to distance themselves emotionally from what they are doing and to avoid feeling personally responsible for their decision. Yes, the faculty members write the test, administer it, score it and report the results, but in doing each of these things, they see themselves as clerical workers, not as judges. It is the nonpartisan third party that judges the student. Faculty members are generally sympathetic, but detached, as the neutral third party snuffs out the student's aspirations in a clean, mechanical, businesslike way.

Qualification systems almost always allow for repeated attempts at success—and repeated occasion for failure. The student has the right to retake the qualifying examination even when the faculty doesn't encourage the student to do so. This right to try again is always presented in terms of the opportunity it provides, not in terms of its main purpose, which is to let down the hopes of the unwanted slowly, rather than in one abrupt, alienating, and potentially explosive step. When students are failed for the first time, they begin to admit thoughts of revising their goals. By the time the exam comes around again, they are more prepared to accept its judgment of their ability to learn the tricks of the trade. The faculty is more persuasive this time, now that it is backed up by another piece of "objective evidence." The facts get increasingly hard for the student to explain away.

Students whose attitudes and values clash with those of the faculty are obviously at a disadvantage when the faculty meets after the examination and considers "the whole student." But they are also at a disadvantage on the examination itself. These students come away from the test feeling frustrated. They feel that the test didn't give them an opportunity to show much of what they could do in the subject but instead focused on a narrow range of skills. The test's focus within the subject, of course, is dictated not by the subject itself, but by the faculty's attitudes and values, and so these lie at the heart of the student's frustration with the test.

However, most students who feel that the exam is underestimating them never manage to get to the heart of the problem. They grope for an understanding of why they failed but end up offering explanations that they themselves don't find satisfactory—I didn't do my best work, the questions were unusually difficult, I ran out of time, I wasn't feeling well. Such explanations, which are the best that students can come up with when they don't question the neutrality of the test, do have a bit of credibility after the first test. You won't hear them after the second test, though.

Even when students do figure out that attitudes and values play a key role in qualification, and even when they also feel that their own conflict of outlook with the faculty has tipped the balance against them, they hesitate to protest. There are two reasons for their timidity. First, they have no way to prove that the conflict of outlook has made any difference. Second, trying to get ready for the all-encompassing examination has left them in a state of very low self-confidence. Because the test knows no bounds, the more students study for it, the more they discover they don't know. Students go into the marathon examination feeling unsure of themselves and come out of it ready to believe just about anything the faculty tells them about how well they did. The student who is failed, of course, suffers an even further reduction in self-confidence. "Maybe I'm really not good enough," thinks the student. "Maybe the faculty is right and I'm just making excuses." In the end, even the most perceptive students may be unable to speak out.

Students who are willing and able to conform to the faculty's attitudes and values, which usually favor the status quo over social change, are less likely than others to get cooled out of professional training. They are also less likely to go on to challenge the field's role in the status quo—or the status quo in the field. Among those who do get cooled out, individuals who would be uncompromising advocates for clients and the public—but a lot of trouble for employers—are overrepresented. This cleansing of the ranks is a great loss not only to the individuals involved, but to society as well. Indeed, the biggest losers in the game of professional qualification are not those shut out of professional careers, but working people in general, who are deprived of the allies they would have in the professional ranks if the politics of professional qualification were different.

NOTES

1. Pick up a card lengthwise between your thumb and fingers. With the same hand, pick up a second card in the same way, so that you are now holding two cards, one atop the other. Move your hand as if you are gently throwing the second card back onto the table, but let the first card slide off instead. Shaving the first card makes it easier. The illusion is almost powerful enough to fool the person performing it. The mark's consolation prize—a free chance to win $20—is worth only a few dollars because of the power of the sleight of hand.

2. Erving Goffman, "On Cooling the Mark Out," *Psychiatry*, vol. 15, no. 4 (November 1952), pp. 451–463.

3. Burton R. Clark, "The 'Cooling-Out' Function in Higher Education," *American Journal of Sociology*, vol. 65 (1960), pp. 569–576.

4. In 1997, 2.8 million youths graduated from high school and half a million dropped out. Of the graduates, 1.2 million enrolled in four-year colleges; 630,000 in two-year colleges. See "College enrollment and work activity of 1997 high school graduates," news release USDL 98-171, U.S. Bureau of Labor Statistics, Washington, D.C. (1 May 1998).

5. Telephone conversation with George Prather, research analyst, Office of Research, Planning and Analysis, Los Angeles Community College District, 14 September 1990.

6. Laura I. Rendón, "Eyes on the Prize: Students of Color and the Bachelor's Degree," *Community College Review*, vol. 21, no. 2 (Fall 1993), pp. 3–13, especially p. 8.

7. Arthur M. Cohen, "Analyzing Community College Student Transfer Rates," U.S. Department of Education, Educational Resources Information Center, ERIC ED354940 (14 April 1993), p. 2 (ERIC p. 4). Even students who have some success tend to get cooled out. A nationwide study found that only half of the students who enter community colleges with no prior college experience manage to complete at least 12 degree-credit units within four years. Of that somewhat successful half, only 1 in 4 transfers by the end of a four-year monitoring period. See Arthur M. Cohen, "Orderly Thinking about a Chaotic System," U.S. Department of Education, Educational Resources Information Center, ERIC ED382248 (February 1995), pp. 8–9 (ERIC pp. 10–11).

8. *Student Profiles, 1998*, report number 98-4, California Postsecondary Education Commission, Sacramento, Calif. (December 1998), secs. 2-2 and 6-3 (updates of September 1998).

9. This is true (or an understatement) at two-year colleges, four-year colleges, graduate schools and, if you use applicants as the baseline, professional schools. Although the credentialing rate is higher back at the secondary school level, a significant number of students—one in seven—leaves high school without a diploma.

10. See note 3.

SUBORDINATION

"The (expletive deleted) computers." When an interviewer asked young nuclear weapons designers at Lawrence Livermore National Laboratory to name the worst thing about their profession, this gripe about uncooperative computers was a typical answer.[1] The goddamn computers. They don't have enough capacity and they're always going down. What's a designer of weapons of mass destruction to do?

The physicists' startlingly narrow answers were not the result of any pressure to respond quickly, without giving careful consideration to the question—the interviewer reports that nearly all of them did think for a while before answering. Rather, a narrow focus comes naturally to such individuals, who, as good products of the system of professional training, give higher priority to carrying out their assignments than to questioning them, and in any case are not prepared to second-guess the political and ideological framework that engenders and guides their technical work. In the final analysis, the physicists' narrow answers are a sad sign of their subordination, of their approval of a work life that will ultimately give them insufficient satisfaction: a work life in which their employers define the big picture and they innovate safely within it, and in which attempting to alter the picture is not a legitimate on-the-job activity.

If an individual professional did have an independent political agenda, it would undermine the ideological discipline and assignable curiosity that ensure that he works in his employer's interest. This is why the system of professional training, and the examination that stands at the center of that system, favors the individual who sees himself as having a technical orientation rather than a political one. Of course, the technical is itself political—the technically best solution to a given problem is often one thing from the point of view of those with an interest in maintaining the hierarchy but something quite different from the point of view of those without power. However, the favored individual sees no class interest in his own work: Because he *internalizes* the requisite ideology, he doesn't see himself as following an ideology at all, but as simply doing what he judges to be technically best. The politics usually enter his work not through conscious plotting or calculation, but automatically, when he does what "feels right." The result is an ironic situation in which this very political worker sees "politics" as a dirty word, a word that means not doing what is technically best.

Having long ago purged himself of his own political agenda, and having internalized the dominant ideology, the expert sees the problems of the world as fundamentally technical in nature (although certainly exacerbated by politics, but not the other way around). As a 28-year-old Livermore physicist working on third-generation nuclear weapons (which aim to knock out attacking nuclear weapons) said about the buildup of nuclear arsenals, "Why not find technical solutions to a technical problem?"[2] Whatever the issue, the rebel and the expert stand out in sharp distinction to each other. In any discussion, the expert's lack of political independence—his loyalty—becomes apparent immediately, as he confines his thinking to technical solutions—making adjustments, fine-tuning the system. He may offer a multitude of ways to deal with a problem, but, as if by magic, not a single one would reduce the flow of profits or otherwise disturb the hierarchical distribution of power.

PROFESSIONALISM

Professionalism—in particular the notion that experts should confine themselves to their "legitimate professional concerns" and not "politicize" their work—helps keep individual professionals in line by encouraging them to view their narrow technical orientation as a virtue, a sign of objectivity rather than of subordination. This doesn't mean that experts are forbidden to let independent political thoughts cross their minds. They can do so as citizens, of course, and they can even do so as experts, but then only in the "proper" places and in the "proper" way. The expert is probably a member of a professional association that has a "committee on social implications" or a "forum on the profession and society." Such a group may take up a political issue, but only after it takes a debilitating bow to power, usually in the form of a protracted debate in which those who want to take up the issue must succeed in repackaging it as a "legitimate professional concern," often as a technical issue. Members of the group can then take a position on the sanitized issue without "being political" in the sense of acting like they don't know their place. Politically timid professionals fear that their organization will look like part of a social movement, and so they try to limit their organization's actions to those of a narrow special-interest group.

As part of their very identity, professionals subordinate themselves to power on ideological matters. Thus, professionals can't take a stand on an unsanitized issue without going through a genuine identity crisis. Indeed, they respond with

"I wish you'd learn to spend your time more destructively!"

Frank Cotham

great fear and trembling whenever anyone proposes that they take such a stand. Even on life-or-death issues, professional associations can rarely muster the courage to take a position that they think might displease employers. Professionals don't want anyone to think that their own views might affect their work, because that would be insubordinate and therefore unprofessional. So even off the job (in professional associations and elsewhere), independence of thought feels out of line. As a result, the typical professional doesn't stand for anything.

Thus, for example, it was sad but not surprising when the National Lesbian and Gay Journalists Association decided not to participate in the massive 25 April 1993 gay rights march on Washington, an event that drew several hundred thousand people, making it one of the largest civil rights demonstrations in American history. Leroy Aarons, the group's president, explained that members didn't want to endanger their "credibility in the industry."[3] As good little professionals they adjust their very identity for their employers: Both on and off the job they act like journalists who happen to be gay, not like gays who happen to work as journalists.

Consider the behavior of the National Association of Black Journalists in the case of Mumia Abu-Jamal, a well-known journalist convicted of killing a Philadelphia police officer. A passionate voice for the black community, Abu-Jamal had worked as a radio and print journalist, doing news reports and commentary for a number of radio stations and networks, including National Public Radio, which aired his pieces on *All Things Considered*. The incident that landed Abu-Jamal in prison occurred in 1981, while he was president of the Philadelphia chapter of the National Association of Black Journalists. Late one night Abu-Jamal happened upon the scene where a police officer had stopped Abu-Jamal's brother for a traffic violation. In the events that followed, the officer shot Abu-Jamal and was fatally shot himself. There is no agreement about who fired first or who shot the officer. Many people felt that Abu-Jamal, a radical and longtime activist with no criminal record, did not receive a fair trial.[4] But years of appeals through the courts were fruitless, and on 1 June 1995 the governor of Pennsylvania ordered prison officials to kill Abu-Jamal by lethal injection at 10 p.m. on 17 August 1995.

This touched off a worldwide outcry involving hundreds of thousands of people. Demonstrations, rallies, teach-ins, celebrity speak-outs, op-ed articles, and letter-writing and petition campaigns—100,000 signers in Rome alone—demanded that Abu-Jamal at least be granted a new trial. Scores of organizations—from Amnesty International and Human Rights Watch to the NAACP Legal Defense and Education Fund and the Southern Christian Leadership Conference—supported this demand and opposed Abu-Jamal's impending execution.

But not the National Association of Black Journalists. In a written statement following a vote by the group's 18-member board of directors, NABJ president Dorothy Butler Gilliam said: "As an organization of journalists, [NABJ] does not see this unfortunate circumstance as an issue of journalism upon which it feels compelled to take a stand at this time."[5] In spite of Gilliam's attempt to make her position sound more reasonable by calling NABJ "an organization of journalists" rather than an organization of blacks, the group's stand infuriated many people, especially in the black community. One critic spoke for them all when he attributed the group's decision to its domination by members "attuned to the subtle grunts and imagined nods of their employers in the corporate media."[6] In response to the barrage of criticism that it received, the NABJ latched onto and took an extra-strong stand on a sanitized issue: restrictions that prison officials had put on Abu-Jamal's communication with the outside world after he contracted to write *Live From Death Row* (Addison-Wesley, 1995), a book sharply critical of the justice and prison system. Thus the NABJ was "outraged" not because the state planned to kill Abu-Jamal, but because it was violating his First Amendment rights, "which we find to be a legitimate issue," the group explained.[7]

The judge in charge of Abu-Jamal's case was a tough, cop-on-the-bench type who had sentenced 32 people to death—more than twice as many as any other judge in the country. He had never before granted a stay of execution and was, in the words of the *New York Times*, "openly contemptuous" of Abu-Jamal.[8] Yet, ten days before the planned execution, he succumbed to the growing popular pressure and granted Abu-Jamal an indefinite stay, allowing Abu-Jamal's lawyers to appeal once again to higher courts for a new trial.[9]

Generally speaking, the greater the power, whether corporate or state or even oppositional, the more eager professionals are to subordinate themselves to it. The power's morality or immorality usually has only a secondary effect on the professional's eagerness to serve, because good subordinates don't make moral judgments about their superiors. This is the unfortunate but invaluable lesson of history. Historian Konrad Jarausch notes, for example, that "in the spring of 1933, most German professionals rushed to curry favor with the new Nazi government." The prestigious German engineering association, the prominent lawyers association, the secondary teachers association and hundreds of other groups all across Germany pledged their loyalty.[10] The behavior of people in my own field, physics, has been far from exemplary. Before and during World War II, the world's top physicists were German, and these individuals typically accepted invitations to work in support of the Nazi war effort. Two decades later, during the Vietnam War, the world's top physicists were American, and these individuals typically jumped at the invitation to become members of the Defense Department's Jason organization and work in support of the U.S. side in Vietnam. (Jason is still active.)

At the workplace, experts can be somewhat independent in informal discussions, but almost never within their professional work itself; it is considered "unprofessional" for experts to bring independent political thinking to bear in their work. On the job, their "legitimate professional concerns" are largely confined to carrying out their assignments. Thus, while some of the nuclear weapons designers mentioned at the beginning of this chapter worried about computer troubles, others—also well trained in confining themselves to their "legitimate professional concerns"—worried that international agreements might further restrict testing and thereby make it more difficult for them to carry out their assignment of weapons design.[11] They did not allow the notion that such restrictions on nuclear testing might actually represent social progress to interfere with their work.

This view of what is legitimate holds hegemony over professionals in every major area of their employment. It is extreme in some cases, such as the aerospace industry, employer of thousands of scientists; the very notion of an aerospace scientist bringing a critical social perspective to his work is so unusual as to be jarring. The social function of the individual produced by the qualification system is to work uncritically within the political hierarchy, bolstering it through his example of eager participation as well as through his actual work product. When the professional leaves unchallenged the moral authority of his employer to dictate the political content of his work, he surrenders his social existence, his control over the mark he makes on the world.

These days one finds students and professionals who have some awareness of the big picture but who *cynically* adjust their behavior for the system. This is quite acceptable to the hierarchy because these individuals, even as they blast distant power figures such as the president, carefully avoid any confrontation with those who hold immediate power over them. As Max Horkheimer said in 1946, in what may be taken as one of the most succinct criticisms of many professionals on today's postmodern scene, "Well-informed cynicism is only another mode of conformity."[12]

However, more than professionalism or cynicism, it is lack of social vision that assures conformity, and professional training does anything but produce people who envision a more democratic social order. Professionals may complain to you about the unfair treatment that they witness firsthand at work, and they may tell you in excruciating detail about the latest cases of corruption in business and government, just as they read it in the newspaper. But most of them are unable to move from concern to action. Professionals are angry about such abuses of power, but having no vision of how power in the schools, in the workplace and in the larger society could be distributed more democratically, they naturally look for ways to make the present hierarchical power structures work. Here the choices are limited—restaff the hierarchy with "better people" or give those at the top even more power so they can "act decisively." So even the most well-meaning individuals end up reinventing some such elitist or authoritarian solution.

Group action by the rank and file is disobedient and antithetical to making hierarchical authority structures work, so many professionals who are well-informed and concerned about abuses of power will nevertheless not engage in collective acts of solidarity with the victims. They don't seek solidarity even when they themselves are the victims, and it is not unusual to see them leave their jobs rather than speak out openly and improve the situation through collective action. For the same reason, they will not identify with a specific movement or work with organizations that have independent social agendas.

Those who have no vision of greater democracy are paralyzed even further by the individualism inherent in their outlook. They retreat in fear at the mere suggestion of joining with others in struggle, for those who act as part of a group admit to being less than autonomous individuals and give up the comforting fiction that they meet their bosses as equals.

CONFLICTS WITH EMPLOYERS

The professional, like any employee, does have conflicts with his employer, but because he is an intellectual employee, he is not free to arrive at just any understanding of the root cause of these on-the-job disputes. Specifically, under normal circumstances he cannot allow himself to view his problems with his employer as an outgrowth of a fundamental conflict of interest, for to do so would sabotage the ideological discipline that allows him to serve his employer's interest in his work and keep his job as a professional. Thus, the professional sees his clashes as originating in conflicting technical judgments over how best to pursue universal interests. He sees conflicting strategies or personalities but doesn't see himself as having a fundamental conflict of interest with his employer—or with the powerful in society in general. That is, he doesn't see his own conflict with his employer as part of a larger conflict between labor and capital. When those who wield power act against his and his fellow employees' interests, the professional does not see them as opponents acting against employee interests, but as incompetents acting against universal interests. Thus, he calls not for breaking down the hierarchy and distributing the power democratically to those who do the work, but for more "intelligence" at the top—an elitist approach, which weakens alliances with nonprofessionals. He challenges the staffing, not the structure. He fumes, "Incompetents! Stupid bureaucrats! Those idiots don't know what they're doing!" In the eyes of the professional, those with authority at worst lack intelligence or information; he dare not admit to himself that those he serves may be smart and well-informed but simply have different class interests—that is, he cannot risk admitting to himself that he has been hired to serve interests that conflict with his own.

This restricted understanding renders the professional weak as a force for his own defense and impotent as a force for change in society. His protestations are impotent because, no matter how militantly stated, they are not threats to break ideological discipline. They don't threaten to affect the political content of his work, as having an independent political agenda certainly would. Even his strongest indictment of decisions made by management—"It's all political!"—suggests a mythical nonpolitical approach rather than an alternative distribution of political power. The louder he shouts his carefully restricted criticisms, the more he proclaims his subordination.

No professional maintains perfect ideological discipline, and every straying leads to a run-in with management. Of course, some professionals have more clashes than others. In particular, those who are the least strict about subordinating their own vision to that of the institution that employs them are the ones who find themselves in trouble most often. But these conflict-plagued employees rarely understand that their poor ideological discipline is the source of their clashes. They avoid such an understanding because it is inherently radical: It exposes their employer's ideology and is critical of it.

To avoid taking such a radical step, professionals come up with other, often far-fetched, explanations of their conflicts with management, as the following discussion of two common types of workplace conflicts suggests. Let's look first at conflicts over employees' demands for excellence and then at conflicts over employers' demands for conformity.

Employers reward mediocrity and punish excellence—at least that's what many disillusioned professionals have concluded. In reality, of course, management has no such operating principle. Yet countless professionals have found that when they take initiative on the job and work with dedication to further the ends they thought they were hired to further, they get criticism from the boss, or they are treated as some sort of threat. Meanwhile, they see that coworkers with take-the-money-and-run attitudes are hassled less.

When devoted professionals complain that they are given grief for doing outstanding work, you usually find that they have decided for themselves which aspects of their jobs deserve the highest priority and the most attention. This assertion of their own agenda, not the excellence with which they pursue it, is what gets them into trouble. The chance to work toward their own goals renews their enthusiasm and inspires them to do what they feel is unusually excellent work. Coworkers typically agree, as do clients, but management is unhappy. Professionals bewildered by their bosses' negative reaction to their special efforts, but unable to recognize the difference between their agenda and their employer's, conclude that the problem is that management is too stupid to recognize quality work. What is really a conflict over goals appears to these professionals to be a dispute over excellence. Other professionals escape such disputes; these are the individuals whose goals match those of the institutions that employ them or who are willing and able to subordinate their own goals.

Institutions demand conformity and obedience and yet hire professionals to do work that requires creativity and questioning. Does this make employer–employee conflict inevitable? Liberals say yes. They enjoy believing that intellectuals are unbridled thinkers and therefore a threat to those in power. (This is a corollary of their elitist belief that nonintellectual workers support the status quo.) But I would argue that institutional demands for political conformity lead to conflict only when individual creative workers have independent political agendas and are not willing to subordinate them. For if professionals adopt their employers' agendas, then their creativity and questioning work toward meeting their employers' goals. The work product in that case is essentially the same as it would be had the employers done the creative work themselves.

The sad fact is, mainstream professionals don't need political freedom to do their creative work. And they don't demand that their employers allow them to exercise political freedom in their work. Only when professionals have an independent political agenda do they need and demand freedom, because only then might their creative work displease their employers.

Scientists are a good example. During Josef Stalin's reign of terror in the Soviet Union, tens of thousands of scientists and engineers were arrested, imprisoned and sometimes executed. Yet Soviet science advanced rapidly and came to lead the world in many fields, including mathematics and theoretical physics. Until the mid-1950s, some of the Soviet Union's most eminent scientists worked in prison laboratories. At the height of the repression, Soviet physicists did work that won them five Nobel prizes. One of those physicists, a Soviet citizen named Pyotr Kapitsa, had been living in England for thirteen years when, upon a routine visit to the Soviet Union to attend a conference, Soviet authorities seized him on Stalin's orders and wouldn't let him return home to England. Within a few years of this kidnapping, Stalin had Kapitsa running a Soviet laboratory and doing the most creative work of his career.

As Loren R. Graham, a science historian at Harvard University and the Massachusetts Institute of Technology, has documented, scientists do not require academic freedom to do their creative work—they just need funding. One haunting image that Graham describes is that of the young scientist Andrei Sakharov sitting at his desk at Arzamas-16 doing his famous work in theoretical physics and gazing out the window at brutal armed guards marching rows of political prisoners to their jobs at the scientific installation, which was the Soviet equivalent of Los Alamos National Laboratory in the United States. Years later Sakharov became a dissident, but that was unusual for a scientist. As Graham notes, even when the Soviet Union was on the verge of collapse, the leaders of Soviet science sided with the old order.[13]

Those naive enough to believe that the professional's creative thinking alone leads to conflict with management probably also subscribe to the myth that the intellectual worker's "professional obligations" lead to conflict, too. No one illustrates better than the mainstream journalist that there is no tension between fulfilling a "professional obligation" or doing a "professional job" and institutional demands for conformity and obedience. The reporters who write front-page stories for the *New York Times* are considered to be among the top journalists in the profession. It is abundantly evident that the paper they work for requires that the stories be written within a framework of general support for the U.S. political and economic system (and that the stories anticipate and head off any possible faith-threatening interpretations of the facts being reported). *Times* reporters conform strictly to the paper's politics and at the same time feel that they are fulfilling their professional obligation to "get the story." There's rarely a serious complaint from either side.

Only when professionals have an independent political agenda do they argue with their bosses about what constitutes a "professional job." When *Times* editors assign one of their politically reliable, top-of-the-line journalists to cover a sensitive story, they don't worry that professional obligations will lead their reporter to frame the story in a way that skewers the paper's fundamental tenets. Thus, for example, most mainstream media in the end reported the Watergate affair not as evidence of the political system's tendency toward corruption, but as evidence that the system works and cleanses itself.

PREPROFESSIONALS

As we know, not all students become clones of the prototypical professional described above. But those who are headed in that direction are easy to spot, because their subordinate attitude is conspicuous early on at the training institution. These students scramble to figure out the rules of the game in their university graduate department or professional school, and then they literally compete to adjust themselves appropriately. Being not merely adjustable, but self-adjusting, they are good students in the eyes of the faculty. For the same reason, they will be good professionals in the eyes of their employers. These students do not simply refrain from acts of insubordination, such as challenging the training institution's agenda or criticizing the ways that agenda reflects the needs of the larger system. Rather, they enthusiastically embrace the system of professional qualification and defend the qualifying examination. The personal strategy of these skilled submissives is to play the game: to use the qualifying examination to demonstrate on the system's terms that they are "good" (that is, well-adapted), to be certified with a credential and to get a job with a new set of rules to submit to. In short, this means integrating themselves into the system, being dwarfed by it but surviving, if not as independent forces for change in society, then at least as well-fed biological entities serving the status quo.

These students also subordinate the dreams they once had of experiencing the totality of their subject in all its technical and social dimensions. In what can be seen as a sad attempt to imitate this forgone experience, some students treat the small problem parts assigned to them as if they were interesting enough in and of themselves to play the role of a surrogate totality. Today these assignments are the catechism-like test-preparation problems, tomorrow the narrow thesis problem and thereafter the corporate problem segment.

Many students do resist making the appropriate adjustments and heading down the designated road: Unwilling to reorient their outlook and goals, they find themselves in conflict with one or another action or policy of the training institution. These students usually struggle individually and indirectly, misunderstanding their problems in the training program as simply personal and not the inevitable result of the system-serving nature of the training institution's goals. Though they often leave the training program, they should not be looked upon as "losers," for they have not necessarily been broken and may go on to struggle elsewhere.

The system of professional training is set up to turn students into good self-adjusters or else get rid of them. Through the mechanisms of pressure and scrutiny that I have described in this book, it usually succeeds in doing one or the other. However, students can and sometimes do frustrate the system by both confronting it *and* remaining, but this is accomplished only through politically conscious, organized action, as I discuss in the next two chapters. At the core of the conflict is an unstated but highly contentious issue: Who will the student become? Professional training programs work routinely, methodically and often consciously to turn students into very different persons, and so individuals who want to control who they are must fight to do so.

NOTES

1. "Popping the 'Strangelove' Myth," *Newsline*, Lawrence Livermore National Laboratory, University of California, vol. 7, no. 5, September–October 1976, pp. 16–17. Parenthetical words in original.

2. "The Young Physicists: Atoms and Patriotism Amid the Coke Bottles," *New York Times*, 31 January 1984, pp. C1, C5; or William J. Broad, *Star Warriors*, Simon and Schuster, New York (1985), p. 47.

3. "For Some Gay Journalists, 'No Marching' Orders," *Washington Post*, 9 April 1993, p. D1.

4. For a thorough description of the facts of the Mumia Abu-Jamal case, and for what I consider to be the most honest judgment of those facts, see Stuart Taylor Jr., "Guilty *And* Framed," *American Lawyer*, December 1995, pp. 74–84.

5. News release of 27 June 1995, National Association of Black Journalists, Reston, Va.

6. Glen Ford, "The Final Betrayal of the NABJ," *Philadelphia New Observer*, 26 July 1995, pp. 11–12; this is an insightful, biting description of the NABJ's history. See also Wilbert A. Tatum, "Mumia Abu-Jamal and the death knell of Black journalists on white newspapers," *New York Amsterdam News*, 15 July 1995, p. 12.

7. News release of 12 July 1995, National Association of Black Journalists, Reston, Va. "Journalist group criticized for snub of Death Row inmate," *News Dimensions* (Washington, D.C.), 14 July 1995, pp. 2, 17. "Pending Execution of Former Radio Reporter Divides Organization of Black Journalists," *New York Times*, 17 July 1995, p. B6. For a chronology of NABJ actions in the Mumia Abu-Jamal case, see Tatsha Robertson, "Taking a stand," *Star Tribune* (Minneapolis), 28 August 1995, p. 6A.

8. "Black Journalist Granted Stay of Execution by the Judge Who Sentenced Him," *New York Times*, 8 August 1995, p. A10.

9. For reactions to the effectiveness of the pro–Abu-Jamal political campaign, see Hugh Pearson, "Is Jamal Guilty? What the Trial Record Says," *Wall Street Journal*, 23 August 1995, p. A13, and Doug Grow, "Graffiti thwart executioner, at least for the time being," *Star Tribune* (Minneapolis), 8 August 1995, p. 3B.

10. Konrad Hugo Jarausch, *The Unfree Professions: German lawyers, teachers, and engineers, 1900–1950*, Oxford University Press, New York (1990), p. 3.

11. At the time, the tests had already been confined to underground and limited in size. Further restrictions would have forced the bomb designers to put an even greater emphasis on computer modeling, a less reliable technique (now being pursued with vigor).

12. Max Horkheimer, *Eclipse of Reason*, Oxford University Press, New York (1947), p. 113.

13. Loren R. Graham, *What Have We Learned About Science and Technology from the Russian Experience?*, Stanford University Press, Stanford, Calif. (1998), pp. 55–57, 67–69, 91, 130.

PART THREE

RESISTANCE

14

RESISTING INDOCTRINATION

The professors were egotistical bastards who tried to impose their perspectives on others. In class, most of them didn't even pretend to want the students to have input. It was like, boom boom boom, these are the points, class is done after I'm done talking.[1]

—Former graduate student

I, as the instructor, would say, "Save your questions until the end of the last session of the course. Because if you have a question now, it will probably be answered in some later session." That's the first thing the group controlled—that you're not allowed to ask questions. And recruits would go, "Well, yeah, it's probably going to be answered better in the class."[2]

—Former cult indoctrinator

The strange idea that cult indoctrination might shed light on professional training emerged from my interviews with students. Many of their experiences in graduate and professional school sounded like what goes on in organizations that are accused of "brainwashing" their members into unthinking clones. Here I am referring to groups that demand total, and therefore unquestioning, commitment—which, of course, amounts to complete subordination. Such "totalist" organizations include military boot camp, gangs, some prison programs, and cults of all types—religious, New Age, human potential, self-help, self-awareness, psychology, therapy, health/nutrition, personality, political, commercial sales and so on. Most organizations in today's society, of course, are not totalist. Organizations ranging from corporations to mainstream unions are hierarchical and undemocratic, but they don't expect to control the totality of their employees' or members' lives. In other words, they are authoritarian, not totalitarian. But it is the totalitarian organizations that give insight into professional training, and so they are the focus of this chapter.

One might not expect organizations as different as the Unification Church and the U.S. Marine Corps[3] to have much in common, but rank-and-file Moonies and Marines are the same in one important way: They are not distracted by ideas of their own. In fact, all groups of the type listed above seek to produce such ideologically subordinate beings, who, of course, make obedient followers. When groups have ends that are the same in such an important way, we shouldn't be surprised to find that their means are the same in important ways, too. Indeed, according to the psychology and anticult literature, the same psychological themes dominate life in all groups that "brainwash" their members.

Professional training programs feature these same themes of obedience and subordination. In this chapter I describe the themes, which can be boiled down to a list of eight. Like a cult or other totalist organization, a given professional training program will feature most of these themes, but rarely all eight of them. The particular subset varies from one totalist organization to another and from one professional training program to another.

Each theme can manifest itself in a variety of ways, and I quote former students to illustrate at least one manifestation of each in professional training. Readers will surely be able to fill in other examples. (For examples in a totalist organization, see note 3, which describes U.S. Marine Corps basic training camp, a single organization that features all eight themes.) The themes operate simultaneously and complement one another—they constitute a system—and so readers will find evidence of more than one theme in each of the quotes below.

But am I claiming too much? Is the typical university program really as repressive and subordinating as a cult? My answer is yes, it is—but not for all students. Students in the same program experience different degrees of subordination. Some students live in fear and work like slaves, while others enjoy a taste of autonomy and set their own pace. Each student negotiates his or her own deal. The same negotiation goes on in cults. But students are in a stronger position than cult members to resist subordination—they can organize, for example—and so students end up with a greater variety of levels of subordination than do cult members. Thus, I do not argue that professional training is always the same as cult indoctrination. Rather, I argue that life in graduate or professional school *can* be very much like life in a cult—and that for students who aren't careful, it *will* be.

Of course, a few faculty members are exceptions to the rule and support students who resist the strong pressure to conform. Unfortunately, because professors themselves are a product of the selective system of weeding out and transformation that they now operate, faculty members who refuse to get with the program are few and far between. They can usually be identified by their participation with student activists in struggles against university authorities—and by their own tenure battles.

Just because professional training programs are structured like brainwashing schemes does not at all mean you should stay away from them, for you can defeat their subordinating features and achieve the opposite of the usual outcome. Graduate or professional school can be fun and fulfilling—or arduous and alienating—depending in part on how you handle it. For me it was the former; graduate school amounted to getting paid to pursue my own interests. I learned some more physics, taught undergraduates as a teaching assistant, did research, audited interesting classes outside the department, did a lot of work with other activists—basically, had a great and rewarding time. Yet for many other students in the very same program, graduate school was unrelentingly stressful; they emerged looking and acting like broken versions of their former selves.

Graduate or professional school can enlighten and empower you personally and boost your self-confidence and self-respect. But that is not its purpose, and so these things will not happen automatically. In fact, the process of readying you to play a subordinate role at work acts against such goals. However, students who understand the subordinating themes that pervade the training environment can resist subordination and make their professional training a transforming experience in the *positive* sense of the term. Thus my purpose in describing the features common to all brainwashing schemes is to help immunize students against them. Simple awareness of how indoctrination systems work is a big step toward undermining their effectiveness. As psychiatry professor Louis Jolyon West noted in a report about training Air Force flight crews to resist brainwashing as prisoners of war, "A realistic, undistorted, truthful account of what a man can expect constitutes a major protection for him."[4] Familiarity with the subordinating measures reduces unreasonable fears, opening the door to resistance.

BRAINWASHING AND RESISTANCE

"Brainwashing"—also known as "coercive persuasion," "thought reform," "mind control" and "menticide"—might jokingly be defined as activity that persuades people to adopt beliefs that you don't like. Indeed, people *are* more likely to label an activity "brainwashing" if they don't like the beliefs it advances. However, if one has a clear definition of the word, then one can both avoid name-calling when a process isn't brainwashing and confidently say "That's brainwashing" when it really is.

I use the word brainwashing to mean activity that pushes people toward unquestioning acceptance of any ideas and away from critical thinking (defined on page 41). Brainwashing, then, is the opposite of education, which is activity that develops a person's critical faculties. Why choose critical thinking as the litmus test for brainwashing? Because it is what makes a human being an individual. People are individuals biologically, of course, but they are individuals socially only if they maintain an independent perspective, and doing this is an ongoing creative process based on critical thinking.

And why is it so important that people be individuals? Because the thinking that people do when they create their own ideology—their own vision for society—is broader than the thinking involved in following a perspective that is given. The demands of this intellectual independence make individuals savvier thinkers and therefore the best able to take care of themselves, serve others and work for a better society. Because of their broader perspective, individuals make better personal decisions and take better advantage of whatever opportunities arise. And, ironically, true individuals are the only people strong enough to overcome individualism—the self-centered orientation encouraged by those who favor the status quo. They alone have the strength to place unity above self and to work effectively for the good of the community.

Only individuals—working together—can stand up to the forces of the status quo and make the world a better place. Any social movement populated by brainwashed followers is inherently weak and will eventually fail, for two reasons. First, the movement's leaders aren't always around, and dependent thinkers have difficulty taking initiative on their own. They can't seize opportunity, because they don't have the creativity to even recognize it. And even when their leaders show it to them, they can't do the creative thinking, innovation and on-the-spot decision-making necessary to make the most of it. Second, a movement of dependent thinkers is easily disabled; one need only take out the leaders, or, more typically, co-opt them, and the faithful will be neutralized en masse.

All groups that brainwash their members use the same basic process. They simultaneously break down the recruit's existing identity and rebuild the person as a follower. Any system working toward that end will have many of the eight features listed below. Robert Jay Lifton's classic study of brainwashing, *Thought Reform and the Psychology of Totalism*,[5] provided the basis for this list, to which I've added items one and seven. Learning to accept a totally subordinate role is the unifying theme of the eight features.

To illustrate a few of the many ways in which the features manifest themselves in professional training, I've included first-person accounts from former students. I deliberately selected four people who made it through professional training with their values mostly intact, and they describe some of the steps they took to accomplish that. Ian, Rod and Jon are sociologists, and Ted is a physicist, but the kinds of problems they faced occur in every field. (For their protection, I am not using their real names.) Examples of the eight subordinating themes, and of resistance to them, could come just as easily from professional training in law, psychology, history, medicine or any other field.

1. *Big promises.* People do not let organizations take charge of their lives and change their personal identity unless they are dissatisfied with who they are and desperate to do something about it. Totalist organizations offer a new and appealing identity: that of a self-actualized person doing work of supreme importance. Desire for the promised new identity motivates the recruit to go through

the difficult and abusive process of conversion. The new you will do big things, for yourself and for the world:

- Become a disciple of Jesus Christ and evangelize the entire world within this generation. (The International Churches of Christ, formerly the Boston Church of Christ)
- Foster economic and scientific progress, the republican form of government, and the inalienable right to life for all peoples. (The Lyndon LaRouche movement)
- Enrich your life with a higher understanding of truth—the Divine Principle—and find true love and lasting solutions to the social and national problems facing the world today. (The Unification Church)
- Clear your mind of the impediments that prevent you from realizing your true potential, and thereby help clear the world of war, pollution, mental illness, illiteracy, drugs and crime. (The Church of Scientology)
- Step beyond the limits of your identity—break through to new levels of performance and ability in every area of your life. (The Forum, formerly Erhard Seminars Training, or est)
- Be all you can be. Defend the nation. (The U.S. Army)
- Realize your true spiritual self beyond your body, and thereby free yourself from anxiety, attain a state of pure, unending, blissful consciousness, and help free our society from conflict. (The International Society for Krishna Consciousness—the Hare Krishnas)
- Be saved and come to know the truth by studying the word of God; keep evil at bay and hasten the return of Jesus Christ by moving God's word over the world. (The Way International)

Leaders of totalist organizations claim to be breaking with tradition. Indeed, their groups appear to be very different from the spiritless, missionless organizations that make the mainstream so unappealing. However, beneath its novel and innovative surface, the totalist organization is ultratraditional and ultraconservative, often to the point of being feudalistic. Typical features include an unelected leader whose decisions can't be appealed, exploitive practices that often amount to de facto servitude, a traditional repressive personal moral code (followed obsessively by members and violated grossly by leaders), and a military-style hierarchy of subleaders appointed from above.

Another way in which totalist organizations appeal to people is by offering an immediate benefit: community. Life in today's alienating and atomizing society leaves people searching for meaning and longing to belong. Many groups "love bomb" disconnected and lonely people, giving them a sense of belonging. This deceptive recruiting technique begins with disingenuous friendliness: a flirtatious style of talking, touching, hugging, kissing, flattery. Next come group activities in which doubt and critical thinking feel out of place: singing, chanting, recitation, prayer, rituals, games. Swept away, recruits find themselves with an instant family-like community that seems too good to be true. Indeed, it is a false community, and any member who tries to have a say in how it is run, or who stops giving money or free labor, is out. In an undemocratic organization the price of belonging is one's individuality.

Lack of solidarity is another sign that the community is artificial. When a dispute arises between a member and a leader, fellow members don't come forward with support. Nor do members band together to empower themselves within the organization. Rather, they compete to subordinate themselves to the leaders, angling to gain security that way.

As recruits get more and more attached to their new "family," the group's leaders gain an increasingly powerful tool for controlling their behavior: the threat of loss of community. Any threat of exclusion from the community terrifies the member with the prospect of personal annihilation, because the member now draws his or her identity and very sense of being exclusively from the group. Thus, shunning or shaming or humiliation is stronger than loss of privileges as sanction for deviance from group norms. Likewise, praise from group leaders becomes inordinately important to the member, and more effective than material payment as a reward for conformity. Peers cheer recruits on and praise them whenever they take a step toward total commitment.

I added "big promises" to Lifton's list to emphasize that people who submit themselves to mind-control organizations typically do so voluntarily. Contrary to the popular image of how brainwashing works, recruits take an active part in the process that leads to their conversion. Becoming a full member of the group is seen as a tremendous personal achievement and is marked by celebration. In his novel *One Flew Over the Cuckoo's Nest*, Ken Kesey draws attention to the common yet surprising phenomenon of voluntary submission to abusive systems of personal change. Recall that the story's main character, R. P. McMurphy, is incredulous when he discovers that almost all of his fellow inmates in the totalitarian psychiatric hospital are there by choice.[6]

Joining a totalist organization is a kind of self-institutionalization. It provides a refuge from a frightening world, time to gain strength, and the encouraging illusion of holding one's own in society. Of course, just because you join a totalist organization voluntarily doesn't mean the organization won't change you in ways you wouldn't have expected and wouldn't have wanted. Voluntary psychosurgery and shock treatment are apt analogies in this regard. At best, the organization's brainwashing, like hypnosis, will take you only as far as you were initially willing to go. But there are no guarantees. Submitting yourself to a totalist organization to cash in on its promise of a better life is risky business, because, ironically, the group will attempt to assault your identity, disempower you and make you less of an individual.

Ian went through the master's degree program in sociology at a large university in Ohio and went on to the PhD program in social work there. He told me about the promise and the reality of sociology graduate school:

> I was really excited when I entered graduate school. I was going to get a better theoretical understanding of the world—knowledge and research skills that could be

applied in social activism. U.S. foreign policy was one of my major concerns. As an undergrad I had been active in opposing U.S. support for the "Contras" in Nicaragua. But also, I saw a lot of domestic problems and was concerned about poverty and the polarization of the United States along economic lines.

Before I entered the sociology program, I talked to some of the professors and to the chair of the department. They gave me a message that was close to what I wanted. They said, We've got great resources here; we've got all these scholars with all these different perspectives; you can find your niche; and so on. The thing that really stood out in my mind was a brochure they sent me. When you opened it up, there was a picture of a student sitting underneath a tree with a professor, engaged in conversation. That's my first image of the department. I'm thinking, Oh, great, there's going to be this informal exchange of ideas. I had this image of professors, that they're wholly committed to knowledge and understanding and aren't that concerned about salaries and status. You know, "You speak the truth."

But once I got there, there was no pretense anymore. I recognized the student from the brochure, and he told me the picture had been staged. Professors didn't even pretend to do anything like Socrates sitting with students. They weren't open to different perspectives. It was, This is the way you do research, and any other way is improper. I felt an imposition from day one. They didn't talk about people; they talked about "respondents" to surveys. And they never once mentioned anything about community involvement.

What I saw was just a lot of careerism. Faculty members worked to pump out articles in accord with the canon so they could get them published in mainstream journals. They would talk about how you could turn one article into fifteen, and sneak them by. No one even *spoke* about working for social change. That was far from their minds. Many graduate students quickly left the program or adapted to the crass careerist perspective. I stayed but didn't adapt, and so I experienced a lot of conflict.

For example, I was in a statistics class and I raised a question about the philosophical basis behind t tests. It was simple stats, but I wanted to know the basis for the assumption that humans work the same way as the objects of study in the hard sciences. Basically the instructor said, "Well, I can't answer that. We're just here to learn the techniques."

About a week later, I was in the elevator and met the student who had won the student-of-the-year award. She had heard through the grapevine about my questioning and said to me straightforwardly, "People like you don't make it here." I said, "What do you mean, people like me?" She said, "Qualitative researchers who ask all these questions." Then she just stepped out of the elevator and walked off without waiting for my response. She is now a professor at some Big Ten school.

Incidents like that really made me see that students were lined up with different professors, trying to get their little assistantships and their research grants and so on. They weren't a unified front. They were the opposite of that. That bothered me. It wasn't like we were sitting together and saying, "Well, OK, they're full of shit, but we gotta get through, so let's cooperate to get through."

The department chair ran a proseminar class for first-year students. In our first meeting, the professor told us the "tricks" of the trade. He told us how to pad our vitae. He made comments like "Controversial work is hard to publish," and "Find projects that don't require much time." He sounded like a crass efficiency buffoon. Issues of quality were skirted through the entire quarter. Students would ask a lot of questions like, "So our whole goal is just to write articles for journals?" Basically, the response was, There are only five good journals in sociology. You want to publish in those. And you're right, that's all that your work in sociology is. Someone would ask, What about teaching? Or, What about community work? Well, you can throw that in, but that's not really what matters.

This was only the first quarter, and I'm getting all these messages, and I'm thinking I'm about ready to quit. But I didn't quit. I think one of the reasons was that I didn't see any alternative spaces where I could go. I had my whole identity with it. Without seeing anything better, I stuck it out.

While sticking it out, Ian did things that kept his values alive:

I don't know if I would have made it if I hadn't found like-minded friends in other departments. We had an informal group, where we would discuss ideas and readings in much greater depth than in class, and we would edit each other's papers. I could get help from them and there wasn't any catch in it. This group was very important to me.

In my own department, two other students and I organized the graduate students around a departmental issue, and this created an atmosphere of solidarity. Students were upset that not everyone got financial support. The teaching and research assistantships were given out by a mysterious A–B–C ranking of students. A-rank people automatically got funding. B was like maybe. C meant probably not. Several of the students, including me, started asking, What's the criteria? Finally, we got a meeting with the head of the graduate program. One of the 40 or so angry students at the meeting asked why the department had all this money for computers but not enough for students. The professor answered that the department couldn't do anything about that, because the money comes in in chunks designated for specific purposes.

I thought, let's look this up. And I did. And at our next meeting of graduate students I presented information indicating that he was lying. Everyone at the meeting was getting all pissed off. We were going, "Yeah, maybe we'll go on strike!" We were really working together. But then one of the students who was in the A group raised his hand and said, "I don't know if I can be a part of this organization anymore, because it sounds like we're going to have a tyranny of the majority." He was thinking that if we challenged the way funding was done, he was going to lose his. He got up and left, just walked out. But no one else did.

We decided that instead of going to the chair, we would go out and make this a public event. We organized an eight-hour rally with leaflets, petitions, signs and people with megaphones. Almost all of the participants were women. We pretended that what the department had told us was true, and said that undergraduate education was suffering because the state and university weren't providing enough money for teaching assistants. We used the sociology department only as an example. TV, radio, newspapers—they all came out. They talked to us and then went and talked to the sociology department. The chair was scared shitless. Mysteriously, a week later we found a memo in our mailboxes saying that everyone got funding.

It was great to work together, and we ended up creating a small ongoing coalition of students within the department.[7]

Ian's participation in the study group and student organization, both of which were independent of his university department, allowed him to experience some of the free intellectual development and fair treatment that the university promises but doesn't automatically deliver. His experience illustrates how a university graduate program, like any organization whose real priority is to get people to play a subordinate role, keeps its recruiting promises only to the extent that it is forced to do so.

2. *Milieu control.* Totalist organizations establish considerable control over their members' social environment and time. They undermine sources of social support outside the group, abridging members' contact with family, friends and anyone else who doesn't share the group's attitude. They may foster economic dependence on the group. In any case, they isolate members from the outside world and often encourage or require them to live or socialize only with other group members. Privacy, and the opportunity for reflection it provides, is reduced. Communication is highly controlled. The organization influences what its members see, hear, read and experience.

People in this managed milieu become detached from society. Socially isolated and lacking outside references, they lose their ability to make reality checks, judge circumstances independently and, therefore, maintain a unique identity. The group becomes their dominant source of reality, and they adopt behavior and beliefs that make sense within that reality.

The controlled environment, by design, produces a narrow, intense focus on work. Members put in long hours for little or no pay. By limiting the opportunity for critical thinking, the all-consuming activity facilitates indoctrination into the group's beliefs and rules of behavior. For example, recruits are typically expected to assimilate large amounts of the group's written material quickly, which precludes critical examination and therefore amounts to indoctrination. The group's exploitive demands have consequences that further limit the member's ability to contemplate the big picture and notice personal change: an exhausting schedule, sleep deprivation, often poor nutrition and eventually physical and psychological deterioration.

The group maintains a strong barrier between members and outsiders. Members-only meetings and rituals reinforce this. When talking with outsiders, members are often secretive or deliberately vague about what they believe and about what goes on inside the group. Members act this way not just to protect the group's deceptive recruiting practices, but also because they are not confident that they can make their beliefs and activities sound reasonable to outsiders. They look enthusiastically to charismatic group leaders to do that.

Members remain in their own world even when they interact with outsiders, as they must when selling or recruiting or engaging in normal everyday activity. An encounter with a member may at first seem to be a genuine two-way interaction. But the member has a hidden superior attitude and the single goal of advancing the group's doctrine, and so remains personally unaffected by the interaction.

Rod is a sociologist trained at Louisiana State University, in Baton Rouge. He told me how the structure of the PhD program there favored an uncritical approach:

> Reading assignments of 300 to 400 pages per week per seminar were normal, and frequently they went far beyond that. Add to this the weekly writing assignments, usually done under such a timeline that little critical thinking was possible. This structure ensured the hegemony of orthodoxy. I spent from 8 a.m. till 10 p.m. in the office and in seminars, then home or to the library to read and write until 2 or 3 a.m. Needless to say I drank a lot of coffee during this time. And the pressures took a big toll on my marriage.

Despite the pressure, Rod took action to stay in charge of his perspective:

> The development of informal grad student groups actually was one of the few areas in which discussion could go beyond the strict orthodoxy. I organized a reading group which included graduate students and young faculty members, who were more politically progressive than older faculty members. About ten of us would pick a book to read and then get together in someone's home for several nights of discussion and debate. This proved to be quite fruitful for those of us taking part in it. Unfortunately, the group became a point of contention with senior faculty members, who felt it was keeping some of the best students from working with them.[8]

The sheer workload of graduate school leads to social isolation and limits the opportunity to explore new lines of thought. However, members of Rod's reading group consciously appropriated some very scarce time, put it outside the control of the department and used it to think in unprescribed directions.

3. *Unquestioned authority.* The self-appointed leaders of totalist organizations claim they deserve special respect and authority for any of a number of reasons: They have achieved the highest level of enlightenment; they understand the governing principles of society, life or the cosmos; they have been chosen by God; they have the gift of prophecy; they have the greatest dedication to the cause; and so on. Members, in turn, trust that the seemingly mysterious dictates of the leaders come out of the leaders' deeper understanding of the world and further a higher purpose—the same purpose the members have signed on to further. Willing subjects of this "mystical manipulation" are reminiscent of children. And like children, they are vulnerable to abuse.

Totalist organizations are authoritarian because a total commitment precludes questioning. And without questioning, an organization can have no internal mechanism that limits its leaders' use or abuse of authority. Clearly, then, a totalist organization cannot be democratic. Members do not choose and cannot fire the leaders of the organization that directs their lives. Authority is centralized, orders work their way down from above, and leaders at no level tolerate dissent. Anyone whose dissent threatens to influence the thinking of other members is quickly removed from the group.

Leaders of totalist organizations treat their own power as more important than the group's mission, even though the mission is supposedly of overriding importance. Thus, they often squelch members who take initiative on their own and organize people to advance in some way the stated mission of the organization. The leaders would rather have total control of a group that does a poor job of fulfilling its all-important mission than be rank-and-file members of a democratic but more effective organization.

The people who run totalist organizations are personally intimidating figures, and frightening to challenge. Members try to anticipate their wishes and scurry to fulfill those wishes even before the leaders express them.

Jon is a sociologist who went through graduate school at a midwestern university. He told me about an incident that brought out how people felt about the faculty's authority:

One professor was a statistician who did a lot of research in spousal abuse. Unfortunately, I totally had problems with both his methodology and his conclusions. He concluded that, in essence, it's just as likely for the woman in a relationship to be abusive towards the male as it is for the male to be abusive towards the female. Which I have to say flies in the face of almost every other study on this issue. But he believed fervently that he could disprove them. He was almost zealot-like about it—you know, Don Quixote, on a mission from God, and all that.

Although I give him high marks for being concerned about his teaching and being conscientious, he was just as egotistical as the others. And he was just as arrogant about his approach. I mean, it wasn't just "This is a really cool way to go," but "This is THE—capital T, H, E—way to go. It's this or die."

Well, one evening some of the students put stickers on his picture. You know how departments will have on public display pictures of all the professors with their names and what kind of work they do. One sticker said "This is offensive to women," and another said "This is offensive to people of color." A friend of mine and I were up there studying, and we saw the stickers just after they were put on. We talked about taking them down, and I felt like, no, somebody really wants to make this statement. We've got to let it stay.

The professor took incredible offense. And boy, did it get ugly. I had no idea. I was probably naïve. There was talk like, "We know who did it. They must be thrown out of the department," when they had no clue who did it. That really conveyed, like, "How dare they defile the sacred temple." There was a real kind of almost theological overtone to the statements, how these people had "defiled," how they had impugned the character of this righteous man.

That was the reaction of most of the faculty—*and* the students who shared the mainstream orientation, which was most of the students. That orientation was toward quantitative methods. I was in the department's small program in studies of social conflict, which took a more qualitative approach to understanding. The general reaction to the incident was, "This must be a conflict student. We must purge ourselves." In fact, within a year of this incident the faculty had dismantled the conflict program.

Despite the repressive environment, Jon took steps that allowed him to maintain an independent point of view:

> One of the best things I did in graduate school was to organize a brown-bag lunch group that brought together about eight graduate students with similar interests. This was invaluable. We talked about what was going on in the department and in the world, organized a reading group, initiated seminars and helped bring speakers to campus. We complained about professors who had unreasonable expectations, professors who may have done things that we considered unethical and illegal. There is a great deal of exploitation of graduate student workers. We organized a couple of political actions inside and outside the department and wrote letters to campus and local newspapers about disputes inside the department and about campus-wide graduate student issues. The group was something that was positive about graduate school. We had to create that. It helped me to graduate in spite of many attempts by faculty to dissuade me out of getting a PhD.[9]

Professors can be personally intimidating figures that students fear to challenge. But as Jon discovered, creating an oppositional community changes that drastically, by shifting the balance of power.

4. *Guilt tripping and shaming.* The charismatic leaders who run totalist organizations are seen by members as superior human beings. This puts the leaders in a position to judge the members and make them feel guilty and ashamed for their morally tainted personal histories and current personal shortcomings. Members are expected to adopt the position that they are not good enough human beings.

The leaders spell out the model good person's behavior and use guilt and shame to push members in that direction. Thus, members feel that they are not living their lives in close enough accord with the official ideology; not studying that ideology hard enough or knowing it well enough; not working hard enough for the global, social or personal change that the group is dedicated to bringing about; not giving up the sins of their former lifestyle; not recruiting enough; not selling enough; not raising enough money; or in one way or another, not showing sufficient commitment to the group's vital work.

Guilt-ridden members hostilely denounce the outside influences that prevent them from getting with the program totally.

Ian, the student who went through the master's degree program in sociology at an Ohio university, told me about one professor's attempts to make him feel unworthy, and how he overcame them:

> The professor who ran my seminar class on political sociology had a pretty big name, and his head was even bigger. One day he was arguing that level of education was the best measure of social class. I said I thought occupation was better. We debated it back and forth politely for about five minutes. But then he started saying, "Have you read this book? Have you read that book?" Finally, he said, "Mr. [Surname], see me after class." His voice was fluctuating, and I was like, Oh my

God. So I met him in his office right after class, and he closes the door and says, "I've never had such an obstinate student in my whole life. I don't think you should be in sociology." I said, "I didn't mean to be obstinate, but, you know, there are different ways of doing things." He said, "No, you just do not have the right persona to be a sociologist." I got really quite upset. I felt like, what am I going to do, stand here and prove that I'm a good human being? Say "Yes, I really can act like a sociologist"? I didn't know what to do, so I left his office.

Later in that class, he assigned me a tricky research project. I knew it was a setup, but I took it and said to myself, I'm going to prove this motherfucker wrong. I'm going to go out there and write the best paper.

He gave me a B on it. He wrote that I showed good library research skills but didn't think out the premise. I took that to mean, you work hard but you can't think. I was so upset that I jumped on the bus and went out to the country, to get away from the university and the city. I was walking around and this cow came up, and I gave my paper to the cow. And the cow ate it. I took the staple out, and the cow ate the whole paper. I think a lot of us who have these problems do symbolic things to fight back. The cow ate the professor's comments as well. I was hoping it wouldn't kill her.

In spite of my anger, there was a lot of self-blame. I left Ohio and went back home, supposedly to write my master's thesis. My family treated me as if I were still a good human being, but I did nothing for six months. Then I got involved with [Persian] Gulf War protests and decided to do my thesis on that. There was this transformation where all of a sudden I got connected. I found an alternative community away from the university. They were street intellectuals—articulate people who really cared and knew much more about the world than all these highly formally educated folks. Integrating my community organizing with my research allowed me to write a thesis that I could be proud of. I did the interviews and drafted the thesis within four months. I took it back to Ohio and said, "You're gonna pass this. But in return, I won't apply for your PhD program." They read it and gave me the master's degree.

Later I entered the PhD program in social work and did my dissertation on another aspect of the antiwar protests.[10]

By connecting to an oppositional community (the street intellectuals), Ian gained a real and independent source of self-worth. This limited the university's ability to lower his opinion of himself.

5. *Total personal exposure.* Totalist organizations push their members to reveal everything possible about themselves—their personal relationships, activities, thoughts, likes, dislikes, personal goals and plans. The tacit understanding is that each member is property of the group. Within the totalist organization, having independent memory, emotion, imagination or aspiration is seen as selfish and highly immoral.[11] Personal activities or plans that don't give priority to the group are viewed with suspicion. The group dictates—sometimes in great detail—how members should think, act and feel. It may prescribe what type of clothes members wear. Group leaders make members' career and life decisions: whether to change jobs, get married, move to another city.

In the environment of total exposure, guilt leads obviously to confession, which is a major activity in totalist organizations. Members admit sins and imperfections and describe the latest situation in which they were held back by their failure to put sufficient trust in the group's leaders or doctrine. In general, the actions or thoughts they confess boil down to failures to subordinate themselves to the organization or its stated ideology. The confession is an implied pledge of future subordination, and as such puts the member back in the good graces of the group's leaders. Members sometimes exaggerate their failures or weaknesses, or even confess to sins they haven't committed, as a convenient way of reaffirming their subordination.

As recruits become more open with the group and begin to confess all to leaders, they become less open with outsiders, including family and friends. Because they can't fully share with outsiders the most important activity in their lives, and because they don't offer much in the way of individuality, members of totalist groups have difficulty forming emotionally intimate relationships with people outside the organization. Even a close relationship between two members is limited in depth, because every member's most intimate relationship is with the organization.

At meetings, the group focuses in turn on each member's "case." The upshot is that organizations that expect a total commitment are not only authoritarian, but also totalitarian, because they do expect to control the totality of the member's life.

Rod, the sociologist who went through graduate school at Louisiana State University, told me what some students did to limit the program's power over them:

There were graduate students who wouldn't say certain things about their personal lives around certain faculty. They had seen enough of the politics and things that went on that they were wary of letting people know anything, because it had the potential for political use.

A fellow graduate student and very good friend of mine was a single parent. Being a graduate student is tough enough. Being a single parent is tough enough. But combining the two is almost an impossible task. Things happened to her that were devastating in her personal life as she went through battles with her ex-husband. He showed up and took her son to visit with him for a couple of days in another state and then called her and said, "Sorry, you're never going to see him again." You can imagine the kind of crisis that that was for her, and it happened in the middle of a semester. But she didn't want me to mention this to faculty members. She said, "Let's keep this quiet." You know, "Don't let this be known. I don't need that."

Faculty might have said, "Her biggest priority is making sure that her son is taken care of," or "Being a good mother is not conducive to being a good scholar." I know that those kinds of things are said and are used against people in terms of getting tenure and everything else.

She did get her son back. And she did get her PhD. She was part of our reading group and part of a small informal support group.[12]

Rod's fellow student knew the difference between sharing personal information with her friends, which can lead to support and bonding, and revealing personal information to people who want to keep her in a subordinate position, which can give those people added power to do just that. Those who are more naive expect that sharing personal information with someone in charge will prompt that person to think on a "one-human-being-to-another" basis, putting aside his or her usual priority on furthering the organization's goals. That seldom happens.

6. *"Scientific" dogma.* You can't commit yourself totally to an organization if you have to look outside the group for help in understanding the world or finding your proper role in it. And you can't stay totally committed to a group unless you have a way to avoid genuinely grappling with facts and ideas that challenge the group's practices. Totalist organizations solve both of these problems by giving you a dogma capable of explaining everything.

Teachings that can make sense of everything call out not for improvement but for worship. Indeed, members of totalist organizations never question their group's basic doctrine, and therefore never push to improve it in any fundamental way. Yet the typical group boasts that its views are "scientific." "Sacred" would be a more accurate description. As Lifton notes, the totalist organization demands "reverence . . . for the originators of the Word, the present bearers of the Word, and the Word itself."[13]

The group's doctrine, being sacred rather than scientific, is not subject to falsification. That is, it is a higher authority than experience. And indeed, such primacy of doctrine over person is a characteristic of totalist organizations. Members deny the validity, truth and even reality of any experience that contradicts the doctrine—even their own personal experience. In this way the doctrine maintains the group's subordinating presence in the lives of its members even when the group's leaders are absent.

A single charismatic individual or a small core of leaders has complete control over the group's doctrine and can change it at will. If the group professes belief in an unchangeable set of writings such as the Bible, then the elite dictates the group's interpretation of those writings. This interpretation will differ from that of all other groups that profess to follow the same writings. The group is ultimately ruled by a few individuals, not by principles as its leaders claim.

The existence of the "sacred science" helps to keep members in their place and maintain the hierarchy of power within the group. The group treats its teachings as unfathomable and always yielding new truths—especially in the hands of the leaders. Members give a person respect and authority in proportion to the person's facility with the all-explaining doctrine. This empowers leaders in the lives of members and disempowers others. Nonmembers, for example, are seen as pitifully unenlightened. As a result, nonmembers find that nothing they say, no matter how sensible, influences a member's thinking or actions. That is, they find members to be closed minded. The group's leaders, on the other hand, automatically know the doctrine better than any member ever can, because what they say defines it. They are the only people more enlightened than the members, and so, conveniently, they are the only people able to influence a member's thinking or actions. Because the doctrine's range of application is unlimited, those who know it best have authority in all areas of life and presumably act out of the deepest understanding of the world. Hence, in totalist organizations members do not criticize leaders, no matter what the issue.

"Scientific" dogma always comes with a set of thought-terminating clichés, which help believers hide their closed-mindedness—mainly from themselves. Totalist organizations have their own language—an "in-group" lingo that allows members to describe the world in terms of the group's all-explaining "science," often by being prematurely abstract in their analysis. The thought-terminating cliché is one such premature abstraction. Thus, for example, "War is the work of Satan," ends the potentially revealing debate about the politics of a particular war. Describing or merely labeling something using this language counts as understanding it, ending any need for further consideration. Hence, new points of view or troublesome events do not provoke reflection but are quickly explained and dismissed. The jargon that expresses key concepts seems profoundly meaningful within the group, yet members cannot translate it into ordinary language to their own or anyone else's satisfaction. Being isolated from society, however, they are rarely called upon to do so.

Jon, the sociologist who got his PhD at a midwestern university, told me about the role of doctrine in the graduate program:

> The faculty saw the whole world through numbers. They were pretty rigid statistical methodologists. They felt that quantitative methods could explain just about everything. The way I saw it, these methods are just a tool in someone's arsenal. I had an interest beyond the numbers and sought to understand society through a variety of tools and theories, including history and qualitative ethnographic research, in which the "subjects" speak for themselves. But the faculty really did not think of the world in terms of anything other than social relationships that could be explained via statistics. If you had conversations with these people, even on a personal level, it invariably became: "What do the numbers show?" "What does the survey show?" "What does the polling information show?" "Is it statistically relevant?" It gets to be difficult to just have a sane conversation with an individual who thinks like that, because they don't turn it off.
>
> Within the faculty, people with a quantitative orientation carried more weight or had more prestige or more honor, what have you. They pretty much controlled the department. The chair, the graduate advisers, the people on the key committees, were all quants. Quants represent a large fraction of the field as a whole, too.
>
> The faculty had a notion that "We are going to turn you into professional sociologists." And what a professional sociologist is, is this quantitative person. The area that you look at may vary somewhat, but your methodology and your general orientation should be this. They had an ideologically rigid notion of what sociology is about. If you didn't do statistics, or if you didn't have a positivistic framework, then

in their minds you weren't a "real" sociologist. They had clear views on who was the superior person and student. They did everything they could to either encourage you to focus on stat methods or discourage you from getting your PhD.

Their best applicants were interested in theory, interested in social conflict, interested in social movements. So they would encourage these students with non-quantitative interests to come in. They believed they could turn these people around, show them the light, as it were. Indeed, I saw several people switch majors or switch focus to have an easier time and fewer problems in graduate school. I saw people leave conflict to go to criminology or demography or stat methods. There was a favored orientation, a clear doctrine.[14]

Jon identified, understood and critiqued the "scientific" dogma pushed by those in charge. By doing so, he pinpointed the origin of his conflicts with the powers that be and their followers. Had his conflicts bewildered him, it is unlikely that he would have survived the program.

Of course, not all departments within a field are the same, and so students have some leeway to select less ideologically rigid programs. However, exercising this choice often means attending a less prestigious institution, which can have serious negative consequences for a career in the field.

7. *Taking away true self-confidence.* You can't become totally committed to an organization that you don't totally trust. And you can't trust an organization totally if there are occasions when you feel confident that your judgment is better than that of the group's decision-makers, or that part of the group's doctrine is wrong. Hence your self-confidence stands in the way of total commitment. Totalist organizations work to remove this obstacle.

Leaders belittle members, usually by confronting them in areas where they feel insecure—in knowledge of the group's doctrine, for example, which one can never know deeply enough. Members end up with so little self-confidence that they trust the group—both its leaders and its doctrine—more than they trust themselves. As their time in the group increases, members become more and more confident when they are acting with the approval of group leaders or in accord with group doctrine, but less and less confident about taking initiative outside of that safe framework. They end up acting self-confident to the point of being arrogant or cocky—except where it matters most: in their dealings with the leaders of the group, the people who set their direction. Members check an increasing proportion of their life activities with group leaders. They become increasingly dependent upon the group, returning to a situation like that of the child under adult authority.

This lack of true self-confidence causes members to ignore anomalies that challenge the group's doctrine. Whenever a world event or personal experience appears to contradict the organization's dogma, those without the self-confidence necessary to listen to their own intuition, let alone stand up to the leaders of the group, will discount their observations and stick to the doctrine. Members of totalist organizations show little spontaneity, imagination, creativity or sense of humor, all of which grow out of self-confidence. Their lack of self-confidence also makes it difficult for them to leave the group.

Jon told me what he saw graduate school do to the self-confidence of his fellow students:

> Graduate school shook some. People felt like, Gee, should I really be here? Some people had their self-concept challenged and their self-confidence at least questioned, if not challenged.
>
> Students with the "right" orientation ultimately had their self-confidence boosted. However, at the same time that these students got higher status and honor than someone like myself, they also learned that it's not a good idea to challenge the department chair or a committee member or a professor in class. There's a certain kind of deference that they learned at [university name], a whole attitude of deference. It's probably a natural tendency among undergraduates that is reinforced in graduate school. I don't think they'd stand up to a big name. Whereas in a professional meeting I might say, "I don't care how many more books you've written than me, I still have a problem with what you're saying," they would defer more to that individual's authority, that individual's perspective.[15]

Jon saw the system give people confidence in proportion to their adoption of dominant values and their willingness to play a subordinate role. This confidence, of course, is not the true self-confidence that Jon had to develop to survive as an independent thinker.

8. *The only path to salvation.* Every totalist organization claims to be committed to one or another mission of supreme human importance. And each group views the work it is doing as the most important work being done by anyone, anywhere. Furthermore, the totalist organization believes that no one else grasps the principles that are the key to achieving the vital personal and social goals to which the group is committed. Hence, the individual, and indeed humanity as a whole, is doomed without the group and its insights.

Members therefore feel an enormous responsibility to spread the word and recruit, and to do so urgently. They feel that the group's mission is more important than their own lives, and so, with encouragement from their leaders, many work like slaves, even though that takes a physical and psychological toll. At the same time, they are arrogant and elitist toward outsiders.

From the perspective of the most extreme totalist organizations, those who reject the group's truth stand in the way of humanity's opportunity for true existence and thereby forfeit their own right to exist. This belief establishes a heavy atmosphere in the group. It justifies extreme measures, especially against those who leave the group. In the condemnatory atmosphere, insecure or guilt-ridden recruits are drawn to a conversion experience as a way of establishing their right to exist.

Leaving the group is seen as a sign of personal weakness that will have disastrous personal consequences, such as an end to personal growth, reappearance of prior personal problems, social failure, failure to get ahead economically or failure to survive looming big changes in the world.

Ted is a physicist who got his PhD at a university in the Southwest. He told me about the arrogant attitude of members of a research group there. The group specialized in the subfield of elementary-particle physics, or high-energy physics:

> Our department decided to start a high-energy-physics program, which would have a close connection with the SSC [the Superconducting Super Collider particle accelerator, which Congress later canceled]. They hired a fairly good high-energy guy, and later two more.
>
> One of the first things the head of the new high-energy group did was arrange a meeting with the grad students to introduce himself and his program. It was supposed to be a friendly get-to-know-each-other meeting, and I am sure he wanted to try to use it as a recruiting tool. At the meeting, the first thing he said was, "I am here to bring this department into the 20th century." Not the 21st, but the 20th!
>
> Wow, this ticked a lot of faculty off when they heard about it. We did not have a big department, but we did have people doing up-to-date research, including a good group of solid-state physicists. We had five or six laser jocks doing cutting-edge stuff—atomic and molecular, Raman and diamond anvil, picosecond spectroscopy, biophysics and more.
>
> But the HEP [high-energy physics] people respected no one but the other HEP people. They thought that HEP was where all the new physics was going to come from and that people in the other subfields were on a futile search. The way the HEP people talked to us definitely led us to believe that they felt superior.
>
> They took an arrogant approach to everything, from the curriculum to the PhD qualifying exam to tenure decisions, all of which they wanted to control. They always said, "Let us decide. We know what is best for the department." This is a direct quote.
>
> Whether they knew what they were talking about or not, the HEP people tried to stop almost every person who came up for tenure. One person they tried to stop was one of the best in a major subfield and brought in the most money to the department. Their thinking was, why give this person tenure when we could get someone better—say, an HEP person.
>
> Most of the new HEP people were junior in rank, yet they spoke their minds and told us how stupid we were. After insulting us, they asked us to help them support the SSC. They were almost in tears at times.
>
> And what was really funny, they did not have a clue as to how or why we were doing research in other fields. They always asked, What good is this? They knew nothing about anything other than high-energy physics. Sheltered lives.
>
> The problems in the department weren't limited to the HEP people. A lot of the faculty treated students unfairly and like children; they didn't respect us as human beings or as individuals. An extreme example was the abuse of Chinese students by Chinese faculty, who induced fear in their students and then made unethical demands on them. The department didn't stop even such extreme mistreatment.

Despite the subordinating atmosphere, Ted took action that allowed him to maintain his dignity:

> One day I said to myself, What the hell, I've worked outside of school, in the "real world," and so I'm not going to be treated like a child. The straw that broke the camel's back was a relatively minor issue involving the department's seminar, which was a weekly talk attended by faculty and students. Students liked the spirit of the seminar, which was learning because you wanted to learn, and we enjoyed hearing speakers from other institutions. This suddenly changed when an authoritarian faculty member became seminar coordinator and demanded that students write summaries of the talks. This did not go over well at all.
>
> So we, the students, decided to have a meeting of graduate students. We organized it and set a date. Word spread like wildfire, and soon the seminar coordinator was at our door, trying to head us off at the pass. He told us in no uncertain terms that he could do what he wanted with the "course." And he wanted to come to our meeting. He was told that that would be up to the students. The students said no.
>
> As the day of our meeting approached, pressure around the department started to show its ugly head. We learned later that a split in the faculty had developed. Some supported us 100% and wanted us to kick his butt, and others were amazed that we would even think of questioning a professor. No one acted openly to help us, but people did intervene to try to stop us. Some of the students got pressure from their advisers not to have anything to do with us. This united us more.
>
> At the meeting we decided to fight the seminar and to form a Physics Graduate Student Union. The seminar coordinator told us not to threaten him. Some students caved in to the pressure and did what he asked, but our union took off. We elected a president, vice-president, U.S. student representative and foreign student representative. The union gave us an unofficial voice in the department and in how it was run.
>
> To keep us quiet on the seminar issue, the faculty pulled the new coordinator after just one semester, dropped the writing requirement and even reduced pressure on students to attend.[16]

Ted's outside experience helped him see through the local powers that be. It helped him imagine standing up to people feared by others and rejecting their totalist expectations. He could then take action.

Here then, in summary, is a list of symptoms of a totalist organization:

1. Big promises.
2. Milieu control.
3. Unquestioned authority.
4. Guilt tripping and shaming.
5. Total personal exposure.
6. "Scientific" dogma.

7. Taking away true self-confidence.

8. The only path to salvation.

Any organization that wants people to play an ideologically subordinate role—be it a professional training program, a cult, a military unit or an employer—will use these techniques. But, as we have seen, the organization does not always get what it wants.

When any of these subordinating features are present in an organization, intellectually honest people will recognize them easily. The hard part is mustering the courage to fight them. Hence, any successful resistance, such as that carried out by Ian, Rod, Jon and Ted, should be publicized to inspire others. As we will see in the next chapter, even seemingly insignificant resistance can play a vitally important role in preserving one's identity.

The four individuals quoted in this chapter are exceptional in that they survived professional training without adopting mainstream values. When I interviewed them, I discovered that all four had accomplished this in part by organizing and creating an alternative community. As we will see in the next chapter, this is not a coincidence.

NOTES

1. Interview with former sociology graduate student by e-mail and telephone, 23 August 1995 to 6 November 1995. He asked me to withhold the name of the university. I have chosen to withhold his name as well.

2. Interview with a former member and leader of The Way International, 30 August 1995. She asked me to withhold her name.

3. For an excellent description of the U.S. Marine Corps's cult-style indoctrination system, see *Wall Street Journal*, 27 July 1995, p. 1.

4. Louis Jolyon West, "Psychiatric aspects of training for honorable survival as a prisoner of war," *American Journal of Psychiatry*, vol. 115 (October 1958), pp. 329–336, especially p. 331. West's work was sponsored in part by the U.S. Air Force.

5. Robert Jay Lifton, *Thought Reform and the Psychology of Totalism*, Norton, New York (1961), ch. 22. My eight features overlap with Lifton's eight (in parentheses) as follows: 1. Big promises. 2. Milieu control ("Milieu Control"). 3. Unquestioned authority ("Mystical Manipulation"). 4. Guilt tripping and shaming ("The Demand for Purity"). 5. Total personal exposure ("The Cult of Confession"). 6. "Scientific" dogma ("The 'Sacred Science'"; "Loading the Language"; "Doctrine Over Person"). 7. Taking away true self-confidence. 8. The only path to salvation ("The Dispensing of Existence").

6. Ken Kesey, *One Flew Over the Cuckoo's Nest*, Viking, New York (1962), about seven pages before the end of pt. 2.

7. See note 1.

8. Interview with sociologist by e-mail and telephone, 14 August 1995 to 2 October 1995. He asked me to withhold his name.

9. Interview with sociologist by e-mail and telephone, 11 August 1995 to 20 October 1995. He asked me to withhold his name and the name of the university.

10. See note 1.

11. See note 5, p. 426.

12. See note 8.

13. See note 5, pp. 427–428.

14. See note 9.

15. Ibid.

16. Interview with physicist by e-mail, 13 October 1995 to 13 November 1995. He asked me to withhold his name and the name of the university.

15

HOW TO SURVIVE
PROFESSIONAL TRAINING
WITH YOUR VALUES INTACT

On 30 December 1981 the United States Army issued a survival manual for graduate school, but no one recognized "Field Manual No. 21-78" as anything of the kind. True, the 108-page how-to book wasn't written for graduate students. It was written to show soldiers how to resist brainwashing and exploitation as prisoners of war.[1] But in light of what we saw in the previous chapter, students in graduate or professional school should be able to put such resistance techniques to good use.

In fact, in a crucial way the military manual is superior to civilian advice books written specifically for students in graduate or professional school. The problem with the civilian guidebooks is that they simply help you conform successfully to the demands of the training institution. You get your credential but lose your identity in the process. The Army manual, on the other hand, shows you how to survive the training program *and* keep control over your identity. The military calls this "honorable survival,"[2] and in this chapter I will quote extensively from the Army manual about how to achieve it.

Mere survival is, of course, a precondition for honorable survival, but it does not get you even halfway there. In graduate school, as in the POW camp, the toughest struggle is not over whether you will survive the process, but over what sort of person you will be when you get out. Thus, if you want to become a professional to be in a better position to pursue your own vision, then the most difficult step is making sure that you will still *have* your own vision after going through professional training. Here I am assuming that you are not a fan of the status quo, with its tired old ways that make work boring, its bureaucracy that takes the fun out of innovation, its decision-making that defies common sense, and its "Just fine, thank you" old guard that sets the cautious tone. Rather, I assume that your vision is forward-looking, and that one reason you want to become a professional is to have some power to further it. But after professional training, will your attitude still be critical and independent, or will it be uncritical and subordinate?

If you don't think attitude is the big issue in professional training, take a look at the civilian guidebooks. In his popular graduate-school survival guide, Robert L. Peters makes rare use of italics to warn that if you want to "get what you came for," then you had better *make it a firm rule never to say bad things within the university community.*"[3] Every conscientious guidebook author who accepts the training system for what it is comes to this same conclusion, which speaks volumes about the true nature of graduate education. This requirement of strict attitude control is reminiscent of cult indoctrination, in which the rules for survival are the same, only more explicit. Here's how a former member of The Way International described it:

> All the time you have to think positive and speak positive. You can't have negative emotions; you battle any negative feelings. You become out of touch with your feelings. You don't go by your feelings; you go by the word of God.
>
> The people who run the group are the spiritual leaders. So they can say, "When you write your diary, don't write anything negative," and you just do it. You write the positives; you write the word of God. They can have your twig coordinator [local group leader] read your diary and make sure you didn't write anything negative. They can do that when you're in The Way Corps, the leadership training program that I was in. The Way Corps is like a 100% commitment. The people in it are considered the top of the line, the cream of the crop.[4]

With or without guidebooks, a lot of students make it through professional training but give up the heart of their identity in the process (I'll call these students group 1). Many others don't finish the program but do hold on to who they are (group 2). Only a fortunate few get through graduate or professional school with their attitude and values intact (group 3). How do they do it?

Students in all three groups have run-ins with the faculty. Even students who follow a mainstream guidebook and make a conscious effort to adopt the favored attitude and values eventually find themselves targeted for a hard time, because they inevitably underestimate just how thoroughly they are expected to conform. Those headed for the first two groups defend their identity unconsciously, never recognizing that their attitude and values are at the root of their conflicts with the faculty. Bewildered by the trouble they are having, and therefore unsure about their own culpability, these students don't feel they have the right to demand that the faculty accept them for who they are. So they either back away from who they are (and end up in the first group) or back away from demanding acceptance (and end up in the second group).

The few individuals who make it into the third group have one thing in common: At some point during their professional training they stand up for their values, fight it out with the faculty and win the right to be different. Attitudes and values atrophy if not acted upon, and so students make it into the third group only if they find a survivable way to take a stand for their beliefs. Because of the disparity in power between students and faculty, the student can't go it alone. Hence, the formula for surviving professional training with your attitude and values intact is, in a word: Organize. Work with others and fight for your values *consciously*. You are going to have conflict in any case, and so you might as well do it right and retain control of your identity. The same word—organize—summarizes the military's advice.

PRISONER OF WAR RESISTANCE

Simple reasoning led me to the Army field manual. I figured that because professional training shares so many essential features with brainwashing, somewhere there must already exist a uniquely insightful survival manual for professional training—in the form of instructional material on resisting brainwashing. All I needed to do was find it. I expected the military to be knowledgeable in mind control, running as it does a massive indoctrination program of its own, in which it turns fresh recruits into people with a military mentality. In particular, I expected the military to know effective resistance techniques that captured troops can use if they don't want to be reindoctrinated.

So I called the Pentagon, and sure enough, soon I was talking to Col. John Chapman, head of the Joint Services Survival, Evasion, Resistance, and Escape Agency. The colonel explained that his 100-person organization, which is headquartered at Fort Belvoir, Virginia, debriefs returned captives; produces survival, evasion, resistance and escape training material; and oversees "SERE" training in the various branches of the military. He offered the assistance of the head SERE psychologist, Lt. Col. Bruce Jessen, PhD. ("I keep him out at Fairchild, because we do some training out there," said Chapman, referring to the Air Force base in Washington state.[5]) He asked Jessen to put together a bibliography on resistance. When Chapman faxed me the result, he explained that "we build our training around these references and some of our own experiences."[6] The bibliography contained publications that were clearly (though inadvertently) relevant to professional training and that in turn led me to other such documents. Two major themes run through these publications: commitment to ideals, and solidarity among the targets of indoctrination.[7]

The Army field manual is the best of the documents, as it synthesizes everything into one practical guide. Titled *Prisoner of War Resistance*, its contents come from debriefings of former prisoners of war as well as from researchers who have studied the subject.[8] After the Army issued the manual, it tightened its restrictions on revealing its resistance techniques, and so the second edition of Field Manual 21-78 (issued in 1989) is a classified document. "We don't want the people who potentially will hold our individuals as captives to know what we teach them to do to deal with it," Jessen told me.[9] But the first edition of the manual had already let the cat out of the bag. This chapter presents some excerpts from it.

If you are a student in graduate or professional school, you should have no trouble seeing how the military's hard-won lessons apply to the situation in your particular program. In fact, you will likely find it hard not to make the connections. But you don't have to be a student for this subordination resistance manual to strike a resonant chord in your life, because its insights apply to all social hierarchies. If you are an employee, for example, applications to your workplace will leap out at you.

I have divided the excerpts into five overlapping subtopics: knowing what you are up against (in the military's words, "Some basic captor approaches"); preparing to take action ("Resistance training"); working with others ("Make a team effort"); resisting subordination ("Resist!"); and dealing with weak links ("Willing collaboration").

Keep in mind that every subordinating institution has its own way of bringing about the oppressive conditions discussed in the manual. In a professional training program, for example, time pressure, insecurity, stress and an overly demanding schedule can lead to lack of sleep, junk-food diets and social isolation. In a POW camp, by contrast, an indoctrinator might simply arrange for sleep deprivation, poor nutrition and isolation. The mechanism is different, but the result is similar.

Because of the essential similarity of hierarchical institutions, tailoring the POW resistance manual to your school or workplace requires nothing more than a few simple word substitutions—a frightening fact when you think about it. Graduate students, for example, might substitute

— "graduate or professional school" for "PW camp"
— "student" for "soldier," "PW" or "man"
— "institution" or "faculty" for "captors"
— "expel" for "kill"
— "upheld values" for "honor"
— "graduate with your values intact" for "escape" or "honorable survival"
— "job" for "big ticket item"
— "being obsequious" for "bowing"
— "institutions" for "nations"

and so on.

Use your imagination—and have fun.

Prisoner of War Resistance

The battle in the prisoner-of-war camp is for the mind.[10]

As a PW, your most powerful and valuable weapon is resistance. It is the only honorable course of action.[11] Resistance . . . can mean the difference between:

• Respectful or disrespectful treatment.
• Walking out of a PW camp or coming out feet first.

- Returning with honor or returning in disgrace.
- Failure or success, as escape.
- Pride or shame (looked up to or down on by the other PWs, family, and friends).[12]

Resistance is the ability to mold the PW environment to your needs and objectives.[13]

Work and cooperate with the other PWs. "Every man for himself" does not work in a PW camp. The only way to defeat your captor is to unite and organize.[14]

Knowing What You Are Up Against

There are only a few ways to get people to adopt the "right" attitude within a set amount of time—say, during the course of a professional training program or during a probationary period on a job. The methods are simple, and people who are given power over others—say, the power to deny degrees or fire employees—quickly rediscover them on their own. Students and employees who are familiar with these attitude-altering techniques and setups, some of which are mentioned below, will be better able to hold on to their values.

Some Basic Captor Approaches[15]

As a PW, you must meet the challenges of loneliness, fatigue, fear, anger, monotony, isolation—a hostile, enemy-imposed environment.[16] The psychological effects of captivity may be greater and last longer than the physical effects.[17]

Your captor [will work] to try to break you—to try to weaken your belief in yourself and your will to keep your identity and maintain your lifetime code of ethics, decency, and standards of behavior.[18]

Generally, the enemy does not want to kill PWs for one major reason, among others: *A dead PW cannot be exploited.*[19]

Enemy can bring about disordered mental function. No amount of willpower can prevent it. Your captors don't have to use physical brutality. Extreme fatigue, lack of sleep, and pain, for example, can cause it. . . . Complex mental functions are lost first: the ability to carry out highly creative activities. . . . There is less concern about "morality" and "right and wrong." Generally, socially oriented behavior falls away.[20]

Your captor will try to disgrace you in the eyes of others, especially your fellow prisoners. Or he will try to make you feel disgraced and ashamed of yourself.[21]

What's-the-use-of-resisting technique. . . . Using this approach, your captor tries to make you quit [resisting] by saying, for example, "What's the use of holding out? Why suffer? You are at our mercy. We can do what we want with you." . . . Or he may put it to you this way: "You're not going anywhere. You'll be here a long time.

Why not make it easier on yourself; cooperate, and we'll see that your stay here is pleasant."[22]

Method: Shows power over life and death.

How they do it: Captor show of power, i.e., executions, torture, starvation, favors, good clothing, medical care, food, and shelter; or deprival of food, medical care, etc. Complete control of physical conditions in camp.[23] Uncertainty of not knowing when or why treatment will change is a threat.[24]

What it does: Makes PW know who is boss, "who runs the show," "who pulls the strings." Breeds extreme caution among PWs. Evidence of power over life hits home.

Method: Deliberately caused physical deterioration.

How they do it: Extremely long interrogation and forced writing sessions, making the PW overly tired. . . . Insufficient, poorly prepared, unpalatable, nonnourishing, monotonous, strange food. . . .

What it does: Drastic lowering of PW's resistance level to interrogation, indoctrination, exploitation. . . .[25]

Method: Now-and-then kind of treatment.

How they do it: Favors—now and then . . .

. . . Better living conditions—food, clothes, shelter, surroundings.

. . . Easy interrogations.

. . . Teases with a small desirable item, letting the PW know that he can get a "big ticket item" for complying with captor wishes.

. . . Promises other rewards for compliance.

What it does: . . .Tries to build a "he's-not-such-a-bad-guy" attitude in the PW. Makes resistance seem like a bad time and undesirable compared with the "luxuries" the captor can give.[26]

The indoctrination process may be gradual. . . . They know that a person who convinces himself that something is right or wrong, good or bad, is a better and more lasting convert than one who has ideas "stuffed down his throat."[27] Your captor . . . wants to make you, the captured soldier, both the propagandist and the object of propaganda.[28]

Preparing to Take Action

People in subordinate positions naturally ready themselves to deal with those above them in the hierarchy, but they don't always admit to themselves that that is what they are doing. Students and employees, for example, take a keen interest in any information they can get about the professors or managers they must face. They eagerly share their information and their analyses of it. They learn from individuals who have more experience dealing with the authorities and teach those who have less. Stories of past struggles at their schools or workplaces, and at other schools or workplaces, are of special interest. The excerpts below assume that serious, conscious study of your situation is wise.

Resistance Training[29]

Training should . . .

. . . Make the soldier self-reliant and a team worker. He must understand that both are needed for success on any battlefield.[30] Proper training . . . impresses personnel with the value of and need for group loyalty, unity, and action while training them to understand the full extent of their own abilities.[31]

. . . Teach him not only to reach deeply within himself for courage and initiative in times of stress, but to reach out to his fellow soldiers to help them, to assure that he lives and succeeds through their survival and success.[32]

. . . Give each soldier confidence in his ability to deny the enemy information and resist interrogation, exploitation, and indoctrination.[33]

. . . Emphasize the psychological aspects of interrogation, indoctrination, exploitation, and isolation so that the trainee, if captured, will know what to expect and can better resist the enemy. . . .

Life–Sanity–Reputation may depend upon the quality and thoroughness of this training.[34]

To resist successfully, a PW must know his captor's—[35]
- Culture, customs, social standards, economic way of life, political structure, system of justice, relationships with other nations.[36]
- Overall strategy regarding the handling of PWs.
- Long-range plans.
- General methods for gaining objectives; i.e., torture, mental stress, the "carrot and stick" approach, etc. . . .

With this information a PW can plan suitable resistance.[37]

Be familiar with the captor's reasons for and methods of attempting to indoctrinate prisoners politically. Be familiar with the methods of resisting such indoctrination.[38]

Working with Others

Organizing is almost magically empowering, but it is very difficult, even under the best circumstances. The difficulties remain essentially the same even when the individuals to be organized are subordinate in very different ways. Janitors in an office building, doctors employed by an HMO, students in graduate school, minorities in a racist institution—any subordinate group can benefit from solidarity and can learn valuable principles and tactics from the struggles of other groups. The politics of power are universal.

Make a Team Effort[39]

Prisoners of war must present a united front to the enemy.[40] While individually they may be weak, as a unified group they are strong.[41]

Help each other and make sacrifices whenever necessary. A PW environment puts a man and his will to the test. Keep your differences to yourself; work them out quietly. If you don't, your captor will try to exploit them.[42] *Do not bring upon a fellow prisoner that which you would not have him bring upon you.*[43]

Place unity above self. Unified PWs represent a serious threat to the enemy—to their plans and achievement of objectives.[44] Live and work as a member of a co-operating, cohesive unit.[45]

Use US names and ranks in addressing each other, not names or ranks conferred by the enemy.[46]

Wherever there are several or many PWs, communication and organization are possible and necessary. To resist the enemy effectively and to give each PW a better chance to escape, it is important to set up a PW organization.[47] Learn the names and locations of other PWs. . . . Learn the status and state of well-being of each. Learn their relationship with the enemy—collaborators, informers, traitors, neutral and noncommitted, or *okay all the way.*[48]

Experience has proven that some individuals are not blessed with sufficient levels of education, training, faith, character, or pride on which to draw for defenses. These people cannot be discarded or left to flounder by themselves. They must be helped. . . . They must be brought into and made an integral part of the PW unit. They must be given responsibilities within their capabilities—perhaps a little beyond their capabilities—and helped to achieve them, by encouraging and actively assisting if necessary. To bring them into the mainstream of the PW activities and unit is a major test of leadership and unity.[49]

At some time or other, a feeling of remoteness hits every PW. Away from family and friends, he gets that feeling of being away from it all. It is a dangerous feeling. It can bring about a complete separation from reality. It may make the PW feel he has been forgotten and abandoned. . . . And his captor makes every effort to make the PW believe it; he tries to instill a feeling of being alone and abandoned. But as a PW . . . *you are a part of something*, some group, some organization. . . . You are not remote from your responsibilities toward that outfit. They are real. Carry them out; others will work with you. As long as that happens, you are in the real world; you will stay in touch with reality.[50]

You may, regardless of rank or grade, become a key figure among the other PWs, looked to for leadership, guidance, and advice. The PW camp is a place where each soldier proves his courage.[51]

Resisting Subordination

Those who impose hierarchy make conflict inevitable, because people resist subordination. Even people who profess belief in the undemocratic distribution of power in the organizations where they study or work—even those people resist their own subordination in practice. Inevitably, at some point in your career as a graduate student or employee, you will come into conflict with those who have authority. If you have already reached that point, then you have probably already discovered on your own some of the points below. The more you know about the tactics of resistance, the better you will do at it.

Resist![52]

Do not allow your captor to establish himself as the audience upon whom you depend for establishment/reinforcement of your self-image. Fix in mind someone you love and respect. Gauge your actions by the question: "What would he/she think about what I'm doing?" Remember: *If the enemy doesn't like you, you're doing well.*[53]

You can survive with honor and retain self-respect by aggressive but discreet and timely resistance as a member of a working PW organization. . . .[54] When you feel you can't do anything about a situation, you get depressed. The best way to overcome depression is to do something that gives you a sense of controlling a situation—a sense of victory, a sense of success.[55] Try to win a victory over your captors every time you can, no matter how small. Then, pass the word to your fellow PWs as quickly as you can. Every victory you win will be a great morale booster for you and for those PWs you tell about it; let them savor the details.[56] In a PW compound, a small victory is really a big victory.[57]

Gripe to your captors at every opportunity, about every aspect of your treatment.[58] Demand your captors adhere to the letter and spirit of the GPW [Geneva Convention].[59] Try to improve the conditions for you and your fellow PWs.[60] Obtain improvement in camp life—better food, living conditions, appropriate clothing, proper shelter, sufficient medicines and medical treatment, religious services, welfare and sports activities, educational opportunities, adequate sanitary conditions, and a congenial environment.[61]

Exert strenuous and continued efforts to assist in the administration of the camp.[62]

It's humbling. All prisoners are bound to feel some degree of humiliation at some time or other. A prisoner may feel humiliated because he was captured. The stripping and processing procedures can be humiliating. Your captor does all he can to make you feel humble and unworthy, and to make you lose face. An excellent defense is: *Don't take it personally! Don't let it get to you! Keep your pride! Know that they, your captors, are beneath you! Ridicule them in private; Assign ludicrous nicknames.* But don't be contemptuous. You may begin to believe that you are smarter than they are and open yourself to exploitation.[63] *Don't get cocky or careless.*[64]

Be coldly proper. If respect for rank is due, show it. Do not, *however, bow or in any manner show subservience.*[65] Move in formations.[66]

Keep a sense of humor. Humor is a highly effective weapon. Use it. It makes living easier if you can find some humor in your situation,[67] ironic and macabre (dark humor) as it may be.[68] It breaks tensions. A sense of humor is really hope with a smile. Humor drives away fear; it gives spirit to the dispirited, courage to the discouraged, strength to the weak, hope to the "down and out." Humor is an invaluable PW weapon. Its use indicates that the challenges of captivity are being squarely and positively faced.

Razz the enemy privately. In the privacy of your cell, in the exclusive company of your PW buddies, *under any conditions where your captors are not present and you can safely do so without risking reprisal,* mock the enemy, ridicule him, make him the butt of your humor and jokes. It does wonders for morale and increases the effectiveness of resistance. Ridiculing the enemy, even if only in one's mind, puts him on a lower psychological level. Psychologically, it makes him less formidable, lessening your apprehension of him.[69]

If you recognize the enemy is using a technique for exploitation, let all the other PWs know as soon as possible, as some of them might not realize what the enemy is doing. Do the same as soon as you become aware of any other techniques, schemes, or objectives the enemy has come up with to exploit, indoctrinate, propagandize, or gain information.[70]

Share any special gifts, items, or favors you receive with the more needy PWs— the sick, injured, dispirited, shackled, etc. Spread the wealth. Each PW is a link in a chain. Keep them all equal in strength—physical, mental, moral, emotional, spiritual—so that there are no weak links at which the chain will break.[71]

If you held out as long as you possibly could—that is, until you reached a point just before physical, mental, or emotional collapse—you have no reason to be ashamed of yourself or to feel guilty. *Suicidal resistance is not demanded of you.* A good PW unit, SRO [senior ranking officer], and staff can help each PW see his actions in the right light and can help increase individual and group resistance.[72]

Dealing with Weak Links

You've disliked snitches and brownnosers ever since you first encountered them—in elementary school if not earlier. They are a by-product of social hierarchy, and so can be found, for example, in every graduate school and every workplace. But with conscious action, you can handle them easily and organize successfully.

Willing Collaboration[73]

Informing, or any other action detrimental to a fellow PW, is despicable and is expressly forbidden.[74] A volunteer informer or collaborator is a traitor to fellow prisoners and country.[75] Prisoners of war must especially avoid helping the enemy to identify fellow PWs who may have knowledge of value to the enemy and who may, therefore, be made to suffer coercive interrogation.[76] Take punishment before . . . informing on or giving information on fellow prisoners, the command structure, the communication system, or US internal camp or compound PW policy, tactics, and procedures.[77]

There is a difference between cooperation and collaboration. PWs cooperate with the enemy when they work with their captor for the welfare of all the PWs. . . . PWs collaborate with the enemy when they work for the benefit of the enemy and when what they do or say helps the enemy achieve his goals. *Collaboration is unacceptable.*[78]

An informer or collaborator should be insulated from sensitive information concerning PW organization, but . . . continuing efforts should be made by members of the PW organization to encourage and persuade the collaborator to cease such activities. Welcoming a repentant collaborator "back to the fold" is generally a more effective PW organization resistance technique than continued isolation, which may only encourage the collaborator to continue such treasonous conduct. There is a significant difference between the collaborator who must be persuaded to return and the resistant who, having been physically or mentally tortured into complying with a captor's improper demand (such as information or propaganda statement), should be helped to gather strength and be returned to resistance.[79]

The collaborator really does not do himself much good, if any. He doesn't live much better. Whatever rewards the enemy gives him do not pay for the harm he has done to his country, the other prisoners, and his own self-respect. And even while he is collaborating, the enemy despises him.[80]

[The prisoner of war] must know that captivity is not forever. He must know that he will escape or be released, and that when this happens, he will emerge as either more of a man or somewhat less of a man than he was before capture. He must know that he will have to live with this knowledge, and that he will forever be judged by those who knew and know him. He must realize he will always carry his own mirror—his conscience.[81]

CONFRONTATION OR OBLITERATION

When your identity is under attack, working with other resisters is the key to keeping control over who you are. An institution cannot brainwash active opponents of its point of view as long as the opponents' organization is democratic and independent of the institution itself. Institutions find such individuals frustrating to "educate," because they have a strong independent sense of reality and a strong base of support.

Students who try to go it alone, no matter how strong they appear to be, end up transformed and afraid to challenge those in power. The tactic of trying to trick the training institution by pretending to have adopted its values commonly backfires. As discussed earlier, an independent outlook won't survive long-term disuse; temporary adjustments of thinking become permanent if they go on long enough. This is especially true when the prescribed ways of thinking must be flawlessly and cleverly applied, as professional training programs demand.

One might expect that in the university, a freethinking atmosphere pervades, where students routinely challenge the dominant ideology, the faculty and the curriculum. In fact, especially in graduate school, such challenges are rare, because the atmosphere in university departments is not freethinking, but repressive. When the establishment's dominance over a field goes unchallenged, students are reluctant to handicap themselves in the competition for jobs by showing less than total commitment to the dominant outlook. Thus, the system's facade of power works to wither any hidden dissenting ideas that the student may have.

Remember also that professional training is preceded by at least 16 years of preparatory socialization in the schools. Students who go on to professional training tend to be the "best" students—those who, among other things, excel at playing by the rules. Over time, playing by the rules becomes part of their personal identity, a feature of who they are. Engaging in an act of resistance is a frightening step for such people, and therefore many never try. Taking a stand would break with the long-rewarded behavior that got them into graduate school in the first place. (For an unrepressed critique of those 16 disempowering years of preprofessional schooling, see Jerry Farber's *The Student as Nigger*.[82])

It is not easy to maintain a nonconforming outlook within an institution. If you do, you stand out at all times, even when you are not expressing your views. Those in charge try to imagine—and think they know—what you must be thinking about whatever establishment-serving idea they happen to be expressing at the moment. They see your deviant outlook as a constant challenge, and they respond with unrelenting pressure to get you to adjust, making at least a few serious confrontations inevitable. Any student with a non-mainstream outlook discovers this quickly and senses that it could be costly to challenge the institution that judges who deserves professional credentials and who doesn't. No student in a professional training program maintains an independent outlook casually.

Alone in a large program designed to mold you, you cannot uphold an independent outlook for long. By yourself you can't even maintain a point of reference against which to sense that your outlook is drifting and to gauge how far it has drifted, because the training system, so as not to sabotage itself, excludes sources of critical distance. Students who want to survive professional training as independent thinkers need a way to take breaks from the otherwise ruinous conformity, self-censorship and ideological discipline that is required—that is, they need a foothold outside the training system. The only way to maintain such a foothold is to work with other independent thinkers in organized oppositional activity. Only by playing a creative role in some organized form of opposition can an individual gain perspective on what otherwise appears to be an all-encompassing, total system. The system is forced to reveal its true nature to those involved in such struggles.

Professional training manages to take a political toll on nearly everyone who goes through it. It lessens people's sensitivity to elitism, weakens their commitment to fundamental change and decreases the militancy with which they pursue their ideals. But by becoming part of an active group in which you can be open about your politics, you will stay aware of what is happening to you and to others, and you will emerge from professional training less separated from your political origins than you would otherwise be. While the oppositional activity is organized to achieve its stated worthwhile reforms, it serves the equally important function of allowing its organizers to maintain their sanity and grow personally.

Organized oppositional activity means confronting the system. At least some of this activity must focus on issues within your own training program. Of course, independent thinkers often have to remain "underground" for a time in their programs. But professional training really *is* training and does rehearse future behavior, and so those who *never* emerge and dissent openly at any time during the entire training process will probably never emerge as independent thinkers after graduation either—when, for example, they could take a stand not to the establishment's liking at work or within a professional organization. Those taking the easy road avoid pain only in the short run, because they are headed for a lifetime of personally stressful political and intellectual subordination.

Thus, the student in professional training faces a tough choice: Organize or conform; confront or be obliterated. Neither alternative is easy, but there is no third choice. In one way or another, everyone chooses. Those who do not face the issue directly allow the training system to decide for them; they end up conforming without missing a beat. Those who take what appear to be third choices, such as informed cynicism, dodge confrontation through disguised forms of self-adjustment to a life that on balance serves the establishment.

This is not to suggest that you must confront the system directly every day. It means being active in maintaining the public presence of an independent outlook—that is, maintaining an environment of opposition, even though those running the training institution will see that (correctly) as radical. It means study and participation with others in a radical organization. It means identifying personally, if not publicly, as a partisan rather than as an observer, through membership in such an organization. It means maintaining independent sources of information and constant awareness of fundamentally independent points of view through the reading of radical periodicals, which, as a practical matter, only subscriptions will provide on the necessary regular basis. Without this foothold, the individual cannot withstand for the necessary years the system's pressure to adjust as its ideology pops up in a multitude of unpredictable disguises.

Such oppositional activity does involve personal risk. However, if one is a member of a local organization—even a small group with an oppositional outlook—then one has a tremendous amount of protection, usually more than even members themselves realize. Those in charge know that such a group can focus public attention on any repressive action they might take. Nevertheless, some risk of reprisal remains. The lesson here is that the greatest threat to the survival of the individual as a potential force for change comes, ironically, from *not* taking this risk. Those who act are the ones who will survive as independent thinkers. They fight without demanding guarantees of victory or immunity from attempts at retribution. They know that the individual is obliterated not by confronting the system, but by conforming to it.

MY OWN CASE

I managed to get through graduate school with my non-mainstream attitude and values mostly intact. I will describe some of that experience as an example of how one graduate student handled the inevitable conflict.

When I arrived at the physics department at the University of California, Irvine, I found fearful and stressed-out graduate students and a generally repressive atmosphere. I knew that if I adopted the favored mainstream behavior, even as a disingenuous act, my thinking would slowly and insidiously become more and more mainstream as well. As an undergraduate campus activist, I had seen how students who sat out the struggles of the day slowly became more and more conservative. So I decided to fake the favored attitude, but not the favored behavior. I would behave in accord with my real beliefs whenever I could get away with it.

I decided to lie low at first so that the faculty would pass me on the physics PhD qualifying examination. I didn't want them to look at my test papers and "find" that I didn't know enough physics. So before the test, I limited my participation in campus life to writing a few op-ed articles in the student newspaper. I knew that physics faculty members would disagree with the radical point of view that I took in those articles, but I also knew that if I chose topics far from the world of physics, the liberal professors would see the articles simply as a nice exercise of free speech by one of their students, who, after all, had the proper subordinate attitude where it counted—within the physics department. I also signed on with a faculty member and started collaborating with him on a research project (my dissertation project) so that I might have an advocate at exam evaluation time.

After they passed me on the exam, I knew it would be more difficult for them to find an excuse to get rid of me, and so I slowly increased my political activity. Another physics graduate student and I organized an unofficial science and society seminar series in the department, focusing mainly on the politics of science. We brought in progressive faculty members from other departments, or gave talks ourselves, to stimulate lunchtime discussions, which attracted undergraduate and graduate students and occasionally faculty members.

Eventually I encouraged students from physics and other departments to form a local chapter of the activist organization Science for the People. Our group was strong and sponsored a number of study groups and well-attended events that allowed a radical point of view to be heard on controversial issues as diverse as sociobiology, faculty military research and U.S. foreign interventions.

Many of our actions hit close to home in the physics department, which we used as a base of operations in part because many of our members were physics students. The faculty knew I was one of the organizers, but they had to be careful because the mere existence of the organization constituted a threat that any repressive action on their part would be publicized and would mobilize people against them.

In one of our many actions, we confronted the head of the Los Alamos nuclear weapons laboratory when he spoke on campus before a large audience at a colloquium sponsored by the physics department. Harold Agnew, then director of the New Mexico laboratory, had been invited to campus by his friend Frederick Reines, an Irvine physics professor who had worked on the hydrogen bomb at Los Alamos.[83] Agnew had been a strong advocate of developing the neutron bomb, a nuclear weapon capable of killing people inside buildings while leaving the buildings perfectly intact. He had explained to a Senate subcommittee what this bomb would do to a person: "In a very short time, he would become very ill and would be incapacitated; in a day or so he would be dead." When Agnew took questions after his talk, we demanded that he explain why, as head of a supposedly politically neutral national laboratory, he had assigned what he described as a "very elite group" of scientists to lobby "very aggressively" in favor of the neutron bomb.[84] He refused to give details. Later, at the beginning of the postcolloquium wine-and-cheese reception for him, I and others questioned him in an unfriendly way about the morality of his nuclear weapons work. Agnew lost his temper, and Reines had to hustle him out of the room.

Reines was extremely embarrassed by our violation of the protocol for how to treat the director of a national laboratory, and he was furious with me in particular for leading the attack. As a member of the Los Alamos old-boys network and a big-time grantsman, Reines had a lot of power within the physics department. Faculty members were afraid to challenge him even though they didn't think he was very good at physics. Reines's anger was of more than academic concern to me, because he paid my salary as a research assistant. (Reines had agreed to allocate a tiny chunk of money from one of his multimillion-dollar Department of Energy research contracts to finance a small project directed by my dissertation adviser, Riley Newman, and my salary was paid out of that.) But Reines limited his retribution to a verbal attack against me at the next meeting of his research group.

Another incident involving our organization hit the faculty closer to home. One of Reines's own graduate students, Scott Nakamura, suffered a fatal cerebral hemorrhage while working in one of Reines's laboratories. Scott was from a working-class family in Hawaii and had gone much farther in school than anyone else in his family. His many friends and fellow Science for the People members knew that it would mean a lot to Scott's parents if the department were to recognize his eight years of graduate work by awarding his PhD posthumously. When another student and I approached Reines with the suggestion, he rejected it out of hand, explaining that the PhD is "the coin of the realm" and must not be devalued. The department issued a master's degree instead, but we argued, to no avail, that that represented only the first two or three years of Scott's graduate work.

So we circulated a petition, which forced the chairman of the physics department to appoint a committee—chaired by Reines—to decide the matter. Reines was furious, as were the department chairman and other senior faculty members, that the petitioners had not accepted Reines's initial decision as final and were drawing ever-wider attention to a denial that made the department look coldhearted. The committee invited the students to testify (under the icy glare of its chairman) and ended up issuing Scott a C. Phil., which ranks between a master's degree and a PhD.

The senior faculty members, angry that their authority had been successfully challenged, moved to discipline the graduate students involved. Each student was punished in some way and warned by his dissertation adviser that if he wanted to get his own degree, he should mind his own business and concentrate on his work. My adviser, Riley Newman, happened to be in Oxford, England, on sabbatical leave at the time all this happened, and so the department handled my case somewhat differently. They saw me as a more dedicated opponent than the other students involved, and clearly wanted me out. But by then I was only a couple of months from completing my dissertation, and so the only practical way to get rid of me was, ironically, to *help* me finish it. In Newman's absence, physics professor Jonas Schultz had been checking the chapters of my dissertation as I completed them. Schultz had always been rather slow to respond, but suddenly and mysteriously my dissertation seemed to become his highest priority. One Friday Schultz told me that Reines had phoned from Los Alamos to ask if my dissertation could be typed by Monday. Schultz knew that many weeks' worth of work remained to be done, and so told Reines regretfully that his suggestion was impractical. When Monday came around, Reines tried to take possession of my dissertation from my typist. He wanted to put *two* typists to work on it simultaneously, give me a PhD and get me out of the department without my adviser even seeing the dissertation. But the typist, his former secretary whom he was paying to do the job, knew about my conflict with him and refused to hand it over. I finished it six weeks later.

At the same time, without Newman's approval, Reines fired me, taking me off the payroll as a research assistant. I claimed this was retaliation for exercising free speech, and after I completed the degree I demanded six weeks' pay, because standard practice in Reines's research group had been to employ students until they completed their degrees. When my adviser returned from sabbatical and asked Reines about my dismissal, Reines told him in a voice of finality, "He can have his vacation pay, but that's all." (This was a small concession, because department practice was to cheat research assistants out of their vacations by asking them to report vacation days on their monthly time sheets without actually taking any time off.)[85] Seven physics graduate students wrote a letter to the department chairman supporting me. And when I mentioned the dispute to the head of the faculty union, mathematics professor Joel Westman, he offered to take up my case. It was highly unusual, of course, for the faculty union to take a case *against* a faculty member, but the union didn't want to see any university employee fired for political activity. Reines at first rebuffed Westman, but then capitulated and asked Newman, "What do I have to do to settle this?" Newman told him the amount I had calculated, and Reines paid up. I donated the money to the faculty union.

My history of troublemaking didn't interfere with my getting a job after graduation. By the time word of it got to my boss at *Physics Today* magazine, which had hired me as an associate editor, I was already through the probationary period and was again busy making trouble for managers who deserved it.

The one who belatedly outed my bad attitude to the *Physics Today* management was Irvine physics professor Gregory Benford, a plasma physicist with military connections (discussed in chapter 5), whose attempt to join my dissertation committee I had blocked. In a telephone conversation that I learned about accidentally, Benford spelled out my political beliefs to my very interested boss, Gloria B. Lubkin, then editor of *Physics Today*. He also gave her details about my political activities. Lubkin put this information into my personnel-matters file in her office. Example: "He believes in revolution in all countries."[86]

The notion that in the United States an employee's political views are not a personnel matter is, of course, only a pretense. As we have seen, the bosses' high priority on control over the workforce and control over the political content of the work *requires* them to be concerned about the attitudes and values of their employees. I oppose political dossiers on employees not because their content is so often inaccurate, but because their content often *is* accurate and facilitates this control. Files and finks, however, rarely change the final outcome of conflicts.[87] The amount of solidarity or potential solidarity is the determining factor.

Yes, people who favor the status quo tend to get treated better than their less conservative colleagues. However, at the same time, people willing to take a stand often get treated better than people with a butt-kissing attitude, who often get taken advantage of. Hence, for example, despite my radical views, as a student and then as a working professional, I have found myself harassed and exploited *less* than other students and coworkers. The faculty and bosses have treated me with greater respect, gotten on my case much less frequently, given me greater autonomy and accepted less work from me, making my daily life much less stressful. They tend to do the most to those who will take the most.

INDIVIDUAL VIOLENCE

Most people don't expect professional training programs at institutions of higher education to be the scene of cold-blooded murder. They are naive.

When they think of professional training, they probably think of kindly, bearded professors conveying important knowledge to eager young students. They don't think of institutions attempting to break students in to a lifetime of political subordination, or of institutions holding students' futures hostage to encourage them to get with the program. The stakes in professional education are clearly high enough that grievances can lead to violence.

The chance of violence is increased when the students in a university department have no independent organization to fight for power within the department. Then students have no way to lessen the fear and isolation that pervade so many programs. The power gained through organizing reduces insecurity, the source of the fear. The fight itself builds solidarity, reducing the cutthroat competition that is the source of the isolation. And the organization can represent individuals with grievances. But without an independent organization, students who feel unjustly treated must either swallow the injustice or take on those with power alone. As a result, there is enough violence that some weeks parts of the *Chronicle of Higher Education* are reminiscent of big-city tabloids. "Wayne State Professor Gunned Down in Class," read one recent headline, on an article reporting that yet another graduate student had killed his doctoral adviser.[88]

Students who carry out deadly violence don't all have the same depth of understanding of their problems' origins. Thus the violence follows all of the possible patterns: suicide, killing/suicide and killing. A brief look at one example of each shows how at least three students perceived the issues.

- Jason Altom killed himself on 15 August 1998. He was the fourth chemistry graduate student at Harvard University to commit suicide since 1981. Altom was considered the top graduate student in the research group headed by his adviser, Nobel Prizewinner Elias J. Corey, a prominent chemist known for his work on the synthesis of organic molecules.

  Nevertheless, in a handwritten letter that he left behind, Altom blamed his suicide on Corey and the system that fails to protect "graduate students from abusive research advisors." Indeed, Corey's relationship to Altom resembled that of a cult leader to a member. Like a cult leader, Corey was both revered and feared—revered for his chemistry and feared for his ability to make or break the careers of his graduate students. To Altom, Corey "was like God," said one chemistry graduate student, a friend of Altom's. "The only opinion about chemistry that mattered to Jason" was Corey's, said another.[89] Throughout the department, students commonly worked with religious fervor, toiling late into the night, seven days a week. In many research groups, no amount of work was seen as sufficient. Thus some students tried to create the illusion that they were always around— by leaving the lights on in their labs, by leaving a decoy coat in a prominent spot, by keeping a magnetic stirrer spinning in a beaker of liquid. Altom often worked 13 or more hours per day, always scrambling to come up with something new to say to Corey, who was checking on his progress twice a day.

"Professors here have too much power over the lives of their grad students," wrote Altom, who was almost 27 years old and had devoted five years of his life to graduate school in preparation for an academic job. To have a chance of success in the looming, highly competitive academic job market, Altom needed Corey's full support. But some harsh criticism from Corey convinced Altom that such support was not in the cards.

Altom's suicide helped push the chemistry department to accept a student proposal that slightly diluted the power of advisers over their students. Now students can ask two additional faculty members to play a small advisory role. The professors who run the department had rejected the same proposal three years earlier.

But those in charge still don't want fundamental change. In a telling effort to have their cake and eat it too—that is, to avoid violent attrition without fundamentally changing their stress-inducing approach to education—the professors arranged to offer their graduate students psychiatric help, off campus and at department expense. Yes, the Harvard chemistry department now has its own on-call psychiatrist.

• Gang Lu killed his physics dissertation adviser on 1 November 1991—along with three other physicists, a university administrator and himself.[90] The physics faculty at the University of Iowa considered Lu to be among the top five graduate students ever to enroll in their department, which has a worldwide reputation in space physics research. Lu dispatched each of his preselected targets with execution-style gunshots to the head, without speaking a word about what he was doing. However, the night before the shootings, Lu wrote a goodbye letter to his sister and composed a long public statement, in which he discussed his personal history, his six years as a physics graduate student and each of the people he killed the next day. (The unreferenced quotes below are from those writings.[91])

Lu's adviser, space physics theorist Christoph K. Goertz, drove his graduate student research assistants relentlessly. Lu was a hard worker, but Goertz, a NASA grantsman, thought he wasn't working hard enough. Goertz got on Lu's case and began pushing him, by piling on the work and making spot checks on him in his office. Lu felt that Goertz exploited his research assistants, and Lu didn't hide his views from others in the department.

Goertz could be extremely tough on students whom he perceived as lagging, and so his students competed for his favor. Linhua Shan, another outstanding student in Goertz's group, beat Lu in this competition by working longer hours, by frequently soliciting Goertz's advice—and by better concealing his own very real dislike for Goertz. "I've been honest and frank for my whole life, and I've suffered for being that kind of person," said Lu, who saw Shan as a butt-kisser.[92] "I have most of all detested cunning, fawning sycophants and dishonest bureaucrats." Shan was one of the physicists whom Lu killed.

After the killings, one graduate student in the department was brave enough to say that if Goertz hadn't pressured Lu and Shan so much, the two "might have had a different, less competitive relationship."[93] But they did compete, and Goertz ended up showing favoritism toward Shan. This left Lu feeling targeted for mistreatment, in both small and big ways.

—When one of Lu's calculations didn't turn out as Goertz had expected, Goertz immediately assumed that Lu had made a mistake. This upset Lu, especially when it turned out that Goertz was the one who had made a mistake.

—For the typical student, the defense of dissertation is just a ritual, because the professors on the student's dissertation committee have already read the dissertation and brought any concerns to the student's attention. At Lu's dissertation defense, however, professors raised new questions, and they did so in a way that humiliated Lu. The department chairman was particularly harsh. To address the committee's new questions, Lu had to work day and night for a week redoing calculations, only to find that his results were right in the first place.

—Lu was hoping to win a university prize for his dissertation, but he discovered accidentally that the department chairman had consulted with the faculty and decided which student to nominate two-and-a-half months before the contest's deadline—and before all of Lu's committee members had seen his completed dissertation. The prize went to Shan, the favored student. Lu appealed the chairman's procedure to university officials but was repeatedly rebuffed. At every level, the investigation of Lu's complaint consisted of a university official talking to the physics department chairman and getting his assurance that the department had given Lu's dissertation fair consideration.

—Lu felt that the department wasn't enthusiastic about helping him get a job, and that Goertz wouldn't write good letters of recommendation for him. Goertz heard about Lu's concerns and insisted on writing the letters, but then missed several deadlines, invalidating Lu's job applications. Thus, at age 28, and after ten years of intense undergraduate and graduate study, Lu had no job prospects.

Lu's sister holds the university responsible for the six deaths. One of her insights about her brother certainly applies to many other aspiring scholars who have taken violent action, and to many who haven't: Because he devoted his entire being to his studies (as the university demanded), blocking his way was tantamount to destroying him.[94] Thus Lu destroyed the people whom he felt had destroyed him.

"Usually an ordinary individual is too weak, both politically and financially, to oppose a giant organization," observed Lu. "There exists no justice for little people." But "guns make every person equal," he noted. "Extraordinary action has to be taken to preserve this world as a better place to live."

So on an overcast November day, Lu made his way to room 309, a windowless seminar room in Van Allen Hall. (James Van Allen himself, the renowned space physicist whose name is also attached to the earth's radiation belts, sat in his office up on the seventh floor.) Lu took a seat and waited for the regular Friday afternoon meeting of the space physics theory group to begin. About ten minutes into the session, with a physicist at the chalkboard giving a talk, Lu stood up and to everyone's surprise pulled out a gun and shot Goertz, Shan and Robert Alan Smith, another member of Lu's dissertation committee. Lu then walked down to the second floor and killed Dwight R. Nicholson, the physics department chairman. Lu's final stop was the administration building, where he killed T. Anne Cleary, the associate vice chancellor for academic affairs, who was the highest-level administrator to reject Lu's dissertation prize appeal. Lu then killed himself.[95]

- Theodore Streleski murdered Stanford University mathematics professor Karel deLeeuw on 18 August 1978. At the time of the murder, Streleski was in his 16th year as a graduate student in Stanford's mathematics department, an experience that had left him feeling disrespected and ripped off. From the beginning, attending the prestigious private school had been a financial struggle for Streleski, who had very little money. Early on, he says, he was told by deLeeuw that he would have to give up his part-time job at Lockheed Corporation while studying at Stanford. But the department didn't give Streleski any financial support, and so he had to attend Stanford intermittently, between low-paying jobs.

Streleski was socially naive. He didn't play the games that would have ingratiated him with the department. Honest and straightforward, he thought he would be rewarded simply for "achieving the technical mastery" of mathematics required by the department. So he was disillusioned when, after passing the qualifying examination, the department still didn't offer him financial support. He felt that deLeeuw didn't even take his inquiry seriously.

Relegated to permanent outsider status, Streleski had a difficult time finding a thesis adviser, and he suffered a series of casual "put-downs" by deLeeuw, from whom he took seven mathematics courses. These seemingly minor incidents alarmed Streleski, because they indicated that he didn't have the professorial favor needed to get good letters of recommendation—or even to be awarded a PhD. Thus, after years of sacrifice and slavish study, it was becoming apparent to Streleski that he would have no future in mathematics, the field to which he had devoted his life. Moreover, his marriage collapsed under the financial and academic pressure, which transformed him from a gentle person into a sometimes violent one. Stanford had left him with nothing—and with nothing to lose.

The turning point came when an abstract of Streleski's discoveries in mathematics was deemed publishable—a sign to him that his troubles were the result not of his failings as a mathematician, but of the department's abusiveness. It was time to act. Furious about the years of unfair treatment, he was willing to pay any price "to be able to bad-mouth Stanford and do it with some impact." He considered going to the alumni, the students or the media, but he felt he had no standing. "The media don't cover struggling graduate students," he noted. "But they do cover murderers."[96] (Of course, one should take issue with this reasoning. But more social means of fighting back are unlikely to look feasible to socially isolated individuals like Streleski. Because different people respond to frustration in different ways, some violently, institutional injustice makes violence inevitable.)

Streleski decided to target the professor whom he felt had done the most to block his career and his life. He envisioned the killing as both a real and a symbolic act of "self-defense" against an individual and an institution that had virtually destroyed him. He brought a two-pound sledgehammer to campus, found deLeeuw in his office grading exams, and bashed him on the head. Streleski then turned himself in to the police. He maintained that the killing was a "morally correct action" and "a political statement" about the way Stanford treats its graduate students.

After his arrest, Streleski refused to submit to psychiatric examination, and he pressured his court-appointed lawyer into entering a simple "not guilty" plea instead of the "not guilty by reason of insanity" plea that the lawyer wanted to use. Streleski considered the Stanford math faculty to be "arrogant and powerful," and so he also made his lawyer agree to put them on the witness stand as a way of putting them on the spot. Streleski took the stand himself and testified about his reasons for killing deLeeuw.

In the end, the jury was unable to see Streleski as an inherently bad person, and so convicted him of second-degree, rather than first-degree, murder. Although the prosecutor was outraged, calling the verdict "almost illegal," Streleski got a short sentence, which prison officials made even shorter by awarding him time off for good behavior.

Ironically, it was only in prison that Streleski was finally able to devote all of his attention to mathematics, just as his wealthy or financially supported fellow students had been able to do at Stanford. Thus he described prison as "utopia with constraints" and joked that he had a "tenured" position with a "state institution."

To the distress of many, Streleski achieved his goal of criticizing Stanford "with some impact." He got wide media coverage, including a sympathetic profile in *People* magazine and a guest appearance on the *Phil Donahue Show*.[97] Imprisoned for seven years and twenty days, Streleski has been a free man since 8 September 1985.

NOTES

1. United States Department of the Army, *Prisoner of War Resistance*, Field Manual FM 21-78, Headquarters, Department of the Army, Washington, D.C. (1982), Superintendent of Documents number D 101.20:21-78.

2. Ibid. See also Louis Jolyon West, "Psychiatric aspects of training for honorable survival as a prisoner of war," *American Journal of Psychiatry*, vol. 115 (October 1958), pp. 329–336, especially p. 331.

3. Robert L. Peters, *Getting What You Came For: The smart student's guide to earning a Master's or a Ph.D.*, revised edition, Farrar, Straus and Giroux, New York (1997), p. 145.

4. Interview with a former member and leader of The Way International, 30 August 1995. She asked me to withhold her name.

5. Telephone conversation with Col. John Chapman, 16 November 1995.

6. Telephone conversation with Col. John Chapman, 5 December 1995.

7. For a study that details the role of commitment in resistance to brainwashing, see Harold G. Wolff, "Every Man Has His Breaking Point—(?)[*sic*] The Conduct of Prisoners of War," *Military Medicine*, vol. 125, no. 2 (February 1960), pp. 85–104. The following are other interesting items: George Winokur, "'Brainwashing'—A Social Phenomenon of Our Time," *Human Organization*, vol. 13, no. 4 (Winter 1955), pp. 16–18; see also the editorial, "'Brainwashing' and the Teaching Process," pp. 3–4. Joost A. M. Meerloo, *The Rape of the Mind*, The World Publishing Company, Cleveland (1956), see pp. 268–269. U.S. Department of the Army, *Communist Interrogation, Indoctrination, and Exploitation of Prisoners of War*, pamphlet number 30-101, Department of the Army, Washington, D.C. (1956), Superintendent of Documents number D 101.22:30-101. For a book by a psychologist who conducted SERE training for the Navy, see Douglas S. Derrer, *We Are All the Target: A Handbook of Terrorism Avoidance and Hostage Survival*, Naval Institute Press, Annapolis, Md. (1992). For a study by a former prisoner of war concluding that solidarity is more important than leaders, see Galand D. Kramer, *POW Leadership in North Vietnam*, study number 1345-78, Air Command and Staff College, Air University, Maxwell Air Force Base, Ala. (May 1978).

8. See note 1, p. ii.

9. Telephone conversation with Lt. Col. Bruce Jessen, 27 December 1995.

10. See note 1, p. 18.

11. Ibid., p. 46.

12. Ibid., p. 1.

13. Ibid., p. 46.

14. Ibid., p. 49.

15. Ibid., p. 31.

16. Ibid., p. 24.

17. Ibid., p. 27.

18. Ibid., p. 41.

19. Ibid., p. 31.

20. Ibid., p. 17.

21. Ibid., p. 32.

22. Ibid., p. 35.

23. Ibid., p. 21.

24. Ibid., p. 20.
25. Ibid., p. 21.
26. Ibid., p. 20.
27. Ibid., p. 42.
28. Ibid., p. 41.
29. Ibid., p. 1.
30. Ibid., p. 2.
31. Ibid., p. 47.
32. Ibid., p. 2.
33. Ibid., p. 3.
34. Ibid., p. 4.
35. Ibid., p. 22.
36. Ibid., p. 3.
37. Ibid., p. 22.
38. Ibid., p. 80.
39. Ibid., p. 49.
40. Ibid., p. 45.
41. Ibid., p. 71.
42. Ibid., p. 49.
43. Ibid., p. 102.
44. Ibid., p. 95.
45. Ibid., p. 49.
46. Ibid., p. 100.
47. Ibid., p. 51.
48. Ibid., p. 100.
49. Ibid., p. 30.
50. Ibid.
51. Ibid., p. 29.
52. Ibid., p. 23.
53. Ibid., p. 29.
54. Ibid., p. 23.
55. Ibid., p. 28.
56. Ibid., p. 38.
57. Ibid., p. 29.
58. Ibid., p. 100.
59. Ibid.
60. Ibid., p. 38.
61. Ibid., p. 93.
62. Ibid.
63. Ibid., p. 28.
64. Ibid., p. 100.
65. Ibid., p. 96.
66. Ibid.
67. Ibid., p. 49.
68. Ibid., p. 29.
69. Ibid., pp. 49–50.
70. Ibid., p. 49.
71. Ibid., p. 95.

72. Ibid., p. 45.

73. Ibid., p. 44.

74. Ibid., p. 8.

75. Ibid., p. 78.

76. Ibid., p. 8.

77. Ibid., p. 101.

78. Ibid., p. 43.

79. Ibid., p. 79.

80. Ibid., p. 44.

81. Ibid., p. 29.

82. Jerry Farber, *The Student as Nigger*, Contact Books, North Hollywood, Calif. (1969). Unfortunately, Farber's critique remains valid today.

83. In 1995, long after the events described here, Reines shared the Nobel Prize in physics for a particle detection experiment that he and another physicist did while Reines was employed by the Los Alamos laboratory. Reines died in 1998.

84. All three quotes are from the testimony of Harold Agnew, 16 April 1973, in *Military Applications of Nuclear Technology*, pt. 1, hearing before the Subcommittee on Military Applications, Joint Committee on Atomic Energy, 93rd Congress, First Session, U.S. Government Printing Office, Washington, D.C. (1973), p. 49.

85. For more detail on the posthumous-degree fight, see the article by Eric Chase, Doris England, Keith Skotnes, Katy Basile, Dan Levinson, Cecily Stewart, Alak Ray and Pat Kerig in the University of California, Irvine, student newspaper, *New University*, 30 September 1980, p. 11.

86. Telephone conversation between Gloria B. Lubkin and Gregory Benford, 26 October 1989. For good measure, Benford told Lubkin that I was "actually pretty good at physics"—the word "actually" apparently indicating some sort of surprise that a radical could be good at physics.

87. Even though my dossier has not been of much use to management, I don't want to take a chance on any future use. So I ask that Benford's assertions and any other dope about my political views and activities be removed from the file and turned over to me. (I take the unusual step of making this request publicly for reasons explained in the next chapter.)

88. "Wayne State Professor Gunned Down in Class," *Chronicle of Higher Education*, 8 January 1999, p. A8.

89. "Lethal Chemistry at Harvard," *New York Times*, 29 November 1998, sec. 6 (magazine), pp. 120–128. See also "Harvard Faces the Aftermath of a Graduate Student's Suicide," *Chronicle of Higher Education*, 23 October 1998, pp. A12–A14. "After suicide, Harvard increases graduate-student supports," *Boston Globe*, 20 October 1998, p. A1.

90. Edwin Chen, *Deadly Scholarship*, Birch Lane Press, New York (1995).

91. For transcripts of Gang Lu's letter and statement, see note 90, pp. 146–156.

92. "The Physics of Revenge," *Los Angeles Times Magazine*, 7 June 1992, pp. 26–28, 32, 46–48.

93. See note 90, p. 95.

94. Ibid., p. 191.

95. For details on many of the points discussed above, see note 90, pp. 53, 85, 93–96, 100, 105–107, 112, 115–117, 130, 133, 151, 152, 156, 159.

96. *People Weekly*, 23 September 1985, pp. 60–65.

97. "Student Sentenced for Bludgeon Death," *Los Angeles Times*, 4 May 1979, pt. 1, p. 26. "The Graduate Degree: Is It Worth It?," *Los Angeles Times*, 16 August 1979, pt. 4, p. 1. Paul Ciotti, "Murder In the Math Department," *New West*, 28 January 1980, pp. 38–54. "Slayer can't vow he will never kill," *San Diego Union*, 28 January 1984, p. A-3. "Killer's Freedom Stirs Coast Fear," *New York Times*, 19 February 1984, sec. 1, p. 32. "Professor's Murderer, Still Unrepentant, Is Free Man," *Los Angeles Times*, 9 September 1985, pt. 1, p. 15. Sita de Leeuw [*sic*]"Widow of Slain Professor Speaks Out," (letter) *Los Angeles Times*, 5 October 1985, pt. 2, p. 2.

⓰

NOW OR NEVER

You are doing socially significant work. That's one big reason why you wanted to become a professional in the first place—and now you're doing it. However, all is not well. You find that your assignments do little more than service some part of the social structure. It's socially significant work, to be sure, but not in the way you had in mind. You wanted your work to contribute to *progress* in the social structure—to more equality and democracy, to less hierarchy and authoritarianism—but now you realize that you have been hired to serve as a strut in the very structure you wanted to change. You feel like part of the problem. What do you do?

Simply put, you must become a radical professional.[1] That may sound extreme, but it's the only way to be honest to your goals. Your egalitarian aims make you a radical. The fact that your priorities are so different from your employer's priorities is one big hint of that. So there is no easy way out of your predicament at work: Either you sideline your goals or you are a radical professional. But exactly what is a radical professional? If a radical is someone who undermines authority (by developing and propagating new, more democratic ideologies) and a professional is someone who bolsters authority (by following assigned ideologies), then what is a "radical professional"? Clearly, the best definition is not immediately evident, and as a result, the label has been used cavalierly. Experience has taught me to reserve the term radical professional for professionals with three characteristics, each of which is absolutely necessary. Thus, to be a radical professional . . .

- Your primary self-identification must be "radical," not "professional." By my definition, radical professionals are professionals who think of themselves as radicals first—as radicals who happen to be working as professionals, rather than as professionals who happen to be radicals. Individuals who call themselves radical professionals, but who think of themselves as professionals first, are in essence liberals. Such people make the social-reform movement unattractive by bringing to it the same elitism, the same inequality of authority and ultimately the same hierarchy of "somebodies" and "nobodies" that turns people off to the status quo in the first place and sparks their interest in the opposition.

- You must hold a very critical view of the social role of your profession and of the institution that employs you. As a radical professional you always look beyond the children's-story and public-relations images of the profession and institution, and see clearly the roles they actually play in society. For example, every time you think of the institution that employs you, you see an institution that plays a particular role in maintaining and reproducing the social structure. As a result, your response to issues that come up at work is always in part a response to the institution's role in maintaining the status quo. You see the contradiction between the institution's work and the work that would be best for society, and you try to do as little of the former and as much of the latter as you can get away with. You don't identify with the institution, and so you speak of it as "they," not "we." Individuals who call themselves radical professionals, but who identify with the institutions that employ them and see no conflict between what they have been hired to do and what they think should be done, have been neutralized through incorporation into the system. (As explained in chapter 1, by "the system" I mean the social hierarchy.)

- Your politics must make a difference in the world. You must make your radical outlook count for something somewhere; it must guide you in some activity, on or off the job. The fact that you are a radical makes no difference, and is therefore wasted, when you do things that would be done anyway. So you must do things that otherwise would not be done. At work, you get little satisfaction when you do essentially the same thing that would be done by a nonradical replacing you, even when the boss tells you "good job." You are not satisfied even if the work is socially beneficial. Yes, it feels nice to be one of those who do some of the socially beneficial work the system orders, but you are truly satisfied only when you do something that increases the total amount of socially beneficial work that is done. You increase this total in many ways, ranging from making direct contributions yourself by taking extra time to better serve clients and the public while on the job, to fighting for structural changes in the system while off the job. (I use the term clients broadly: for teachers, they are students; for journalists, readers; for doctors, patients; and so on.)

This third point is a subtle one, and failure to understand it has taken a toll on the social reform movement. From a global point of view, what matters is not who does work that changes society for the better, but how much of such work is done. Nevertheless, it is understandable that newly graduated professionals who identify not with the system but with the opposition want to be the ones who do this work. However, some feel that they *must* be the ones to do this work; they feel that unless they get a job with a reform-oriented organization such as a human-rights group, public-interest law project, union, alternative media outlet or political group they are not really genuine members of the opposition.

Such an assessment is doubly wrong. First, if one has to get hired by the opposition to be a full-fledged member of it, then the opposition is doomed to weakness, because it does not and never will employ more than a minute fraction of the workforce. It does not need to, of course: Oppositional organizations get their strength from their active members, not from their office staffs. A union with many truly active members is very strong even if it employs only a relatively small number of people. Second, many reform-oriented organizations are hierarchically organized, and staff members are basically expected to follow the policy set by those at the top. If, for example, those at the top of a union decide that cooperation with management is the union's new strategy, as happened with the United Auto Workers' "jointness" program, then the union's organizers and other staff members are not free to take a different approach.[2] The problems faced by radical professionals working in such reform-oriented organizations are in essence the same as those faced by radical professionals working for mainstream organizations.

When individuals fail to get reform-oriented jobs and instead join the staffs of establishment organizations (as the vast majority must because of the relatively small number of reform-oriented jobs), they often identify with the opposition less and less as time goes by, because they feel they are not a part of it. They fail to see that although it would be personally pleasant to work for a flawless outfit, a willingness to struggle to make an imperfect one better might do the world more good. And so their original assessment that they are not genuine members of the opposition tragically fulfills itself.

You can avoid this fate, but as a professional in a mainstream organization there are tremendous forces acting on you to adopt a more conventional frame of reference and thereby drift away from the opposition. To remain a radical in this situation requires a deliberate and continuing effort. Simply put, you must anchor yourself in the opposition. You must connect yourself with radical organizations. You must subscribe to radical publications. Such connection with the movement for social change, and only such connection with the movement, allows you to work in the system without being *of* the system. Experience shows that there simply is no other way.

So you are a radical professional. Now, how do you pursue your own vision on a professional job, where, in essence, you have been hired to help fulfill someone else's vision? There is no universal technique. Basically you do as much as you can get away with. Whenever you have the opportunity to influence a decision, you tilt in the direction that advances your larger social goals.

You find, however, that even in carrying out the work assigned to you, you can't get away with much out of the ordinary before you are seen as breaking ideological discipline. And so you constantly find yourself doing more or less the same thing in more or less the same way as your nonradical coworkers. You simply aren't making much of a difference. Most of the social change that you do introduce isn't really your own doing, but is the result of changes in the larger society, to which the institution would soon conform even in your absence. These changes, such as increased attention to minority issues, are brought about through the struggle of independent organizations, such as civil rights groups. You soon realize that as far as having an effect on the social structure goes, your entire institutional "career" is of little value: You can do much more for democratic social progress by participating in the movement for social change and by engaging in other independent oppositional activities than through your salaried professional work.

Nevertheless, there are many things you can do at work to advance your goals. Below are 33 suggestions. Out of necessity, many are quite radical. I can't say how risky each one is, because that varies greatly from workplace to workplace, some workplaces being more repressive than others. However, your gut feeling about each suggestion probably gives a safe estimate of the risk it carries where you work. In the most repressive workplaces, getting caught trying even the mildest of the suggestions could jeopardize your job, because even the tiniest deviation from "normal" behavior can indicate that you have adopted a critical attitude and therefore can't be trusted to uphold an assigned ideology. In my own work experience I managed to follow most of the suggestions without getting fired. How much you do along the lines of these suggestions—ranging from nothing at all to as much as you can get away with—depends upon how radical you choose to be: The corresponding spectrum ranges from mainstream professional to radical professional. Thus, as a radical professional employed by an establishment organization, to the extent you can get away with it, you . . .

- . . . help coworkers look beyond your employer's public-relations image as serving the public. You help them to see the organization for the institution of the status quo that it is and to understand the particular role it plays in perpetuating the social hierarchy.
- . . . encourage coworkers to connect themselves with radical organizations and to read and subscribe to radical publications. You circulate antiestablishment periodicals, or selected articles from them, to professional and nonprofessional coworkers who might be interested.
- . . . break down discipline to your employer's ideology. You encourage coworkers to take a critical view of the assigned ideology, and you support them whenever they make progressive challenges to that ideology. You win every crumb and token that can be won.
- . . . assign your own curiosity. On the job, you develop and pursue your own goals while supposedly pursuing your employer's goals. You steal as

much time and as many resources as possible to do this. You encourage the hiring of more employees to give everyone more time to pursue their own goals.

- ... overcome your need for the boss's compliments on your work. You judge your work yourself, by very different criteria, based on the goals of the oppositional movement to which you are connected.
- ... give priority, during working hours, to helping coworkers with their own self-assigned, politically progressive projects. You collaborate on such projects whenever possible.
- ... resist taking on extra work or special projects for the bosses unless you will have control over the ideological content of the work. Otherwise the extra work will simply crowd out your own, more socially beneficial, projects.
- ... channel as much useful information as possible, especially inside information, to opposition groups, publications and individuals. As someone who is a radical first, you see this as your responsibility. In this and in a number of other activities listed here you may have to act anonymously to protect yourself from employer reprisals. But acting anonymously does not mean acting alone—that you do only when there is no other way. Anonymously here means acting with as many coworkers as possible, but without management's knowledge.
- ... blow the whistle and sabotage projects that are against the public's interest. You act for a fairer social structure even at your employer's expense. You do this, for example, by leaking plans and other information to opposition organizations or to the press. In the case of the press, you make it the radical press not only to avoid an innocuous treatment of the issue, but also to build the radical press. When this activity becomes widespread, all segments of society will see the radical press as required reading.
- ... air your institution's dirty laundry in public. When you make public an internal fight over the nature or quality of the institution's products or services, you expose your bosses to pressures that make an outcome in the public interest more likely and the usual outcome that serves elites less likely. This pressure can be strong, because even members of the public who seem to be apathetic perk up when let in on what is going on behind the scenes; they can see where the decision is being made and can, for a change, imagine themselves influencing it.
- ... sharpen general awareness of the political nature of professional work by drawing attention to the specific places in the work where ideology plays a role and where management acts to set the tone. When research scientists claim that their work is politically neutral, I think of the cartoon by Sidney Harris in which one researcher in a laboratory coat says to another, "If only there were some *peaceful use* for nerve gas."[3] Even professionals who do liberal political work off the job often fail to recognize that their professional work on the job is just as political, that neither what is

done nor the way it is done nor the result is neutral or serves universal interests. Hence, you encourage coworkers to reflect critically on the political nature of their work.

This is not at all as easy as it sounds. The notion that professional activity and political activity can be thought of separately is very convenient for the liberal professional, because it allows for unfettered career-building. When you challenge this notion you confront the individual's careerism. For scientists, the convenient way of looking at things is that there is nothing inherently political about any particular piece of science (including nerve gas), but that what is political is the completely separate question of whether the piece of science is to be used in a socially beneficial way or is to be abused, the piece of science itself being no better suited for one than for the other. This career-protecting point of view, known as the "use–abuse" school of thought, has been discussed and refuted elsewhere.[4]

- . . . debunk the myth of the objectivity or neutrality of the profession and its working principles. You challenge the social role of the profession.

- . . . encourage coworkers to see it as their business to pass judgment on the ideological content of their work assignments, and not just to accept the assigned ideology uncritically. You encourage informal workplace discussions, without managers, to critique the ideological content of the work at hand. You want these discussions to become the locus of the most lively, interesting, unrestrained, uncensored, honest, free-flowing and democratic debates about the content of the work. Such discussions will prepare people to work in concert for common goals during the repressed discussions of work content that take place at the official staff meetings run by management. You strive to make the nonmanagement discussions regular and formal (and inclusive of nonprofessionals). In most workplaces this would be a very bold move.

- . . . conspire with radicals in your workplace and in other workplaces to tilt your professional work and theirs to the left, so that it favors as much as possible those with less wealth and power. Also, you recommend knowledgeable radicals for nonradicals to consult in carrying out their assignments.

- . . . help coworkers understand that their conflicts with local authority (their department or division managers) have more to do with the actual social function of the institution as a whole than with the personalities of the managers. When managers are not around and coworkers get together and talk informally, the most common topics are office politics, rumors, gossip and personalities, all of which tend to focus on power in the workplace: Office politics addresses the subject directly; rumors often concern what those in power are planning to do; gossip many times has to do with the things coworkers may be doing to escape their "place"; and when personalities are the topic, the bosses get much more than their fair share of attention as their personalities are analyzed and reanalyzed ad infinitum. You participate in these discussions, understanding that those with little power and information must for their own protection monitor every move of those who have more power and information. But as a radical you also try to broaden the discussions to deal with the systemic origins of the conflicts—why they persist even as various management personalities come and go. You help coworkers understand how many of their grievances have their origin in the workplace hierarchy and the assigned ideology that goes along with it—the very ideology that guides their work. You explain how the workplace hierarchy goes hand-in-hand with the assigned ideology, so that the struggle against one must involve a struggle against the other. As a workplace radical you are more than someone who favors militancy in the fight for your coworkers' "economic" demands; you draw connections so as to spread understanding of how the system works and why it must be changed.

- ... help coworkers and others to acknowledge the forbidden (and difficult-to-accept) truth pointed to by their own conflicts and frustrations: Hierarchical organizations are fundamentally flawed. This acknowledgment will in turn stimulate them to develop their own vision of how the workplace should be organized, making them harder to manage and, ultimately, forcing management to make democratic concessions. Most situations that cause employees anxiety and stress would be only minor problems if the individuals involved had equal shares of power. Thus, to those who have experienced conflict, your radical democratic views will at least make sense. You offer these individuals all the hard-won lessons of how structural inequality is bad news. Six examples:

—First, hierarchical organizations take the fun out of work. They centralize decision-making, so that most people involved in an activity or project are deprived of creative control, alienating them from their own work and killing their enthusiasm. This makes individuals less productive (Ever notice how people work hardest on self-assigned projects?) and leaves them less fulfilled. Nobody says, "Wow, you work in a hierarchy; that must be fun!"

—Second, hierarchical power structures twist people's personalities. The skills people develop for surviving in hierarchies are different from those they would develop in a democratic setup. As one secretary where I work confided proudly to another, "I know whose ass to kiss around here."

—Third, hierarchical power structures are necessarily secretive. Executives make key decisions behind closed doors. The hierarchical structure keeps people in the dark—even about issues that affect them directly—and engenders rumors.

—Fourth, hierarchical power structures create repressive environments. They produce fear and insecurity, killing free expression and spontaneous activity. People huddle and talk in hushed tones; "C.Y.A." governs their work. Criticism of the status quo and trial and error are necessary for progress, and so hierarchical power structures slow progress.

From The Wall Street Journal, by permission, Cartoon Features Syndicate

"I learn more from originals left in the copier than
I do from the employee newsletter."

—Fifth, hierarchical power structures stunt personal development. They cause conformist behavior by increasing the personal risk associated with creativity, independent thinking and dissent. They narrow the scope of each individual's work, ensuring that most people do not experience a wide variety of activity. In these and other ways hierarchy deprives individuals of the environment of freedom and experimentation necessary for personal growth.

—Sixth, hierarchical power structures are inherently violent. The few can't maintain their authority over the many through rhetoric alone. Although bosses, for example, rarely use guards or police, their right to do so influences people's behavior, most obviously during individual confrontations and strikes. More importantly, on a daily basis, hierarchies subordinate and humiliate and, as mentioned, make people's working lives a grind, warp their personalities, perpetuate their ignorance, repress their spontaneity and stunt their personal development, amounting to a kind of violence against the individual. Some individuals respond with actual violence; those pushed over the edge tend to "go crazy" in a particular way, aiming their guns up the hierarchy more often than down. But more commonly, people respond with many nonviolent forms of resistance—or with redirected violence such as alcohol and drug abuse and domestic brutality.

All six problems mentioned here, and certainly others, are endemic to hierarchy, and so you point out that they will eventually arise in every hierarchical system, be it an economic system such as capitalism (which is inherently hierarchical because authority originates in ownership) or a hierarchical workplace, political organization, social or volunteer organization or personal relationship. Any such social grouping can be organized nonhierarchically—and is always more human when it is.[5]

• . . . write and publish an exposé of the organization that employs you. You do this as a public service, to demystify one of society's institutions and to give insight into the workings of such organizations in general. You detail the way the bosses treat employees and the way they fashion the organization's products or services for clients and the public, showing the objectives that explain both. This look behind the scenes will not only entertain readers and enlighten them about the true nature of the organization, but will also force the bosses to curb some of their excesses. You make this a group effort if you can, and probably publish the result under a pseudonym.

• . . . sharpen and deepen your coworkers' dissatisfaction with the restrictions on their work. If a coworker shows no such dissatisfaction, stir some up. Through its misrepresentation of the nature of the professional, the culture instills in those who aspire to go to professional school expectations of autonomy and of creative and fulfilling work. Professional training itself, however, is a process not of building up such expectations but of cooling them out, and it usually succeeds in getting individuals to be "realistic"— that is, to accept strict limits on their expectations. You encourage any expectations that have survived. You explain that boring or narrow jobs are not "natural" but are the result of the way the system divides labor to serve employer interests (at the expense of both employees and clients). You support individual professional and nonprofessional coworkers in their struggles to be allowed to do work that is more interesting, more challenging, more fulfilling or better for furthering their personal development—but you bring out how such struggles are fights with the system. You encourage coworkers to experiment and innovate in carrying out their work assignments, and you support their struggles to be allowed to exercise initiative, explaining how the restrictions on such activity originate in the hierarchical system rather than in the style or personality of one or another manager. With the same explanation, you fight against dead-end jobs and support people's struggles for work that will further their careers. It is not possible to draw a line that separates political and economic demands.

- . . . help lay bare the intimate details of management's decision-making about the content of the work. Because workplace secrecy increases the power of the bosses by ensuring that they are the only ones with a comprehensive knowledge of what is going on, you work to spread around as much information as possible. When you know the details of how the bosses made a particular decision, you inform people inside and outside of the organization, and you encourage coworkers to do the same. This helps reveal management's politics and enables people to predict its decisions in the future.

- . . . encourage openness in personnel matters, specifically, in individual terms of employment. Secrecy allows management to avoid the pressure of precedents, so that it can give each employee the cheapest deal it can get away with. With openness, all employees would have the precedent of the best deal. Hence, you encourage coworkers to reveal the details of their deals with management. And yes, you advocate making lists of salaries public. The bosses strongly discourage such openness and are often extremely angry when it occurs, not because they are out to "protect your privacy," but because they are out to protect themselves—from the cost of satisfying employees who have discovered the details of how they are being taken advantage of.

- . . . encourage openness in personnel matters, specifically, in individual disputes with management. When you have a dispute with management, the bosses insist on discussing it with you behind closed doors not because they want to protect your privacy, but because they want to deny you the support of coworkers. Behind closed doors you stand alone against the institution. Hence, you try to handle conflicts with the boss in front of coworkers to whatever extent possible. In any case, you recount the details of your disputes to coworkers, and you encourage coworkers to do the same when they have disputes with management.

- . . . encourage coworkers to use their collective strength to maintain their individual dignity. You encourage employees to take their grievances to management collectively rather than individually. In the typical one-on-one meeting in the manager's office, the boss pretends to treat the employee as an equal, and the employee either plays along with the pretense to avoid humiliation or is disarmed by it out of desperation for an ego boost. In either case the indignity is there. In a collective meeting, power is more equal. In general, you support nonprofessionals and other professionals when they go up against the institution alone.

- ... fight to get professional organizations to handle grievances—that is, to consider it their business to intervene in personnel matters on behalf of individual members. The availability of such backing would put members in a much better position to challenge their employers on the political content of the work.
- ... help organize a union. After all, management is organized and sticks together to defend *its* interests.
- ... undermine management's ability to manipulate employees: You become an expert on management tactics and tricks, you become an expert on the principles of resistance, and you spread this knowledge throughout the workplace. The excerpts in chapter 15 from the Army field manual are a great starting point. (That chapter discussed the manual primarily in terms of the training institution, but I am sure that every reader who has ever worked as a professional immediately recognized the manual's relevance to the workplace as well.)
- ... hire coworkers on the basis of character. When there are job openings at the workplace, managers sometimes ask professionals on the staff to meet some of the applicants and comment on them. Typically, the bosses will have already filtered out the ones who don't have the technical ability to do the job. So you need ask only one question, and if you can talk to the candidates outside the presence of managers you can ask it directly: "What do you stand for?" Or, perhaps even more to the point in a world where "flexibility" has become the key to "marketability," "Do you stand for anything?" You are simply trying to find out what the person will fight for, if anything. The managers will be sorting the interviewees by character, too, looking for "team players"—management's euphemism for people who stand for nothing of their own.
- ... fight elitism, authoritarianism and hierarchy by resisting a professional self-identity. Your academic degree and job title do a lot to shape your workplace identity. But you don't let your fancy credentials go to your head and shape your self-identity. Whenever you have a choice in your interactions with coworkers and clients, and with people in your life outside the workplace, you downplay your formal education and your position within the system, recognizing that it would be elitist to imply that such credentials make you even a bit more deserving of respect than other people. When you identify yourself, you don't adorn your name with titles such as "Dr.," "PhD," "Professor" or "Esq."

Because fighting elitism is at the top of your agenda as a radical, you realize that no matter how much further you might advance your progressive views on one or another issue by flaunting your credentials, such elitist behavior would do even more to set back your ultimate goals. In fact, even if all you cared about was prevailing on just the one issue at hand, and you didn't care if you promoted elitism in the process, arguing from authority would still be counterproductive. For if your own degree and job title lend validity to your conclusions, then the paper credentials and positions of your establishment-oriented colleagues lend validity to the opposite conclusions. And there are more of them than there are of you. For every radical in your field there may be dozens of establishment-oriented professionals, many with academic degrees and job titles fancier than yours, and so any implication that a person's formal education or position within the system lends validity to that person's political views does more for the other side than it does for yours. Hence, the use of system-based authority against the system itself, always a temptation for some, is a double loser.

As a radical, you realize that the system of authority works against you—some of the most backward things that you have ever heard have come from well-educated "authorities"—and you realize that you therefore have no choice but to work against the system of authority. (Take it from me, an authority on expertise: You can't trust experts.) Your gut reaction to system-based credentials is more one of suspicion than of respect, because you see their underside: A person's flashy diploma or job title, for example, brings to your mind the degree to which the person has been processed by the system, is trusted by the system or is concerned about keeping the system's trust. In your own case, you don't worry about being "respectable" by the system's measure. You give respect—and expect to receive it—according to your own measure, in which commitment to the opposition counts and success within the system does not. And you are careful not to give the system credit for such commitment: You understand the politics of professional qualification too well to think that the progressive outlook of oppositional professionals is due to the enlightening effect of their extensive formal education. You know that when professionals have good politics it is not because of their professional training, but *in spite of it*.

Finally, you don't let rank within the system determine rank or authority within the antisystem movement, as often happens in professional associations. Many people check out the opposition because the elitist system turns them into "nobodies." Opposition groups that do the same thing by honoring system-based credentials, and thereby importing hierarchies from the system, should not wonder why few people stick around. People subordinate themselves to authority at work because they are paid to do so, and even then they resist. Few are about to do so voluntarily.

- . . . work to democratize your field, to break down the hierarchy within it. You draw attention to the establishment connections of the field's establishment.

- . . . use your position within the system to help other radicals. Commitment to the opposition usually involves career and financial sacrifices. You help counterbalance these by helping radicals to get jobs, by supplying them with references and recommendations, by giving them access to the resources and products of the organization that employs you, by making available to them free or at-cost professional services and by helping them get anything else you can from the system. When you give someone this kind of help, you don't see yourself as doing the individual a personal favor, but as helping the movement. You expect no return favor or special thanks, because you see yourself as simply fulfilling the obligation of a radical who has a professional position within the system. You expect to receive such help yourself when you need it, and you recognize the right of radicals to expect it from you.
- . . . work to abolish professionals. That is, you work to eliminate the professional/nonprofessional division of labor, not only because it stunts the intellectual development of people on both sides of the division, but also because it works against democracy in society. If knowledge is power, then a truly democratic society is impossible without the broad distribution of expertise throughout the population.[6] Thus, you encourage nonprofessional coworkers, clients and others to gain some technical understanding and skills of your profession. Many of the most useful skills are simple and can be learned quickly. You take the time to apprentice people, to minimize their dependence on professionals. You "give away" your skills.
- . . . build solidarity between professionals and nonprofessionals by encouraging your professional coworkers to see themselves as labor and by discouraging them from seeing themselves as superior to labor. Salaried professionals are workers who have been hired to carry on intellectual labor under the guidance of an assigned ideology. The mental contortions that professionals have to perform to maintain the pretense that they are superior to labor and that they are ideologically self-directed are stifling and unhealthy. Dropping the pretense and acknowledging that you are a rank-and-file member of the ideologically directed intellectual workforce opens the door to many forms of resistance and is personally empowering.

The staff professional's universal complaint, "They treat us like wage laborers here," should lead not to demands for special privileges for professionals, but to specific demands for better treatment of all the institution's employees. To strengthen professionals for this struggle you encourage them to identify not with the institution, but with labor: to see themselves as renting their abilities to the system for a certain number of hours per week; to resist working longer hours than nonprofessionals in the organization and to expect overtime compensation when they do; but most important, to take the attitude that they do not want to serve the assigned ideology a minute longer than they have to.

Finally, you avoid subtle put-downs of nonprofessionals. For example, when you argue that a particular group of professionals deserves higher salaries, you don't use arguments that imply that professionals have some sort of natural or moral right to have a higher standard of living than non-professionals. You argue that the professionals deserve a raise because they are exploited (that is, because the value of their work to their employers is greater than that of their pay), not because plumbers or bus drivers outearn them. You don't subscribe to the notion that someone who has been privileged enough to spend many years in college and who gets to do work that offers many nonmonetary rewards should naturally be rewarded with a salary higher than that of nonprofessionals—that is, "reward privilege" is not part of your ideology.

- . . . undermine management's information advantage. Management's knowledge of what is going on in workplaces throughout the industry, throughout the country and throughout the world gives it a tremendous advantage over labor in its own workplace, allowing it to judge rather precisely just how much it can get away with. Its historical knowledge of struggles with labor allows it to fine-tune this judgment. To cut management's advantage, you arm your coworkers with as much information about the big picture as possible. You simply want your fellow employees to know and use to their advantage what top management already knows and uses to its advantage: that their grievances are not unique, that their own workplace is just one of many battle sites in a widespread contest between labor and management, and that they have much to gain by following the overall struggle.

You get a lot of your information by reading the very same publications that your institution's top management reads to get its broad perspective. These almost certainly include the *Wall Street Journal*, as well as the appropriate trade publications. If the institution deals with academics, for example, the *Chronicle of Higher Education* would be required reading. The best way to judge a publication, and at the same time determine how useful it might be to you, is to figure out its role in society. The above-mentioned newspapers make good examples.

The *Wall Street Journal* is for decision-makers—not just those in business, but all decision-makers throughout a society that is dominated by business. Unlike the *New York Times* and other newspapers for wider audiences, and contrary to popular mythology, the *Journal* does not push the establishment's side in its reporting. It serves the establishment in a different way: by informing its members from an above-the-fray perspective, trusting them to come to their own conclusions. One of its most important functions is to give top managers the comprehensive social intelligence they must have if they are to boss their employees effectively and market to the public successfully. Thus the *Journal* keeps its subscribers up-to-date on contemporary sociology and popular culture, giving the bosses the intimate details of the lives and aspirations of individuals at each and every level of society, from skid row on up, while always quickly reporting on anyone who is doing something out of the ordinary. The fact that the *Journal* does not use photographs, together with the widespread but incorrect belief that it contains only boring financial data and articles that praise the system, help keep the wrong eyes from seeing the big picture.

The *Chronicle of Higher Education* is a weekly intelligence report for university bosses, focusing primarily on ideology. It keeps administrators on top of the ideological battles that are going on within each of the many fields of research, and it reports on newly produced ideology the moment it appears in books, journal articles or talks. It also keeps administrators up to the minute on student culture, reporting in great detail the attitudes and activities of college students across the country and around the world. And, of course, it briefs administrators on academic labor disputes.

If reading such establishment publications keeps you as informed as local management, then adding the opposition press to your reading list propels your awareness beyond that of your bosses—but you don't give them any tips.

- . . . help liberate nonprofessionals, and professionals themselves, from the mystique of the professional. One way that you demystify professionals is by making clear their role in the system of production, whose cast can be analyzed like this:

Nonprofessional employees: Follow assigned procedures.

Professional employees: Follow assigned ideologies.

Employers: Critically assess ideologies and develop ideologies to assign.

And, undermining this not-so-happy hierarchy from within, a subgroup of nonprofessional and professional employees:

Radicals: Critically assess ideologies and develop and propagate democratic ideologies that challenge the employer's elite-serving ideologies.

You also explain the politics of professional qualification—that the criterion for certification as a professional is not just technical knowledge, but also attitude, specifically, an uncritical attitude. You want everyone to understand the politics of professional qualification at least as well as those who hire and fire professionals understand it. Note from the descriptions listed above that the radical, of all people, is on an intellectual par with the employer. Both see the big picture and know the utmost importance of ideology. Only the radical, however, wants to bring other employees up to this higher level of understanding. Explaining the division of labor and the politics of professional qualification is a step in that direction.

At stake is not only the nature of the workplace and society, but your own nature as well—your very identity. The system of education and employment works to redefine who you are in the deepest sense, pushing you away from developing and acting upon your own vision and guiding ideas. Hence, if you want to stand for something and avoid vanishing as an independent force in society, you have no choice but to resist. Certainly, resisting the system carries some risk, but not resisting is a far deadlier course for your individual identity.

NOTES

1. For a discussion of the problems of being a radical professional, see Barbara Haber, Al Haber, *Getting by with a little help from our friends*, a 20-page pamphlet written after the July 1967 Radicals in the Professions Conference in Ann Arbor, Mich., New England Free Press, Boston.

2. One place where the "jointness" attitude showed up clearly was in the national pact between the UAW and Chrysler laying out the framework within which individual plants could negotiate a "Modern Operating Agreement" that grouped hourly employees into work teams. Each local MOA had the same preamble, which set the tone for the new workplace order: "We the workers, the union and the management recognize that we are competing in a global market and dedicate ourselves to successfully meeting this competitive challenge. . . . To achieve our desired goal, it is . . . recognized by all concerned that both the management and the union must set aside the traditionally accepted roles each have played in the past and embark upon a new non-adversarial working relationship for the mutual benefit of all concerned." *The Road to Industrial Democracy: Joint UAW–Chrysler Modern Operating Agreements*, a fold-out brochure published by the United Auto Workers and Chrysler Motors (undated, around 1990). In a booklet explaining the MOA, workers learned that company and union officials would be expecting them to "get rid of the old grudges and conflicts of the past—the Us versus Them kind of thinking." *The MOA & Me*, a 12-page booklet published by the United Auto Workers and Chrysler Motors (undated, around 1990), p. 9.

3. Sidney Harris, *Wall Street Journal*, 17 November 1987, p. 39.

4. See, for example, John Vandermeer, "Coming to terms," *Science for the People*, March–April 1987, pp. 20–21, 32. Bob Young, "Science *is* social relations," *Radical Science Journal*, no. 5 (1977), pp. 65–129, especially p. 103.

5. For tales and analysis of hierarchy and people's responses to it, see Chris Carlsson, Mark Leger, editors, *Bad Attitude: The Processed World Anthology*, Verso, London (1990).

6. See Charles Derber, William A. Schwartz, Yale Magrass, *Power in the Highest Degree*, Oxford University Press, New York (1990).

INDEX

ABOUT THE AUTHOR

Jeff Schmidt is an editor at *Physics Today* magazine. He has a PhD in physics from the University of California, Irvine, and has taught in the United States, Central America and Africa. Born and raised in Los Angeles, he now lives in Washington, D.C.